THE PSYCHOLOGY
OF LEARNING AND MOTIVATION

Advances in Research and Theory

VOLUME 7

CONTRIBUTORS TO THIS VOLUME

M. R. D'Amato

J. A. Deutsch

Henry C. Ellis

Nancy Frost

Stewart H. Hulse

Earl Hunt

George R. Kiss

Clifford Lunneborg

John R. Platt

John Theios

Thomas Tighe

THE PSYCHOLOGY
OF LEARNING AND MOTIVATION

Advances in Research and Theory

EDITED BY GORDON H. BOWER

STANFORD UNIVERSITY, STANFORD, CALIFORNIA

Volume 7

1973

ACADEMIC PRESS   New York   San Francisco   London

A Subsidiary of Harcourt Brace Jovanovich, Publishers

ACADEMIC PRESS, INC.
111 Fifth Avenue, New York, New York 10003

United Kingdom Edition published by
ACADEMIC PRESS, INC. (LONDON) LTD.
24/28 Oval Road, London NW1

LIBRARY OF CONGRESS CATALOG CARD NUMBER: 66-30104

PRINTED IN THE UNITED STATES OF AMERICA

CONTENTS

GRAMMATICAL WORD CLASSES: A LEARNING PROCESS AND ITS SIMULATION

George R. Kiss

REACTION TIME MEASUREMENTS IN THE STUDY OF MEMORY PROCESSES: THEORY AND DATA

John Theios

INDIVIDUAL DIFFERENCES IN COGNITION: A NEW APPROACH TO INTELLIGENCE

Earl Hunt, Nancy Frost, and Clifford Lunneborg

STIMULUS ENCODING PROCESSES IN HUMAN LEARNING AND MEMORY

Henry C. Ellis

SUBPROBLEM ANALYSIS OF DISCRIMINATION LEARNING

Thomas Tighe

DELAYED MATCHING AND SHORT-TERM MEMORY IN MONKEYS

M. R. D'Amato

PERCENTILE REINFORCEMENT: PARADIGMS FOR EXPERIMENTAL ANALYSIS OF RESPONSE SHAPING

John R. Platt

PROLONGED REWARDING BRAIN STIMULATION

J. A. Deutsch

PATTERNED REINFORCEMENT

Stewart H. Hulse

LIST OF CONTRIBUTORS

Numbers in parentheses indicate the pages on which the authors' contributions begin.

M. R. D'Amato, Department of Psychology, Rutgers University, New Brunswick, New Jersey (227)

J. A. Deutsch, Department of Psychology, University of California, San Diego, La Jolla, California (297)

Henry C. Ellis, Department of Psychology, University of New Mexico, Albuquerque, New Mexico (123)

Nancy Frost,[1] Department of Psychology, The University of Washington, Seattle, Washington (87)

Stewart H. Hulse, Department of Psychology, The Johns Hopkins University, Baltimore, Maryland (313)

Earl Hunt, Department of Psychology, The University of Washington, Seattle, Washington (87)

George R. Kiss, Medical Research Council Speech and Communication Unit, University of Edinburgh, Edinburgh, Scotland (1)

Clifford Lunneborg, Department of Psychology, The University of Washington, Seattle, Washington (87)

John R. Platt, Department of Psychology, McMaster University, Hamilton, Ontario, Canada (271)

John Theios, Department of Psychology, University of Wisconsin, Madison, Wisconsin (43)

Thomas Tighe, Department of Psychology, Dartmouth College, Hanover, New Hampshire (183)

[1] Present Address: Department of Psychology, Princeton University, Princeton, New Jersey.

CONTENTS OF
PREVIOUS VOLUMES

Volume 4

Volume 5

GRAMMATICAL WORD CLASSES: A LEARNING PROCESS AND ITS SIMULATION

George R. Kiss

MRC SPEECH AND COMMUNICATION UNIT
UNIVERSITY OF EDINBURGH, EDINBURGH, SCOTLAND

I. Introduction

The objectives of this article are to present a detailed description of a model for a learning process, proposed as an account of the learning of word classes by the child, to relate this model to other theories and empirical findings, and to describe the results of a computer simulation which uses recorded speech of some mothers to their children as the input corpus. I wish to emphasize at the outset that this model is proposed purely as an account of learning grammatical word classes. It is *not* a complete theory of language acquisition, only an intended component of such a theory. It is important to keep this firmly in mind, since the mechanisms which are incorporated in this model are in all likelihood incapable of accounting for language acquisition in its totality. This, however, should not detract from their usefulness in accounting for part of that process. The relationship of the proposed mechanism to other component subsystems, believed to take part in language acquisition, will be indicated.

1

Since there is at present no general theory available to us, the account of these other subsystems has to be vague at the moment. It is not the purpose of this article to describe a detailed formulation of them, and they will be mentioned only to delimit the boundaries of the mechanism for word class learning. It is necessary to emphasize this at the outset in order to forestall criticisms, which could be justified only if the model were to be put forward as a general theory of language acquisition. No such claims are made here, and for this reason criticisms which attack associative mechanisms for their inadequacy as a general account of language acquisition are simply not applicable, unless it is shown that this inadequacy in toto entails inadequacy as an account of some subsystem.

The main preoccupation of this paper is with detailed *mechanisms*. While there is now an abundance of abstract theorizing in psycholinguistics, mainly motivated by recent advances in linguistics, there is a considerable neglect of the specification of detailed psychological mechanisms which could serve as feasible realizations of the theories. This neglect hinders both relevant experimental research and the execution of "sufficiency tests" by computer simulation. Accordingly, this article will start with a detailed description of the proposed mechanism and only in a later part shall it be related to other theories and to behavioral data. Great care will be taken to explain the information-processing concepts used in constructing the model, in order to avoid confusion with associative theories based on stimulus-response (S-R) psychology. Apparently, the use of terms like "associative learning" evokes powerful associative reactions like "S-R psychology" in at least some psychologists, leading to a conclusion that any model containing associative mechanisms is an S-R model. There is no reason why this should be the case. The model presented here is *not* one based on the ideas of S-R psychology. We shall return to this point in a later section.

II. Description of the Model

A. Learning Word Classes: A Component of Language Acquisition

This article does not attempt to present a complete theory of language acquisition. It is nevertheless necessary to indicate how the process of learning word classes fits into the complex developmental process of language acquisition. What follows, in this respect, is an outline of an attitude and of a research strategy, rather than a detailed theory.

Language acquisition has justifiably been claimed to be the most complex learning task a human being has to face. It is not to be expected that a single, self-contained psychological mechanism could account for it. Rather, learning a language is to be conceived as a process in which all of the cognitive resources of the organism are utilized to the fullest extent. Some of these resources are general-purpose, also taking part in processes other than language learning, while others are perhaps specific to this task. In trying to understand how the child learns a language, it is a reasonable strategy to regard his intellectual resources as parts of a complex system which interact with each other. I shall refer to these parts as *subsystems*. Such subsystems may be specified either functionally or by the mechanism which realizes them. An example of a functionally defined subsystem may be the machinery which deals with the learning of referential properties of words. An example of a subsystem based on a single mechanism may be the auditory perceptual machinery responsible for pitch perception. The degree of autonomy a subsystem has is variable, particularly in the case of functionally defined systems. Sometimes no sharp boundaries can be drawn, and the subsystem is simply a convenient device for collecting together, from a uniform point of view, the various aspects of a complex process.

The complexity of these subsystems may vary according to the tasks they carry out. Some of them may contain very simple learning processes, others may incorporate very complex high-level manipulations of symbolic entities.

The model described in this article relates to the subsystem dealing with the formation of word classes. This subsystem is assumed to be a part of the subsystem dealing with the learning of syntax, which is in turn only a part of the total system for learning the language. This latter probably involves all of the cognitive resources of the child. The subsystem for word class learning is a *functional* one. It is composed of several learning processes, including among other things, simple associative learning, testing of a tentative word class system using the syntactic and semantic subsystems, modification of the tentative word class system in the direction of overall optimization with respect to criteria like simplicity, efficiency, and the like.

The model to be presented is aimed at the first two components of this subsystem: associative learning and classification. The role of these two components is to derive from the input corpus of the child a series of primitive, *tentative* classification systems for the words of the corpus. These two components on their own may not be capable of deriving a word class system which is adequate by the criteria mentioned above. If this is the case, the other components will have to be called in to make the adjustments when conflict arises. It is to be noted, however, that these more complicated processes can only operate once the learning process is sufficiently advanced on the basis of the first tentative classifications. Evaluation of the word class system by syntactic criteria cannot be made unless a tentative syntax has been formed. This in turn is not possible without *some* kind of word class system, for a syntax can only be formulated in terms of such a system. I am arguing here for a kind of "bootstrapping" process, which gets under way using some simple machinery, and then makes use of the results to improve itself. Let us now turn to a detailed discussion of two basic mechanisms which will be shown to be capable of deriving such tentative classification systems.

B. Accumulating Distributional Evidence

The basic assumption of the model is that a tentative word class system can be derived by observing statistical regularities in the input corpus. These regularities yield what is known as distributional evidence, indicating certain patterns in the occurrence of word tokens. In this section I shall describe a mechanism for the accumulation of such distributional evidence. The mechanism which will derive a classification system from the distributional information will be described in subsequent sections.

The proposed mechanism for accumulating distributional evidence is an associative one. In order to specify it, I shall need to use two concepts: that of an internal representation and that of an associative link. I shall now discuss these in detail.

An internal representation is defined as a symbolic entity, containing symbolic elements in defined relationships to each other, which is constructed by the organism and is stored in its memory. For example, the internal auditory representation of a word may consist of symbolic internal representations of its constituent phonemes in defined temporal relationships to each other. An internal representation is not a stimulus, although it may be constructed by processing stimuli. It may also be constructed entirely through internal processing and may thus have no one-to-one mapping into an externally observable stimulus or response. Internal representations may have an arbitrary degree of complexity due to the possibilities of cross-referencing, embedding, and any other compositional mechanisms which can be used to construct new internal representations from others which already exist. Internal representations can contain descriptive information, like attributes and their values, or they may contain descriptions of procedures to be executed by some specified mechanism. For example, the internal representation of a word may contain a pointer to a procedure which, when executed by the articulatory mechanism, produces the pronunciation of that word. The coherence of an internal representation derives from the fact that its constituent symbolic elements are stored in such a way that given some of the elements, others can be retrieved. This aspect can be described by using the concept of an associative link, to which we now turn.

An associative link is a symbolic entity (and for this reason it could be regarded as a special kind of primitive internal representation). I shall say that an associative link exists between two internal representations if there is a mechanism (function) such that given one of them, the other one can be retrieved. An associative link is thus seen as a property of the memory retrieval mechanism. Associative links can be quantified with respect to their "strength," which can be interpreted through parameters of the retrieval mechanism, like the time taken by, or the amount of processing involved in, or the probability of success of the retrieval process.

Various mechanisms have been proposed in the literature for the implementation of the retrieval mechanism itself. I shall make use of the one described by Kiss (1967, 1969) as a memory model for words. Lack of space prevents a detailed description of that model to be given here. If the reader finds the following compressed description obscure, he may consult the two papers for more detailed discussion.

In the "word store" model of Kiss (1967, 1969), the internal representations of words are interconnected by physical transmission links, capable of carrying "activation" into a network. Each word can be in a quantified state of activation (the concept of activation resembles that of the "trace strength" of other theorists). The transmission links can carry a part of this activation to other word representations, depending on their transmission capacity. The current state of the word store is defined by the current state of activation of all word representations in it. This state can be changed by injecting activation into some of the representations from outside the word store (for example, by the perceptual systems), or due to the transmission of activation between representations via the transmission links. The word store can produce an output in the form of readings of activation levels of specified word representations. The output is a description of the activation pattern existing in the word store, taking the form of a state description vector. The elements of this vector are pairs, consisting of the symbolic names of the word representations, and their current activation levels, respectively. (The symbolic name of a representation is to be understood as a pointer which identifies that word representation.)

Note that the transmission links of the word store provide a mechanism for the implementation of associative links, as defined above. When activation is injected into a word representation, it spreads to the other representations linked to it, making them available to some other mechanism for further processing.

Using these concepts, let us now return to the description of the mechanism for the accumulation of distributional evidence. I shall postulate that the word store mechanism described above is used for representing this information. The basic mechanism is thus a network of internal representations. The word store will be extended, however, by permitting the incorporation of representations for entities other than words. For example, representations can be constructed for entities like continuous or discontinuous word sequences, phrases, and also for word groups defined in any arbitrary manner by internal processing. This last point will be discussed in greater detail in the next section. For the time being, it is important to note that even complete temporal word sequences can have their own internal representation.

The distributional information is stored using a learning mechanism which can adjust the strengths of the transmission links. This will be assumed to be a simple reinforcement scheme which increments the strength of the corresponding transmission link every time two words occur in temporal contiguity with each other, i.e., one occurs in the context of the other. Context can also be defined in a number of other ways (see, e.g., Fries, 1952; Harris, 1951). Most often the contextual event is taken as a sentence frame. It is also possible, however, to take the nearest immediate constituent of the sentence, or the neighboring words on the left, on the right, or both, as the context. Whichever definition is adopted, it will be assumed that an internal representation exists for that kind of contextual event, and that a transmission link can be built and incrementally reinforced between it and any word representation.

Our strategy will be to take first the simplest kind of definition of context and examine its power in supporting a word classification system, and then to progress to more complex definitions if it is found wanting. The model proposed in this article does not, however, depend on the nature of the context, although its performance of course may well vary accordingly.

For the time being, the context will be defined as the *immediate successor* of a word. For our purposes here the input corpus is represented as a temporal string of words. Each word (except the last one) has an immediate successor, which is the word just following it. A symbol marking the end of a sentence will also be assumed. (This is perhaps a moot point, since this symbol would be represented in the auditory modality by stress, pause, and intonation, so that internal representations have to be postulated also for these kinds of information as well. At the moment it is not known whether a sentence terminator is essential or even beneficial to the word classification mechanism. This is a problem for empirical research.)

The word-to-word transitions of the input corpus will be mirrored in the word store by the transmission links according to the particular reinforcement scheme adopted. The strengths of the links will be determined by the frequencies of the corresponding transitions in the input corpus. Notice that the network built up by the learning process is a particular physical representation of the Markov chain inherent in the input corpus. The words are states of this Markov chain, and the transmission links correspond to the transition probabilities.

Owing to the fact that the connecting transmission links can carry activation, this memory structure is capable of a certain amount of parallel processing. When a word representation is activated, the activity spreads along the links to other representations, the magnitude of the activation reaching them depending on the strengths of the links, i.e., their activities will represent the frequencies with which they have been paired with the word in question. A simple mechanism is thus provided for ascertaining all the different contexts for any word. The mechanism is to inject activation into the corresponding node of the network, and then to read off the activations reaching all neighboring nodes. In what follows, I shall refer to this set of readings as the *distribution vector* of a word. [The distribution vector is thus the state description vector of the word store after the activation of a word, provided that initially the system is cleared and only one state transition takes place. For more details on the word store model see Kiss (1969)].

C. The Classification Mechanism

The next step is to specify a mechanism which can form groups of words using the distribution vectors in making judgments of similarity. Two words are to be assigned to the same group if they are similar to each other in terms of their distribution vectors. The groups are to be formed in such a way that words belonging to the same group are in some sense more similar to each other than words belonging to different groups. The groups may, however, overlap, since a word could belong to several groups.

My purpose in this section of the article is to describe the nature of the computations required for such a grouping process and to suggest one particular implementation of a mechanism which can carry out these computations. The discussion will be at the psychological level and, except for some suggestive remarks, no attempt will be made to pursue the nature of these mechanisms to the neurophysiological level.

The first essential component of the classification mechanism is the computation of some measure of similarity between words in terms of their distribution vectors. This requires that the distribution vectors be matched against each other and some comparison performed on their elements. A large number of suggestions have been made in the literature of numerical taxonomy for the measurement of similarity between objects described by attribute vectors (see, e.g., Sokal & Sneath, 1963).

An example of a dissimilarity measure, which was found to work well with these data, is the so-called Canberra metric, defined as

$$C_{ij} = \sum_k |x_{ik} - x_{jk}| / \sum_k (x_{ik} + x_{jk}) \tag{1}$$

where x_{ik} is the value of the kth attribute for object i. In our case the x's represent the transitional frequency or probability from word i to word k. It can be shown that the corresponding similarity measure, obtained by subtracting Eq. (1) from one, is

$$1 - C_{ij} = 2\sum_k \min(x_{ik}, x_{jk}) / \sum_k (x_{ik} + x_{jk}) \tag{2}$$

which is related to an "overlap" measure used by Deese (1965) and others for the measurement of associative relatedness between words. I am grateful to Jim Piper for deriving this relationship.

As will be seen in a moment, the model needs the construction of transmission links with strengths determined by Eq. (2). As a suggestion toward neurophysiological implementation, this requirement can be formulated as the need for some "connector" element, shown in Fig. 1. It has four terminals, two of which are connected to word i and the other two to word j. The unidirectional input connections going into k (the connector element corresponding to word k) are determined by the distributional information. The operation of the

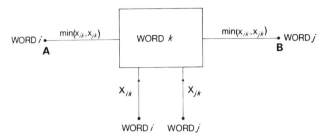

Fig. 1. The connector element. The function of this element is to establish a non-directional path with a strength corresponding to the smaller of the two inputs x_{ik} and x_{jk}, between the terminals A and B.

connector element is to establish the two bidirectional links of k, with a strength corresponding to the smaller of the two input connections. The logical AND operation between two ordered sets of binary elements will provide the required operation.

The second essential component of the classification mechanism is the construction of separate internal representations for the word groups whose members are similar to each other. The postulation of internal representations for word classes is an important characteristic of the theory put forward in this article, since such a representation does not correspond to any physical object or stimulus event in the environment, but is a representation of an abstraction about the environment (the input corpus). It is at this point that we part company with traditional associationistic or mediation theories. The postulation of representation for a word class introduces an element which is not part of the behavioral vocabulary (see Bever, Fodor, & Garrett, 1968, p. 583).

The internal representation of a word class is assumed to contain associative links to the words which have been assigned to it as members. The strength of such a link corresponds to the degree to which a word is similar to the other members of the class. For example, the strength of the link may be determined by the average similarity of a word to other members of the group.

Word classes are built up by interconnecting the words which have similar distributions. This grouping process is applied to any word pairs which occur together within the distribution vector of another word. The process comes into operation for each occurrence of every word in the input corpus. The process can be described in more detail as follows.

The occurrence of any word in the input activates the corresponding internal representation. This activation now spreads to all words in the distribution vector through the transmission links built up during the accumulation of distributional evidence. At this point in time all the words in the distribution vector are, therefore, simultaneously active. Using the mechanism for deriving measures of similarity between words, which has just been described, associative (bidirectional) links are built and reinforced between these words according to the degree of similarity between them. The strength of such a link between a word pair will be a function of the frequency with which they *both* follow some other words in the corpus, and also of the degree of similarity existing between them, as determined by their own distribution vectors at the time.

Thus, each word event in the input makes a small contribution to the process of grouping and organization. The initially diffuse system of words will be gradually organized into coherent groupings. Notice that the grouping process can only get under way once the distribution vectors are reasonably well established, so that they can provide useful similarity information. This agrees with the behavioral evidence which will be discussed later. The grouping process itself, and the resulting memory organization, will also be described in more detail in the section on computer simulation.

Once coherent sets of words have been established by the grouping process, internal representations can be constructed for the groups. These will be the internal representations of the corresponding word classes. They will contain as components associative links to all words which have a large enough degree of cohesion with each other as a result of the grouping process. Notice that membership of a class is a matter of degree, not of binary decision. The concept of a word class is seen to correspond to some characteristic "modes" in the input data, rather than to well-defined sets of words with clear-cut boundaries. Indeed, as will be discussed later, the learning process results in the discovery that words can have certain characteristic distributional features, i.e., that they can be more or less nounlike, verblike, etc. Once the existence of such features has been learned, actual assignment of features to individual words probably comes under the control of other than distributional properties (for example, inflections, syntactic relations, etc.).

Let me now point out that this model can correctly reflect some known characteristics of the word class system of a natural language. First, a word can belong to several word classes, which is represented in the model by having connections with several word class representations. Second, the model reflects the "graded" assignment of a word to a class by the strength of the link. The "fuzziness" of the word class system is a characteristic of natural languages (see Crystal, 1967, for discussion): the classes have a core of clear-cut cases, surrounded by less and less definite assignments. Insofar as this gradation depends on distributional properties, the model correctly captures this characteristic.

III. Empirical Background and Relation to Other Theories

All studies of early language learning come up against the problem of word classes, simply because any attempt at systematic description and explanation requires the use of grammatical categories of this kind.

Several early studies were aimed at the description of regularities and patterns in the speech of the child. Thus, Braine (1963a, 1963b) introduced the pivot *vs.* open class (P-O) distinction, which has been widely used ever since. The terminology rests on the finding, confirmed by Brown and Fraser (1963), and Miller and Ervin (1964), that most of the earliest word combinations by children consist of a noun (a member of the open class) and a modifier (the pivot). The concept of a pivot class can be criticized on both linguistic (McNeill, 1970b) and distributional grounds. A class of pivots can be separated out only as a "second-order" class, if we assume that the open class words are equivalent to each other, otherwise no distributional overlap can be established, due to the relatively low frequency of occurrence of the open-class members.

Subsequent developmental changes in the patterns of word combinations were described by Brown and Bellugi (1964) as a progressive differentiation of the pivot and of the open classes. The procedures which have been followed in arriving at such a conclusion are set out in more detail by Brown and Fraser (1963), and can be briefly summarized as follows.

The basic principle used was the method of shared contexts. The contexts were defined either as complete utterances taken from the corpus, or else descriptions of such utterances in terms of classes already established. We thus see the application of a "recursive" principle leading to "higher-order" classes. The problem of setting up a criterion in terms of the percentage of shared contexts out of the total possible for the assignment of two words to the same class is discussed, but no systematic solution is suggested. The authors comment that very large speech samples would be required for the application of a mechanical (i.e. nonintuitive, rigorous) shared-contexts procedure. Since such samples are not available, intuitive heuristics are followed to derive classes first from the words occurring at least twice in the first position of two-word utterances and then from the second words. Next, utterances of length three or more are used to split up Class 1 into subclasses. At this point, descriptions of class sequences are used to make further adjustments to Class 1. Finally, the existence of Class 1 is used to assign all recurrent words in the second position of two-word utterances to Class 4. We thus see that a relatively unsystematic mixture of principles and procedures have been used in arriving at the word classes ascribed to the child. I suggest here that more systematic classification procedures should be employed in further studies of child language development to provide consistent descriptions of longitudinal changes in the word class system of the child. Until this is done, attempts at the construction of detailed explanatory theories of such changes, like those of McNeill (1966b, 1970b) and the one put forward in this article, suffer from a lack of well-defined data which such theorists purport to explain. Apart from their potential usefulness as a research tool, methods of numerical taxonomy (Jardine & Sibson, 1971; Sokal & Sneath, 1963) are also more likely to provide fruitful hypotheses as to the processes taking place in the child.

Another set of phenomena have been observed in word association data, taking the form of a shift from syntagmatic to paradigmatic responses, which are relevant to the problem of word class learning. The evidence provided by these phenomena is only tangential, insofar as the syntagmatic-paradigmatic (S-P) shift continues to an age level where the grammatical learning process is almost complete, or is well advanced. It is quite clear therefore that the process responsible for the S-P shift cannot be the one leading to the *discovery* of word classes: by that time the child can correctly use, and so has presumably discovered, the classes. However, it is likely that the S-P shift is due to a continuation of the process of organization and reorganization in the child's subjective lexicon, and to some changes in the response process, and as such it will be interesting to see how far the proposed model could account for it. I shall return to this point during the following discussion of theories.

THEORIES OF WORD CLASS LEARNING

The purpose of this section is to indicate the relation between the model and other theories which have been put forward in this area.

It is not intended as a comprehensive and detailed review (for which the reader should see Clifton, 1967).

Explicit theories of word class learning have been put forward only by Braine (1963b), Jenkins and Palermo (1964), and McNeill (1966b, 1970a, 1970b). The theories of Ervin (1961) and Brown and Berko (1960) were formulated for word association phenomena, although for the reasons mentioned above they are highly relevant. I shall now consider each of these in turn and relate them to the model.

The problem of word classes is only dealt with directly in Braine (1963b). In his later paper (Braine, 1963a), the main preoccupation is with the learning of phrase structure through contextual generalization of positional learning. In his answer to criticisms by Bever, Fodor, and Weksel (1965), Braine points out explicitly that his theory would have difficulty with word classes (Braine, 1965, p. 487), and suggests that "Jenkins and Palermo do provide a reasonable theory of word-class formation that is at least theoretically capable of explaining covert categories [Braine, 1965, p. 489]."

The discussion of word classes in Braine (1963b) is in terms of the P-O distinction. As mentioned in the previous section, the P-O distinction cannot be fully supported by distributional evidence from child speech. In order to establish the pivot class it is necessary to extrapolate from this evidence, using the intuition of an adult speaker. This is not a satisfactorily objective procedure. From a completely different point of view, McNeill (1970b) also criticizes the P-O distinction and suggests that "The distinction necessarily appears in a distributional analysis because a child's lexicon is derived from the three basic grammatical relations of modification, predication and main verb, and sentences constructed from this lexicon are limited to two or three words [p. 1098]." Thus we see that the status of pivot and open classes, as such, is, to say the least, dubious. It would be better to talk about a single open class at this stage of development, for the only clear distinction is that members of the open class can appear on their own as single-word utterances, or in combination with each other in two-word utterances, while members of the pivot "class" cannot. At this stage, therefore, we can say that there is an open class, but there would be little justification in grouping everything else into a class, especially if the basic definition of a class as words sharing similar privileges of occurrence is to be maintained.

Braine (1963b) postulates that children learn to place the pivots in fixed positions in utterances. I have just argued that the concept of a pivot *class* is not a sound one. Braine's theory therefore has to be interpreted in terms of *pivot words* rather than a pivot class, if it can be interpreted at all. There is, in fact, a considerable amount of evidence that during this phase of development children pick up a pivot word and rapidly combine it with a large variety of open class words (Braine, 1963b; Weir, 1962). There is no doubt that this "pivoting" process forms part of the algorithm by which the child *generates* utterances and practices them to himself. The combinatorial play process described by Weir, in particular, may provide the child with a method of selectively building and reinforcing associative connections of the kind required by my theory. The pivoting process does not, however, say anything about the mechanism by which the child extracts word classes from the corpus presented to him by others.

Furthermore, according to Braine, position is to be defined relative to phrase structure elements. Since at the earliest stages of learning the part of speech units for the description of phrase structure are not yet available, position learning relative to units cannot be the mechanism for early learning of word classes. This criticism is quite independent from those of Bever *et al.* (1965) who criticize Braine on the grounds that positional learning does not illuminate "how the child learns the deep syntactic structures." That aspect of language learning is considerably beyond the scope of the present article.

In summary, Braine's theory of positional learning relative to phrase structure units cannot form the first phase of word class learning. It may, however, form a later stage in development, once the phrase structure elements can be identified by the child. Some simpler mechanism is needed, however, to get the "bootstrapping" under way. The theory proposed in this article provides such a mechanism when context is defined in terms of neighboring *words*. Once primitive classes have been formed using this context, other learning processes can operate on them to find a grammatical description in terms of these classes. Higher level (possibly phrase-structure) elements so identified can then be used to refine the word classes. At this point some mechanisms of the kind proposed by Braine may turn out to be useful. Braine's theory (insofar as word class formation is concerned) is thus a special case of my theory, and is obtained from it by defining context in terms of phrase structure elements.

A theory based on mediation processes has been proposed by Jenkins and Palermo (1964) for the learning of word classes and the development of syntax. The theory rests on the use of three kinds of mediation processes: S-R chaining, response equivalence, and stimulus equivalence. The existence of these processes is usually demonstrated by transfer effects using paired-associate or conditioned-response learning. While the application of these principles to associative learning, and to some other experiments with artificial linguistic situations, is admirably clear in Jenkins and Palermo (1964), the discussion of actual language acquisition in these terms is not very detailed. The reason for this is probably the complexity of the situation, clearly recognized and commented upon by the authors (Jenkins and Palermo, 1964, p. 163).

The explanation of *word class* formation (but not the learning of syntax in general) proposed by Jenkins and Palermo is obviously a very plausible idea. There is general agreement about this in the literature, even among those severely critical of the use of S-R associative principles in psycholinguistics, as the following quotations show:

Though *the formation of word classes can perhaps be accounted for by such* (mediational—GRK) *paradigms,* they throw no light whatever upon the assimilation of even such relatively superficial syntactic features as phrase structures [Bever *et al.,* 1965, p. 475 (italics mine)].

It is however, unreasonable to deny *a priori* that in learning his language the child may take advantage of distributional regularities in his corpus. Such regularities would be good guides to the tentative analysis of the corpus into classes, and it is precisely such tentative analyses that are required if he is to employ rules that project putative descriptions of underlying structure [Fodor, 1966, p. 118].

However, the potential of this idea has apparently never been realized, possibly because this whole direction of research came under heavy criticism from the Chomskian school. It is my view that the application of some extended form of the mediation theory to word class formation has been abandoned prematurely. For example, Palermo (personal communication) no longer adheres to the views described above.

Two major differences exist between the Jenkins and Palermo theory and mine. First, the Jenkins and Palermo theory is formulated in S-R terms, so that there is no room for a specific internal representation for a class, in contrast to the explicit postulation of such an object in my theory. This aspect of the Jenkins and Palermo theory has been justifiably criticized by Bever (1968), and by Bever *et al.* (1968). Bever *et al.* crystallize their objection in terms of the so-called "terminal metapostulate":

Associative principles are rules defined over the "terminal" vocabulary of a theory, i.e., over the vocabulary in which behaviour is described. Any description of an n-tuple of elements between which an association can hold must be a possible description of the actual behaviour [Bever *et al.*, 1968, p. 583].

As I have argued earlier, the internal representation of a word class is an element which is not part of the behavioral vocabulary, so that my theory violates the terminal metapostulate, while that of Jenkins and Palermo does not. As a consequence of this, since internal representations are assumed for elements not in the behavioral repertoire, the objections raised by Bever *et al.* cease to be applicable to my theory.

Secondly, my theory postulates a classification mechanism, which is an additional component beyond the associative learning process of the Jenkins and Palermo theory.

Let us now turn to theories of McNeill, whose views were first formulated as an explanation of the S-P shift (McNeill, 1966b) and were later elaborated into a theory of word class learning (McNeill, 1966a, 1970a, 1970b). I shall come back to the problem of the S-P shift in a moment but will now discuss McNeill's present theory of word class learning. McNeill (1970b) maintains that words are classified by the child through the use of the basic grammatical relations of predicate, subject, main verb, object, modifier, and head. These grammatical relations are expressed as syntactic features which can be attached to words. For example, for adjectives one might have the feature $(+\text{Det}, +\_\_\text{N})$, expressing a modification of a noun (the red ball), or the feature $(+\text{VP}, +\text{NP}\_\_)$, expressing a predication (the ball is red). The child forms classes by deriving these features from an understanding of adult speech, attaching them to words and entering this information into a lexicon (McNeill, 1970b, p. 1096). At this point McNeill's theory becomes subject to the same objection as Braine's, i.e., it cannot serve as an explanation of the very earliest stages of word class formation, since it presupposes the availability of feature components like N (noun), V (verb), NP (noun phrase), etc., whose acquisition the theory is trying to explain.

Again, as in the case of Braine's theory, the feature-based classification might be used for the refinement of classes, once the required categories are available to the child through previous simpler learning processes. Let us point out that if this is the case, then McNeill's views are *not* contradictory to the kind of theory proposed in this article, in spite of the apparently general tendency to contrast such theories as incompatible alternatives (see, for an example of this attitude, Clifton, 1967). I have argued in a previous section that internal representations can be constructed for phrases in terms of word class representations, and also for incomplete contextual sequences. Associative links can then be built between words and such higher level representations, making it possible to compare and classify words in terms of contextual noun phrases, verb phrases, etc. (giving the grammatical relation in which they participate). This, as I understand it, is exactly the substance of McNeill's theory.

Let us now turn to word association phenomena and to the S-P shift. The S-P shift itself is now a well-documented phenomenon (Entwisle, 1966). Moreover, a good deal of evidence is available to show that the shift is a gradual evolutionary process which occurs in synchrony with the increasing linguistic experience of children (Brown & Berko, 1960; Ervin, 1963; Jenkins, 1965; McNeill, 1963). The shift occurs at different times for different parts of speech, and is correlated with the variety of contexts in which words occur in sentences. Even in adults, stimuli belonging to different parts of speech elicit a varying degree of paradigmatic responding, and within any part of speech absolute frequency of occurrence has a similar effect. For example, high-frequency adjectives elicit a great deal of paradigmatic responding, whereas low-frequency adjectives elicit syntagmatic responses. Brown and Berko (1960) reported that paradigmatic responding correlates with the ability to recognize the part of speech assignment of a nonsense syllable in a sentence context. Ervin (1963) found a correlation between substitutability of words in sentences and their associative frequency, and also that words which were followed by a large variety of contextual words tended to elicit paradigmatic associates. McNeill (1963) obtained evidence showing that paradigmatic associations depend on the use of words in the same contexts, by using artificial words in identical sentence frames. Jenkins (1965) found that when subjects were asked to choose words to replace a specified word in a sentence, the words chosen were generally the most frequent paradigmatic associates of that word.

Ervin (1961) put forward the theory of "erroneous anticipation" of common substitutes of words in sentence contexts as an explanation of paradigmatic associations. Clifton (1967) argues, correctly, that the erroneous anticipation theory is a special case of mediation through the response equivalence paradigm, so that it can be treated on the same footing as the Jenkins and Palermo theory. McNeill (1966b) carried out a direct test of the erroneous anticipation theory with equivocal results (they were in the right direction, but did not reach significance). Although the results were highly similar to those of his earlier study (McNeill, 1963), McNeill interpreted the results as disconfirming Ervin's theory. Instead, he constructed a theory in terms of the accumulation of semantic features which are gradually attached to words. Word associations were then said to be generated by finding words with a minimal semantic contrast to the stimulus. Due to the incomplete development of semantic features, however, words in minimal contrast for the child may belong to different grammatical classes and are thus pseudosyntagmatic. McNeill (1966b) attempts to support this view by showing that paradigmatic responding increases with increasing ability to use nonsense words correctly in word substitution after appropriate training as to part of speech membership. These experimental results, however, do not contradict the argument that paradigmatic responding is dependent on increasing experience with contextual variety. They merely demonstrate that once the relevant experience has been accumulated, it can also be used appropriately in word substitution—a result which has already been obtained by Jenkins (1965). Thus it might be said that McNeill's (1966b) Experiment I disproves the erroneous anticipation hypothesis (although it needs replication, in view of the above remarks), but it does not affect the view that contextual variety is the determining factor in the development of paradigmatic responding. It is also the case that McNeill's Experiment II does not provide direct evidence for a featural theory.

There is thus a great deal of evidence available, showing that increasing experience of words in a variety of contexts leads to paradigmatic responding in word association, which is in turn related to the ability of using various parts of speech correctly in analyzing and constructing sentences. All of this evidence can be regarded as supporting the theory put forward in this article, for the correct operation of the classification mechanism presupposes the availability of enough distributional evidence for the words; this evidence is gradually accumulating during experience with input received from outside, later with the construction of output sentences, and with the combinatorial play of the kind described by Weir (1962). The greater the contextual variety, the more refined the classification system which can be supported by the distribution vectors. However, I have not as yet specified the mechanism for generating word association responses. Since this mechanism goes beyond the scope of this article, only a brief outline will be given here.

The stimulus given in a word association experiment places the memory depicted in Fig. 2 (which will be discussed in detail in the next section) into a certain starting state by activating its representation in the first and second planes simultaneously. Activation now spreads along the transmission links both within and between planes.

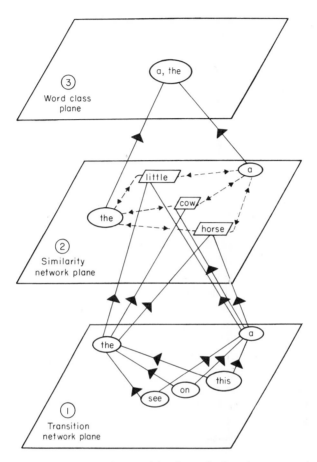

Fig. 2. The memory organization resulting from the learning process described by the model.

The result of this process is that an activation pattern is created over the words in the first and second planes (the plane of the transition network and the plane of the similarity network), and also over the word classes in the third plane. The evolution of these activation patterns can be described and treated mathematically by regarding the memory planes as separate subautomata of the system and investigating the input-output relationships between them. The internal states of each subautomaton are governed by its transition function (see Kiss, 1972). The response to be emitted by the subject in the word association experiment is now assumed to be determined by the state of the overall system (shown in Fig. 2) at some point in time after the presentation of the stimulus. The states of each of the sub-automata will contribute to the making of a final decision as to which word is to be emitted. Suppose, for example, that the response will be the word with the highest level of activation in planes one and two, or rather that the probability of its emission will be a function of these activation levels.

Early in the development of the system connections exist only in the transition network plane, so the response is fully determined by this plane. Later in the development the connections in the similarity plane will become much stronger than those in the transition network plane, since they are reinforced much more often. The reason for this is that the similarity links are reinforced whenever the occurrence of (a possibly very frequent) word simultaneously activates two words. With increasing learning experience, therefore, the similarity plane becomes dominant in determining the response. The degree of dominance will also be dependent on the variety of contexts in which the words occur, since the greater this variety, the greater the number of similarity links between them.

It can be seen, therefore, that the phenomenon of S-P shift can be fitted quite naturally into the proposed theory. Notice also that the theory accommodates the possibility of syntagmatic responses even late in development, by permitting the domination of the response process through a very strong transition link in the absence of strong links in the similarity plane. This is presumably the case with word association responses of the *Yankee-doodle* type.

IV. Computer Simulation

The theory of word class learning described in this article has been formulated with computer simulation in mind. It is worthwhile to pursue a computer simulation approach in the study of language acquisition for several reasons.

The first reason is that it can handle the logical complexity involved in working out the consequences of some fundamental assumptions about mechanisms. Under the same heading one can include the beneficial effects of the need for explicitness and detail in the formulation of theories.

The second reason is that simulation can, at the very least, provide a "sufficiency test" for a set of mechanisms: it can decide whether the specified mechanisms can in fact produce the required results. The simulation described in this article establishes that simple asso-

ciative learning and classification are sufficient for the extraction of
word classes from a corpus. Further work will be required to show
that the child uses just the mechanisms built into the programs, i.e.,
to show "strong equivalence" between the simulation and the biologi-
cal system, in the sense used by Fodor (1968).

The third reason is that simulation supplements the limited pos-
sibilities of experimental research into the linguistic competence of
very young children, and the work done by writing grammars based
on the record of children's speech.

The description of the simulation programs can be conveniently
divided into two parts which correspond to the two components of
the theory: associative learning and classification. These will be now
discussed in detail, together with the resulting memory organization
which is sketched in Fig. 2.

A.   ASSOCIATIVE LEARNING

The associative learning program reads an input corpus and es-
tablishes associative links between the words and their contexts. In
the current program the context is defined as the immediate successor
of a word. This program therefore builds a word-to-word transition
network for the input corpus. The links of the network are trans-
mission links of the kind described earlier.

Each word is looked up in a data structure representing the tran-
sition network, as soon as it is read. If the word already has a repre-
sentation, the next word is read and a link is created between them.
If the link already exists it is reinforced by adding a constant incre-
ment to it. If a word has no representation in the data structure, then
the representation is created and added to the transition network
as a new node.

When the whole of the input corpus has been read the transition
network is normalized so that the values of all arcs which emerge from
a node sum to one. This normalization is done in order to eliminate
the influence of absolute word frequency, which would cause cluster-
ing of words according to frequency.

The distribution vectors of the words can now be obtained by
looking at the lists of links attached to each word. The program has
provisions for truncating the distribution vectors to items whose
values are above a specified threshold. This truncation reflects in a
simplified way the property of forgetting in memory, and it elimi-
nates the influence of word transitions which are rare and are there-
fore unreliably estimated by the transition frequencies.

At the end of the associative learning phase the information about the corpus is held as a list of words, each with its distribution vector, appropriately truncated. The corresponding memory structure in Fig. 2 is the "transition network plane." The classification program comes into operation at this point.

B. CLASSIFICATION LEARNING

The purpose of the classification learning program is to establish internal representations for groups of words which are distributionally similar to each other. This process has two components. In the first component associative links are built between distributionally similar words, and in the second component associative links are built between the members of such a group and the internal representation of the word class which is formed by them.

The process of interassociating distributionally similar words relies on the simultaneous activation of such words by the occurrence of a common predecessor. In the child this grouping process takes place simultaneously with the associative learning of transitional information. However, the classification process cannot really get under way until a substantial amount of information is contained in the distribution vectors. For this reason, and also for computational convenience, the classification learning program operates after a complete pass over the input corpus by the associative learning program described in the previous section.

The first component of this program computes the following approximation to the grouping process described earlier (on p. 8). The total strength (T) of the connection between any two words i and j is

$$T_{ij} = (1 - C_{ij}) \sum_s f_{si} \cdot f_{sj}$$

where C_{ij} is the Canberra metric [see p. 8, Eqs. (1) and (2)]; f_{si}, f_{sj} are the transitional frequencies from some common predecessor p to words i and j; and S is the set of common predecessors of i and j.

The result of this grouping process is a second memory "plane" containing word representations and connections between them. The connections have strengths determined by the degree of similarity between the words and by the degree to which they tend to occur together after a common predecessor, i.e., the degree of similarity based on their "left contexts."

The second phase of the classification learning consists in constructing a third "plane" (see the "word class plane" in Fig. 2) from internal representations corresponding to whole groups of strongly interconnected words on the second plane. Connections are then built and reinforced between the second and third planes by connecting each member of a group to the corresponding group node on the third plane. This process simply consists of activating a word node in the second plane and observing the set of other nodes in the same plane which also become active. Each of these nodes are then connected to a common node in the word class plane. The strength of the connection from a word (in the second plane) to the representation of the group (in the third plane) may, for example, correspond to the average adhesion of that word to other members of the group. This process was simulated by using standard numerical taxonomy algorithms, to be described below.

The number of nodes on the third plane may still be quite large at first, although considerably smaller than the number of words on the second plane. Fusion of group representations into more inclusive groups could be organized on the same principle if additional memory planes are introduced into the system. An alternative possibility is, however, that the groups are not represented by single nodes, but by the activation pattern of a set of nodes. The hierarchical organization of groups is then reflected by the similarities between such patterns of activation over the group nodes.

C. Using Numerical Taxonomy

The process of establishing internal representations for word classes corresponds to the process of classifying a set of objects according to their characteristics, which is the subject matter of numerical taxonomy. This field is at present undergoing rapid development (Jardine & Sibson, 1971; Sokal & Sneath, 1963). There is a great proliferation of methods and a rigorous mathematical foundation for them is only beginning to be formulated. For lack of space I cannot give a detailed discussion of this area here; the reader is referred to the references given.

For the purposes of the work described here, numerical taxonomy provides a set of methods for exploring the structure of the grouping which results from the process described in the previous section. While the use of numerical taxonomy in other areas like ecology may be governed by different criteria, my purpose of using these methods is to ascertain whether any of them can lead to classes which are intuitively and grammatically satisfactory, and then to investigate whether the computational algorithm of such a method can provide some hypothesis as to the nature of the classification process in the human brain. The conclusions drawn will be, however, functional. The detailed elaboration of neural mechanisms which could carry out the relevant computations is a task for neurophysiologists.

A considerable range of classification methods have been tried out in the course of this work. It is not possible to describe in detail all of the results of this exploration. Only the general conclusions and the most interesting results will be presented here.

Among the large variety of classification methods certain characteristics can be found according to which the methods can be differentiated and grouped together. One such characteristic is that a method can be aimed at the discovery of a hierarchical classification (in which the route along which an object can be reached in the classificatory hierarchy is optimized), or else it can be aimed at the discovery of clusters, so that some property of the clusters is optimized (for example, the intracluster variance). It is generally desirable that the classification method should yield a stratified clustering, by which we mean that a sequence of clusterings be arranged according to some numerical level representing the strength of clustering in the data. Hierarchical classification necessarily has this property. Nonhierarchical methods are usually aimed at the description of the data at one particular level of clustering strength, although several of them can be used to obtain a stratified sequence in which each member of the sequence is optimized according to some criterion.

Hierarchical methods are discussed by Lance and Williams (1966a,b, 1967), Johnson (1967), and many others. The agglomerative hierarchical classification methods operate by calculating interobject dissimilarities and by successively merging the nearest objects into groups. The differences between the methods reside in the way in which interobject dissimilarities are determined. In the so-called "nearest-neighbor" sorting (also known as single-linkage, or as Johnson's minimum method), intergroup dissimilarity is defined as the dissimilarity between the closest pair of objects in the two groups about to be merged. In "furthest-neighbor" sorting (complete-linkage, or Johnson's maximum), intergroup dissimilarity sorting is the dissimilarity between the most remote objects of the two groups. In the centroid or average-linkage methods, it is the dissimilarity between the group centroids, or the average of all intergroup dissimilarities, respectively. All of these methods have been used in exploring the word classification data.

A large variety of nonhierarchical methods exist. Some of these are described by Wishart (1969), MacQueen (1967), and Ball and Hall (1965). Jardine and Sibson (1971) describe methods which yield over-lapping clusters. The methods of MacQueen, Ball and Hall and many others can be characterized as variance-minimization methods. MacQueen's method has the advantage that it can be used with very large populations of objects. Wishart's "mode analysis" tries to find dense regions of data points instead of variance minimization. The B(k) method of Jardine and Sibson is particularly attractive in the case of the word class data, since multiple class membership of a word is the rule rather than the exception in natural languages. Un-fortunately, this method is very laborious to use and is useful only for an examination of subsets of the data in order to clarify inter-cluster overlap relationships. All of these methods have also been used in exploring the word classification data.

V. Experimental Results

In this section an empirical test of the theory will be described. The theory was tested by writing computer programs which embody the processes required by the theory; by collecting an input corpus through tape recordings of mothers talking to their young children; and by processing this corpus with the simulation programs to the stage of the classification learning. The resulting word classes will be discussed in the light of several criteria, such as the word classes recognized by contemporary and earlier grammars, information from word association studies, information from studies of language acquisition in young children, and the approximations involved in the simulation.

A. THE INPUT CORPUS

The input corpus was derived from tape recordings of seven mothers talking to their children. These data were collected by Dr. Ann Carswell of the Speech and Communication Unit at the University of Edinburgh, and I am greatly indebted to her for permitting me to use it in this study. A detailed analysis of this corpus is to be presented in a separate paper, so that only the major characteristics will be described here.

The recordings were made in the families' homes in short (5 to 30-minute) sessions. An assistant, Mrs. Myrna Kaplan, who was familiar with these children and their mothers, was present to handle the tape recorder. The occasions were made as informal as possible. In order to avoid making the mothers self-conscious, they were told that the main interest is in the child's speech. To provide some focus for the interaction, Mrs. Kaplan took with her either a book or a set of toys relating to farm animals and their surroundings. The tape recorder was switched on, the toys or book presented, and then the mother was left to communicate with the child in as natural a fashion as possible without further interference.

All seven families can be described as middle class in social status. The degree of linguistic sophistication and average rate of speech varied considerably. The total recording times for the mothers were 53, 48, 41, 35, 15, 14, and 5 minutes, respectively, giving a total recording time of 211 minutes. During this time interval the mothers emitted a total of 15,317 words, distributed as follows: 3,828; 2,705; 3,172; 2,713; 1,189; 1,458; and 252. The average rate of speech is 1.2 words per second. The average utterance length for the first and third subjects combined was 7 words.

The ages of the children in months were: 21, 8, 30, 35, 23, 22, and 20, respectively. The recordings were made during a period of 1 to 2 months in 1971.

It is hoped that this 15,000 word corpus is a fairly representative sample of the kind of speech a child hears between the ages of 1 and 3 years. Little is known about the general characteristics of the child's input, particularly as to its total volume. It is likely that the 15,000 words recorded in 3½ hours of time represented only a very small fraction of the total speech input to which the child attends (and even less of what he hears) during its first 2–3 years of life. This should be remembered in evaluating the results of the simulation. As a very rough guess, a 2-year-old child of middle-class background with a not overly communicative mother could be expected to receive this amount of input in a matter of a few weeks.

Detailed analyses as to word frequencies, characteristic syntactic patterns, types of utterances, and other features of the corpus will be presented elsewhere. Here I shall discuss only whether this corpus could be regarded as typical. As far as the so-called function words are concerned, they would have a high frequency of occurrence, whatever the topic of discussion. This would also be true of many content words as well, like *see, look, think, big, small, nice,* etc. Some other content words will have a higher frequency in this corpus than would be expected in a larger sample, because the topic of discourse was biased toward the "farmyard" environment by using these particular toys and picture books. For example, the frequency of *horse* was 68, of *cow* 45, of *pig* 45, and of *hen* 14. It would not be expected that within a few weeks (which we assume to be the equivalent time for receiving a corpus of this size) the frequency of *horse* would be as high as this. However, two points must be made here. First, it is very likely that *some* nouns would have a rather high frequency if they regularly turn up in everyday life in the child's environment. This would be particularly true for the second year when the child begins to learn words, and his life is largely confined to a fixed and well-defined environment in the home. These high-frequency words would then be used for the discovery of the noun class which, once discovered, can be characterized by other than distributional criteria. This point will be discussed further in later sections.

Second, the operation of the learning processes required by the theory do not depend on the high-frequency occurrence of certain words *within a short period of time,* since the accumulation of distributional information can take place even if particular occurrences of a word are far from each other in time.

The total vocabulary which has been used by the mothers is quite large. For example, the first subject used a total of 376 different words. Of these 76 had a frequency greater than 10. Because of the restricted computational resources it has not been possible to include all, or even all of the high-frequency words in the simulation so far. Instead, 31 high-to-medium frequency words were selected for detailed study. They are presented in Table I, together with their total frequencies in the 15,000 word corpus. They include nouns, adjectives, verbs, auxiliary verbs, personal pronouns, demonstrative pronouns, articles, and prepositions.

TABLE I

THE 31 SELECTED WORDS AND THEIR FREQUENCIES

the	673	he	111	pig	45
a	543	I	99	cow	45
you	381	can	91	over	39
that	198	think	78	big	38
see	185	little	78	sheep	36
is	176	this	74	nice	35
it	175	horse	68	she	33
are	147	house	67	farmer	27
in	135	on	66	hen	14
look	123	put	50	into	13
do	112				

B.   PROCESSING THE CORPUS

The complete corpus of 15,000 words was transcribed from the recordings to punched cards. After a preliminary word frequency counting of the subsets of data belonging to subjects 2 and 3 (which were the first two to become available), the 31 words of Table I were selected for further study. The complete corpus of 15,000 words was now scanned and all occurrences of these words were found, together with their immediate successors. A small segment of the resulting transition graph is described by Table II. In this table the numbers are transition probabilities. The list following one of the 31 selected words is the distribution vector of that word. The vectors have been truncated at the .01 level of transition probability. This truncation was done to reflect forgetting. Note, however, that a more realistic reflection of forgetting would apply something like an

TABLE II

A SEGMENT OF THE TRANSITION GRAPH

Node: the

Connected to: house .041; horse .034; little .032; farmer .032; sheep .025; chickens .022; man .02; baby .02; animals .019; cow .017; cows .017; big .017; mummy .017; farm .016; boy .016; doggy .016; donkey .014; water .014; other .014; sky .014; pig .013; dog .013; pigs .011; book .011; tree .011; shed .011; doggy's .01; farmer's .01; same .01; cow's .01.

Node: a

Connected to: baby .047; horse .042; little .04; duck .038; nice .033; big .029; tree .029; house .029; cow .027; donkey .018; bit .018; pussy .016; car .016; baa .014; dog .014; doggie .012; tractor .011; door .011; boy .011; pig .011.

Node: put

Connected to: the .3; him .24; them .12; it .08; that .06; all .04; those .04; on .04; these .04; her .02; down .02.

Node: look

Connected to: "comma"[a] .308; at .268; "stop"[a] .187; there's .073; what .032; very .024; Simon .016; he's .016.

Node: farmer

Connected to: "stop"[a] .518; "comma"[a] .074; is .074; ride .037; will .037; isn't .037; right .037; over .037; like .037; a .037; got .037; says .037;

Node: horse

Connected to: "stop"[a] .573; "comma"[a] .191; then .029; do .029; doing .029; isn't .029; instead .014; some .014; go .014; you .014; is .014; Martin .014; there .014; will .014.

---

[a] The punctuation marks "comma" and "stop" (period) were treated in the same way as words throughout the processing.

exponential decay function in time. The present method of thresholding is a rough approximation.

A 31 × 31 similarity matrix was now calculated using the so-called Canberra metric described earlier. (This is a dissimilarity measure, and it was converted to similarity by subtracting the values from 1.) A small segment of this matrix is shown in Table III. The values vary between 0 and 1.

The resulting similarity matrix was itself taxonomically analyzed. The results of this analysis will not be given here in detail for lack of space. In brief, the resulting clusters were showing organization of the right kind, but of weak strength. Some of the expected clusters did not separate from each other. For example, the following classification was obtained by the iterative relocation method:

> *you I;*
> *this that;*
> *think look can;*
> *a the nice big little;*
> *sheep pig house horse hen farmer cow he she it;*
> *see put is are do in on over.*

It can be seen that the articles and adjectives, the nouns and personal pronouns, and the verbs and prepositions are not separated from each other. The clustering is in general rather weak and is detected only by sensitive methods. This result is to be regarded as the classification which can be supported by the information in the "right-context" distribution vectors after a 15,000 word corpus. While this information seems sufficient to separate nominals from modifiers and verbs, it cannot distinguish verbs from prepositions, pronouns from nouns, and adjectives from articles. It was clear at this stage, therefore, that further information from the "left context" is required. This is provided by the grouping process described in the previous sections.

Ideally, the grouping process ought to be applied to the distribution vectors of all words in the corpus. It is clear, however, that the largest contribution to the grouping will come from the high-frequency words. The distribution vectors were in any case only available for the 31 selected words. The process was therefore applied to these words and also to the vectors of the full stop and the comma (which were usually the highest frequency items). The latter two vectors were obtained by extrapolation from the processing of the first and third subjects.

TABLE III

A SEGMENT OF THE SIMILARITY MATRIX
(ENTRIES ARE 1-CANBERRA METRIC)

	you	this	think	the	that	sheep	she	see	put	pig	over	on	nice	look	little	it
the	0	.102	0	1	.079	0	0	0	0	.015	0	0	.169	0	.162	.165
a	0	.109	0	.421	.082	0	0	0	0	0	0	0	.223	0	.204	.017
put	0	.013	.128	0	.022	0	0	.41	1	0	.23	.36	0	0	0	.018
look	.17	.225	.149	0	.25	.251	.194	.313	0	.355	.239	.251	.207	1	.013	.264
farmer	.236	.367	.102	0	.589	.453	.353	.336	0	.614	.227	.262	.159	.271	.012	.666
horse	.195	.271	.117	0	.479	.503	.256	.297	0	.788	.274	.242	.2	.392	.012	.639

A small segment of the results for the grouping process is given in Table IV. The grouping process is applied to the un-normalized distribution vectors, so that the numerical values in Table IV result from summing the products of two (integer) frequencies and of the corresponding similarity metric from Table III, the sum taken over all words which have the two words together in their distribution vectors. Notice again that a further element of approximation is introduced here by using only the selected 31 words, the full stop and the comma for the grouping process. It is possible that some of the other high-frequency words which have not been included may have an appreciable influence on the grouping. Further computation of distribution vectors will be needed for a check.

The results of the grouping process are presented in the form of a graph in Fig. 3. This method of presentation gives perhaps the clearest impression of the nature of organization in the data. This graph shows only those connections which are above the value of 40. There are many more connections in the complete data, but it would be rather difficult to incorporate them in a drawing. The numbers give the strengths of the connections established by the grouping

TABLE IV

SEGMENT OF THE GROUPING RESULTS

Node: the
Connected to: a 728; that 84; this 72; it 17; little 6; cow .076.

Node: a
Connected to: the 728; this 19; little 13; that 9; it 6; nice 2; big 1.

Node: put
Connected to: see 83; are 19; is 14; in 9; think 6; into 6; do 3; in 1; can 1; this .148; it .093.

Node: look
Connected to: see 91; you 64; are 37; horse 36; cow 22; house 22; do 19; he 16; nice 14; is 14; think 11; hen 8; pig 8; this 4; I 4; big 3; she 3; farmer 2; sheep 2; can 2; little 1; on 1; in 1; it .792.

Node: farmer
Connected to: house 403; horse 395; cow 187; sheep 171; pig 129; hen 22; big 15; little 6; nice 5; look 2.

Node: horse
Connected to: house 695; cow 496; farmer 359; pig 272; sheep 219; nice 82; hen 67; look 36; big 34; little 13; is 1.

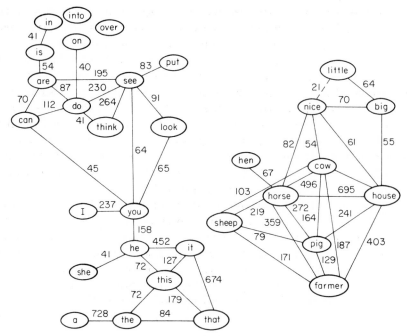

Fig. 3. Graph of the grouping results. The numbers show the strengths of the connections. With one exception, only links above the threshold of 40 are shown. The positions of the words are *not* to scale.

process. The strongest connection is that between *a* and *the,* with a value of 728. The weakest connections are below the value of 1, and of course are not shown here.

The graph shows clear-cut organization of the nouns into a densely interconnected coherent network. The group of adjectives shows organization within itself, but also a fairly strong adherence to the nouns. This is not surprising in view of the similarities in the distributional properties of nouns and adjectives. This relationship is also well known from the history of development of the word class system in general. Many grammarians treat nouns and adjectives as a subdivision of a general nominal class (Robins, 1966).

Another class to show clear organization is that of the verbs. Notice, however, that the cohesion of this class is considerably lower than that of the nouns. The fact that this is not merely a frequency effect, can be seen from a comparison with the data in Table I. Although there are not enough examples in this set, it is possible that a differentiation of transitive and intransitive verbs is beginning to emerge.

A rather interesting group is formed by the pronouns and what may be called determiners. The definite and indefinite articles show the strongest coherence in the whole data. The demonstrative pronouns are also strongly linked. The first and second person singular pronouns *I* and *you* are strongly linked to each other, while the link to the third person pronouns via *he* is weaker. This may reflect the distinction drawn by Huxley (1970) between the pronouns for participating *vs.* nonparticipating agents in the discourse. A strong connection also appears, not surprisingly, between the demonstrative and personal pronouns. More interesting is the very strong linkage between *it* and *that*. This linkage reflects the deictic or anaphoric uses of these words, discussed at length by Huxley (1970). The relationship between the articles and the demonstrative pronouns is another connection which can be traced back to historical origins, according to Huxley, in Old English. Apparently the same word was used for the definite article and the demonstrative pronoun (*se*), and the modern English *that* derives from the neuter form of the demonstrative pronoun and definite article (*þæt*).

Finally, the organization among prepositions is very weak. No connections among them appear over the threshold of 40, and the only connections which do exceed the threshold go to the verbs. The reason for the lack of coherence is the great deal of variability shown by these words in their distributions, coupled with their generally low frequency. The linkages to verbs appear because of the similar positions of prepositions and verbs in prepositional and verb phrases. Both tend to be followed by a noun phrase.

C. Taxonomic Analysis of Grouping Results

Let us now turn to the results of applying well-defined methods of taxonomic analysis to the results of grouping. These methods enable us to explore the nature of organization in the data, and also provide us with hypotheses as to the possible nature of the process which constructs internal representations for word classes. Space does not permit a detailed description of all the different methods and results which have been used in this study. Fortunately, the various methods do not yield widely different results, so that it can be said with reasonable confidence that the results are not artifacts due to the particular properties of any one method of analysis. For this reason only the results of the best known methods will be given here.

Some of the most satisfactory classes are obtained by using a hierarchical merging process with the Canberra metric and the group-average procedure. The results of this are shown by the dendrogram in Fig. 4. Since such a method will eventually force all objects into a single group, the higher levels of the dendrogram are not very informative. The full tree is given here merely for the sake of completeness. The optimal grouping of items is probably obtained at the level of 957.2 clustering strength. The clusters existing at this level are the following:

> (hen(sheep(pig(farmer(cow(house horse)))))),
> (can (are (do (think see)))),
> (little(big nice)),
> (this(he(that it))),
> (a the),
> (you I).

Here the bracketing is used to indicate the merging structure within the cluster, giving a two-dimensional representation of the dendrogram of Fig. 4. The unassigned items at this level are: *she, put, look, in, is, on, over,* and *into*. It can be seen from the dendrogram that *put* and *look* are correctly attached later to the verb cluster, and *she* to the pronoun cluster. The assignment of the other items is at a high level only, and is correspondingly arbitrary. This reflects the lack of sufficient information about their characteristics at this stage of learning.

For comparison, let us look at the results obtained by the complete linkage (Johnson's maximum) method:

> (sheep(pig(farmer(cow(house horse))))),
> (are(can do)),
> (think see),
> (big nice),
> (this(he(that it))),
> (a the),
> (you I).

This clustering is obtained at the level of 929.3. Finally, the results obtained by the single-linkage (Johnson's minimum) method:

> (sheep(pig(farmer(cow(house horse))))),
> (put(look(can(are(do(think see)))))),
> ((a the) ((you I) (this(he(that it))))),

obtained at the level of 916.4. It can be seen that main features of these results are highly similar, within the limitations of the methods.

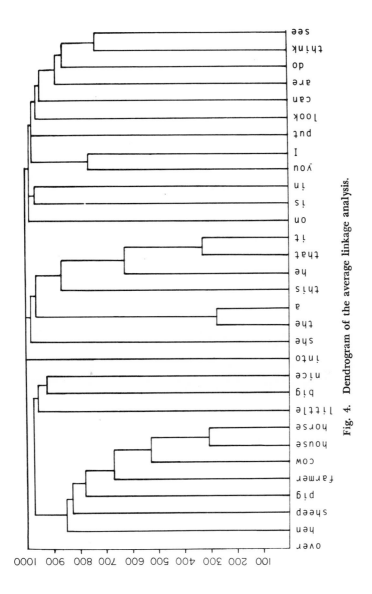

Fig. 4. Dendrogram of the average linkage analysis.

It can be concluded from these results that a process like the group-average fusion can detect the noun, verb, adjective, pronoun, and article clusters.

D.   Discussion of Empirical Findings

Should one expect a classification system to emerge from the simulation, containing no misclassifications and a perfect differentiation of the expected grammatical classes? The answer to this question is certainly negative.

First of all, a number of approximations have been made in the computer simulation which may have an influence on the results. Examples of this are the process of forgetting distributional information, and the use of a limited number of words in the grouping process.

Secondly, grammarians themselves do not agree about the details of a word class system. Such agreement could only be reached if a uniform set of classification criteria could be set down. Linguists usually use a set of varied criteria, like distributional properties, inflectional paradigms, notional definition, and the like. Of these only the distributional criterion is taken into account by the simulation. While the other criteria would presumably contribute to the formation and refinement of a classification system by the child, it is my view that they are processes which come into play at a later stage of development.

Thirdly, the simulation reflects the stage of development in forming a classification system somewhere during the early part of the child's third year. It is well known that at this stage the child's classification system is far from being in complete agreement with the adult grammatical classification system, let alone the classifications proposed by grammarians. The development of the word class system is to be regarded as an evolutionary process of imposing organization on what is initially a diffuse, unsystematic assembly of words. This process of organization continues in step with the growth of general linguistic competence far into the later years of life and is presumably reflected in the S-P shift in word association. The proper question to ask as to the success of the simulation is whether it shows a similarity with the kind of classification system that can be detected in the child's output when he begins to combine words.

Before we turn to a discussion of this question let us restate the assumptions made in this article about the nature of the process leading to the final word class system in the child. It must be kept firmly in mind that there are two distinct problems involved. The first of these is the *discovery* of the word classes, i.e., the discovery of the fact that from the syntactic point of view words have certain characteristics according to which they can be more or less similar to each other. Using such characteristics words can be grouped together if they are similar. For the purposes of early development the characteristics used for this grouping process must be simple and commensurate with the state of general cognitive development in the young child. This is the reason why the distributional properties only are used in my theory. Once groups have been found by using the simple criteria, others can be used to refine and change the system if it is inadequate. Put in other words, the *discovery* of the word classes consists in learning that words can be nounlike, verblike, adjectivelike, etc., to varying degrees. Moreover, a word may have several such properties simultaneously. The first stage of development is therefore the discovery of these features, or factors, or components. This process will be presumably based on the words which occur with the highest frequency in the input.

The second problem is that once the child has discovered that words can be nounlike, verblike, etc., (i.e., that they can have various word class features), he is faced with the problem of assigning such features to newly acquired words. This is generally called the problem of *diagnosis* in taxonomy. The discovery of word class features and the diagnosis of new words obviously interact with each other in early development. New features have to be added to the list if new words are learned which cannot be adequately classified on the basis of existing features. Once the feature system is in its final form, the diagnosis of new words consists in checking some prominent distributional, inflectional, or notional characteristics of the word in order to assign to it some word class features.

With this formulation of the problem firmly in mind, let me now discuss the success of simulation. My expectation is to find the emergence of some word class features in the results in the same order as they are known to be recognized by the child. Clear-cut evidence of this kind is found. The results given in the previous section show that the simulation results in the detection of noun, verb, adjective, article, and pronoun features. At the stage represented by the simulation, the preposition feature is not yet detected.

These findings agree well with the findings of several studies of early linguistic development in the child. Brown and Bellugi (1964) found that the earliest classes to emerge were the articles and demonstrative pronouns followed later by the adjectives and possessive pronouns. These represent the subdivision of the so-called modifier class, while nouns were found to constitute a class from the beginning. Braine (1963b) shows evidence for the early emergence of noun, verb, adjective, deictic pronoun, and possibly preposition classes. Miller and Ervin (1964) found evidence for the early emergence of nouns, verbs, adjectives (although they were not clearly differentiated from the nouns), adverbs, and prepositions (although these last two classes were not clearly differentiated from each other and evidence about them was relatively meager in the corpus studied).

It should be remembered that the conclusion of these studies were not based on a rigorous quantitative analysis of large amounts of outputs from children. It is not very clear therefore how much reliance can be placed on these findings. Nevertheless, it seems generally the case that the sequence of emergence for the classes starts with the nouns (in the form of single-word utterances), continues with modifiers like articles, deictic pronouns, adjectives, and verbs, and terminates with prepositions and adverbs. There are wide variations from child to child in the actual order, but there is some support for placing nouns and deictics earlier, verbs and adjectives in the middle, and prepositions and adverbs later in the sequence. Examination of the coherence of clusters in the simulation results agrees with these findings. The clearest and strongest organization is shown by the nouns and deictics, with verbs and adjectives coming next, while that of the prepositions lags behind.

Looking at particular features of Fig. 3, we see that the strongest link is between *a* and *the,* one of the best documented early classes for all children. Among the pronouns, *it* and *that* has a surprisingly strong linkage, stronger than the one between *that* and *this.* This is a feature often observed in children. For example, for the two children studied by Huxley (1970) "The use of *it*(NP), and the demonstrative pronouns, particularly *that,* seem to show a close relationship for both children [p. 153]."

Furthermore, even with adults, word association data show a strong associative relationship between *it* and *that.* For example, *it* elicits *that* with a probability of .08, and *this* with a probability of .01 (Kiss, Armstrong, & Milroy, 1972).

To summarize, the simulation shows that the proposed learning process is capable of detecting word class features in the input corpus; that the features are grammatically plausible ones; and finally that both the order in which they emerge and some particular relationships between them agree well with the findings of empirical studies of early language acquisition.

VI. Summary

A model of a learning process has been presented for the early learning of word classes by the child. The model is an extension and modification of the mediational theories of Palermo, Jenkins, and Ervin. While those theories were couched in the terms of S-R psychology, the model is an information processing formulation. Close attention has been paid to the detailed *mechanisms* which could carry out such a learning process. None of the proposed mechanisms are neurophysiologically implausible. Most of them are very simple conceptually. They require only the construction and reinforcement of transmission links between internal representations of words, either directly or through "connector" elements, and the capability of making comparisons between activation patterns over a set of internal representations.

A detailed comparison was made between the model and other theoretical formulations. It was found that with the exception of the mediation theory, none of the formulations was capable of accounting for the earliest stage of word class learning. The differences between the proposed model and mediation theory are that the model is worked out in much more detail, that the model violates the "terminal metapostulate," and that it contains a classification process which was not present in the mediation theory.

The model was related to empirical findings, and it was shown that it can account for them. In particular, the S-P shift is a natural consequence of the memory organization in the model.

Due to the amount of detail and explicitness with which the model was specified, it was possible to implement the model as a computer program. This program was then tested by a small but realistic input corpus derived from tape recordings of mothers talking to their young children. The size of this corpus is probably very small compared with the amount of input received by a child in a normal middle-class social environment. The output of the program is a classification system, or more precisely, a set of features, for word classes.

Analysis of this output from the program showed that it contains grammatically appropriate classes and exhibits certain aspects known to be characteristic for the word class systems of young children.

REFERENCES

Ball, G. H., & Hall, D. J. ISODATA, a novel method of data analysis and pattern classification. SRI Project 5533, 1965, Stanford Research Institute Technical Report.

Bever, T. G. Associations to stimulus-response theories of language. In T. R. Dixon & D. L. Horton (Eds.), *Verbal behavior and general behavior theory.* Englewood Cliffs, N.J.: Prentice-Hall, 1968.

Bever, T. G., Fodor, J. A., & Garrett, M. A formal limitation of associationism. In T. R. Dixon & D. L. Horton (Eds.), *Verbal behavior and general behavior theory.* Englewood Cliffs, N.J.: Prentice-Hall, 1968.

Bever, T. G., Fodor, J. A., & Weksel, W. Theoretical notes on the acquisition of syntax: A critique of contextual generalisation. *Psychological Review,* 1965, **72**, 467–482.

Braine, M. D. S. On learning the grammatical order of words. *Psychological Review,* 1963, **70**, 323–348. (a)

Braine, M. D. S. The ontogeny of English phrase structure: The first phase. *Language,* 1963, **39**, 1–3. (b)

Braine, M. D. S. On the basis of phrase structure: A reply to Bever, Fodor and Weksel. *Psychological Review,* 1965, **72**, 483–492.

Brown, R. N., & Bellugi, U. Three processes in the child's acquisition of syntax. In J. A. Fleming, J. T. Fleming, & H. M. Popp (Eds.), *Language and learning.* New York: Harcourt, 1964.

Brown, R. N., & Berko, J. Word association and the acquisition of grammar. *Child Development,* 1960, **31**, 1–14.

Brown, R. N., & Fraser, C. The acquisition of syntax. In C. N. Cofer & B. Musgrave (Eds.), *Verbal behavior and learning.* New York: McGraw-Hill, 1963.

Clifton, C. C. The implications of grammar for word association. In K. Salzinger & S. Salzinger (Eds.), *Research in verbal behavior and some neurophysiological implications.* New York: Academic Press, 1967.

Crystal, D. English. *Lingua,* 1967, **17**, 24–56.

Deese, J. *The structure of associations in language and thought.* Baltimore: Johns Hopkins Press, 1965.

Entwisle, D. R. *Word associations of young children.* Baltimore: Johns Hopkins Press, 1966.

Ervin, S. M. Changes with age in the verbal determinants of word association. *American Journal of Psychology,* 1961, **74**, 361–372.

Ervin, S. M. Correlates of associative frequency. *Journal of Verbal Learning and Verbal Behavior,* 1963, **1**, 422–431.

Fodor, J. A. How to learn to talk: Some simple ways. In F. Smith & G. A. Miller (Eds.), *The genesis of language.* Cambridge, Mass.: MIT Press, 1966.

Fodor, J. A. *Psychological explanation: An introduction to the philosophy of psychology.* New York: Random House, 1968.

Fries, C. C. *The structure of English.* London: Longmans, Green, 1952.

Harris, Z. S. *Structural linguistics.* Chicago: University of Chicago Press, 1951.

Huxley, R. The development of the correct use of subject personal pronouns in two children. In F. d'Arcais & W. J. M. Levelt (Eds.), *Advances in psycholinguistics.* Amsterdam: North-Holland Publ., 1970.

Jardine, N., & Sibson, R. *Mathematical taxonomy.* New York: Wiley, 1971.

Jenkins, J. J. Mediation theory and grammatical behavior. In S. Rosenberg (Ed.), *Directions in psycholinguistics.* New York: Macmillan, 1965.

Jenkins, J. J., & Palermo, D. S. Mediation processes and the acquisition of linguistic structure. In U. Bellugi & R. Brown (Eds.), The acquisition of language. *Child Development Monographs,* 1964, 29, No. 1.

Johnson, S. C. Hierarchical clustering schemes. *Psychometrika,* 1967, **32**, 241–254.

Kiss, G. R. Networks as models of word storage. In N. Collins & D. Michie (Eds.), *Machine intelligence*. Vol. 1. Edinburgh: Oliver & Boyd, 1967.

Kiss, G. R. Steps toward a model of word selection. In B. Meltzer & D. Michie (Eds.), *Machine intelligence*. Vol. 4. Edinburgh: University of Edinburgh Press, 1969.

Kiss, G. R. Long-term memory. *British Journal of Psychology*, 1972, **63**, 327–341.

Kiss, G. R., Armstrong, C., & Milroy, R. *An associative thesaurus of English*. (Microfilm Version) Wakefield, Eng.: EP Microforms, 1972.

Lance, G. N., & Williams, W. T. Computer programs for hierarchical polythetic classification. *Computer Journal*, 1966, **9**, 60–64. (a)

Lance, G. N., & Williams, W. T. A generalised sorting strategy for computer classification. *Nature (London)*, 1966, **212**, 218. (b)

Lance, G. N., & Williams, W. T. A general theory of classificatory sorting strategies: I. Hierarchical systems. *Computer Journal*, 1967, **9**, 373–380.

MacQueen, J. B. Some methods for classification and analysis of multivariate observations. *Proceedings of the 5th Berkeley Symposium on Mathematical Statistics and Probability*, 1967, **1**, 281–297.

McNeill, D. The origin of associations within the same grammatical class. *Journal of Verbal Learning and Verbal Behavior*, 1963, **2**, 250–262.

McNeill, D. The creation of language by children. In J. Lyons & R. J. Wales (Eds.), *Psycholinguistics papers*. Edinburgh: University of Edinburgh Press, 1966. (a)

McNeill, D. A study of word association. *Journal of Verbal Learning and Verbal Behavior*, 1966, **5**, 548–557. (b)

McNeill, D. *The acquisition of language*. New York: Harper, 1970. (a)

McNeill, D. The development of language. In P. A. Mussen (Ed.), *Carmichael's manual of child psychology*. New York: Wiley, 1970. (b)

Miller, W., & Ervin, S. The development of grammar in child language. In U. Bellugi & R. Brown (Eds.), The acquisition of language. *Child Development Monographs*, 1964, 29, No. 1.

Robins, R. H. The development of the word class system of the European grammatical tradition. *Foundations of Language*, 1966, **2**, 3–19.

Sokal, R. R., & Sneath, P. H. *Principles of numerical taxonomy*. San Francisco: Freeman, 1963.

Weir, R. H. *Language in the crib*. The Hague: Mouton, 1962.

Wishart, D. Mode analysis: A generalisation of nearest-neighbour which reduces chaining effects. In A. J. Cole (Ed.), *Numerical taxonomy*. London: Academic Press, 1969.

REACTION TIME MEASUREMENTS IN THE STUDY OF MEMORY PROCESSES: THEORY AND DATA[1]

John Theios

DEPARTMENT OF PSYCHOLOGY, UNIVERSITY OF WISCONSIN,
MADISON, WISCONSIN

[1] This article is dedicated to the memory of Robert R. Bush who not only provided me with encouragement, direction, and reinforcement during a critical time in my career, but whose life as a scientist and scholar has had a lasting influence on me and many others.

Many of the theoretical ideas presented in this article grew out of long conversations and collaborative theoretical work with Jean-Claude Falmagne. His influence on this article is so great that he should be considered a precursor if not a coauthor. Acknowledgment is also due to Dominic W. Massaro who influenced the sections on the stimulus identification and naming processes. Finally, much appreciation is due to my research staff, Diane Flakas, Melvyn C. Moy, Peter G. Smith, Jane Traupmann, and Dennis Walter, who worked very hard on this research over a number of years.

The research reported in this article was conducted in part during the author's tenure as a John Simon Guggenheim Memorial Fellow and was supported by Public Health Service Research Grant MH 19006 from the National Institute of Mental Health. Computing time and other support was made available from the Wisconsin Alumni Research Foundation in part through funds from the National Science Foundation.

I. Introduction

The research reported in this article investigates the human memory process through the use of reaction time measurements. Traditional human information processing tasks such as stimulus naming, choice reaction, and stimulus classification are related to current conceptions of short-term and long-term memory and subsumed under a single information processing theory. The guiding principles in this endeavor are the following assumptions:

1. To respond discriminatively to a stimulus, an observer must first identify (or classify) the stimulus and then determine the particular response which is appropriate. For very familiar stimuli such as alpha-numeric characters, stimulus identification is a relatively automatic process which is independent of the probability and number of stimuli in the experimental ensemble.

2. Human memory can be partitioned into a very large capacity long-term store and a number of very limited capacity short-term (working) stores. Representations of all stimulus-response codes are stored in long-term memory, and these are always potentially retrievable. Retrieval of information from long-term memory is assumed to be relatively slow and take a constant amount of time. As such retrieval from long-term memory can be thought of as a *content addressable* (essentially parallel) search process.

3. In many situations (especially in artifically contrived learning, memory, and information processing tasks), a small set of stimuli and responses recur at a fairly high frequency. In these situations, it is convenient to assume that "copies" of the memory representations of the recurring stimuli and responses may be held and organized into serially scanned, short-term stores or memory buffers. Retrieval from the short-term memory buffers is relatively fast since the serial scanning is assumed to be fast.

A basic thesis of this article will be that in serial human information processing tasks, the short-term stores become completely filled up with representations of the occurring stimuli and responses, and that to the extent that there is any structure in the sequence of physical stimuli and required responses, that structure will be mirrored in (or at least affect) the structure and organization of the serially searched, short-term stores. In particular, it will be postulated that the organization of the short-term stores will be greatly influenced by the sequential (recency) properties of the recurring stimuli and responses.

A. CONTINUOUS INFORMATION PROCESSING TASKS

Given the assumption of serial short-term stores in human memory, it is our conjecture that there are tasks which can completely tie up one's short-term stores. If this is true, then these tasks can give the experimenter a great deal of control in studying the short-term memory systems of humans. We will call these tasks *continuous information processing tasks*. One example of this type of task is the classic serial, choice reaction time situation (e.g., Falmagne, 1965). In this type of experiment, the subject monitors a serial sequence of two or more different stimuli, differentially reacting to each stimulus as quickly as possible after it is presented. The next stimulus is usually presented very quickly after the subject's response. From the subject's point of view, the task is essentially continuous if the response-stimulus interval is about .5 seconds or less.

Another group of continuous information processing tasks are the stimulus identification experiments in which the subject is asked to identify, name, or read each of a sequence of stimuli. Character naming experiments (e.g., Davis, Moray, & Treisman, 1961; Morin & Forrin, 1965) are good examples of stimulus identification. If the response-stimulus interval is made short enough, the task can be made to appear continuous for the subject, and the experimenter can "drive" or completely engage the subject's short-term memory system.

A final example of an "attention-locking" continuous information processing task is a speeded version (Theios, Smith, Haviland, Traupmann, & Moy, 1973) of Sternberg's (1967) character classification experiment. Here the subject is required to keep a constant set of stimuli in memory, and to classify each of a sequence of stimuli as being a member or not a member of the memory set. Nickerson (1972) has recently reviewed the experimental studies of this type of binary classification. Again, if the response-stimulus interval is kept short enough, the experimenter can "lock up" all of the subject's attention or short-term memory capabilities. We use the terms "tie up," "drive," or "lock up" the subject's attention or short-term memory because if a subject is distracted or thinks about something else in these speeded types of identification-reaction time tasks, he will be unable to perform the task quickly, and reaction times become long. Presumably, the reaction times become long because the subject's short-term memory is being filled by information extraneous to the task, so that in order to respond differentially to the incoming experimental stimuli, the necessary internal stimulus-response representations now have to be retrieved from long-term memory. This will take much longer than if they had been temporarily stored in short-term memory. Of course, the more traditional way of saying this is that the subject's "attention" is being diverted away from the experimental task. Thus, in this article we will occasionally equate "attention" and "short-term memory."

B. Use of Reaction Time to Measure Cognitive Processing

1. *History: Donders' Subtractive Method*

Over a hundred years ago, Franciscus Cornelis Donders introduced the use of reaction time to measure the speed of unobservable, internal human events. Given the current revival of the use of reaction time measures in psychological research, Donders' (1868–1869) theoretical analysis and his experimental conceptualization seem incredibly advanced. In a typical experiment, Donders used plosive consonant-vowel clusters (ka, ke, ki, ko, ku) as stimuli, either presented auditorially (spoken) or visually (rapid illumination), and the subject's task was to repeat the stimulus as quickly as he could. He tested the subjects under three experimental conditions:

a. Simple Reaction Time. Using a tone as a warning signal, the stimulus ka, for example, would be presented for many trials, and an estimate of the subject's mean and minimum reaction time to the stimulus ka would be obtained. This simple reaction time estimate, t_a, would be the time to respond with a known response to an expected stimulus. Presumably, t_a would simply be a measure of stimulus input and response output time, and would not contain decision time components for stimulus identification or response selection. Thus,

$$t_a = t_i + t_o \tag{1}$$

where t_i represents stimulus *input* time and t_o represents response *output* time.

b. Choice Reaction Time. Using the same subjects and the same stimuli, Donders would also measure reaction time to an uncertain stimulus. For example, on any trial, one of the five consonant-vowel sounds would be selected more or less at random, and the subject had to repeat it as soon as he determined what sound it was. Choice reaction time, t_b, thus had four additive components; stimulus input time t_i, stimulus identification time t_s, response selection time t_r, and response output time, t_o. Thus,

$$t_b = t_i + t_s + t_r + t_o. \tag{2}$$

From the assumption that the times of the various psychological events are additive, Donders argued that they would also be subtractive. Thus,

$$t_b - t_a = t_s + t_r \tag{3}$$

which is a measure of the decision time for both stimulus identification and response selection.

c. Selective Reaction Time. In a third testing condition, Donders had his subjects monitor an uncertain, random sequence of stimuli and respond only when a particular (memory or target) stimulus occurred. Donders theorized that reaction time in the selective task, t_c, would be composed of three additive components (stimulus input time t_i, stimulus identification time t_s, and response output time t_o), but would not include response selection time. Thus,

$$t_c = t_i + t_s + t_o. \tag{4}$$

It follows by subtraction that an estimate of response selection time can be obtained as

$$t_r = t_b - t_c \tag{5}$$

and an estimate of stimulus selection time can be obtained as

$$t_s = t_c - t_a. \tag{6}$$

In a typical experiment on himself, Donders (1868–1869) estimated stimulus identification time to be about 47 msec, response selection time to be about 36 msec, and combined stimulus-input and response-output time to be about 201 msec.

There are problems with Donders' subtractive method. The conjecture that the times are additive (subtractive) is based upon the assumption that all the component times are constant from task to task. This is not likely to hold across the three methods, but rather, the means for a given time component will probably vary from method to method. For example, in all probability the t_a estimates will be too short because in the simple reaction time task the subject can anticipate the signal. Effectively, the main objection is that using Donder's subtractive method, one has no or little control over the subject's response criteria (in the signal detectability sense).

2. Sternberg's Additive Factor Method

The reasoning behind Sternberg's (1969, 1971) *additive-factor* or *serial-stage* method is very similar to that of Donders. However,

Sternberg's analysis of variance approach enables one to evaluate the independence or covariation among various experimental variables affecting reaction time. If two variables are *independent* they are assumed to affect separate processing stages, and their effects on reaction time means and variances are *additive*. If two variables *interact* they are assumed to affect at least one stage in common, and their effects on reaction time are not additive. Sternberg (1969, 1971) has postulated four serial stages which seem necessary for many information processing tasks:

a. Stimulus Encoding. Presumably, this stage involves sensory input time and the time to transform the sensory information into a form which can be operated on in memory. Encoding time is affected by such variables as stimulus detectability, intensity, and quality. Sternberg has not been clear on whether or not this stage involves stimulus identification (cognition).

b. Memory Search and Comparison. In this stage, properly encoded stimulus representations are evaluated as to class membership. This stage could involve the identification or cognitive interpretation of the stimulus. The memory search and comparison time is affected by the size of the stimulus ensemble, nature of the task, and instructions to the subject.

c. Response Decision. Depending upon the task, the subject is required to differentially respond to different stimuli. The results of the prior memory search and comparison operations are evaluated, and a decision to make a particular response is made. The response decision stage may be affected by speed-accuracy instructions and the types of permissible responses.

d. Response Selection and Evocation. Once a decision as to the appropriate response has been made, a response evocation "program" is selected and executed. Sternberg (1971) has called this the *translation and response organization* stage. Its duration is affected by such variables as response relative frequency, number of response alternatives, and stimulus-response compatibility.

e. Cautionary Remarks. A number of excellent presentations of the additive factor method have been made (Sternberg, 1969, 1971), and we will not further explicate it here. We do, however, wish to make the following cautionary remarks. The linear analysis of variance model has often been used in conjunction with the additive factor method. In these cases it suffers from all the restrictive assumptions of the analysis of variance, namely, the requirement of identically distributed (equal variance) normal distributions. In point of fact, empirical reaction times are not normally distributed but are skewed with a high positive tail. Further, and more importantly, the means and variances of empirical reaction time distributions are most often positively correlated, a direct violation of the equal variance assumption. Much of the research using the additive factor method (Sternberg, 1969, 1971) has centered around demonstrating additivity (the independence of variables affecting different processing stages), and this has been done by showing *lack* of significant interactions in analysis of variance tests. With the large variances of reaction time measurements and the typically small number of subjects used in information processing experiments contributing to low power of the analysis of variance, failure to find significant interactions has been interpreted as indicating additive (independent) effects of experimental variables where the noninteracting variables affect separate processing stages. Thus, any Type II decision errors (accepting the null hypothesis when it is in fact false) in the interaction tests favor an independent stage–additive factor interpretation. One does not know how often it is the case that two variables really interact to *a small degree,* but the power of the analysis of variance is too low to detect the interaction. To avoid this "acceptance of the null hypothesis" problem, we propose that investigators construct precise, well formulated mathematical models to describe the processes which they are investigating, and that they continually modify the models as new data are made available. One primary purpose of this article will be to show that specific descriptive models with strong assumptions about processing operations can provide much more information about human information processing and memory than can the additive factor method used alone. The main point of this theoretical difference is that one asks different questions about the data and does different experiments if one is looking for additive factors than if one is looking for specific processes. The additive factor (functionalist) approach essentially asks "What variables have effects, and how do they interact?" The specific descriptive model (process) approach essentially asks "What are the processes involved, and how do the variables affect the process?" In the remainder of the article we will introduce and test a very robust descriptive process model of human memory and information processing.

II. Self-Terminating Memory Scanning Model

A. Stimulus Encoding

Stimulus encoding time (t_e) is assumed to be composed of two components. The first component (t_i) is the time it takes for the physical stimulus energy to be input and transformed in the brain to information which can be used to identify or classify the stimulus. The second component (t_s) is the time it takes to identify the stimulus given the coded information from the physical stimulus. It is assumed that to identify the stimulus, contact must be made with long-term memory by matching the stimulus to a stored representation or by uniquely specifying the stimulus as a member of some class following an analysis operating on the features of the coded stimulus. The identification process is assumed to be a content addressable or a net discrimination process so that for sets of well-defined stimuli such as numbers or letters, encoding time averaged over the experimental ensemble of stimuli should be essentially a constant, independent of size of the experimental ensemble. Encoding time, of course, may vary from stimulus to stimulus, due to unique features.

B. Response Determination

The response determination stage of processing follows stimulus encoding. If the task involves reading or naming the stimulus (a highly compatible response), then a simple transformation is made on the stimulus information which will enable a relatively direct output of the response. The stimulus-to-name transformation will take a constant amount of time. Essentially, it is assumed that names (and perhaps other highly compatible responses) are stored in long-term memory in or near the location of the stimulus code, and that little or no additional memory searching (for a response) is necessary for reading, naming, and other highly compatible responses.

With responses that are not naturally related to the stimulus, a *response determination search* must take place before the appropriate response can be selected. For button pushing or other types of indicator responses, it is assumed that the set of stimulus-response codes are stored in a list or "dictionary" in some other location in long-term memory. Further, in speeded tasks, the set of stimulus-response codes may be organized into a short-term, serially scanned, limited capacity buffer. In fact, elements of the long-term "dictionary" may be sequentially loaded into the short-term buffer for processing. To the extent that the fast-access, serial, short-term buffer is used, response determination time (t_r) will be an increasing function of the number of stimulus-response pairs. The short-term buffer is conceived of as a dynamic stack or hierarchy in which representations of the stimulus-response pairs are changing positions from trial to trial and are probabistically ordered on the basis of recency and frequency of stimulus occurrence according to a process similar to that proposed by Falmagne and Theios (1969) and Theios *et al.* (1973). The scan of the stimulus-response buffer is assumed to be serial and self-terminating. Thus, representations of recent and more frequent stimuli are more likely to be located faster, since they are more likely to have favored buffer positions (be higher in the stack). Infrequent and nonrecent stimuli are more likely to have their representations stored further down in the buffer. In that the buffer is of limited capacity, infrequent and nonrecent stimuli may not be represented in the buffer at all, and thus, retrieval of their responses must be made from the slower, long-term memory dictionary. The size of the serial buffer may be variable (in part under the control of the observer) and may be influenced by instructions and the demands of the specific task at hand. With a one-to-one assignment of stimuli to responses, response determination may be a simple transformation taking a small, relatively constant amount of time.

C. Response Evocation

After the stimulus has been identified and the appropriate response determined, the response must be output by the observer. Response output time can be decomposed into two components. The first is the time to select the appropriate response output program. The response output programs may be organized into a dynamic, serial, self-terminating response output buffer which is probabilistically reorganized from trial to trial on the basis of frequency and recency of response occurrence. Output programs for most recent and more frequent responses are located faster than programs for infrequent and nonrecent responses. The second component of response evocation time is simply the motor time involved in making the response.

D. Flow Chart of the System

Figure 1 presents a flow diagram of the self-terminating memory system. Information in the physical stimulus S is input to the sensory receptors and transformed and coded by the nervous system into a form usable by the memory process. This takes time t_i, and the result is coded information about the stimulus which we represent as s. The coded information is then processed by the long-term memory identification system which either finds a coded representation of the name of the stimulus (n) as a result of a content addressable memory retrievable process or a sequential feature testing, net discrimina-

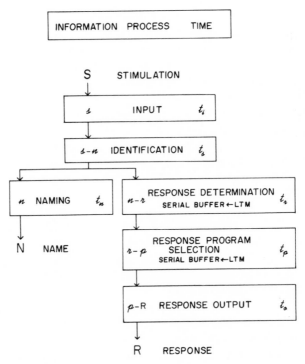

Fig. 1. Flow of information through the human memory system. Physical stimulation S is input to the memory taking time t_i to be converted to a sensory code s. The sensory code s is fed into the identification process, taking time t_s to determine the name code n of the stimulus. (s-n denotes the link from s to n). If the task requires naming the stimulus, the name code is fed into a naming process which outputs the name of the stimulus, taking time t_n. The total time it takes to name a stimulus is $t_i + t_s + t_n$. If the task requires making some other response to the stimulus, the name code n is fed into the response dictionary which determines the appropriate response code assigned to the stimulus, taking time t_r. For tasks with a compatible one-to-one stimulus response mapping, t_r is effectively a constant near zero. In tasks with a many-to-one stimulus-response mapping, a serially searched, self-terminating buffer may be set up which is fed response codes by a long-term store. The response code r is fed into a system which selects a response program taking time t_p and outputs a response taking time t_o, yielding an overt response R. The total time it takes to respond to a stimulus is $t_i + t_s + t_r + t_p + t_o$.

tion process. The stimulus identification process takes time t_s. If the task at hand requires a simple name response, a transformation is performed on the coded name information n to produce an overt name response N. If some other indicator response is required by the task, the coded name information n is fed into the response determination system which has two components which operate in parallel. One component is a content addressable (or sequential feature testing) long-term memory system which can produce the required response for any stimulus. The other component is a limited capacity, short-term buffer which determines the response by a serial, self-terminating scan of the buffer. The coded name information n is compared sequentially to each of a small set of name-to-response (n-r) pairs stored in the buffer until a match is obtained. If a buffer match is obtained, coded information about the response (r) is fed into the response output buffer where a response is selected and executed. There are two ways to think about the operation of the long-term memory response determination process.

1. Parallel Operation

As soon as the long-term response determination system "computes" the response, the response code r is fed directly into the response output system for response selection and execution. This may happen before the serial scan of the short-term buffer has located the response. Thus, the time to retrieve a response from long-term memory may determine the effective capacity of the short-term buffer. If the time it takes to retrieve a response from long-term memory is t_L and the scan rate of the short-term buffer is t_S, then the effective short-term buffer capacity is $K = t_L/t_S$.

2. Yoked Operation

This process was suggested by Jean-Claude Falmagne. Assume that the long-term memory system loads the short-term buffer with the representations of potential n-r pairs, and that the actual response decision is made by the self-terminating, serial buffer scan process. At the beginning of a trial the buffer is already loaded with the (locally) most likely n-r pairs in sequential order. During the buffer scan, the long-term memory system continues to load likely n-r pairs into the buffer. The effective capacity of the short-term buffer is determined by the average time it takes for the long-term memory to feed the correct n-r pair to the buffer. If the estimated capacity of the buffer were K, this would mean that the average time for the long-term memory to retrieve and feed the correct n-r pair to the buffer would be $(K - 1)t_S$, where t_S is the buffer scan time for a single pair.

After the appropriate response code r has been determined, it is fed into the response output system. The response output system may work very similarly to the response determination system, having both a long-term and a short-term memory component. The response output programs may be selected by a fast, serial, self-terminating scan of a dynamic, response buffer or by a slower long-term memory retrieval process. The time to select the response program can be designated as t_p. The time to output an overt response can be designated as t_o.

E. Specific Representation of the Model

This section may be skipped by readers who understand the model as conceptually presented in the previous sections. The following presentation is given to resolve ambiguities that may result from the inexactness of the English language, and to help investigators who wish to obtain quantitative predictions from the model or to do further mathematical and computer research with the model.

Suppose a set S containing I ($I \geqslant 2$) stimuli $\{S_1, S_2, S_3, \ldots, S_i, \ldots, S_I\}$, a set R containing M ($2 \leqslant M \leqslant I$) responses $\{R_1, R_2, R_3, \ldots, R_m, \ldots, R_M\}$ and a binary function of the form $\{(S_i, R_m)\}$ which is a subset of the cross product of the sets S and R which maps the set S onto the set R.

Definition 1: Stimulus Input

The time to input a stimulus S_i to the system and convert it to a usable representation s_i is t_i which is a random sample from a distribution $f_i(t)$ having mean μ_i and variance σ_i^2. This distribution may vary somewhat from stimulus to stimulus.

Definition 2: Stimulus Identification

The time taken by the system to determine the name code n_i of representation s_i is t_s which is a random sample from a distribution $f_s(t)$ having mean μ_s and variance σ_s^2. This distribution may vary somewhat from name to name.

Definition 3: Naming

The time to convert the name code n_i to an overt name response N_i is t_n, which is a random sample from a distribution $f_n(t)$ having mean μ_n and variance σ_n^2. This distribution may vary somewhat from name to name.

Axiom 1: Naming Time

The time to overtly name a stimulus S_i is

$$NT_i = t_i + t_s + t_n \tag{7}$$

where t_i, t_s, and t_n are random variables defined in Definitions 1–3.

Definition 4: Memory Stack Response Dictionary

If the stimulus-response mapping is not one-to-one, then at each trial there is an ordering of appropriate name-response pairs (n_i-r_m) in memory such that every pair can be given a position k, where $1 \leqslant k \leqslant Z$, and $Z \leqslant I$.

Axiom 2: Response Determination

If the stimulus-response mapping is not one-to-one, and if stimulus S_i is presented, and if K is the dictionary position in which the matching memory pair n_i-r_m is stored, then the time to determine the appropriate response code r_m is

$$t_r = \sum_{k=1}^{K} t_k \tag{8}$$

where t_k is a random sample from a distribution $f_k(t)$ having mean μ_k and variance σ_k^2. With a one-to-one stimulus-response mapping, the dictionary position may equal one for all name-response codes.

Definition 5: Response Output Buffer

At any time there is an ordering of the response output programs such that every response program can be given a position j, $1 \leqslant j \leqslant W$, in memory, with $W \leqslant M$.

Axiom 3: Response Output Program Selection

If the execution program for response R_m is stored in position J of the output buffer, then the time to select the program is

$$t_p = \sum_{j=1}^{J} t_j \tag{9}$$

where t_j is a random sample from a distribution $f_j(t)$ having mean μ_j and variance σ_j^2.

Definition 6: Response Output Time

Given that the response output program has been selected, the time to output the overt response R_i is t_o, a random sample from a distribution $f_o(t)$ having mean μ_o and variance σ_o^2. This distribution may vary somewhat from response to response.

Axiom 4: Reaction Time

The reaction time to stimulus S_i is the sum of the times to input and identify the stimulus and the times to determine the appropriate response and select and output the response

$$RT_i = t_i + t_s + t_r + t_p + t_o. \tag{10}$$

For a one-to-one stimulus-response mapping, t_r may equal a nonnegative constant.

Axiom 5: Memory Differentiation

Positions 1 through $Z - 1$ of the serial response dictionary each contain only one name-response code pair $(n\text{-}r)$ whereas the long-term response dictionary may be considered as position Z which contains all the relevant $n\text{-}r$ codes.

Likewise, positions 1 through $W - 1$ of the serial output buffer each contain only one response output program, whereas the long-term response output memory may be considered as position W which contains all the relevant response output programs.

Axiom 6: Dictionary Position Changes

Let $X_{i,N}$ be a random variable indicating the dictionary position of name-response pair $n_i\text{-}r_m$ on trial N. If $n_i\text{-}r_m$ is represented at memory position K and if stimulus S_i is presented on trial N, then the probability that pair $n_i\text{-}r_m$ moves up to position K' $(K' < K)$ before trial $N + 1$ is

$$\Pr(X_{i,N+1} = K'|X_{i,N} = K) = (1 - a_i)^{K'-1} a_i. \tag{11}$$

The probability that pair $n_i\text{-}r_m$ remains in the Kth memory position is

$$\Pr(X_{i,N+1} = K|X_{i,N} = K) = 1 - \left[\sum_{k=1}^{K-1} (1 - a_i)^{k-1} a_i \right]. \tag{12}$$

The parameter a_i represents the conditional probability that pair $n_i\text{-}r_m$ will replace pair $n_j\text{-}r_o$ in the kth position of the dictionary stack given it did not replace any pair higher in the stack. If memory pair $n_i\text{-}r_m$ moves up to memory position K' from position K following the presentation of stimulus S_i on trial N, then all the intervening pairs in positions K' through $K - 1$ move down one, to positions $K' + 1$ through K, with their order preserved.

Axiom 7: Output Position Changes

Let $Y_{m,N}$ be a random variable indicating the buffer position of the response output program for response R_m on trial N. If response R_m was made on trial N and its output program was located at buffer position J on trial N, then the probability that the program moves up to position J' $(J' < J)$ before the next trial is

$$\Pr(Y_{m,N+1} = J' | Y_{m,N} = J) = (1 - b_m)^{J'-1} b_m. \tag{13}$$

The probability that the program remains in the Jth position is

$$\Pr(Y_{m,N+1} = J | Y_{m,N} = J) = 1 - \left[\sum_{j=1}^{J-1} (1 - b_m)^{J-1} b_m \right]. \tag{14}$$

The parameter b_m represents the conditioned probability that the response output program for response R_m will replace some other program in the jth position of the buffer given that it did not replace any program located higher in the buffer. Following a response R_m, if the response program moves up to position J' from position J, then all the intervening programs in positions J' through $J - 1$ move down one to positions $J' + 1$ through J with their order preserved.

Axioms 6 and 7 are not fundamental to the system. They could be replaced by other axioms which determine memory positions for the name-response pairs and the output programs. What is crucial is that the time to locate a name-response code and an output program be directly related to the number of intervening stimuli and responses since the last occurrence of the stimulus and response in question.

A number of testable hypotheses follow directly from the definitions and axioms, assuming standard statistical theory and reasonable simplifying assumptions. The simplifying assumptions which will be made in this treatment are:

1. All the component time distributions $[f_i(t), f_s(t), f_j(t), f_k(t),$ and $f_o(t)]$ are statistically independent of each other.

2. Mean stimulus input time (μ_i), mean stimulus identification

time (μ_s), mean naming time (μ_n), and mean response output time (μ_o) are independent of stimulus presentation probability and the size of the experimental set of stimuli.

3. Dictionary comparison time t_k and output buffer comparison time t_j are independent of memory positions k and j.

4. Dictionary position change probabilities a_i are equal for all stimulus names assigned to the same response.

5. With a one-to-one stimulus-response mapping, the dictionary process cannot be differentiated (mathematically) from the response buffer process. Thus, in situations with a one-to-one S-R mapping, it will be assumed that the response determination time t_r will equal a nonnegative constant.

III. Experimental Tests of the Model

A. STIMULUS NAMING AND CHOICE REACTION TIME WITH EQUALLY LIKELY STIMULI

Prediction 1: Mean Stimulus Name Time. Given the above definitions, axioms, and assumptions, the mean time to name a stimulus S_i is independent of the number of other equally likely stimulus alternatives and is equal to a constant

$$\overline{NT}_i = \mu_i + \mu_s + \mu_n. \tag{15}$$

This result follows directly from Axiom 1.

Our next prediction requires a preliminary result. The derivation of this result is straightforward and will not be given here.

Expected Response Buffer Position. Given I equally likely stimuli with a one-to-one stimulus-response mapping, and a response output buffer capacity of W, the asymptotic expected buffer position for any response program is

$$E(Y_I) = \left(\frac{I - W + 1}{I}\right) W + \frac{1}{I} \sum_{j=1}^{W-1} j. \tag{16}$$

In the present model, the serial buffer capacity $(W - 1)$ is a parameter that must be estimated from the data.

Prediction 2: Mean Reaction Time. Given the above definitions, axioms, and assumptions, the mean time to differentially react to a stimulus with a uniquely assigned response is a linear function of the expected buffer position of the response output program.

$$\overline{RT}_i = (\mu_i + \mu_s + \mu_r) + (EY_i)\mu_j + \mu_o \qquad (17)$$
$$= \mu E(Y_i) + B$$

where B, the reaction time intercept, is equal to $\mu_i + \mu_s + \mu_r + \mu_o$ (the mean stimulus input, identification, response determination, and output time) and $\mu = \mu_j$ is the mean response selection buffer scan time. This result follows directly from Axioms 4, 5, and 7 and Eq. (16).

1. Stimulus Naming Experiment

This experiment was conducted with the aid of Diane Flakas and Peter G. Smith. The subjects were 12 University of Wisconsin undergraduate student volunteers who received $2.00 for participation in the experiment. The apparatus was the same as that described in detail in Theios et al. (1973). Each subject was tested individually on two successive days during a session which lasted less than 50 minutes. On one day the subject was required to name the stimuli (the numerals 0–9). On the other day the subject was required to indicate the stimulus by pushing a response button uniquely assigned to each stimulus. Half of the subjects received the naming task on their first day and half the subjects received the button-pushing task on their first day. In the naming task each subject received six experimental conditions of 300 trials each. The variable was the number of equally likely stimuli (2, 4, 6, 8, or 10). The first condition each subject received was practice with 10 stimuli. Each subject then received the conditions of 2, 4, 6, 8, and 10 stimuli in a random order which was different for each subject.

In the button-pushing task each subject received five experimental conditions of 300 trials each. The variable was the number of equally likely stimuli (2, 4, 6, and 8). The first condition each subject received was practice with eight stimuli. In the next four conditions, the order of the conditions of 2, 4, 6, and 8 stimuli were distributed among the 12 subjects according to three Latin squares which balanced the order of presentation. The eight response buttons were located under the subject's eight fingers, and the stimulus-response mapping was 2–9 with the fingers from left to right. The stimulus sets were (5, 6), (4, 5, 6, 7), (3, 4, 5, 6, 7, 8), and (2, 3, 4, 5, 6, 7, 8, 9).

In both tasks, the response-stimulus interval was .5 second, and the stimuli were presented by an Industrial Electronics Engineers Inc., Series 10 rear-projection visual readout unit. The stimuli were selected and presented by a PDP-8 computer which also recorded

the stimulus, response, and response time on magnetic tape. The
subjects' verbal naming responses were recorded on audio tape, and
a Lafayette voice sensitive relay was used to trigger the naming times.
The subject sat in a sound-attenuated booth and wore earphones
which delivered a wide-band white noise mask.

Figure 2 presents mean response time as a function of number of
stimulus-response alternatives for name responses as well as button-
push responses. As can be seen, the mean name response times are
effectively a constant, approximately 450 msec, independent of num-
ber of stimulus-name alternatives. On the other hand, the mean
button-pushing reaction times increase with the number of stimulus-
response alternatives. This pattern of results was true for each of the
twelve subjects individually, and it is consistent with the results of
many other experiments (e.g., Brainard, Irby, Fitts, & Alluisi, 1962;
Davis *et al.*, 1961; Morin & Forrin, 1965).

The results have three important implications for information
processing models. The first is that of the *locus of cognition*. After
a stimulus has been encoded and before it is used in any serial mem-
ory scan, the stimulus has been identified. The subject "knows" what
the stimulus is since he can report the name of the stimulus fast
without any serial scanning dependent upon the size of the experi-
mental set of stimuli.

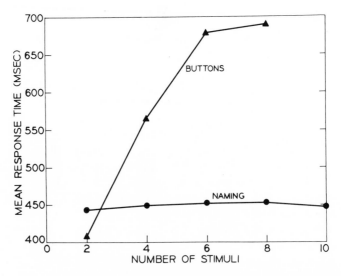

Fig. 2. Mean response time (msec) as a function of number of equally likely
stimulus alternatives for the verbal naming and button-pushing response conditions.

The second implication is that the typical serial component of reaction time is a *response* process such as response determination or response selection. Presumably, in the Sternberg (1967) character classification task, the subject should be able to identify (name) the stimulus before he can determine whether it is or is not a member of the target set.

The third implication is that, in the context of the present model, the response output buffer must be of limited capacity. If the response output buffer was large enough to hold all the output programs, then mean reaction time in the button-pushing condition should be a *linear* function of the number of stimulus-response alternatives. Obviously, the obtained function is not linear. This implies that the response output buffer is of limited capacity. The capacity of the buffer may be estimated by selecting the capacity $W - 1$ which makes mean reaction time a linear function of expected buffer position. In Figure 3 it can be seen that a buffer capacity $W - 1$ equal to three gives a linear relationship between mean reaction time and expected buffer position. The theoretical interpretation of this is that

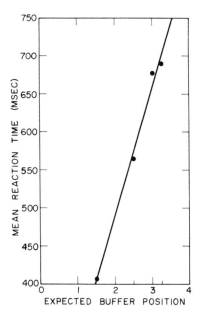

Fig. 3. Mean reaction time (msec) to equally likely stimuli in the button-pushing condition as a function of theoretically expected position in the response output buffer. The four ordered buffer positions indicated by the points correspond to two, four, six, and eight stimulus alternatives.

the buffer can serially scan three positions, before long-term memory will supply the correct response program. The slope of the linear function is approximately 168 msec, which is to be interpreted as the time needed to go from the coded name of the test stimulus to a determination of its response output program.[2] According to the theory, it took long-term memory approximately four times 168 msec or 672 msec after stimulus identification to find the response output program. However, with I equally likely stimulus alternatives, the serial buffer came up with the response program in 336 ± 168 msec on a proportion $3/I$ of the trials when I was equal to or greater than 3. When there was only two stimulus alternatives, the buffer produced the appropriate response program in 252 ± 84 msec on every trial.

Table I presents the mean and standard deviation of the proportion of errors. For the naming condition, the probability of an error was virtually nonexistent, and for the button-pushing condition it was low (.045) and did not vary much as a function of the number of stimulus-response alternatives.

TABLE I

MEAN PROPORTION OF ERRORS

	Number of equally likely stimuli				
	2	4	6	8	10
Naming	.007	.011	.006	.004	.005
Buttons	.032	.042	.057	.054	

B. TWO-CHOICE REACTION TIMES

If indeed the capacity of the serial, short-term output buffer is three response programs, then for a traditional two-choice reaction time task, both response output programs should fit into the response buffer. The theorem that mean reaction time is a linear function of expected buffer position can then be tested by varying stimulus presentation probability, since according to the model, expected buffer position is a function of stimulus presentation probability.

Theios and Smith (1972) have worked out the mathematics for the

---

[2] This estimate of the slope seems unusually high, but it may be understandable in that the stimulus-response compatibility was not high in this task. The stimulus 2 was paired with the first finger, the stimulus 3 was paired with the second finger, and so on. A more compatible S-R mapping would have been to pair the stimulus 1 with the first finger, the stimulus 2 with the second finger, and so on.

two-stimuli case of the model being considered in this article. The asymptotic probability of the response output program for stimulus S_i being in the first position of the buffer is

$$\Pr(Y_i = 1) = (\pi_i b_i)/[\pi_i b_i + (1 - \pi_i)b_j] \tag{18}$$

where π_i is the presentation probability for stimulus S_i, b_i is the buffer position exchange probability for stimulus S_i, and b_j is the buffer position exchange probability for the other stimulus, S_j. The expected buffer position for the response output program of stimulus S_i is then just

$$E(Y_i) = (1)[\Pr(Y_i = 1)] + (2)[1 - \Pr(Y_i = 1)]. \tag{19}$$

According to Prediction 2, the expected mean reaction time to a stimulus S_i presented with probability π_i is simply a linear function of its expected buffer position [Eq. (17)].

1. Remington's Experiment

Remington (1969) varied stimulus presentation probability in a two-choice reaction time task, using probabilities of (.3, .7) and (.5, .5). The stimuli consisted of left and right lights and the corresponding responses were a left- and a right-hand index finger button push. Each trial began with a red warning light followed by a 1-second foreperiod before the presentation of a stimulus light. The inter-stimulus interval averaged about 4 seconds. Each of five human subjects were given 1200 trials on each problem in alternating blocks of 200 trials, and the data considered here represents the last 800 trials for the (.5, .5) problem and the last 1000 trials for the (.3, .7) problem.

For this experiment, the best estimate of the buffer exchange probability (b_m of Axiom 7) was .18 for the .3 stimulus, .22 for the .5 stimuli, and .38 for the .7 stimulus. Thus, according to Eq. (19), the expected buffer positions are 1.17 for $\pi = .7$, 1.50 for $\pi = .5$, and 1.83 for $\pi = .3$. Figure 4 shows mean reaction time in Remington's experiment as a function of expected buffer position. As can be seen, the relationship is linear. The intercept (B) is 209 msec and the slope (scan rate) is 54 msec.

2. Stimulus-Response Sequential Effects

Predictions can be made about stimulus-response sequential effects using the same parameter estimates used to predict the mean reaction

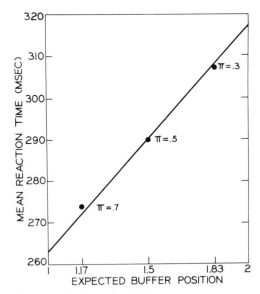

Fig. 4. Remington's (1969) mean two-choice reaction time data as a function of theoretically expected response output buffer position.

times. Equation 17 is again used to predict the reaction times, but instead of $E(Y_i)$ representing the unconditional asymptotic expected buffer position, it represents the asymptotic buffer position *conditional* on a specific sequence of preceding stimuli. For example, during a run of presentations of stimulus S_1, the expected buffer position of response program r_1 approaches 1.0. Likewise, during a run of stimulus S_2 the expected buffer position of response program r_1 approaches 2. Thus, depending upon the previous sequence of S_1 and S_2 stimuli, the asymptotic expected buffer position will be somewhere between 1 and 2, and an entire space of sequential effects is possible. The first four orders of sequential effects are represented in Fig. 5 as a tree. A sequence *ijkl* should be interpreted to mean that we are considering the average reaction time to stimulus S_i on all occasions on which it was preceded by stimulus S_j on the previous trial, preceded by stimulus S_k two trials before, and by stimulus S_l three trials before. Predictions were made for each stimulus probability (.3, .5, .7) separately, and then pooled together, as were the observed conditional mean reaction times. As can be seen, the predictions of the model are closely approximating the data. The square root of the weighted mean squared error between ob-

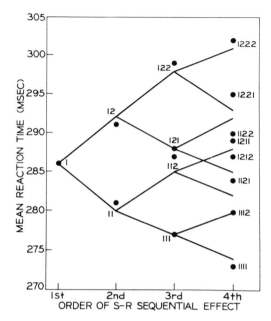

Fig. 5. Sequential effects in Remington's (1969) two-choice reaction time experiment. Observed (points) and predicted (lines) mean reaction times conditional on the sequence of preceding stimuli, averaged over the three stimulus probability values. For example, the point 1212 represents the mean reaction time to a stimulus (call it S_1) given that the other stimulus (call it S_2) occurred on the previous trial, S_1 occurred two trials before, and S_2 occurred three trials before.

served and predicted conditional reaction times is less than 3 msec. Thus, the model can account for sequential effects in two-choice reaction times.

C. Two-Choice Naming Times and Stimulus Probability

We have just seen that two-choice (button pushing) reaction times decrease markedly as stimulus probability is increased. According to the model presented in Section II, the time to name a stimulus in a two-choice task should not be a function of stimulus presentation probability. This prediction follows since naming is assumed to be a content-addressable process or a feature testing process.[3] To test this

[3] The feature-testing process envisioned here is one in which, for sets of basic verbal-linguistic stimuli such as numerals or letters, the identification process is automatic with respect to all the elements of the set, irrespective of how many elements the

prediction, ten human subjects were tested in a two-choice naming experiment in which stimulus presentation probabilities were varied as (.2,.8), (.3,.7), (.4,.6), and (.5,.5). After a practice session with probabilities of (.5,.5), each subject was given 300 trials at each of the four pairs of presentation probabilities, in a different random order. The stimuli were the digits 4 and 5, and the experimental method was similar to that of the naming experiment described in Section III, A. For stimulus probability increasing from .2 to .8 in steps of .1, the obtained mean naming times were 356, 356, 351, 357, 348, 347, and 346 msec. The obtained naming times did not differ significantly from their overall mean of 351 msec [$F(6,54) = .27$]. Thus, there is no evidence for a stimulus or response probability effect in two-choice naming of stimuli such as exists for two-choice button-pushing reaction times. The results of this experiment constitute further evidence in support of the hypothesis that stimulus identification is a process that occurs early, before any serial, self-terminating memory scanning.[4]

D. THREE-CHOICE REACTION TIMES

Consider an experiment with a one-to-one stimulus-response mapping in which there are three uncertain stimulus events, S_1, S_2, S_3 which recur with constant probabilities of $\pi_1 = \pi$, and $\pi_2 = \pi_3 = (1 - \pi)/2$. For this special case, the following result follows from Axiom 7 if it is assumed that $b_m = b$ for all responses.

Asymptotic buffer position probabilities for special case of three stimuli and responses: As N becomes large, the probabilities that

---

experimenter is presenting in the task. Thus, identification time will be effectively a constant irrespective of the size of the *experimental* ensemble of alpha-numeric characters. For less basic sets of stimuli such as colors, pictures, and words, the identification process is less automatic, and identification time may depend upon the size of the experimental ensemble of stimuli. This analysis is supported by the results of experiments by Morin, Konick, Troxell, and McPherson (1965).

[4] In the present two-alternative experiment, the naming times were approximately 100 msec faster than in the two-alternative condition of the previous experiment. This difference is due to differences in the level of accuracy used by the subjects. In the first naming experiment, the error percentage was less than 1% for the two-alternative equally likely condition. In the corresponding condition of the second experiment, the error percentage was 2.3%. This is in the neighborhood of the error percentage of the two-alternative button-pushing condition of the first experiment (3.2%). Holding error probability roughly constant, two-choice naming times are faster (357 msec) than two-choice button-push reaction times (408 msec).

response output code $<n_1, r_1>$ is stored in the first, second, or third buffer position approaches, respectively

$$\lim_{N \to \infty} \Pr(Y_{1,N} = 1) = \pi , \tag{20}$$

$$\lim_{N \to \infty} \Pr(Y_{1,N} = 2) = \frac{\pi(1 - \pi)}{.5(1 + \pi)} , \tag{21}$$

$$\lim_{N \to \infty} \Pr(Y_{1,N} = 3) = \frac{(1 - \pi)^2}{(1 + \pi)} . \tag{22}$$

Since the other two stimuli S_2 and S_3 are equally likely, it directly follows that

$$\lim_{N \to \infty} \Pr(Y_{2,N} = 1) = \lim_{N \to \infty} \Pr(Y_{3,N} = 1) = \frac{1}{2} [1 - \lim_{N \to \infty} \Pr(Y_{1,N} = 1)], \tag{23}$$

$$\lim_{N \to \infty} \Pr(Y_{2,N} = 2) = \lim_{N \to \infty} \Pr(Y_{3,N} = 2) = \frac{1}{2} [1 - \lim_{N \to \infty} \Pr(Y_{1,N} = 2)], \tag{24}$$

$$\lim_{N \to \infty} \Pr(Y_{2,N} = 3) = \lim_{N \to \infty} \Pr(Y_{3,N} = 3) = \frac{1}{2} [1 - \lim_{N \to \infty} \Pr(Y_{1,N} = 3)]. \tag{25}$$

Given the asymptotic buffer position probabilities, the expected buffer position for any response code $<n_i, r_i>$ will be equal to

$$E(Y_i) = (1) \lim_{N \to \infty} \Pr(Y_{i,N} = 1) + (2) \lim_{N \to \infty} \Pr(Y_{i,N} = 2)$$
$$+ (3) \lim_{N \to \infty} \Pr(Y_{i,N} = 3). \tag{26}$$

Given the expected buffer positions, Eq. (17) can be used to generate predictions for mean reaction time.

1. Three Stimuli Experiments

In order to test the predictions from the model, two choice reaction experiments each involving three stimuli and responses were conducted. The experiments were conducted with the aid of Jane Traupmann and Peter G. Smith. The general experimental method was similar to that used in the button-pushing reaction time experiment described in Section III A. The stimuli were the numerals 1, 2, and 3 which were mapped, respectively to the index, middle, and ring finger of the subject's right hand. The subjects were 48 right-handed

University students, 24 in each experiment. There were four experimental conditions in each experiment, each involving 300 trials. Experiment 1 used stimulus presentation probability schedules (π_1, π_2, π_3) of (1/3, 1/3, 1/3), (1/2, 1/4, 1/4), (1/4, 1/2, 1/4), and (1/4, 1/4, 1/2). Experiment 2 used stimulus presentation probability schedules of (1/3, 1/3, 1/3), (5/12, 5/12, 1/6), (1/4, 1/4, 1/2), and (1/3, 1/6, 1/2). Within an experiment, each subject received his four experimental conditions in a different order.

Obtained mean reaction times as a function of stimulus-response pair and stimulus probability are presented in Table II, along with predictions from the self-terminating memory stack model. The values of the parameters of the model were estimated by having Chandler's (1969) subroutine STEPIT select values for the parameters which minimized the weighted squared error between observed and predicted mean reaction times. For experiment 1, the best fitting parameters were μ (scan rate) = 69 msec, B_1 = 336 msec, B_2 = 346 msec, and B_3 = 353 msec, where B_i is the reaction time intercept ($\mu_i + \mu_s + \mu_r + \mu_o$) for stimulus S_i and response R_i, $i = 1$, 2, 3. For Experiment 2, the best fitting parameters were μ = 78 msec, B_1 = 322 msec, B_2 = 348 msec, B_3 = 332 msec. Condition IV of Experiment 2 does not fall within the special case considered in this section; however, the predictions for this condition were obtained by computer simulation of the process using the same parameter values. In Table II, all 24 predicted means are well within plus and minus one standard error of the obtained mean reaction times. The strong stimulus probability effect should be noted in the data of Table II. For every stimulus-response pair, in each experiment, mean reaction time increases as stimulus presentation probability is decreased. Thus, the serial, self-terminating push-down stack model is able to account for three-choice reaction times with unequal stimulus-response probabilities.

E. N-CHOICE REACTION TIMES WITH VARYING STIMULUS PROBABILITIES

Consider the class of choice reaction time experiments with an arbitrary number N of stimuli and an unequal distribution of presentation probabilities among the N stimuli. Restrict the consideration here to one-to-one stimulus-response mappings. For this class of experiments, the self-terminating model presented in Section II, E does not yield explicit solutions, in general. This is largely due to Axiom 7 in which the expected buffer positions will be functions

TABLE II

THREE STIMULI EXPERIMENTS: OBTAINED (Obt.) AND PREDICTED (Pre.) MEAN REACTION TIMES (msec) AS A FUNCTION OF STIMULUS PRESENTATION PROBABILITY (π) AND STIMULUS-RESPONSE (S-R) PAIR

Experiment 1 conditions

S-R	I			II			III			IV			Mean	
	π	Obt.	Pre.	π	Obt.	Pre.	π	Obt.	Pre.	π	Obt.	Pre.	Obt.	Pre.
1	1/3	471	474	1/2	452	451	1/4	489	485	1/4	484	485	470	469
2	1/3	482	484	1/4	488	495	1/2	463	462	1/4	500	495	480	480
3	1/3	492	491	1/4	507	502	1/4	502	502	1/2	466	469	487	487
Mean		482	483		475	475		479	478		479	479	479	479

Experiment 2 conditions

S-R	I			II			III			IV			Mean	
	π	Obt.	Pre.	π	Obt.	Pre.	π	Obt.	Pre.	π	Obt.	Pre.	Obt.	Pre.
1	1/3	471	477	5/12	455	458	1/4	494	492	1/3	463	471	468	472
2	1/3	499	503	5/12	484	484	1/4	512	518	1/6	532	538	501	504
3	1/3	489	487	1/6	524	525	1/2	478	479	1/2	466	459	482	479
Mean		486	489		479	480		491	493		476	476	483	484

of the exact sequence of stimuli experienced. However, predictions
can be obtained from the model using Monte Carlo simulation
methods. Preliminary investigation has indicated that if the b_m pa-
rameters of Axiom 7 are all set equal to each other ($b_m = b$), then
the asymptotic buffer positions are independent of b, as long as b
is not equal to zero.

1. Falmagne's Six-Choice Reaction Time Experiment

Falmagne (1972) conducted a six-choice reaction time experiment
in which the stimulus presentation probabilities were .32, .25, .18,
.13, .08, and .04. A compatible, left to right, one-to-one stimulus-
response mapping was used with the stimuli being the numerals 1–6,
and the responses being the ring, middle, and index fingers of each
hand. The experiment had a Latin square design such that each of
six subjects received a different distribution of probabilities over the
six stimuli. The subjects were tested on 10 different days, receiving
1000 trials per day. The data reported here are from three asymptotic
days of testing. The obtained mean reaction times are presented
in Table III where it can be seen that mean reaction time increased

TABLE III

OBTAINED MEAN REACTION TIME (msec) FOR FALMAGNE'S
EXPERIMENT AS A FUNCTION OF STIMULUS PRESENTATION PROB-
ABILITY (π) AND CORRESPONDING MEANS SIMULATED FROM
THE PUSH-DOWN STACK MODEL

π	Obtained	Predicted
.32	397	407
.25	438	427
.18	452	454
.13	484	483
.08	529	525
.04	571	575

systematically as stimulus probability decreased. Table III also pre-
sents predictions for the Falmagne experiment obtained from 20
simulations of the push-down stack model. The capacity of the output
buffer ($W - 1$) was set equal to six. The estimated buffer scan rate
was 65 msec with a reaction time intercept of 252 msec. The pre-
dicted mean reaction times given in Table III are close to the ob-
tained mean reaction times. The linear correlation between obtained

and simulated mean reaction times is .994, with the model accounting for .99% of the variance between means. In any case, the model is accounting for the overall stimulus-response probability effect. Thus far we have seen that the self-terminating push-down stack model can account for the data from two-choice, three-choice, and N-choice reaction times.

F. Character Classification

Sternberg (1966, 1967, 1969) has introduced a binary-choice, character classification task which is particularly relevant to the information processing theory proposed in this article. A subject memorizes a small target set of stimuli, and then either one or a sequence of stimuli are presented. After the presentation of a stimulus the subject must indicate as quickly as he can whether the presented stimulus is or is not a member of the target set. In studies of this type, it is typically found that mean reaction time to both target and nontarget stimuli is an approximately linear function of the size of the target set. Further, the slopes of the functions relating mean reaction time to target set size are typically about equal for both target and nontarget stimuli. This pattern of results led Sternberg (1966, 1967) to propose a serial, exhaustive memory scanning process to account for the data in these binary classification experiments. In order to respond correctly, a subject presumably had to compare a representation of the test (or probe) stimulus to those of the target set already stored in memory. The fact that the mean reaction times increased as a linear function of target set size led Sternberg (1966, 1967) to propose that the memory comparison (scanning) process is serial in nature. That is, each stimulus added to the target set added a constant increment of time to the mean reaction time. Secondly, the fact that the slopes of the reaction time functions were equal for target and nontarget stimuli led Sternberg to propose that the search of the memorized target set was exhaustive. Sternberg reasoned that if the subjects were using a self-terminating memory search, the slope of the reaction time function for nontarget stimuli should be twice that of the target stimuli. Assuming that the subject scans only representations of the target set and that the memory scan is self-terminating, the average number of memory comparisons made would be one half the number of target stimuli if a target probe was presented, but would be equal to the number of target stimuli if a nontarget probe was presented. This line of reasoning led Sternberg (1966, 1967) to reject serial, self-terminating memory processes as reasonable for these types of tasks. The key to this rejection is the assumption that the subject scans only the set of target stimuli. In this paper, a serial, self-terminating memory scanning process is proposed in which elements of both the target and nontarget set of stimuli may be represented in the scanning process. This expanded serial, self-terminating scanning process can account for data of the type published by Sternberg (1966, 1967) as well as for stimulus probability and sequential effects which are not easily accounted for by an exhaustive scanning process.

1. Sternberg's Design

Using a constant target set procedure, Sternberg (1967) performed a binary classification experiment in which target set size was varied as 1, 2, and 4. In that experiment, all 10 digits were used as stimuli. The design was such that stimulus presentation probability was confounded with set size, but within a given target set size condition the individual target stimuli were equally likely. The individual target presentation probabilities were $4/15$, $2/15$, and $1/15$ for target set sizes of 1, 2, and 4, respectively. Within the set of nontarget stimuli, the individual stimuli differed in their presentation probabilities. Sternberg (1967) did not report the results of analyses of stimulus probability or of stimulus or response sequential effects. The self-terminating memory stack model predicts stimulus probability and sequential effects for this type of experiment. In order to gain information about the effect of stimulus probability and sequential effects, we essentially replicated the Sternberg (1967) design in our laboratory. Since it is commonly assumed that sequential effects in reaction time occur only with a short response-stimulus interval, the length of the response-stimulus interval was also varied in our experiment.

The experiment was run by Dennis Walter as his masters thesis research. The subjects were 48 university students. The apparatus and general procedure was that described in Theios et al. (1973), but the design of the experiment closely followed that of Sternberg (1967). Using a within-subjects design and blocks of 108 trials, subjects were tested with both a short response-stimulus interval (.5 second) and a long response-stimulus interval (2.0 seconds). Figure 6 presents mean reaction time for target and nontarget stimuli as a function of target set size (the points on the graph). The data are in essential agreement with Sternberg (1967); 97% of the variance is accounted for by the hypothesis of parallel linear functions. The data do, however, differ *significantly* from the best fitting parallel lines and also from their individual best fitting lines (F's > 6.04, $df = 1$, 94). This difference between our replication and Sternberg's (1967) data is most likely due to the fact that the power of the analysis of variance is much greater in our experiment where four times as many subjects were given twice as many trials. In Fig. 6 the lines represent

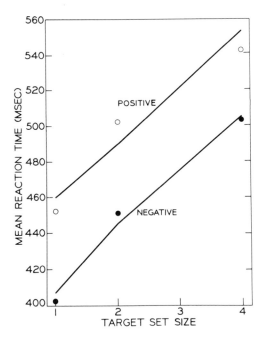

Fig. 6. Replication of Sternberg's (1967) character classification design. Mean reaction time (circles) as a function of target set size. The lines are predictions obtained from a simulation of the self-terminating memory stack model.

predicted means generated from a computer simulation of the self-terminating memory stack model. The simulation procedure followed that described in Theios *et al.* (1973). Table IV presents obtained and simulated mean reaction times for all the conditions in the experiment. The obtained means do not differ significantly from the simulated means $F(10, 912) = 1.06$, $p \gg .05$. The values of the parameter used in the simulation were obtained with Chandler's (1969) subroutine STEPIT and were, for the short and long response-stimulus intervals respectively: mean stimulus input, identification and positive response time (which is $B = \mu_i + \mu_s + \mu_{p,+} + \mu_{o,+}$)

TABLE IV

OBSERVED MEAN REACTION TIMES (Obs.) (msec), STANDARD
ERRORS (SE), SIMULATED MEANS FROM THE SELF-TERMINATING
MEMORY STACK MODEL (Sim.) AND PARAMETER VALUES
USED IN THE SIMULATION

	Short RSI[a]			Long RSI		
	Sim.	Obs.	SE	Sim.	Obs.	SE
Target set size 1						
Positive 4/15	435	434	8	485	471	10
Negative 2/15	384	376	8	429	426	12
Negative 1/15	386	380	8	431	429	11
Target set size 2						
Positive 2/15	468	480	12	512	524	14
Negative 4/15	415	414	10	459	470	12
Negative 1/15	427	430	10	470	482	13
Target set size 4						
Positive 1/15	533	529	10	573	560	11
Negative 4/15	464	472	11	508	510	11
Negative 2/15	489	488	12	530	516	11
Negative 1/15	504	505	12	544	544	13
Parameter values						
Positive response time intercept (mseconds)		379			428	
Negative response time intercept (mseconds)		300			349	
Comparison time		43			41	
Positive stack prob. a_+		.34			.43	
Negative stack prob. a_-		.06			.08	

[a] RSI, response-stimulus intervals.

equals 379 and 428 msec, mean dictionary scan time (μ_r) equals 43 and 41 msec, mean difference between positive and negative responses in response selection and output time $[(\mu_{p,+} + \mu_{o,+}) - (\mu_{p,-} + \mu_{o,-})]$ equals 79 and 79 msec, positive dictionary stack replacement probability (a_+) equals .34 and .43, and negative dictionary replacement probability (a_-) equals .06 and .08. Finally, the capacity of the serial response dictionary ($Z - 1$) was set to equal the target set size.[5]

[5] The rationale for this assumption has been given in Theios et al. (1973). We assume that the subject *attempts* to perform the classification task as instructed, focusing only on target stimuli and programming only $Z - 1$ dictionary buffer positions for the $Z - 1$ target stimuli. However, as a result of the dynamic nature of the buffer and the occurrence of nontarget stimuli, representations of the nontarget name-response codes replace representations of target name-response codes in the buffer.

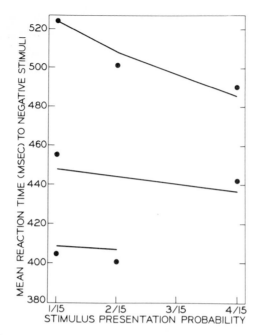

Fig. 7. Replication of Sternberg's (1967) character classification design. Mean reaction time (dots) to nontarget stimuli as a function of stimulus presentation probability and target set size. The lower two points are for a target size of one, the middle two points are for a target size of two, and the upper three points are for a target set size of four. The lines represent predictions obtained from a simulation of the self-terminating memory stack model. Note the significant interaction between stimulus probability and memory set size.

As is clearly seen in Fig. 6, the self-terminating model predicts mean reaction time functions which are close, but not necessarily equal to parallel straight lines.

a. *Stimulus Presentation Probability Effects.* Figure 7 shows mean reaction time to negative stimuli as a function of target set size (M) and stimulus presentation probability. Analyses of variance indicated that there are significant effects due to both stimulus probability, target set size, and their interaction. The stimulus probability effect is especially difficult for an exhaustive scanning model to account for. If scanning is exhaustive over only the target set, then why should there be a stimulus probability effect for the nontarget stimuli? If it is argued that stimulus probability affects encoding time, then the significant stimulus probability by target set size interaction is difficult to handle with an exhaustive scanning process. Set size is assumed to affect the scanning stage, but not the encoding stage (Sternberg,

1969). Thus, stimulus probability effects should be independent of set size. The nontarget stimulus probability by target-set-size interaction indicates that these two variables are affecting a common processing stage, presumably memory scanning. This strongly suggests that nontarget stimuli are on or can get on the list of scanned elements (as postulated in the present self-terminating model). The nontarget stimulus probability effect strongly suggests that the scan is self-terminating on a memory ordered more or less on the basis of presentation probability.

The lines in Fig. 7 represent means simulated from the self-terminating model. Inspection of Table IV and Figs. 6 and 7 indicate that the self-terminating model is giving a reasonable account of the data and easily accounts for the stimulus probability and stimulus probability by set size interaction, the two effects for which the exhaustive model has difficulty accounting.

  b. *Sequential Effects.* According to the self-terminating memory model (especially the Axioms 2, 3, 4, 6, and 7), in tasks like binary character classification which utilize a many-to-one stimulus-response mapping, both stimulus and response sequential effects should be observed. Presentation and repetition of a stimulus should move its name-response code higher in the response dictionary, leading to faster reaction times to that stimulus. Likewise, the occurrence and repetition of a response should move its response output program higher in the output buffer, also leading to faster mean reaction times to stimuli having that response. The converse will be true for a stimulus not presented or a response not made. Figure 8 presents conditional mean reaction times as a function of sequence of preceding stimuli. For example, the upper point DDS represents the mean reaction time over all stimuli to a stimulus S given that a different stimulus was presented on the preceding two trials. The lower point SSS represents the mean reaction time to a stimulus S given that stimulus S was also presented on the preceding two trials. As can be seen in Fig. 8, there are systematic stimulus sequential effects in both the long and short response-stimulus interval conditions. The effects are *slightly* larger for the short response-stimulus interval, but they certainly are large and significant in the long response-stimulus interval condition. The same pattern of sequential effects occurs regardless of stimulus probability, set size, or whether the stimulus is a target or nontarget item.

Figure 9 presents conditional mean reaction times as a function of sequence of preceding responses. The upper point DDS represents the mean reaction time over all stimuli to a stimulus S given that the other (different) response was made on the preceding two trials. The

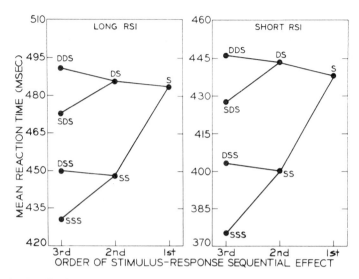

Fig. 8. Replication of Sternberg's (1967) character classification design. Mean reaction time (msec) as a function of sequence of preceding stimuli for both long (2.0 seconds) and short (.5 second) response-stimulus intervals (RSI). For example, the point DDS represents the mean reaction time to a stimulus S given that a different stimulus was presented on the preceding two trials.

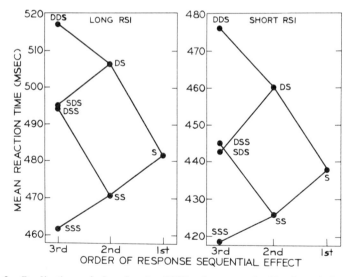

Fig. 9. Replication of Sternberg's (1967) character classification design. Mean reaction time (msec) as a function of preceding sequence of responses for both long (2.0 seconds) and short (.5 second) response-stimulus intervals (RSI). For example, the point DSS represents the mean reaction time to a stimulus S given that the same *response* was made on the previous trial but a different response was made two trials previously.

lower point SSS represents the mean reaction time to stimulus S given that the same response was made on the preceding two trials. Again, there are systematic response sequential effects in reaction time for both the long and the short response-stimulus interval conditions.

While the stimulus-response mapping is not one-to-one in this classification task, it is true, of course, that stimuli and responses are not completely independent. It is possible that the stimulus sequential effects merely reflect the embedded response sequential effects. To check on this possibility, a further sequential analysis was performed. Figure 10 shows mean reaction time over all stimuli to a stimulus S as a function of sequence of preceding stimuli given that the response is the same during the entire sequence. In this analysis, since the response is held constant, we can see the pure stimulus sequential effect, uncontaminated by the response sequential effect.

In Fig. 10 the difference in time between points S and DS is the reduction in response time due to a single response repetition, uncontaminated by a stimulus repetition. The difference between points DS and SS is the reduction in response time due to a single stimulus repetition with the effect due to the necessary response repetition taken

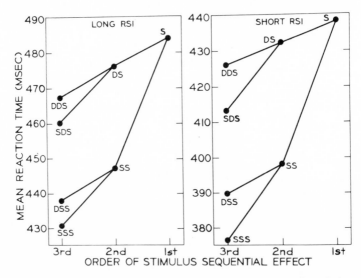

Fig. 10. Replication of Sternberg's (1967) character classification design. Mean reaction time (msec) as a function of sequence of stimuli during runs of the same response. For example, the point DDS is the mean reaction time to a stimulus s given that different stimuli requiring the same response were presented on the two previous trials.

out. As can be seen, the "pure" stimulus repetition effect is larger than the "pure" response repetition effect. These data demonstrating both "pure" stimulus repetition and "pure" response repetition effects are consistent with results published by Bertelson (1965) and Rabbitt (1968) for choice reaction times with a many-to-one stimulus-response mapping. The two types of sequential effects illustrated in Fig. 10 are entirely consistent with the self-terminating memory stack model and are the basis of the assumption of both a probabilistically ordered response dictionary process and a probabilistically ordered response output buffer in choice tasks involving a many-to-one stimulus-response mapping.

As published by Sternberg (1966, 1967), the exhaustive memory scanning model has no mechanisms to account for stimulus sequential effects. If, in the exhaustive scanning model, it were assumed that stimulus repetition lowered encoding time, then in Sternberg's (1967) design (which we replicated) differential frequencies of repetitions for the various stimuli would differentially affect mean reaction time, and the prediction of parallel linear reaction times for positive and negative stimuli as a function of target set size would be lost.

Inspection of Figs. 8, 9, and 10, and Table IV indicate that in the present experiment, response-stimulus interval had little effect on reaction time other than that of generally increasing mean reaction time in the long response-stimulus interval condition. As indicated by the estimated parameters of the computer simulation of the memory stack model, only the reaction time intercept (B) is greatly affected (elevated 49 msec) by the long response-stimulus interval. The values of the other parameters are probably within chance limits for the short and long response stimulus intervals.

2. Stimulus Probability Effects in Target and Nontarget Sets of Equal Size

Using the constant target set procedure and a response-stimulus interval of .5 second, Theios et al. (1973) conducted a character classification experiment in which the size of the target and nontarget sets were equal as target set size was increased. Their experimental design which is given in Table V also varied stimulus presentation probability symmetrically within each stimulus set. In two replications, a total of 40 subjects were given 200 trials at each target set size. The error rate was less than 2.5% and all errors were excluded from the analyses.

Table VI shows that, for both target and nontarget stimuli, mean

TABLE V

DESIGN OF THE EXPERIMENT

	Stimuli	Stimulus presentation probabilities									
		Positive target set					Negative nontarget set				
	Stimuli	s_0	s_1	s_2	s_3	s_4	s_5	s_6	s_7	s_8	s_9
Target Set Size	2	.35	.15				.35	.15			
	3	.30	.15	.05			.30	.15	.05		
	4	.20	.15	.10	.05		.20	.15	.10	.05	
	5	.20	.15	.05	.05	.05	.20	.15	.05	.05	.05

reaction time is a decreasing function of stimulus presentation probability. Using Monte Carlo computer simulation procedures, quantitative predictions were obtained from the self-terminating memory stack model presented in this article. A statistical response protocol corresponding to the self-terminating process was obtained for every response protocol given by a real subject in both replications of the experiment. After specific, restrictive assumptions were made about

TABLE VI

MEAN RT (msec) OBSERVED AND SIMULATED FROM THE SELF-
TERMINATING MODEL AS A FUNCTION OF SET SIZE, STIMULUS
PROBABILITY, AND TYPE OF RESPONSE $(+, -)$ AND
OBSERVED STANDARD ERRORS OF THE MEANS

Set size	Probability	Positive target set			Negative nontarget set		
		Simulated	Observed	SE	Simulated	Observed	SE
2	.35	507	498	10	529	519	10
	.15	533	543	15	548	550	13
	Mean	515	512	11	535	528	11
3	.30	519	522	9	550	546	14
	.15	553	549	16	578	570	18
	.05	590	604	20	597	634	22
	Mean	536	538	13	563	562	14
4	.20	551	546	14	590	589	19
	.15	570	576	18	606	612	21
	.10	594	597	16	616	628	20
	.05	622	609	20	634	626	20
	Mean	572	572	15	604	607	18
5	.20	560	578	16	599	611	20
	.15	581	587	18	614	624	18
	.05	650	630	18	670	658	24
	Mean	593	596	16	625	629	18

the values of some of the parameters of the model, Chandler's (1969) subroutine STEPIT was used to find values of the remaining free parameters which minimized the weighted squared error between the means of the pooled data and the means obtained from the simulation of the self-terminating process. In the simulation, the capacity of the serial response dictionary $(Z - 1)$ was set to equal the size of the target set. The best estimates of the remaining parameters were: mean stimulus input, identification, and response output time $(B = \mu_i + \mu_s + \mu_p + \mu_o)$ equals 429 msec, mean dictionary scan time (μ_r) equals 45 msec, target dictionary replacement probability (a_+) equals .62, and nontarget dictionary replacement probability (a_-) equals .28. The obtained and predicted (simulated) mean reaction times for the various conditions are given in Table VI, along with the obtained standard errors of the means. A goodness-of-fit analysis of variance indicated no significant difference between the simulated and obtained means $[F(19, 936) = .90, p > .50]$.

Figure 11 shows mean reaction time as a function of target set size

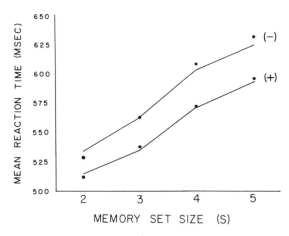

Fig. 11. Obtained mean reaction time (msec) (dots) as a function of target set size for positive target and negative nontarget stimuli, and predictions obtained from a simulation of the self-terminating memory stack model.

for both target and nontarget stimuli. In Fig. 11, neither the obtained means nor the means simulated from the self-terminating scanning model differ significantly from two parallel straight lines predicted by the exhaustive scanning model $(F's < 1.00)$. Again, the self-terminating model is predicting and accounting for the essentially linear, parallel mean reaction time functions, the set size effect, and for stimulus presentation probability effects in both the target and non-target sets. Stimulus presentation probability effects have been reported in this type of task by Hawkins and Hosking (1969) and Krueger (1970).

IV. Summary and Conclusions

In this article, the case has been made that the study of choice reaction times in continuous (serial) information processing tasks can be very useful in investigating human short-term memory. The subtractive method of Donders (1868–1869) and the additive factors method of Sternberg (1969) have been briefly reviewed. A third method which is suggested and illustrated in this article is the construction and testing of specific process models which make clear-cut quantitative predictions for carefully designed experiments which fall within the boundary conditions of the process models.

In this article a serial, self-terminating memory scanning model is proposed to account for human behavior in stimulus identification, naming, choice-reaction, and (memory scanning) character classification tasks. The model assumes that after stimulus information is input, it makes contact very soon with long-term memory, where the information is interrogated and the stimulus is identified. The identification process operates in parallel (or is a net-discrimination, feature-testing process with the property that for well-defined stimulus ensembles, such as letters or numerals, identification time is effectively a constant, independent of size of *experimental* ensemble). The evidence in support of this is that the time to name a character is independent of stimulus ensemble size and stimulus probability (cf. Forrin, Kumler, & Morin, 1966). The serial component of memory scanning which many investigators have found (cf. Sternberg, 1966, 1967), is due to the response determination and selection processes. Evidence has been given here suggesting the existence of a response dictionary process which determines the appropriate response code associated with a stimulus in a specific task. The response dictionary process is especially needed in tasks such as character classification which involve a many-to-one assignment of stimuli to response. Presumably, the response dictionary is also important in tasks involving a one-to-one stimulus-response mapping in which a response transformation is necessary, such as the use of an incompatible as compared to a compatible assignment of stimuli to responses. The response dictionary process has been shown to have a serial component as evidenced by an effect due to stimulus ensemble size. The presence of stimulus probability effects and stimulus sequential effects strongly suggests that the serial component of the response dictionary is a self-terminating process. Evidence from character classification experiments varying the number of stimulus alternatives suggests that the serial component of the response dictionary is of limited (and varied) capacity which may be determined in part by the instructions to the subject and by the nature of the task. After the appropriate response has been determined, the response must be selected and executed. The response output process seems to have a limited capacity serial component as evidenced by response probability effects and response sequential effects.

All in all, the theoretical model, which can be conceived of as a sequence of processing stages with two, limited capacity, serial, self-terminating scanning buffers, makes the following general predictions about performance in human information processing tasks:

1. Stimulus naming times and other highly overlearned compatible responses may be fast and independent of stimulus presentation probability and number of stimulus-response alternatives.

2. With equally likely stimuli (responses), mean reaction time will not, in general, be an increasing linear function of number of stimuli (responses), but will be a negatively accelerated increasing function of the number of alternatives. The function may be effectively linear up to four alternatives.

3. As stimulus (response) probability is increased, mean reaction time will decrease.

4. Mean reaction time in tasks with compatible stimulus-response mappings will be faster than in tasks with incompatible stimulus-response mappings.

5. In character classification (memory scanning) tasks, mean reaction time to target and nontarget stimuli will be essentially linear, parallel functions of target set size.

6. There will be both stimulus and response sequential effects in reaction time data.

The above qualitative predictions from the self-terminating memory stack model cover a number of the major, well-known empirical relationships in the choice-reaction time and character classification research literature. It is felt that the model provides a useful and potentially fruitful theoretical framework within which human memory and information processing can be investigated. As such, the model is viewed as a heuristic which summarizes many known empirical relationships. As it now stands, many details of the model have yet to be worked out, and modifications and elaborations will surely have to be made. In addition, much of the human information processing research literature needs to be reevaluated from the standpoint of the present model.

The weakest point of the theoretical model is that (like most other reaction time models) it has completely ignored response errors. The model is assumed to hold in situations in which the subject is giving errorless or essentially errorless performance. In the reaction time tasks that we have considered, error rates are low (under 2.5%). However, there is an increasing body of literature which suggests that errors can exert a surprising effect on reaction times, and that they cannot be ignored. Clearly, the next important theoretical task is to develop a theory of errors which is consistent with reaction times, so that both response measures may be predicted by the same theory and set of parameter values.

REFERENCES

Bertelson, P. Serial choice reaction-time as a function of response versus signal-and-response repetition. *Nature (London)*, 1965, **206**, 217–218.

Brainard, R. W., Irby, T. S., Fitts, P. M., & Alluisi, E. A. Some variables influencing the rate of gain of information. *Journal of Experimental Psychology*, 1962, **63**, 105–110.

Chandler, J. P. STEPIT: Finds local minima of a smooth function of several parameters (CPA 312). *Behavioral Science*, 1969, **14**, 81–82.

Davis, R., Moray, N., & Treisman, A. Imitative responses and the rate of gain of information. *Quarterly Journal of Experimental Psychology*, 1961, **13**, 78–89.

Donders, F. C. Over de snelheid van psychische processen. Onderzoekingen gedaan in het Physiologisch Laboratorium der Utrechtsche Hoogeschool, 1868–1869, Tweede reeks, II, 92–120. (Translated by W. G. Koster, In W. G. Koster (Ed.), *Attention and performance II. Acta Psychologica*, 1969, **30**, 412–431.)

Falmagne, J.-C. Stochastic models for choice reaction time with applications to experimental results. *Journal of Mathematical Psychology*, 1965, **12**, 77–124.

Falmagne, J.-C. Biscalability of error matrices and all-or-none reaction time theories. *Journal of Mathematical Psychology*, 1972, **9**, 206–224.

Falmagne, J.-C., & Theios, J. On attention and memory in reaction time experiments. In W. G. Koster (Ed.), *Attention and performance II. Acta Psychologica*, 1969, **30**, 316–323.

Forrin, B., Kumler, M., & Morin, R. E. The effects of response code and signal probability in a numeral-naming task. *Canadian Journal of Psychology*, 1966, **20**, 115–142.

Hawkins, H. L., & Hosking, K. Stimulus probability as a determinant of discrete choice reaction time. *Journal of Experimental Psychology*, 1969, **82**, 435–440.

Krueger, L. E. Effect of stimulus probability on two-choice reaction time. *Journal of Experimental Psychology*, 1970, **84**, 377–379.

Morin, R. E., & Forrin, B. Information-processing: Choice reaction times of first- and third-grade students for two types of associations. *Child Development*, 1965, **36**, 713–720.

Morin, R. E., Konick, A., Troxell, N., & McPherson, S. Information and reaction time for "naming" responses. *Journal of Experimental Psychology*, 1965, **70**, 309–314.

Nickerson, R. S. Binary classification reaction time: A review of some studies of human information-processing capabilities. *Psychonomic Monograph Supplements*, 1972, **4** (Whole No. 65), 275–318.

Rabbitt, P. M. A. Repetition effects and signal classification strategies in serial choice-response tasks. *Quarterly Journal of Experimental Psychology*, 1968, **20**, 232–240.

Remington, R. J. Analysis of sequential effects in choice reaction times. *Journal of Experimental Psychology*, 1969, **82**, 250–257.

Sternberg, S. High-speed scanning in human memory. *Science*, 1966, **153**, 652–654.

Sternberg, S. Two operations in character recognition: Some evidence from reaction-time measurements. *Perception & Psychophysics*, 1967, **2**, 45–53.

Sternberg, S. The discovery of processing stages: Extensions of Donder's method. *Attention and Performance II. Acta Psychologica*, 1969, **30**, 276–315.

Sternberg, S. Decomposing mental processes with reaction-time data. Invited address, presented at the annual meeting of the Midwestern Psychological Association, Detroit, Michigan, May 1971.

Theios, J., & Smith, P. G. Can a two-state model account for two-choice reaction time data? *Psychological Review*, 1972, **79**, 172–177.

Theios, J., Smith, P. G., Haviland, S. E., Traupmann, J., & Moy, M. C. Memory scanning as a serial self-terminating process. *Journal of Experimental Psychology*, 1973, **97**, 323–336.

INDIVIDUAL DIFFERENCES IN COGNITION: A NEW APPROACH TO INTELLIGENCE[1]

Earl Hunt, Nancy Frost,[2] and Clifford Lunneborg

DEPARTMENT OF PSYCHOLOGY, THE UNIVERSITY OF WASHINGTON,
SEATTLE, WASHINGTON

I. Introduction

The fact of individual differences in mental functioning cannot be doubted. Their size and nature have such important consequences for our technologically oriented culture that society has demanded a way of measuring intelligence. Psychologists have responded with tests which, by almost any criterion, are a most substantial contribution to technology. What few laymen realize, however, and what few psychologists talked about until recently, is that the intelligence test is a measuring instrument which stands quite apart from any formal

[1] The research reported here was supported in part by the U.S. Air Force Office of Scientific Research Air Systems Command, Grant AFOSR 70–1944, and in part by the National Institute of Mental Health, Grant GB 25979, both to the University of Washington. We are happy to acknowledge the assistance of a number of colleagues. Our thanks go in particular to Lee Roy Beach, John Clavedetscher, Benoît Côté, Philip Milliman, Beth Nyblade, Thomas Nelson, and Susan Nix.

[2] Present address: Department of Psychology, Princeton University, Princeton, New Jersey.

model of the dynamics of the thought process. This article is a collection of theoretical and empirical arguments against the separation of testing from a theory of cognition. We believe that substantial benefits can arise from a rapprochement between the experimental psychologist and the psychometrician and these data now available indicate how this rapprochement may occur.

Before presenting our argument, a look at history is in order. How is it that a science noted for its addiction to Logic of Science ever developed an atheoretical technology? The answer seems to lie in public insistence on socially relevant devices in preference to sound theory. The first modern scientist to study individual differences was Francis Galton, just over 100 years ago. Galton had a theory of cognition. He thought that intelligence was a part of a general, heritable trait of "fitness for survival." Furthermore, Galton was a good scientist; he let his theory dictate the observations to be made. Since "fitness" had mental and physical components, Galton felt that both speed of striking a bag and speed of doing mental arithmetic were valid indicators of genius or lack of it. With the benefit of hindsight, we know that Galton had the wrong theory. His measurements of cognitive functioning were swamped by the much greater extent to which he was measuring motor functioning. As a result, Galton's tests did not succeed in making the identifications he thought they should. For instance, his tests did not distinguish the members of the Royal Society from the rest of London. Galton himself was forced to admit that his measurements of fitness had almost no practical utility.

Galton's scientific approach was effectively forgotten when Binet showed that a pragmatic approach could produce a socially useful intelligence test.[3] The only theoretical assumption Binet made, and which could be tested directly, was that the relative mental ability of individuals in a population was constant over time. To choose his measures, Binet sought advice from experts in children's school behavior. Any item, from any source, was a useful test item if it met the statistical standards for predicting later academic success. Modern psychometric theory has accepted Binet's approach. Factor analysis is a sophisticated tool for discovering the number of different relative orderings needed to account for performance on "intellectual" tasks. Estimates of this number range from 2 (Cattell, 1971;

---

[3] Binet himself realized the desirability of a theoretical test and conducted work much in Galton's traditions before adopting the relative measurement approach (Binet, 1890).

Jensen, 1970) to 120 (Guilford, 1967). There is still no theory of the dynamics of cognition which dictates our choice of what questions to ask. A test item is a good one if it shows the right pattern of correlations.

We believe that Galton, not Binet, had the right approach. Measurement in science should be dictated by theory. What is needed is a better theory.

If theory is necessary, then why has the intelligence test prospered? There are two answers to this question. One is that stable relative orderings are quite adequate for the technological purpose of prediction. This is particularly true when we view testing as a personnel screening technique. If Harvard wants the best available students and IBM the best available sales trainees, then all they need is a way to order the individuals in the populations of interest. The argument for a relative ordering is much weaker if one is concerned with the institution's responsibility to provide a service for members of the population qualified to receive it, but this is a rather recent concern of our society. Is it surprising that as this concern has arisen the intelligence test has become suspect?

A second reason for the success of the present tests is that they do assess certain basic aspects of cognition. We know this because physical changes in the brain affect test scores. It is well know that brain damage causes deterioration of test performance. In fact, specific injuries can be diagnosed by noting the type of test deterioration (Reitan, 1964). Particularly striking examples of the relation between the biology of cognition and test performance are the loss of speech-related abilities following injury to the left temporal cortex (Geschwind, 1970; Lenneberg, 1967) and the loss of the ability to learn new material after damage to the hippocampus (Milner, 1970). The fact that there is a substantial genetic component in intelligence test performance, whatever the size of that component may be, is itself an indication that to some extent the intelligence test measures a basic biological function. The individual differences assessed by an intelligence test provide useful reflections of cultural and biologic differences among men, but the development of those tests has taught us little about the nature of these differences. As a result, intellectual assessment is all too often descriptive rather than prescriptive.

Now let us look at the other side of the coin. Have scientists interested in a theory of cognition learned a great deal about individual differences? They have not. Modern studies of cognition from an information processing point of view have revealed the existence of a very wide range of individual differences, so much so that in many cases "within-individual" designs which control for this inter-subject variability must be used to obtain reliable results. This control has been appropriate because cognitive psychology has sought general laws, applicable to all men. Similarly, the learning theory approach which has dominated experimental psychology for so long does not regard individual differences of central interest, and modern learning theory offers little to explain why subjects react to tasks in such varied ways (Estes, 1970). Indeed, it is something of a tribute to the ingenuity of students of experimental design that cognition has been studied with little concern for the differences between people.

The point of reciting this history is to introduce to the reader our belief that on the one hand theoretically based intelligence tests are needed, and that, on the other, useful models of cognition must take into account established differences in mental functioning. In the remainder of this article we shall try to convert you to our beliefs, by showing that intelligence, as measured by conventional means, is consistently and substantially related to certain of the key variables in a modern theory of cognition. To do this we shall first describe a general model of cognition and present some of its implications for individual differences. We shall then discuss a number of experiments which relate the model to our present tests of intelligence. In the final section we shall consider the implications of these results for both psychometrics and cognitive psychology and indicate some directions for future research.

II. The Distributed Memory Model of Mental Functioning

The theoretical model we shall use is the *Distributed Memory* model (Hunt, 1971, 1973). It is representative of a class of models acceptable to the majority of experimental psychologists interested in cognition, although many would have reservations about certain details—with different scientists having different reservations. No attempt will be made to defend the reasoning which led to the model, or to cite the various experimental results which suggested it, as these were done in the model's original presentation.

The theoretical approach underlying the distributed memory model is that the brain can be thought of as a *computing system* (not as a computer, more narrowly defined), and that as such it has a physical and implied logical construction which is called its *system architecture*. The physical structures comprising the system architecture are exercised by *control processes* analogous to programs in an actual computer. The control processes use the architecture to manipulate information which is stored in a purely logical organization called a *data structure*. To illustrate from psychology, concepts such as "short-term memory" and "permanent memory" are architectural concepts, since they imply fixed storage devices which can be used only in certain ways. A coding strategy, such as rehearsal or conversion of a stimulus consisting of a sequence of zeroes and ones into octal digits, is a control process. Storage of information in connected clusters, such as the subset-superset links between noun terms suggested by Quillian (1968), or the various combinations of subset-superset and attribute-value connections described by Meyer (1970), are data structure concepts. A message from the environment is said to be comprehended if it has been incorporated into a data structure. This is done by the action of architectural components upon input and stored information, under the direction of a control process.

The system architecture of the distributed memory model is shown in Fig. 1. Two broad classes of information holding stages are postulated: *peripheral buffering* stages and *central memory* stages. Information presented from the environment is assumed to pass through a series of buffer stages. Each buffered step involves a recoding, which is essentially an interpretation of the current input in terms of past experience. For example, a printed word must be converted

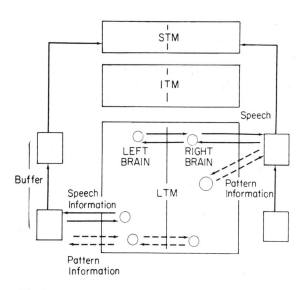

Fig. 1.   A schematic diagram of distributed memory.

from a point by point retinal display into a collection of lines, and then letters, and then a word. Subjectively, however, we see at least the letter, and often the word itself. Note that the recoding process must involve access to information in the central memory areas. This has been illustrated in an excellent series of experiments by Posner and his associates (Posner & Boies, 1971) on the "matching task." They have shown that it takes progressively longer to recognize two stimuli as "same" or "different" depending upon whether identity can be determined by physical shape (e.g., a $\neq$ A) or upon a higher order code, such as letter name (in which case a $=$ A). Obviously name matching is impossible unless the subject knows the alphabet, and it staggers the imagination to assume that the entire alphabet is held in short-term memory. Less scientifically, but perhaps more demonstratively, there are any number of anecdotes about how a person can recognize his own name in the buzz of a cocktail party conversation, yet ignore other discussions which have a louder acoustic signal.

After information has passed through the buffering process, its coded information enters into central memory. The central memory is assumed to have three components, short-term memory (STM), which holds stimulus-bound codes for a period of seconds, intermediate-term memory (ITM), which holds a semantic code for a period of several minutes to perhaps an hour, and long-term memory (LTM), which is a permanent repository. Colloquially, STM provides a word-by-word recall of what was just said, ITM provides a general picture of what the conversation is about, and LTM holds what is known about the world outside of the current discussion. It is likely that the nature of information coding in each of these memories is markedly different. In STM the codes are very much stimulus bound. The sound of words appears to play an important role here. ITM codes are much more bound to semantic relations. It is often useful to visualize ITM codes as graphs tying together basic terms in a lexicon, such as the graphs of episodes or events as proposed by Rumelhart, Lindsay, and Norman (1972), or Schank's (1969) constituent structure analysis of sentences.

LTM codes play a role similar to dictionary terms. These codes are thought to be organized in some form of semantic net, and are perhaps best envisaged as forming data bases for an information retrieval system. In the final stages of comprehension, information is assumed to move from ITM to LTM, where it is incorporated into the data bases of LTM. The organization of the various data bases will determine whether a particular piece of information is difficult to retrieve, and the extent to which the retrieval will be sensitive to the context of the recall situation. Much of the recent work on clustering, proactive inhibition, sentence comprehension, and long-term recall can be thought of as parts of an attempt to discern the nature of the retrieval system. An excellent case can be made for the existence of several data bases, e.g., Tulving's (1972) distinction between episodic and semantic memory and the distinction between retrieval systems for verbal and nonverbal information. The last dichotomy is of special interest to us. Of course, there must be some process by which information in different data bases can be cross-referenced.

The distinction between different types of data bases leads us to a second bifurcation of system components, into right and left hemisphere components. We know that the human brain is markedly asymmetrical in its functioning. Both physiological and clinical evidence has accumulated showing that for most people LTM for speech is located in the left cortex (Gazzaniga, 1969). This functional split has major implications for a theory of cognitive functioning. The fact of asymmetry reinforces the assertion that verbal and pattern memories are anatomically as well as logically distinct. To predict performance on a given task it is necessary to determine the involvement of each hemisphere and the importance of coordination between them, with particular attention to the efficiency of the required information transfers.

Thus far our emphasis has been on the location and communication of different types of information. We must also be concerned with the transformation of information. To continue with the computing system analogy, we must ask what basic operations on data can be performed in the various component units of the model. Compiling a list of basic brain functions would itself be a major undertaking, one which we shall not attempt here. Instead we shall deal with two classes of transformations. The *psychophysical transformations* deal with the conversion of external world signals into internal codes. After all, we can only think about the things we can sense. For our purposes, the chief importance of the psychophysical transformations is undoubtedly in determining the efficiency of the buffer system. The *internal manipulations* in both peripheral and central memory are those operations used to produce new internal codes from other codes. Restle's (1970) studies of mental calculation and Shepard and Metzler's (1971) study of mental rotation of visual images illustrate the sorts of experiments which reveal these processes.

Ideally, in relating the distributed memory model of cognition to individual differences, we ought to develop a precise theory of how the model could be applied to solve a variety of intellectual tasks.

Since a given task could be approached several ways, we should consider a variety of programming solutions for the human computer. We would find that performance on some tasks would be sensitive to the program being used and to some of the parameters of the model, but relatively insensitive to other choices of program and parameters. For example, in most situations word recognition is sensitive to the speed of retrieval and organization of data in LTM, but insensitive to the size of STM; while a digit span task is affected by the amount of space in STM and the codes available in LTM. By the use of analysis and simulation,[4] we ought to be able to find those parameters and programs which are most crucial in determining different types of intellectual performance. Tests could then be derived to measure directly the parameters or programs used. These tests would, collectively, be a theoretically based measure of intelligence. Such a proposal is an ambitious one which should be undertaken only if it has a reasonable chance of success. Here we shall attempt the more modest goal of showing that success is likely. We shall show that there are relationships between our present intelligence tests and some of the major variables in the model. We shall concentrate on the components of memory, since they have been subject to much recent study. Can we find evidence through the study of individual differences, showing that there are separate memory talents which have different relations to the factors of intelligence? It is important to realize that our goal is *not* to show that the parameters of models of cognition might be used to predict intelligence scores, or vice versa. If this were the case, the two measures would be transmitting the same information. We wish to show two things: first, that there is a substantial *but imperfect* relationship between a model of human cognition and our present tests, i.e., that the measures share information but are not identical; and secondly that differences in subjects' reactions to experimental tasks are reliable functions of individual characteristics, and cannot properly be conceptualized as measurement error.

III.   Research Plan

A number of those studies most influential in developing our model of thought were selected for replication, with the addition of

---

[4] The reader is urged to consider the type of simulation that would be needed. It is a sort of hybrid between the purely task-oriented simulation advocated as general models of cognition and the Monte Carlo techniques used by economists.

intelligence as an independent variable. To do this, we required a group of subjects for whom adequate psychometric data were available. If our theoretical approach is correct, we should be able to develop across studies a consistent pattern for an individual's mental functioning. Thus, we restricted our subjects to those whose performance could be examined in a number of experimental tasks. Ideally we would have liked to have drawn our subjects from a population which had a wide range of variation on a number of intellectual factors, as this would have increased the sensitivity of our measurements. Since administrative considerations made this impossible, we used University of Washington undergraduates who, prior to entering the University, had taken a standard battery of intelligence tests known as the Washington Pre-College (WPC) battery. This is part of a program offered to all Washington State high school students, and required of those entering the university. It is normally taken at the end of the junior year of high school. The battery contains nine intelligence related tests: Vocabulary (antonyms), English Usage (grammar, usage, diction, and idiom), Spelling (recognition of misspellings), Reading (providing separate level of comprehension and speed scores), Quantitative Skills (three-part measure of quantitative reasoning), Applied Mathematics (number skills, arithmetic applications), Mathematics Achievement (geared to high school curriculum through junior year), Spatial Ability (visualization of manipulations through three dimensions), and Mechanical Reasoning (application of physical principles). In addition to the scores on the separate tests, two composite measures are reported based upon a factor analysis of the battery. The Verbal Ability Composite (VA) score is a weighted sum of performances on Vocabulary, English Usage, Spelling, Reading Comprehension, and Reading Speed. The Quantitative Ability Composite (QA) score is a weighted sum of Quantitative Skills, Applied Mathematics, and Mathematics Achievement scores. We used the two composite scores to categorize our subjects, as these scores are representative of verbal and quantitative intelligence measures widely employed with late adolescent subjects—the composite measures correlate, .81 and .85, with the Verbal and Mathematical subtests in the College Entrance Examination Board's Scholastic Aptitude test comparable to the test-retest reliabilities for those SAT subscores.

Because of the widespread acceptance of such verbal and quantitative measures as indicators of two of the most important aspects of intelligence, as presently measured, we selected as subjects those students who had extreme scores within the range present in the University of Washington undergraduate population. All freshmen whose composite scores were both in the extreme quartiles for their entering class received a mailed invitation to participate as paid subjects. While these subjects represent extremes among university students, our low subjects scored between the mean and one standard deviation below it in terms of the scores obtained on the WPC by high school students. High subjects, by contrast, had scores exceeding one standard deviation above the mean. These distributions are due to the University of Washington's selection policy. In general, entering students are in the upper third of their high school graduating classes.

Response to the mailed invitations was quite good. More students volunteered than could be studied. Our eventual panel of subjects consisted of 104 freshmen resident in the university in 1971–1972. Table I shows the distribution of subjects into the four groups de-

TABLE I

NUMBER OF SUBJECTS SCORING IN EACH QUARTILE OF QA AND VA COMPOSITES

		Verbal ability score		
		Fourth quartile	First quartile	
Quantitative ability score	Fourth quartile	30	26	56
	First quartile	25	23	48
		55	49	104 Total

fined by combinations of upper and lower QA and VA quartiles. Not all subjects participated in all experiments.

We shall present our results in logical order, initially describing two "global" experiments which tested at once many aspects of memory functioning. We shall then describe other experiments addressed to more specific questions.

IV. General Experiments

A. CONTINUOUS PAIRED ASSOCIATES

Atkinson and Shiffrin (1968, 1971) have developed a detailed two-stage model of the continuous paired associates task. The task requires that the subject keep track of the current association between each of a small set of stimuli and one of a large set of responses, although the current association is changed repeatedly. For example, suppose that the stimuli are the letters A–D, and the responses are selected from among integers between 00 and 99. A sequence of presentations using the anticipation method might be:

A—47	⎫
B—12	⎬ Starting trials
C—39	⎪
D—17	⎭
B—?	First test trial, lag = 2
B—73	First study trial after a test trial
A—?	Second test trial, lag = 4
A—7	Second study trial

The presentation sequence is divided into three types of trials. First we have the "starting" trials, in which each stimulus is paired with a response. These are followed by pairs consisting of a test trial and a study trial. In the test trial, the stimulus alone is presented and the subject is to state the number most recently paired with the stimulus. The test trial is followed by a study trial, in which the just-tested stimulus is paired with a new response. In our experiments 150 massed pairs of study-test trials were presented. The task is quite a demanding one, and error rates are high. The independent variable of interest is the *lag*, defined as the number of pairings intervening between the study trial and test trial for a given stimulus. In the illustration, examples of lag 2 and lag 4 are shown.

Atkinson and Shiffrin's model for the analysis of data from this task provides an estimate of four parameters: α, the probability of entry of an item into STM; r, the number of items that can be held in STM at one time; θ, the rate of transfer of information into ITM;[5] and τ, the rate at which information becomes unavailable from ITM. The model has been shown to fit data very accurately in a number of experiments. It is of particular interest to us to note that substantial individual differences are found when parameters are estimated for each subject (Atkinson, Brelsford, & Shiffrin, 1967).

Forty subjects, ten from each of the four subgroups, participated in a replication of the Atkinson-Shiffrin experiment. The study was conducted under computer control, using an IMLAC PDS-1 display system. The stimuli were four consonant-vowel-consonant (CVC)

---

[5] We will use the term ITM, thus being consistent with our own terminology. Most authors use LTM to refer to any memory from minutes to years.

trigrams, and the responses were digit pairs from 01 to 75. Four study trials were used to initially pair each stimulus with a response, and then 150 study-test sequences occurred. Each study trial lasted for 3 seconds. The test trials were, or course, paced by the subject. The lag between a study trial and its subsequent test varied from 1 to 14. Additional details followed the procedure of Atkinson and Shiffrin (1968).

Parameters were estimated for each subject using a visual chi-square minimization technique developed by Garnatz and Hunt (1973). Table II shows the mean and standard deviation for each

TABLE II

MEANS AND STANDARD DEVIATIONS FOR PARAMETER ESTIMATES IN THE CONTINUOUS PAIRED-ASSOCIATES TASK[a]

	Parameter estimates							
	α		r		Θ		τ	
	$\overline{X}$	SD	$\overline{X}$	SD	$\overline{X}$	SD	$\overline{X}$	SD
High quant:								
High verbal	.50	.56	1.75	1.93	.32	.36	.75	.84
Low verbal	.38	.34	1.65	1.88	.28	.33	.74	.61
Mean for high quant. groups	.44		1.70		.30		.74	
Low quant:								
High verbal	.30	.46	1.60	1.87	.27	.29	.52	.84
Low verbal	.24	.43	1.23	1.44	.32	.38	.30	.40
Mean for low quant. groups	.27		1.42		.30		.41	
	$p < .10$		N.S.		N.S.		$p < .002$	

[a] Results of high-low quantitative significance tests are indicated. No significant verbal composite group differences were found.

parameter for each group, and for the combined low and high quantitative groups. It is readily apparent that there were large individual differences and that some of them were related to WPC scores. The most striking difference is that the rate of loss of retrievable information from ITM (τ) was reliably lower for subjects in the high QA groups. ($F_{1,36} = 14.62$, $p < .022$). There is suggestive evidence that subjects with high QA scores also had a higher probability of placing an item into STM (for α, $F_{1,36} = 5.00$, $p < .10$). None of the other individual differences appeared to be associated with intelligence test scores. It is of interest to note that the parameters

θ, r, and α are considered to be under the subject's control, in the sense that their values can be manipulated by choice of strategy for handling the experimental task (Loftus, 1971). As such, the values of these parameters might be expected to exhibit wide individual differences when subjects do not have sufficient practice to stabilize on a common strategy. Unlike Atkinson and Shiffrin, we did not have our subjects go through an extensive familiarization period. The measure of effective loss of information from ITM, on the other hand, is presumably a measure of the extent to which one is distracted by incoming information *after* an item has been fixed in memory. As such, it may be less under the subject's control.

B. CLUSTERING

The Atkinson and Shiffrin task was chosen because it represents a global task in which several aspects of memory can be tested without regard to the linguistic meaning of the stimuli. Now let us consider a second global task—free recall of an organized list of words. It is well known that in free recall of verbal lists, subjects will attempt to impose some organization upon their responses. For instance, in free recall of unrelated words responses may follow the order of presentation of stimuli, even though the subjects are not instructed to do so. Another common strategy used in free recall is to recall words together if they are semantically related in some way. For instance, words which are free associates of each other, such as THREAD and NEEDLE, will usually be recalled together regardless of their position in the stimulus list. A particularly powerful type of clustering is semantic category clustering (Bousfield, 1953). If a list of words consists of, say, animal, vegetable, and mineral names, then members of each category will be recalled together. The phenomenon is even stronger if the list is *blocked,* i.e., if all terms within a category are continuous when the list is presented (Cofer, Bruce, & Reicher, 1966; Puff, 1966). Puff's study of the blocking effect was selected for replication. Intuitively we would expect performance on such a recalled task to be more sensitive to verbal facility than performance in a paired-associates recall task.

Subjects recalled lists of nouns that were grouped into semantic categories and presented in either categorized or random fashion. Thus this study permits the subject to organize his memory by reference to semantic categories, and allows us to observe the extent to which his recall organization is affected by the conditions of presentation.

Twelve subjects from each IQ group participated. Each subject learned, and then immediately free recalled, two lists of 30 words. Each list contained ten words from each of three categories:

List A—vegetable, occupation, animal

List B—fruit, geographic term, kitchen utensil

In the *blocked* condition all words within a category were presented contiguously; in the *pseudorandom* condition the words from different categories were mixed, so that in only nine cases were two words from the same category adjacent in the list. Presentation order and list organization of lists A and B were balanced over subjects. Each list was presented twice, with immediate free recall after each presentation. Within a list items were shown for 2.5 seconds, with a 1.5 second interitem interval. All other details of the study replicated Puff's original work. Free recall was scored for number correct and number of category repetitions, relative to the maximum number of possible repetitions. The degree to which semantic coding is sensitive to presentation order can be inferred from the category repetition, or clustering, score under the two conditions of list presentation.

Table III summarizes the results. There were no differences in total number of words recalled. Not surprisingly, clustering was high for all subjects in the blocked condition. However, marked differences between groups appeared in the pseudorandom condition. The results were counterintuitive: the high verbal subjects showed a

TABLE III

MEAN CATEGORY CLUSTERING SCORES FOR THE FOUR SUBGROUPS[a]

	Mean clustering score		
Group	Blocked condition	Pseudorandom condition	Difference[b]
High verbal			
High quant.	.96	.70	.26
Low quant.	.96	.68	.28
Mean high verbal	.96 (26.6)	.69 (23.9)	.27
Low Verbal:			
High quant.	.86	.82	.04
Low quant.	.96	.85	.11
Mean low verbal	.91 (25.4)	.84 (23.0)	.07

[a] Mean number of words recalled per list given in parentheses.

[b] $p < .01$ for comparison of high and low verbal subjects.

marked drop in the amount of clustering when the list was not blocked, while the low verbals continued to cluster. The high verbal subjects did not appear to be using a random recall, however. In the words of several subjects, they just "read the words back as they heard them." This was reflected (weakly) in the data by an insignificant tendency of high verbal subjects to respond with items in order of presentation. In any case, whatever the high verbals did, both the data and their reports are consistent in *denying* that they relied on clustering as greatly as did the low verbals.

V.   Experiments on Details

A.   ENCODING

An important concept in the distributed memory model is the idea of levels of stimulus code. We previously illustrated this by reference to the name matching and physical matching tasks developed by Posner and his associates. These studies provided the paradigm for our next experiment. In a sequential variation of the Posner *et al.* method, subjects are shown one letter immediately followed by the second, which is to be identified as "same" or "different" depending on either physical or name identity. It typically takes about 70 msec longer for a practiced subject to make a name match than it does to make a physical match.

Sixteen subjects, four from each of the subgroups, completed a name and physical matching task during a single experimental session. The task requires that the subject look at a letter which is presented for 1 second. After the letter disappears, a second letter is displayed, with an interstimulus interval of zero seconds. In the physical match condition, the subject must then respond SAME if the letters are physically identical (e.g., AA); in the name match condition, subject responds SAME if the two letters have the same name (e.g., AA and aA). Responses were made by pushing marked buttons on a teletype keyboard. The subjects practiced for 160 trials before beginning the experiment, and half of the subjects performed the name match condition first while the other subjects began with the physical match task. Each subject received 40 same trials and 40 different trials in each condition. In all cases the physical form of the second letter was predictable (i.e., Posner's PURE list paradigm was used).[6]

---

[6] The same subjects were also run in conditions where the occurrence of all letters

TABLE IV

NAME-PHYSICAL MATCH TIME DIFFERENCES FOR FOUR SUBGROUPS
(msec)

		Verbal		
		High	Low	
	High	35	63	49
Quantitative				N.S.
	Low	31	109	70
		33	86	

$p < .08$

The data are summarized in Table IV. In spite of the small number of subjects and the brief amount of training (compared to the procedure used by Posner), marginally significant differences ($p < .08$) were found between the high and low VA groups, using the Mann-Whitney U statistic. No other contrasts approached significance. Unfortunately, the advent of summer vacation, and subsequent disappearance of our sample, made it impossible to replicate this study with a larger group, and hence the results can be looked upon as suggestive only. The very large absolute size of the differences suggests that this will be a fruitful area for further study. It should be noted further that the difference is due to a difference in time for *name* matching; in physical matching the high VA subjects are only 12 msec faster than the low VA subjects. In other words, the effect shown in Table IV is due to faster name access by high VA subjects.

B. SEMANTIC CODING AND PI RELEASE[7]

The coding involved in the Posner *et al.* task are physical and taxonomic only. We next consider a type of coding which involves a

---

was unpredictable, but due to a computer malfunction, some data were lost. Since the results of the two types of stimulus presentation did not differ, only the pure list conditions will be presented.

[7] This experiment was part of a B.S. honors thesis by Susan Nix, under the direction of the first two authors.

higher order LTM code, semantic memory. Wickens and his associates have carried out extensive studies of the release from proactive inhibition (PI) phenomenon in STM experiments (Wickens, 1970). It is well known that if a person is asked to hold from three to six "chunks" of information in STM while he performs a distracting task, such as counting backward, then forgetting can be observed in a matter of seconds. The phenomenon depends partly upon proactive inhibition (PI), for it does not occur on the first trial, and then builds rapidly to an asymptote in three or four trials. Wickens has found that the increase in PI is affected by the constancy of stimulus meaning. For example, if a subject is given a series of trials involving CVC trigrams, PI will build up. Suppose the n + first trial uses instead a 3-digit number sequence as the stimulus to be remembered. The subject will not display forgetting on that trial. This is referred to as *release from PI*. PI can be built up again, in our example, by giving the subject a further sequence of trials involving number strings. PI release can be demonstrated either by switching to stimuli with different acoustic or semantic characteristics—e.g., from U, C, D to A, X, R, or from letters to numbers, or even from one category of noun to another. Now consider the results of the name-matching studies. They suggested that the *speed* of encoding linguistic material was related to verbal ability. Would *sensitivity* to the meaning of linguistic coding show a similar relation?

Twenty-four subjects, six from each of the four subgroups of the pool, participated in a PI release experiment. On each trial, the subject read three names of vegetables, counted backward by 3's for 15 seconds, and then attempted to recall the vegetables names. After three such trials the stimulus category was switched from vegetables to occupations, while all other details remained the same. A second group of 24 subjects participated in a no-release control condition, where vegetable names were continued through the fourth trial.

The results are shown in Figs. 2 and 3. Directing the reader's attention first to Fig. 2, it can be seen that PI does indeed build up over the first three trials both in experimental and control groups. The release from PI phenomenon appears to occur most strongly for high verbal subjects. However, the data presented in Fig. 2 were scored correct only if a subject recalled all the words in the order presented. In Fig. 3 one sees the same data rescored for word recall only (errors in serial position ignored). When rescored, the data indicate that release of category PI is strong in both groups. These remarks are supported by an analysis of variance, which indicated a

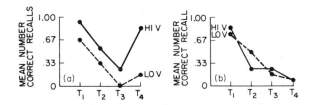

Fig. 2. Proactive inhibition release data, scored correct only if recall in order.
(a) 12 high verbal (HIV) and 12 low verbal (LOV) subjects; experimental condition.
(b) 12 high verbal and 12 low verbal subjects; control condition.

significant interaction ($p < .025$) between verbal ability and method of scoring. The differences in Fig. 2, then, are not due to *categorical* encoding, but to the deterioration of *temporal* encoding over trials in the low verbal groups. This is of interest because temporal encoding and speed of coding are closely related concepts. The data also suggest that in the clustering study low verbal subjects used semantic information because they cannot (rather than do not) retrieve serial position codes. In retrospect, we are reminded of Lashley's (1951) eloquent discussion of the serial position problems in understanding language. A superior memory for order information may well increase the typical verbal IQ score. We also point out that temporal coding may be closely related to speed factors in cognition.

C.   MANIPULATION OF INFORMATION IN STM

In describing a computing system one always states what the memory access time is, as this very largely determines how rapidly data can be processed. Sternberg (1966, 1970) has developed a paradigm for studying the speed with which people can access data in

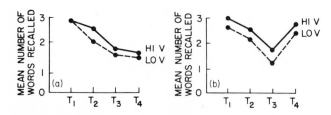

Fig. 3. Proactive inhibition recall data rescored to count as correct word recall regardless of order. (a) 12 high verbal (HIV) and 12 low verbal (LOV) subjects; control condition. (b) 12 high verbal and 12 low verbal subjects; experimental condition.

STM. The subject is first presented with a (small) set of familiar items which are to be held in memory. This is called the *memory set*. Digit or letter strings are frequently used. A probe item is then presented, and the subject is asked to indicate whether or not the probe was in the memory set. It has been found that the time required to answer this question is a linear function of the number of items in the memory set. The slope of the function is interpreted as a measure of the time required to access a single item from STM and to compare it to the probe. Obtained slope figures vary with the type of material, but virtually all studies find marked individual differences.

Eight high- and eight low-verbal subjects were tested using the varied set procedure of the Sternberg paradigm (Sternberg, 1970). From 1 to 5 digits were displayed simultaneously for 3 seconds. The probe digit appeared 2 seconds later. Subjects learned the task rapidly and averaged fewer than 3% errors. Response latencies as a function of set size are plotted in Fig. 4. High verbal subjects had significantly faster search than low verbal subjects, but there was no correlation ($r = .09$) between search rate and subjects' QA scores. Further, there was no evidence of a correlation between slope and intercept, thus demonstrating that the results did not merely reflect the difference between cautious and eager reactors. The results are

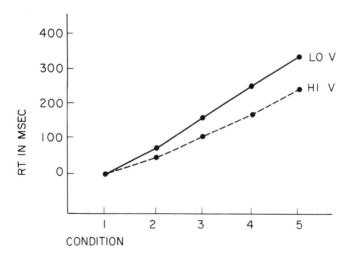

Fig. 4. Reaction time (RT) to correctly recognized probes from the memory set, plotted as a function of number of items in the memory set. Data points represent the mean of RT's at each condition minus the mean RT for Condition 1. Curves for individual subjects were smoothed.

consistent with the results of the name-matching study in indicating that verbal ability is related to the speed of data manipulation in memory.

D. SUSCEPTIBILITY TO INTERFERENCE

In our next study we shift from the study of VA to QA. Recall that the results of the continuous paired-associates study led us to suggest that high QA subjects had high resistence to interference following information acquisition. Let us address this question more directly.

Eighteen high QA and ten low QA subjects participated in a replication of the Brown-Peterson paradigm (Peterson & Peterson, 1959). As the subject sat in a sound attenuated booth, a CCC trigram was presented through earphones, followed immediately by a 3-digit number. The subjects counted backward from this number by 3's, for 3, 6, 9, 12, 15, or 18 seconds, and then, on signal, attempted to recall the trigram. There were four trials at each interval. The study was modeled as closely as possible after Peterson and Peterson's original experiment.

The data are presented in Fig. 5. High QA scorers showed consistently better ($p < .05$) performance at all retention intervals, so the fact that high QA subjects do well in this (nonquantitative) task is clear-cut. The reason for their superiority is not. Three hypotheses occur: that high QA subjects are generally less susceptible to distraction, both when perceiving information and when trying to retain it

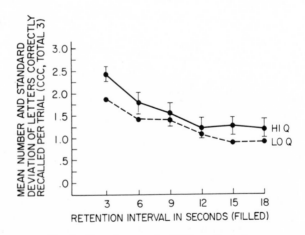

Fig. 5. Data from main CCC recall study.

in memory; that high QA subjects simply have larger STM buffers, and hence are able to hold more information in STM at a given time; or that high QA subjects have a memory process which is less susceptible to interference.

As a check on the first hypothesis, a "noise" condition of the Brown-Peterson paradigm was run, using the same 28 subjects. The experiment was identical to the main experiment, except that the CCC stimuli were presented against a background of white noise, adjusted so that the stimuli were audible at a 0-second interval 50% of the time, for the average subject. If the high QA subjects were able to perceive information in spite of distracting stimuli, then they ought to show a more marked superiority in this condition. The resulting data are shown in Fig. 6. Both groups were dropped to their

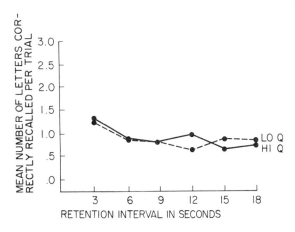

Fig. 6. Brown-Peterson task with white masking noise during stimulus presentation.

"floor" level of perceiving and held only one of the three letters presented. Thus there is no evidence that high QA is associated with an ability to disregard physically distracting stimuli per se.

If high QA subjects have a larger STM, then they ought to be able to retain more information in STM in a digit span task. This question was addressed directly in a separate study, using 18 high and 12 low QA subjects. Digits were presented visually at a rate of one per second. Immediately following the presentation of a sequence of digits, the subject recalled it by typing the sequence on a computer keyboard. The number of digits in the sequence was gradually increased until the subject was no longer able to respond correctly.

High QA scorers had a mean digit span of 7.44, and low scorers, a mean of 7.42. The difference between the groups did not approach statistical significance. Furthermore, a digit span score of this size is well within the normally reported range. Thus there is no support for the proposition that high QA subjects have exceptionally large STM's.

We are left with the conclusion that high QA scorers are better able to hold information in memory in the face of distracting stimuli. It should be noted that in the Brown-Peterson paradigm there are two potential sources of interference: PI from the previous trials and retroactive interference due to the effects of the distracting task (counting backward) required while information is being held in memory. The data do not permit us to distinguish which of these sources has an effect sensitive to QA level. For tangential reasons we suspect it is the latter. Recall that in the "release from PI" study described above it was found that a PI effect was more likely associated with verbal ability. We also examined the QA scores of the subjects in that experiment and found no indication of any relationship between QA and release from PI, or between QA and build up of inhibition over trials. Thus it seems most likely that high QA subjects are less susceptible to distraction while consolidating information in STM, rather than being better able to distinguish between the data from the current and the previous trials, presumably the explanation for the basic PI effect.

E. Acquisition and Retrieval from LTM

We have noted throughout that "long-term memory (LTM)," as the term is used by most authors, often refers to what we prefer to characterize as intermediate term memory (ITM). We now report a somewhat different study which approaches the question of individual differences in memory of a more permanent nature.

Thomas Nelson conducted a paired-associates study[8] in which subjects were asked to learn 24 nouns, verbs, or adjectives paired with numbers. Learning was by a modified study-test method to the criterion of one perfect trial. The subjects were tested for retention of the associates 5 weeks later.

Table V presents the correlations between errors during acquisi-

---

[8] We concern ourselves solely with the correlations between acquisition, retention, and the WPC. Data contrasting the effectiveness of performance in the various groups will be presented by Nelson in a subsequent paper.

TABLE V

CORRELATIONS AND PARTIAL CORRELATIONS OF VERBAL AND
QUANTITATIVE SCORES WITH ACQUISITION AND RETENTION[a]

Psychometric subtest	Acquisition (errors to criterion)			Retention (number recalled)		
	Noun group	Verb group	Adjective group	Noun group	Verb group	Adjective group
Verbal ability (VA)	−51	−45	−29	30	15	21
VA (QA partialled)	−36	−45	−30	14	24	18
VA (Acquisition errors partialled)				27	−22	21
VA (QA and errors partialled)				15	00	18
Quantitative ability (QA)	−44	−18	05	36	−15	36
QA (VA partialled)	−23	15	08	24	−08	35
QA (Acquisition errors partialled)				33	−36	36
QA (VA and errors partialled)				24	−29	35

[a] Correlations of .34 and .46 are significant at the .05 and .01 levels with 24 subjects.

tion, number of associations retained 5 weeks later, and the WPC composites. The results for verbs are somewhat puzzling, and discussion of these data will have to await further study. The finding of interest here concerns the different correlates of acquisition and retention. Acquisition of a paired-associates list requires use of both STM and ITM. VA, which we have found to be related to speed of encoding, was the best predictor of acquisition performance, in both noun and adjective groups, and prediction was not significantly enhanced by the use of QA scores as a second predictor. Exactly the opposite relation held for prediction of retention 5 weeks later. QA was the best predictor of retention, but VA added nothing to predictability. This pattern of correlations is consistent with the observations we have made relating VA to STM and QA to resistance to interference.

F. CORRELATIONAL STUDIES

We have been arguing that the experimental psychologist's tools can illuminate the psychometrician's problems. The fact that the same subjects were used in a number of experiments allows us to reverse this procedure, by studying the correlations between different task measures. The required procedure is somewhat different from the usual psychometric analysis of a test battery, since not all subjects participated in all experiments, but this problem can be handled by applying the usual procedures for missing data.

Table VI shows the correlation matrix for 15 task variables. The correlation matrix was factor analyzed using the principal components technique, and the resulting factors rotated to simple structure using Kaiser's varimax criterion for orthogonal rotation (Harman, 1967). The varimax criterion places the axes defined by the factor analysis at an orientation that tends to maximize high and low factor loadings on each factor, thus rendering the factors more easily interpretable.

Table VII presents the factor loadings for each test on the first five factors. The first factor extracted accounted for 25% of the variance, the next factor about 16%, and the next three factors about 10% each. We shall comment on each in turn.

Factor I, the largest and statistically most reliable factor, appears to be a generalized "efficiency of STM" factor. Tests which have high loadings on this factor, such as digit span at a *low* presentation rate and CVC recall, typically require the recall of meaningless information over brief periods of time. Tests which have intermediate loading, such as Atkinson and Shiffrin's α parameter measuring the likelihood that an item enters STM, or digit span at a *rapid* rate of presentation, involve not only the holding of information, but other abilities, such as coding speed as well. Measures of LTM performance, such as the θ and τ parameters in Atkinson and Shiffrin's model, are independent of Factor I.

The meaning of the second factor is somewhat less clear. It appears to be a measure of the ability to hold meaningful material over a short period of time. The defining test is the number of words recalled in a free recall of an unordered list. The average speed of recall in Sternberg's memory scanning task also has an appreciable loading on Factor II. We suggest that Factor II may be related to the speed with which meaning can be established when a highly overlearned item appears in STM.

Factors III and IV appear to be specific measures of performance in the clustering task. Factor IV, for example, is the factorial equivalent of the experimental result showing that some subjects shift recall strategies when dealing with pseudorandom or blocked lists.

Factor V is defined by a high loading for size of the STM buffer, as measured by the continuous paired-associates task, and by a *nega-*

TABLE VI

CORRELATION BETWEEN TASK MEASURES

Variable name	1	2	3	4	5	6	7	8	9	10	11	12	13	14	15
1. r—Continuous paired associates	1.00	.20	-.12	.22	.08	.16	.01	.23	.25	-.21	.18	-.26	.20	.12	.28
2. α—Continuous paired associates	.20	1.00	-.26	.42	.10	-.10	-.02	-.09	.47	.28	-.05	.36	.52	.43	.47
3. θ—Continuous paired associates	-.12	-.26	1.00	.02	.19	.31	-.10	.24	-.19	-.33	.42	-.17	-.17	-.04	.07
4. τ—Continuous paired associates	.22	.42	.02	1.00	-.05	-.04	-.15	-.20	.13	.09	.13	.07	.12	.25	.03
5. Number of words recalled, unblocked	.08	.10	.19	-.05	1.00	.25	-.01	.24	-.05	-.33	.68	.28	.09	-.25	-.15
6. Number of words recalled, blocked	.16	-.10	.31	-.04	.25	1.00	.24	-.07	-.18	-.05	-.16	-.30	.10	.09	.32
7. Difference, blocked and unblocked	.01	-.02	-.10	-.15	-.01	.24	1.00	-.39	.28	.06	.34	.05	.09	.40	.32
8. Clustering of unblocked words	.23	-.09	.24	-.20	.24	-.07	-.39	1.00	.18	.03	-.11	.20	.32	.28	.28

(Continued)

TABLE VI (Continued)

Variable name	1	2	3	4	5	6	7	8	9	10	11	12	13	14	15
9. Clustering of blocked words	.25	.47	−.19	.13	−.05	−.18	.28	.18	1.00	−.37	.39	.42	.68	.32	.45
10. Slope of memory scan	−.21	.28	−.33	.09	−.33	−.05	.06	.03	−.37	1.00	−.38	.23	.39	.21	.03
11. Intercept of memory scan	.18	−.05	.42	.13	.68	−.16	.34	−.11	.39	−.38	1.00	.03	−.10	.06	.21
12. Digit span, 1-second interval	−.26	.36	−.17	.07	.28	−.30	.05	.20	.42	.23	.03	1.00	.43	.30	.19
13. Digit span, 6-second interval	.20	.52	−.17	.12	.09	.10	.09	.32	.68	.39	−.10	.43	1.00	.47	.72
14. CVC recall, Number correct after 3 seconds	.12	.43	−.04	.25	−.25	.09	.40	.28	.32	.21	.06	.30	.47	1.00	.82
15. CVC recall, Number correct, total	.28	.47	.07	.03	−.15	.32	.32	.28	.45	.03	.21	.19	.72	.82	1.00

TABLE VII

ROTATED FACTOR LOADINGS

Variable name	Factor I	Factor II	Factor III	Factor IV	Factor V
1. r—Continuous paired associates	.21	.04	-.13	.19	.81
2. α—Continuous paired associates	.48	.18	.00	-.10	-.01
3. θ—Continuous paired associates	.01	.13	-.16	.22	-.05
4. τ—Continuous paired associates	.06	-.04	.00	-.05	.07
5. Number of words recalled, unblocked	-.10	.99	-.08	.14	.07
6. Number of words recalled, blocked	.17	.13	.12	.90	.11
7. Difference, blocked and unblocked	.36	.05	.85	.10	-.01
8. Clustering of unblocked words	.40	.12	-.79	-.05	.07
9. Clustering of blocked words	.61	.20	.14	-.54	.41
10. Slope of memory scan	.19	-.20	-.09	.22	-.65
11. Intercept of memory scan	.09	.58	.38	-.25	.27
12. Digit span, 1-second interval	.40	.44	-.09	-.45	-.47
13. Digit span, 6-second interval	.80	.21	-.18	.01	-.02
14. CVC recall, Number correct after 3 seconds	.86	-.22	.10	.01	-.11
15. CVC recall, Number correct, total	.94	-.05	.06	.15	.14

tive loading for slope in the memory scanning task. Both these measures reflect speed of encoding. If a subject can produce a number of compact codes quickly under the stressful conditions of the continuous paired associates task, he will obtain a high value of r. Similarly, a low slope in the memory scanning task represents rapid access to STM. Factor V calls to mind the performance of the mnemonist VP, a man who has been shown to have an amazingly accurate memory (Hunt & Love, 1972a, 1972b). One of the differences between VP and other equally intelligent subjects who do not have unusual memories is the speed with which he is able to produce semantic codes for virtually any stimulus material. In other words, this particular man's performance is almost exactly defined by Factor V.

In closing our discussion of these results, a word of caution is appropriate. Factor I is substantial and probably reliable. It represents an interesting validation of the STM concept outside of the tradition of experimental psychology. The remaining factors are not as large as Factor I, and ought to be considered suggestive but hardly conclusive. Note, however, that there is little difference between factors in this regard. Factor V is nearly as large as Factor III, and not terribly smaller than Factor II, so we suggest that their statistical reliabilities should be considered equivalent.

VI. Discussion

The obvious question is "What does all this mean?" The answer depends on the person addressing the question. These results have different meaning for the psychologist generally interested in individual differences, for the experimentalist concerned with cognition, and for the psychometrician wishing to assess mental functioning.

The general psychologist will have noted that while we have shown significant results, we have not shown strong correlations. Indeed, our initial studies can be criticized on the grounds that we have shown a large number of moderate correlations, rather than having elucidated any one relationship in greater detail. Our data, then, may be more suggestive than conclusive. One of our original points, however, was that low positive correlations are of interest. Although it seems reasonable on *a priori* grounds to expect that the study of individual differences in cognition would locate the same critical underlying variables of human performance that would be revealed by an experimental approach to cognition, this, in fact, has not happened. Psychometrics and cognitive psychology appear to be currently sharing information about man, but by no means do they duplicate each other. At least, we see no other way to account for the pattern of our results. Indeed, we see this as support for our basic proposition. The finding of consistent, though moderate, relations between individual difference variables and experimentally manipulated performance reinforces our position that it is time to begin the development of theoretically oriented tests, and it is time to begin considering the differences between people in our models of cognition.

Our data pose a challenge to the experimental psychologist at two levels. Empirically, we have shown that individual differences systematically interact with treatment effects in a number of the most popular paradigms in modern cognitive psychology. This is a quite atheoretical statement; to disbelieve it you must argue with our data rather than our interpretation of the studies. Quite without theory, the existence of an interaction between treatment effects and subject characteristics establishes a problem for the experimentalist. The logic of most experimental studies assumes that the "error term" represents measurement error and is randomly distributed over observations. Our results call this assumption into question. The challenge is *not* to the legitimacy of statistics, for statistical analysis using the so-called "fixed effects" model is appropriate so long as the assignment of subjects to treatment conditions is random. The challenge is directed toward the generalizations which we might wish to draw from an experimental study. The vast majority of experiments are conducted using students from the experimenter's own institution as subjects. We have shown that within the undergraduate population of a somewhat selective state university there are systematic individual differences by treatment interactions. We would expect to find even larger interactions if we studied populations drawn from varying institutions, say, from a rural community college and an Ivy League university. Inferences from university sophomores to people in general are even more suspect. Psychologists have known, and largely ignored, this fact for some time. The unspoken assumption has been that while levels of performance might vary in different populations, the same relationships would hold between performance and treatment conditions. Our data do not support this assumption. It now seems unlikely that a general model of cognition can be based on the performance of subjects from any narrow range of mental functioning.

Experimentalists interested in cognition may also wish to consider our specific results in the construction of formal models of thought.

The exact interpretation of the data will depend, however, upon how a particular theorist views the experimental situations we have studied. For example, a person who rejected the assumptions of the distributed memory model would probably not accept our discussion of the continuous paired-associates task. The interpretations of the experiments which we favor lead us to conclude, tentatively, that there is a relationship between rapidity of STM processes and verbal ability, and between resistance to interference and quantitative ability. At a more general level, we have demonstrated relationships between psychometrically defined factors of mental ability and the parameters of an information processing model of cognition. This is by far the most important facet of our study. The experiments which we have completed are relatively crude. We have relied on global parameters, used subjects from restricted ranges of mental abilities, and typically used very small numbers of subjects. Even so, we obtained results which present a coherent picture. There are other aspects of the information processing model of cognition and other mental factors which await exploration.

Our results also stress an important point which is often overlooked by both experimentalists and psychometricians. Equivalent results may often be produced by different processes. In our clustering study, high and low verbal subjects recalled almost exactly the same number of items from the unblocked (pseudorandom) lists. To do so, the low verbal subjects, we argue, must semantically cluster, while the high verbals are not dependent upon this strategy.

In a separate study (to be reported subsequently), high and low VA subjects participated in a recognition memory task in which the stimuli were either written names or children's faces. The high VA subjects consistently adopted a naming strategy and, as a result, there was a substantial correlation between their performance in face and name recognition. Low VA subjects seemed to have looked on the task as one of perceptual memory, and their face recognition performance was not correlated with performance in the verbal task. Similar results have been noted in the way in which high and low VA subjects approach a picture recognition task such as the Mooney Closure Test, a test which was designed to measure the ability of subjects to form a Gestalt pattern, and which has been used to assess brain damage associated with loss of the Gestalt ability (Lansdell, 1968). When high verbals take the Mooney test, they convert it to a labeling task, while low verbals deal with the visual material directly.

We find an even more striking example of qualitative differences which can lead to the same level of performance when we consider the case of two mnemonists, Luria's (1968) "S" and "VP," a man who has been more recently studied (Hunt & Love, 1972a, 1972b). It is clear that both men would give outstanding performances in the classic experimental tasks set by the cognitive psychologist interested in memory. How they would go about each task would be quite different. According to Luria's account, S was either an eidetic imager or he relied strongly on memory traces stored as sensory images. He made extensive use of the "memory walk" method of encoding. VP, on the other hand, typically relies on verbal labels and semantic codes. He denies reliance on sensory image. It is particularly interesting that he does this, because VP, in terms of our sample, would be high in both VA and QA. His performance indicates that he is extremely rapid at encoding stimuli, and that he is virtually impervious to retroactive interference. (He has, on several occasions, recalled perfectly for 150 trials in the continuous paired-associates task!) VP is also a chess master, indicating his competence in analytical reasoning. Formal intelligence data are not available for S, but Luria's clinical description of him suggests that he was not unusually intelligent, especially in abstract linguistic or quantitative reasoning. In fact, he solved arithmetic problems by visualization. We can imagine two groups of individuals, one composed of "VP's" and the other of "S's," providing homogenous results on a number of memory tasks, yet performing according to grossly different strategies.

Granted then, that subjects cannot be regarded as random replicates in the study of cognitive functioning, where are we to turn? The only cognitive theorists to be much concerned about this to date have been the developers of computer simulation models, who often propose a distinct model for each individual subject. This surely is not adequate economy of description. We must have a middle ground between the "one model for mankind" and the "one model for one man" approaches. Here is where the psychometrician can help. What are the implications of our results for this area of psychology?

In these initial studies we have provided the psychometrician with a first glimpse of a new theoretical base to intellectual assessment. The challenge is to begin to incorporate this into the web of established empirical relations that forms the base for current psychometric practice. It will be a multifaceted task, involving as it must at least four sets of relations: among existing psychometric measures, among process measures or parameters derived from the cognitive model, between these psychometric and process measures, and between psychometric assessments and subsequent performance in socially significant settings.

Let us first consider, speculatively, the last of these sets of relations. It is well established that verbal ability is a very useful predictor of success in certain vocations. We are now suggesting that verbal ability is related, in turn, to the rapidity of information processing in STM. Can the psychometrician identify situations in which the two relations are consonant, in which speed of STM processing will be predictive of job success? This seems a reasonable prospect and, indeed, we would argue that such new predictive relations may have more significant implications than present psychometric relations even where the new predictive relation may not be quite as strong as the old. Because of the atheoretical, empirical basis of a construct like verbal ability, permitting only relative measurement, few clues are available to suggest how (or if) verbal ability can be changed in the individual. As a result, the temptation is strong to treat people as if they either have it or do not have it. In contrast, a theoretically based predictor, because of the theory, is more likely to carry with it implications about its modifiability. Training of STM processing efficiency, for example, seems more directly approachable than increasing verbal ability. In appears probable to us that a set of new, theoretically based measures of intelligence will move many psychometric predictions from static statements about the probability of success to dynamic statements about what can be done to increase the likelihood of success. Such shifts must await considerably more extensive measurement of model-related cognitive performances than we have been able to attempt to date.

In the more immediate future, then, the challenge to psychometrics will be that of bringing well-developed multivariate analytic tools to bear on the establishment of a measurement multidimensionality based upon a model of cognitive functioning. The model, of course, provides a statement of what theoretically should be measured, but as it as yet does not take patterns of individual differences into account, this may be quite different from a statement of what needs to be measured. We suggest that once extensive assessment is accomplished, the model parameters might be suitable for factorization. For instance, the various encoding speed and time tagging measures could well be a reflection of an underlying "cognitive clock" which cycles at different speeds in different individuals, just as different computers cycle at different times. If this is true, parameters affected by the cognitive cycle time should display an appropriate factorial structure. Also, apart from theoretical considerations, we suspect there may be such strong cultural (educational) constraints on the selection of control processes that, for any practical purpose, not all of the model parameters need to be assessed.

Indeed, a very important problem closely akin to that of determining an appropriate dimensionality for cognitive assessment is that of identifying cognitive types. Above we suggested that the psychometrician could help establish a middle ground between a universal cognitive model and a separate model for each person. Although we can only guess at them at this time, there are almost certain to be logical, physiological, and cultural constraints against the occurrence of certain combinations of parameter values. Which patterns occur, with what frequency, and under what circumstances are questions which, in addition to being inherently interesting to the multivariate psychometrician, have implications for the experimentalist or cognitive theorist. Indeed, we visualize that the successful development of this area will depend upon a recursive cycling between experimental and psychometric work. As the cognitive model suggests experimental measures to be obtained, the psychometric analysis of the relations among those measures will suggest, in turn, modifications of the model, then new measurement, new analysis, etc.

Let us shift from considering how measures can be analyzed to a consideration of the measures to be taken. Our reported measures of cognitive performance were obtained from the replication of neoclassic experiments. Actually running subjects in paradigms which yield one parameter after an hour's work is hardly practical, however. A final challenge to the psychometrician is the development of reliable tests of the model parameters that are of reasonable length. These new theoretically based measures will bear little resemblance to the paper and pencil, multiple-choice format tests in wide psychometric use today. Increasing importance must be given to the measurement of latency of response, to the careful timing of exposure of test materials, and to the recording and scoring of open as opposed to choice responses. Fortunately, we expect an economically feasible technology, computer-directed assessment will be available at about the time new measurements can be constructed. We are pleased to note that a growing number of psychometricians are at work on problems related to the new technology.

VII. Conclusion

We have presented a theoretical argument and supporting data for a new conceptualization of intelligence. The gist of our argument is that intelligence should be determined by absolute measures of aspects of a person's information-processing capacity rather than by measures of his performance relative to the performance of others in a population. If we replace the relativistic definition of intelligenece with a definition in terms of information processing, we will force a change in the way in which we view and utilize intelligence measurement. This may have disadvantages as well as advantages. From the scientific point of view we will be on much firmer footing when we try to relate individual differences to a general model of cognition. Not only is this logically desirable, it is likely to have important consequences for continuing controversies about intelligence testing. For instance, the nature-nurture argument will become one about which parameters of the information processing model are trainable and which are hereditary. At the practical level, intelligence tests will measure what a man can do, rather than what he can do relative to others. Such a change in testing may have some awkward implications. Personnel screening, for instance, has made effective use of a relativistic model of ability. Hopefully the new viewpoint on intelligence will lead to measuring instruments which are diagnostic, in the sense that they tell us how the institution should adjust to the person, instead of simply telling us which people already are adjusted to the institution. The full development of such test is, of course, some time in the future. First we must complete a research trail on which the present report is only a first step. In addition, we must develop a technology of testing which can make use of the techniques of experimental psychology. We are confident that this can be done. The scientific challenge is before us. Once we decide what we should measure, a way will be found to measure it.

References

Atkinson, R., Brelsford, J. W., & Shiffrin, R. M. Multiprocess models for memory with applications to a continuous presentation task. *Journal of Mathematical Psychology,* 1967, **4**, 277–300.

Atkinson, R. C., & Shiffrin, R. M. Human memory: A proposed system and its control processes. In K. W. Spence & J. T. Spence (Eds.), *The psychology of learning and motivation: Advances in research and theory.* Vol. 2. New York: Academic Press, 1968.

Atkinson, R., & Shiffrin, R. The control of short term memory. *Scientific American,* 1971, **225**, 82–90.

Binet, A. La concurrence des états psychologiques. *Revue de la France et l'Étranger,* 1890, **24**, 138–155. (S. Boies translation.)

Bousfield, W. A. The occurrence of clustering in the recall of randomly arranged associates. *Journal of General Psychology,* 1953, **49**, 229–240.

Cattell, R. B. *Abilities: Their structure, growth and action.* Boston: Houghlin, 1971.

Cofer, C. N., Bruce, D. R., & Reicher, G. M. Clustering in free recall as a function of certain methodological variations. *Journal of Experimental Psychology*, 1966, **71**, 858–866.

Estes, W. K. *Learning theory and mental development*. New York: Academic Press, 1970.

Garnatz, D., & Hunt, E. Eyeball parameter estimation with a computer. *IEEE Transactions on Systems, Man, and Cybernetics*, 1973, **SMC–3**, No. 1, 45–51.

Gazzaniga, M. S. *The bisected brain*. New York: Academic Press, 1969.

Geschwind, N. The organization of language in the brain. *Science*, 1970, **170**, 940–944.

Guilford, J. P. *The nature of human intelligence*. New York: McGraw-Hill, 1967.

Harman, H. *Modern factor analysis*. Chicago: University of Chicago Press, 1967.

Hunt, E. What kind of computer is man? *Cognitive Psychology*, 1971, **2**, 57–98.

Hunt, E. The memory we must have. In R. Schank & K. Colby (Eds.), *Computer simulation of information processes in man*. San Francisco: Freeman, 1973.

Hunt, E., & Love, T. How good can memory be? In A. Melton & E. Martin (Eds.), *Coding and memory*. New York: Academic Press, 1972. (a)

Hunt, E., & Love, T. The second mnemonist. Paper presented at the meeting of the American Psychological Association, Honolulu, September 1972. (b)

Jensen, A. R. Hierarchical theories of mental ability. In W. B. Dockrell (Ed.), *On intelligence*. London: Methuen, 1970.

Lansdell, H. Effect of temporal lobe deficits on two lateralized defects. *Physiology & Behavior*, 1968, **3**, 271–273.

Lashley, K. S. The problem of serial order in behavior: In L. A. Jeffress (Ed.), *Cerebral mechanisms in behavior*. New York: Wiley, 1951. Pp. 112–136.

Lenneberg, E. H. *The biological foundations of language*. New York: Wiley, 1967.

Loftus, G. R. Comparison of recognition and recall in a continuous memory task. *Journal of Experimental Psychology*, 1971, **91**, 220–226.

Luria, A. *The mind of a mnemonist*. New York: Basic Books, 1968.

Meyer, D. E. On the representation and retrieval of stored semantic information. *Cognitive Psychology*, 1970, **1**, 201–214.

Milner, B. Memory and the medial temporal regions of the brain. In K. Pribram & D. E. Broadbent (Eds.), *Biology of memory*. New York: Academic Press, 1970.

Peterson, L. R., & Peterson, M. J. Short-term retention of individual items. *Journal of Experimental Psychology*, 1959, **58**, 193–198.

Posner, M. I., & Boies, S. Components of attention. *Psychological Review*, 1971, **78**, 391–408.

Puff, C. R. Clustering as a function of sequential organization of stimulus word lists. *Journal of Verbal Learning and Verbal Behavior*, 1966, **5**, 503–506.

Quillian, M. R. Semantic memory. In M. Minsky (Ed.), *Semantic information processing*. Cambridge, Mass.: MIT Press, 1968.

Reitan, R. Psychological deficits resulting from cerebral lesions in man. In J. Warren & K. Akert (Eds.), *The frontal granular cortex and behavior*. New York: McGraw-Hill, 1964. Pp. 295–312.

Restle, F. A. Speed of adding and comparing numbers. *Journal of Experimental Psychology*, 1970, **83**, 274–278.

Rumelhart, D. E., Lindsay, P. H., & Norman, D. A. A process model for long term memory. In E. Tulving & W. Donaldson (Eds.), *Organization and memory*. New York: Academic Press, 1972.

Schank, R. A conceptual dependency representation for a computer oriented semantics. A. I. Memo 75, Stanford University Department of Computer Science, 1969.

Shepard, R. N., & Metzler, J. Mental rotation of three dimensional objects. *Science*, 1971, **171**, 701–703.

Sternberg, S. High speed scanning in human memory. *Science,* 1966, **153,** 652–654.

Sternberg, S. Memory scanning: Mental processes revealed by reaction time experiments. In J. S. Antrobus (Ed.), *Cognition and affect.* Boston: Little, Brown, 1970.

Tulving, E. Episodic and semantic memory. In E. Tulving & W. Donaldson (Eds.), *Organization and memory.* New York: Academic Press, 1972.

Wickens, D. D. Encoding categories of words: An empirical approach to meaning. *Psychological Review,* 1970, **77,** 1–15.

STIMULUS ENCODING PROCESSES IN HUMAN LEARNING AND MEMORY[1]

Henry C. Ellis

DEPARTMENT OF PSYCHOLOGY,
UNIVERSITY OF NEW MEXICO, ALBUQUERQUE, NEW MEXICO

[1] The research described in this paper was supported by several grants from the National Science Foundation. Preparation of the paper was facilitated by National Science Foundation Grant GB-27413X. A preliminary version of this paper was prepared while the author was Visiting Professor of Psychology at the University of California, Berkeley. The support of Leo Postman and the Institute of Human Learning staff is gratefully acknowledged. Appreciation is expressed to following graduate students who are currently participating in this research program: Charles Grah, Reed Hunt, Frederick Parente, Chandler Shumate, Charles Tatum, and Craig Walker, and to previous graduate students whose works are acknowledged at appropriate places.

I. Introduction

A fundamental problem in the experimental analysis of human learning and memory is the manner by which a subject transforms experimenter-presented nominal stimuli into functional stimuli. In order to understand how a particular stimulus becomes capable of evoking a particular response or class of responses, it is generally agreed that a direct and simple one-to-one relationship between a nominal stimulus and an experimenter-defined overt response represents an insufficient formulation in accounting for many experimental findings. There is now substantial evidence that a subject, when presented with a nominal stimulus, selectively attends to particular features of that stimulus (e.g., Richardson, 1971; Trabasso & Bower, 1968).

In a parallel vein, a closely related problem in human learning is that of stimulus encoding. It is generally held that humans may encode particular aspects of nominal stimuli so as to facilitate the link between a nominal stimulus and an overt response (e.g., Lawrence, 1963; McGuire, 1961; Martin, 1968). Similarly, it is evident that verbal coding can enable the classification and storage of visual pattern stimuli (e.g., Ellis & Muller, 1964; Glanzer & Clark, 1962; Riley, 1962). Except for the simplest kind of stimuli, performance in a variety of tasks involving learning, memory, transfer, and concept identification seems not to depend solely upon physical properties of the nominal stimuli as such, but upon the manner in which the stimuli are encoded.

The purpose of this article is to examine a particular class of problems which can be subsumed under stimulus coding. They concern the role of verbal processes and structural properties of stimuli in the encoding of both visual pattern and verbal stimuli. Although there is little doubt about the encoding function of language in the sense that names or verbal labels encode certain kinds of information in visual patterns, the mechanisms accounting for this class of events are not fully understood. It will be necessary to consider not only how verbal labeling of stimuli enables their efficient encoding, but also how recall of the verbal label or some related verbal code influences memory of the associated stimulus. Moreover, interest is focused on the manner in which acquired encodings function in new learning tasks. Thus a verbal tag cannot only affect the rate or ease with which a subject achieves a stable encoding of nominal stimuli, but the tag may affect subsequent stimulus recognition, recall, or transfer performance.

A. STIMULUS CODING AND SELECTION

Stimulus coding is one of several classes of organizational processes that operate in learning and memory. The concept emphasizes the processing function of the learner in which he transforms stimulus materials presented to him in a variety of ways. Stimulus coding is the process by which a subject changes or transforms any experimenter-presented stimulus into some new "state" or representation. These transformations may be of the one-to-one variety, involving a particular transformation of each nominal stimulus presented to a subject, or they may be composed of a several-to-one arrangement in which two or more nominal stimuli receive the same transformation. The essential feature of the coding concept is that it involves either partial or full replacement of the stimulus input with some new representation, or an elaboration (enhancement) of the stimulus which involves the storage of additional nonredundant information with the unit to be remembered. Several conceptions of this representation will be discussed in subsequent sections.

The distinction between stimulus coding and stimulus selection is most clearly seen by focusing on the nature of what is transformed. Obviously, coding and selection are related processes. The essential distinction lies in the fact that stimulus coding usually refers to transformation of stimulus input into some hypothesized representation, whereas stimulus selection refers to the fact that subjects may select some fraction or portion of a stimulus, once it is perceived, to cue a response. A test of stimulus selection allows the identification of a functional stimulus which can be some portion of a nominal stimulus compound. To the extent that a subject selects some part of the compound rather than its entirety, stimulus selection is a *reductive* process. Moreover, the functional element is usually identifiable. In contrast, stimulus coding is an *elaborative* or reconstructive process involving either rearrangement of elements of the nominal stimulus, or complete transformation to a new state. In some instances the code may be identifiable, as when a subject rearranges anagram stimuli (e.g., Underwood & Erlebacher, 1965), whereas in other instances the code concept remains an inference in the sense that its properties retain a hypothetical status (e.g., Lawrence, 1963; Martin, 1968).

B. STIMULUS CODING AND MEDIATION

In a similar vein it is useful to make a distinction between coding
and mediational concepts while remaining cognizant of their simi-
larities. The theoretical descriptions of mediation have sometimes as-
sumed that a subject makes an implicit response to a nominal stimu-
lus, and that the cue properties of this response become, in turn,
associated with the experimenter-defined overt response. This ap-
proach is quite explicit in McGuire's (1961) multiprocess model of
paired-associate learning, and in formulations that have employed
cue-producing responses (Dollard & Miller, 1950; Goss, 1955; Kend-
ler & Kendler, 1968). Although theoretical divergencies regarding
the nature of such implicit responses exist ranging from stimulus-
response mediational interpretations (Kendler & Kendler, 1968),
perceptual encoding accounts (Martin, 1968), to attentional interpre-
tations (Hake & Eriksen, 1955), there is general agreement regarding
the significance of this class of events.

Coding responses are similar to mediating responses, and indeed,
coding and mediation have on occasion been treated as largely syn-
onymous concepts. They differ, however, in that mediating responses
are treated as being tied in some fairly direct manner to nominal
stimulation. The conception of a cue-producing response (N. E. Miller
& Dollard, 1941) is representative of mediational formulations. The
clearest distinction between the two emphasizes that mediating re-
sponses are stimulus-determined, whereas coding responses are deter-
mined by both sensory input and learner states that involve sets
and instructions (Lawrence, 1963). The principal difference lies in
the contribution of the organism to coding responses, a contribution
which presumably allows for more abrupt changes in behavior than
seem predictable by mediating responses.

C. CONCEPTIONS OF THE CODING RESPONSE

There is growing evidence that a subject must acquire some rela-
tively stable representation of a nominal stimulus if he is to respond
to that stimulus in a consistent fashion on successive trials (e.g.,
Bernbach, 1967; Martin, 1967a, 1967b; Royer, 1969). Although the
nature of this representation remains for the most part either un-
specified or ambiguous, several attempts at specification have been
made. For instance, Martin (1967a, 1967b) has suggested that a
recognition response be considered as a prime candidate, in the
sense that nominal stimulus recognition is regarded as a precursor

to association formation in paired-associate learning. In a subsequent theoretical paper, Martin (1968) refers to this precursor as a perceptual-encoding response, leaving its specification open-ended for the present. Modifying this position, Ellis and Tatum (1973) have proposed that the precursor is some encoding of nominal stimulus events and is not necessarily reflected in nominal stimulus recognition as such. Similarly, both Peterson (1967) and Melton (1967) have considered the characteristics of an "editing" mechanism that might function as a precursor to recall. In a related vein, Ellis and Homan (1968), and subsequently Price and Slive (1970), have suggested that some form of an implicit associative response might be viewed as the precursor to stimulus recognition. Support for this latter view stems from studies showing that the rate of false recognition is influenced by the probabilities of implicit associative responses being elicited by a stimulus (e.g., Underwood, 1965).

Investigators of perceptual memory have also contended that verbal encodings of stimuli govern subsequent memory performance in both recognition and recall tasks. For instance, Glanzer and Clark (1962), in proposing the verbal loop hypothesis, contended that subjects translate visual pattern stimuli into a series of words, and that the retained verbalization controls subsequent memory performance. This hypothesis emphasizes that the encoding of visual information is characteristically verbal, and that retrieval of the visual input is governed by recall of the verbalization at the time of testing. Similarly, Ellis and Muller (1964) have proposed a conceptual coding hypothesis designed to account for the effects of verbal labeling on recognition memory of forms. This position emphasizes that it is not the verbal label itself that facilitates performance, but the fact that the label suggests a conceptual category which governs what is initially encoded. Other accounts have emphasized the role of imagery (Bower, 1972; Paivio, 1969) and the relationship between verbal and image codes (Bahrick & Boucher, 1968).

D. ARTICLE PREVIEW

The purpose of this article is to explore the ways in which stimulus encoding interpretations have been used to account for performance in tasks of memory and transfer. An examination of alternative theoretical conceptions of this process will be made in the context of four classes of experiments. Section II will examine several experiments conducted under the rubric of acquired distinctiveness and acquired equivalence of cues, experiments which examine the role of verbal labeling of visual patterns on their subsequent recognizability. Section III examines the role of response processes in stimulus encoding and focuses on the role of response variables in shape and trigram recognition. The relationship between stimulus recognition and association formation is examined in detail. Section IV pursues this issue and examines the interdependence between recall and recognition. Section V examines the role of stimulus variables in stimulus encoding with an emphasis on stimulus meaningfulness, configurational or grouping rules, and nominal stimulus variability. Section VI views the classic transfer of stimulus differentiation issue as an encoding problem, and evaluates the role of stimulus redundancy and stimulus recoding mechanisms.

II. Verbal Processes in Stimulus Pretraining

The class of research problems categorized under the rubric of verbal pretraining or stimulus predifferentiation is directly relevant to the general problem of the role of verbal processes in the encoding of visual stimuli. Although not all verbal pretraining experiments have dealt directly with the process of verbal encoding, the majority of such studies relate either directly or indirectly to the problem. Moreover, the experimental analysis of stimulus predifferentiation effects bears closely upon the second level of the classic Whorfian hypothesis and upon the general problem of language and thought, because such studies ask how memory and perception of stimuli depend upon language. In general, studies of verbal pretraining have been designed to determine "what is learned or encoded" about a set of stimuli during a pretraining session in which subjects are taught to label the stimuli with verbal labels.

A. Studies of Verbal Labeling

Properties of the verbal labels may be varied in a number of ways in stimulus pretraining studies so that effects associated with specific response features may be examined. Subjects may, for example, learn to associate quite distinctive verbal labels to different stimuli, or they may associate a single label to one set of stimuli and a second label to another set of stimuli. These variations define what are commonly known as the acquired distinctiveness and acquired equivalence of cues paradigms, respectively (Arnoult, 1957; Ellis, 1969). Similarly, properties of the verbal response such as its meaningfulness, or its representativeness of the pretraining stimuli, may also be varied (e.g., Ellis, 1968). Moreover, subjects may also be asked to provide their own unique verbal labels (e.g., Arnoult, 1956) in an effort to allow the development of more unique encodings. Other pretraining procedures which require subjects to observe the pretraining stimuli or to make same-difference judgments of the stimuli are also sometimes used, primarily as efforts either to minimize or prevent covert labeling of stimuli and thus provide control conditions against which to compare the effects of overt labeling practice. Instructions to a subject to inspect or observe the stimuli as such do not, of course, automatically prevent covert labeling (Ellis & Muller, 1964); nevertheless, such procedures do minimize the immediate likelihood of covert labeling activity when the stimuli are complex in formal structure or are low in codability (e.g., Brown & Lenneberg, 1954; Daniel & Ellis, 1972; Ellis & Daniel, 1971).

Following pretraining, subjects are then given one or more test tasks designed to assess the effects of verbal pretraining. A variety of test or transfer tasks have been employed, and features of the test task have usually reflected the theoretical predisposition of the investigator (cf. Vanderplas, 1963). Moreover, Ellis and Muller (1964) and Vanderplas, Sanderson, and Vanderplas (1964) have described the dependency of verbal pretraining effects upon characteristics of the criterion or test task. Before we examine the nature of the test tasks themselves, a few comments on the conceptual origins of these studies are in order.

The majority of predifferentiation experiments have been designed to test empirical implications that presumably derive from stimulus-response mediation theories employing the concept of a cue-producing response (e.g., Goss, 1955; Miller & Dollard, 1941). Alternatively, some of the experiments derived from differentiation concepts of perceptual learning (e.g., E. J. Gibson, 1969; J. J. Gibson & Gibson, 1955) which propose that stimuli become more perceptible, not because of associative processes or verbal labeling per se, but because organisms come to respond to more aspects of environmental stimuli as the result of practice. In addition to (a) stimulus-response mediation theory and (b) differentiation theory, other interpretations of verbal pretraining effects have suggested the role of (c) observing responses (Ellis, Bessemer, Devine, & Trafton, 1962; Spiker, 1963) and (d) attention to cues (Hake & Eriksen, 1955). Only the general features of these accounts need be noted because the analysis of predifferentiation studies will focus on verbal encoding interpretations of the findings with some consideration of observing responses and attention. Thus, despite the divergence of theoretical interpretations given to the findings of predifferentiation experiments, they will be examined for the purpose of determining what conclusions they enable about verbal encoding processes.

1. Mediated Generalization Tests

In studies of stimulus predifferentiation, three kinds of test tasks have typically been employed. One test measures changes in the probability of stimulus generalization following predifferentiation training. This task has been infrequently used (e.g., Birge, 1941; Malloy & Ellis, 1970) and yet is the most directly pertinent to the two formal hypotheses of Miller and Dollard regarding the role of verbal labeling practice (Ellis, 1969, 1970), hypotheses which employ the concept of a cue-producing response. The first, that of acquired equivalence of cues, contends that attaching identical or similar cue-producing responses to two distinctive stimulus events gives them some learned equivalence, increasing the extent to which instrumental response will generalize from one stimulus to another. Thus, attaching common responses to somewhat different stimuli should lead to an increase in stimulus generalization following such verbal pretraining, a prediction which was confirmed by the results of Malloy and Ellis (1970). The importance of this study was that it demonstrated that changes in stimulus generalization following verbal pretraining were not due *simply* to the label encouraging a subject to attend to common features of the stimuli during pretraining.

The second hypothesis, that of acquired distinctiveness of cues, proposes that associating distinctive response-produced cues to two initially similar stimuli provides for learned distinctiveness, decreasing the extent to which instrumental responses will generalize from one stimulus to another. Other than the classic study of Birge (1941), there is no substantial evidence (Malloy & Ellis, 1970) for an acquired distinctiveness of cues mechanism in which generalization tests have been used. Moreover, Maltzman (1968) has noted that Birge's findings may be easily interpreted as the result of attentional rather than mediational processes.

2. Transfer Tests

A second type of test measures the ease with which new responses can be associated with the pretaining stimuli following verbal labeling practice. This type of test is properly seen as a transfer test in the sense that following first-week associative learning, in which subjects must learn to label a set of stimuli with a set of distinctive responses, they must then associate new and quite different responses to the stimuli, thus conforming to an A-B, A-D transfer paradigm. The appropriateness of this test task is that it was first suggested as pertinent by E. J. Gibson (1940) as a way of evaluating her predifferentiation hypothesis. Theoretically, there should be a source of positive transfer in A-D learning associated with the *differentiation* of the relevant stimuli during first-task learning. Thus, if part of what a subject learns during first-task learning is the differentiation of the stimuli, then he should benefit during A-D learning because the stimulus differentiation component is already achieved.

The transfer test has been used in several ways. In some instances (e.g., Gagné & Baker, 1950), experimental subjects have been given verbal pretraining prior to the transfer task and their performance compared with control subjects given no pretraining. Other studies (e.g., Goss & Greenfeld, 1958) have compared the effects of verbal labeling practice with subjects who received instructions to observe the stimuli alone and again have found that verbal pretraining facilitates transfer. Such studies are nonanalytic in the sense that positive transfer effects associated with verbal pretraining may not be due to an increase in "distinctiveness" of the stimuli as such but rather may be due to general transfer effects associated with learning how to learn to associate stimuli and response terms in paired-associate fashion.

The most appropriate use of transfer tests of verbal pretraining effects are those which employ a typical nonspecific transfer control (e.g., Ellis & Shaffer, 1971; Underwood & Ekstrand, 1968), or studies which estimate relative transfer effects with control subjects observing the stimuli (Del Castillo & Ellis, 1968).

3. Recognition and Discrimination Tests

The third type of task designed to assess the effects of verbal pretraining of stimuli has measured either recognition or discrimination of the stimuli subsequent to verbal labeling practice (e.g., Arnoult, 1956; Clark, 1965; Price & Slive, 1970; Robinson, 1955). Here interest has focused on whether the stimuli are indeed more accurately recognized as a result of verbal labeling practice, or if discrimination between training and test stimuli, as say, in a same–different judgment task, is facilitated as a result of verbal labeling of the stimuli.

These tasks, obviously, focus most directly on memory and perception, and hence provide more direct information about the facility with which a subject has encoded the stimuli as a result of verbally labeling them.

It is worthwhile noting that experiments using recognition memory tasks are not directly pertinent to formulations derived from *verbal* cue-producing response mechanisms. This point appears not to have been recognized until recently, and Ellis (1970) has outlined one possible reason, which appears to be the failure to have distinguished between *verbal* and *nonverbal* cue-producing response mechanisms as formulated by Dollard and Miller (1950, p. 103). It is important to note that although the Miller-Dollard formulation was concerned principally with verbal cue-producing responses, they nevertheless recognized the function of nonverbal cue-producing responses that could mediate changes in transfer and discrimination. For instance, this second source of performance changes could be mediated by attention to particular aspects of a stimulus pattern or by orienting responses. One implication of this general failure to recognize that Miller and Dollard had proposed *both* an S-R mediation mechanism and attention mechanism based upon nonverbal cue-producing responses is that much of the controversy between so-called enrichment and differentiation theories of perceptual learning was probably unnecessary (Ellis, 1970). Although this article is not concerned with this theoretical controversy, it is worthwhile noting this point principally for the purpose of recognizing that theoretical studies of stimulus predifferentiation using recognition memory tasks have been, in essence, irrelevant to this particular controversy despite the fact that such studies do provide valuable information about verbal coding processes. The next section considers studies of the effects of verbal labeling of stimuli on stimulus recognition and examines several alternative accounts of this effect.

B. ATTENTION AND OBSERVING RESPONSES

When humans associate verbal labels to shape or form stimuli during a training session, it seems intuitively reasonable to assume that the verbal label may aid the encoding of certain features or aspects of the pattern solely because a distinctive verbal label may encourage a subject to select more distinctive features of a pattern than is likely if no label is present. It is *not* contended here that the label necessarily "enriches" (cf. E. J. Gibson, 1969) whatever encoding a subject may acquire, but only that a task requiring a subject to associate different verbal labels to different stimuli may predispose a subject to acquire somewhat more unique encodings of stimuli than would otherwise occur. In addition, if the verbal labels are in some way "representative" or descriptive of the shape stimuli, such labels would appear to aid a subject in rapidly achieving a stable encoding for each visual pattern. Although classical studies of perceptual memory (e.g., Carmichael, Hogan, & Walter, 1932) indicated that practice in verbally labeling stimuli did produce effects on stimulus recall (reproduction), earlier studies employing recognition or descrimination tests almost always failed to obtain any effect due to verbal pretraining (e.g., Arnoult, 1956; Campbell & Freeman, 1955; Prentice, 1954; Robinson, 1955).

The fact that verbal labeling effects were fairly consistently associated with stimulus recall and not with recognition suggested that verbal labeling practice might produce its principal effects on retrieval processes in memory. An even stronger version of this argument proposes that verbal processes, even if operating during shape-label associative training, are in no way enhancing the storage of information about the stimuli but are producing their entire effects during retrieval. Although this interpretation has recently been shown to be unreasonable (Ellis & Daniel, 1971), the characteristically negative results reported with recognition tests prompted pursuit of this problem in an experiment by Ellis et al. (1962).

In the Ellis et al. (1962) study, subjects were given three kinds of pretraining with random tactual shapes. Tactual shapes were employed in order to obtain some information about how subjects manipulated the stimuli during pretraining and thus determine if exploration of the stimuli was conceivably dependent upon the conditions of verbal pretraining. Random shapes constructed of vinyl were mounted on a circular plywood form and presented to blindfolded subjects who were allowed only to feel the shapes. The shapes were presented in paired-associate anticipation fashion, subjects having 10 seconds to feel the shape and 10 seconds in which to anticipate the response in those conditions in which they labeled the shape. Three conditions of pretraining were administered: One group of subjects learned to associate distinctive and representative verbal labels to each of the eight shapes, defining a *distinctiveness* training group. A second group learned the response "wide" for half the shapes and "narrow" for the remaining half, defining an *equivalence* group. The labels were representative of the shapes, and the shapes could be physically classified as wide or narrow, thus making the task essentially one of concept identification. A third group merely inspected the shapes (by touch) for an equal amount of time without instructions to label them. Following pretraining, the subjects were given a three-item recognition task in which they were instructed to identify the shapes learned during pretraining. A recognition set consisted of a pretraining stimulus and two highly-similar distractor shapes.

Figure 1 presents the recognition results. Two features are of interest. First, there was no superiority in recognition due to association of distinctive and representative labels compared with subjects who merely observed the shapes; quite possibly the observation-instructed subjects were covertly supplying their own unique labels. The second finding was that labeling the stimuli with common responses lead to somewhat poorer performance when compared with the observation condition. Although this difference was not large, it was reliable and it represented clear evidence of differences in recognition memory performance associated with verbal labeling practice.

The principal interest was, however, in the interpretation of this finding. On the surface these data could be regarded as consistent with an S-R mediation interpretation in which the stimuli became less "distinctive" through the addition of common response-produced cues. This interpretation seemed questionable for at least two reasons: First, the acquired equivalence mechanism is concerned with hypothesized changes in the "equivalence" of the stimuli employed in the pretraining set, and does not directly refer to accuracy of stimulus recognition when the training stimulus is compared with

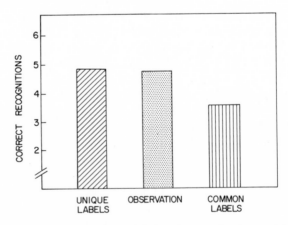

Fig. 1. Tactual shape recognition following three kinds of pretraining: association of distinctive or unique labels, observation practice, or association of common verbal labels to the shapes. Data are from Ellis *et al.* (1962).

highly similar distractor items. Moreover, there was doubtful relevance of such tests to *verbal* mediation mechanisms, a point already mentioned.

Second, two alternative interpretations of the poorer recognition performance following common labeling seemed equally plausible. The first was that the labels, given that they were representative of (or relevant to) the tactual shapes, might simply encourage subjects to observe only certain portions of the stimuli and to ignore other portions. Since the subjects were instructed to label stimuli with responses relevant to the physical features of the stimuli (relative width), they could easily restrict their manipulatory responses primarily to those features of the stimuli which were suggested by the label. Since recognition performance is dependent upon more features than just width cues, the subjects would be expected to show poorer performance simply because they had picked up less information about the stimuli. This account emphasizes, of course, that *peripheral observing responses* could be determined by the relationship between a label and its corresponding shape. An alternative possibility was that the label might influence a subject's *selective attention* to the stimuli, even though peripheral observing responses could remain unaffected. We shall return to a selective attention account shortly but note it here to contrast it with an observing-response interpretation.

A follow-up experiment (Ellis, Feuge, Long, & Pegram, 1964) was conducted with the purpose of determining if verbal labels do control subjects' observing-responses made to stimuli. The procedure was essentially a replication of the Ellis *et al.* (1962) experiment with one critical change. The subjects were given forced practice in manipulating the shapes during pretraining as a first approximation at controlling the amount and type of observing responses that subjects might make to the shapes. It was argued that if an observing-response interpretation were reasonable, then the poorer recognition performance following equivalence pretraining would not occur because the subjects would have been forced to observe the stimuli in the same fashion as subjects who received simple instructions to observe the stimuli. By making the inspection procedures comparable for the various groups during training, no difference in recognition performance should occur *if* the information encoded is influenced by subjects' peripheral manipulatory or exploratory responses. The control of observing responses was accomplished by requiring subjects to trace each shape with the index finger of his preferred hand. Subjects were required to trace the perimeter of each shape in alternating clockwise and counterclockwise directions. Thus the information picked up presumably would not differ at this level of input.

In spite of the fact that both equivalence and observation pre-training groups received comparable amounts and types of practice with the stimuli, the equivalence group still made fewer correct recognitions of the shapes than did the observation group. Figure 2 presents the mean correct recognition for all three conditions and again indicates the poorer performance of the equivalence group. Thus these results indicate that the poorer encoding of the common-labeled stimuli is not directly a result of reduced or limited explora-tion of these stimuli during pretraining.

The pattern of results seriously weakened the proposition that the effects of verbal labeling in enabling a subject to encode visual pat-tern stimuli was due to some peripheral response mechanism. By whatever means the shape-label relationship modifies the encoding of the shape, it did not appear to be due simply to some influence on a subject's observing responses. Two issues emerged at this junction: (a) Why was it that labeling the stimuli with distinctive verbal labels failed to enable subjects to encode the shapes more effectively than did mere observation of the shapes? Do subjects in the observation condition produce their own verbal labels, enabling an equally effec-tive encoding? Are there conditions under which experimenter-supplied labels provide for superior performance? The answer to

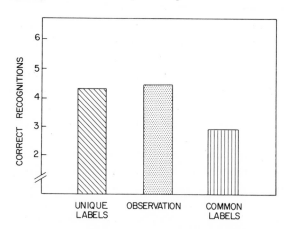

Fig. 2.   Tactual shape recognition following three kinds of pretraining (association of unique labels, observation practice, or association of common labels) under forced-practice conditions. Data are from Ellis *et al.* (1964).

these latter two questions is decidedly positive, based on several studies (Clark, 1965; Ellis & Homan, 1968; Ellis & Muller, 1964; Katz, 1963; Ranken, 1963). (*b*) The second issue concerns the interpretation of the acquired equivalence "effect" described above. An alternative and reasonable account of the reduced recognition performance following common labeling practice emphasizes the process of selective attention. This proposition implies that the common labels may encourage a subject to attend to common features of the set of shapes such that he encodes less unique information about each pattern, information which is important for recognition performance.

An attentional interpretation in its most general form could account for effects due to performance suppression following equivalence labeling and could also account for the effects of associating distinctive and verbal labels to stimuli had such effects been present. Although these experiments (Ellis *et al.*, 1962, 1964) provided no evidence for encoding effects due to distinctive verbal labeling over and above nonlabeling conditions, subsequent studies (Ellis & Daniel, 1971; Ellis & Muller, 1964; Santa & Ranken, 1972) have indicated that this effect does occur in certain circumstances. The next section examines one line of evidence which has led to support of an attentional interpretation.

C. Role of Stimulus Complexity

The failure to find that practice in associating distinctive and representative verbal labels to shape stimuli produced an effect on recognition was an obvious experimental puzzle. This finding was, however, consistent with the negative results obtained by Arnoult (1956), but obviously was at variance with classical studies of perceptual recall (e.g., Carmichael *et al.*, 1932). Therefore, the next line of attack was to vary properties of the stimuli, such as complexity and association value, on the grounds that such properties might well interact with verbal pretraining conditions. Presumably, as stimuli increase in their complexity or in the amount of information that a subject must encode, the importance of verbal labeling would increase.

In order to evaluate the possible role of stimulus complexity and verbal pretraining, Ellis and Muller (1964) extended the basic approach of the earlier studies by giving independent groups of subjects training in either labeling random shapes with distinctive and representative labels, or practice in labeling half the shapes with one label and the remaining half with another, or instructions to merely observe the stimuli for an equivalent duration of stimulus exposure and were then given a recognition test. The subjects learned either shapes of low or high complexity, where complexity was defined as the number of points on straight-sided random shapes (cf. Vanderplas & Garvin, 1959).

The left panel of Fig. 3 shows the effects of verbal pretraining when the stimuli are simple, and the right panel shows the results when the stimuli are complex. This figure shows a comparison of only the distinctive verbal labeling and observation-instructed groups for ease of comparison. In both instances, subjects given common-label pretraining showed poor recognition performance. It is clear from the figure that the effect of verbal pretraining depends upon shape complexity. With simple shapes the verbal labeling subjects are actually somewhat inferior to the observation subjects. This difference is not substantial but is consistent across varying amounts of pretraining. In contrast, subjects responding to the high complexity shapes show superior recognition performance when compared with observation-instructed subjects. The combined panels reflect an obvious interaction between type of pretraining and complexity of the stimuli.

These results were of interest for at least two reasons. First, this was one of the earliest studies to demonstrate the positive effects of verbal labeling practice in enhancing recognition performance, thus paralleling the findings of earlier studies which had obtained positive effects of labeling with recall tasks. Second, the results led us to

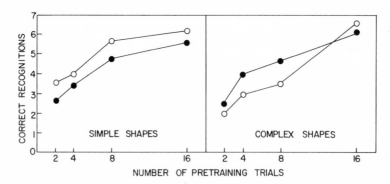

Fig. 3.   The effect of pretraining conditions on visual shape recognition as a function of shape complexity. Observation (O); labeling (●). Data are from Ellis and Muller (1964).

focus attention on properties of the stimulus as important determiners of verbal labeling effects.

D. A CONCEPTUAL CODING HYPOTHESIS

These findings suggested a tentative hypothesis to Ellis and Muller which emphasized the role of conceptual processes in verbal coding. We proposed that when a "representative" verbal label is associated with a stimulus, the label will enable encoding of that form and hence facilitate subsequent form recognition *when* the label allows a subject to relate the form to some available concept which is representative of the visual pattern. The label itself may serve as a concept, or it may suggest a concept which allows a subject to encode the shape. The fundamental assumption underlying this account is that the effect of associating verbal labels to shape stimuli is dependent upon the *codability* of the stimuli, with the *relative* effects of verbal labeling practice being greater with less codable, more complex stimuli.

This account can be characterized as a conceptual coding hypothesis and is outlined as follows: First, it was assumed that when a subject learns to associate a representative label to a simple shape, there is relatively little information present that must be processed. Therefore, a subject does not have to expend considerable effort in scanning the shape and selecting information on which to acquire a stable encoding. Moreover, it was assumed that simple shapes are more familiar than complex shapes, allowing a subject to relate more readily the simple shape to some available concept. This latter assumption was subsequently verified when we found that associative latencies to complex shapes were longer than for simple shapes, and that more associations were elicited by simple than by complex shapes (Ellis, Muller, & Tosti, 1966). As a consequence, it was reasonable to assume that the effect of labeling practice on the recognition of simple shapes, as compared with observation practice, could be minimal since the simple shapes are already relatively distinctive and familiar.

In contrast, complex shapes contain more information and are less readily or easily related to some concept. The effect of a label, if representative of a shape, is either to provide a concept directly or to suggest a concept to which the shape may be related. Furthermore, it was assumed that such a concept will encourage a subject to attend to those distinctive features of the shape which are suggested by the concept. Where no labels are immediately available, as is the case with observation practice, a subject would be required to generate his own concepts or verbal encodings of the complex shapes. This task would require more time on the part of a subject given observation practice and would explain why he, given observation practice, would be inferior in tasks of recognizing complex stimuli compared with subjects who are directly provided with experimenter-supplied labels. Finally, this conception could account for the fact that with extended practice, observation-instructed subjects might begin to generate their own labels, and hence more unique verbal encodings, and would subsequently perform as well as subjects given labeling practice.

The conceptual coding hypothesis emphasized that the contribution of an associated verbal label to the encoding of visual pattern stimuli is dependent upon the codability of the visual input. *To the extent that the visual pattern is initially difficult to encode, to that extent is the greater relative contribution of the label in assisting this process.* It is the relative contribution that is emphasized because stimuli which are initially easy to encode are, of course, more likely to be recognized regardless of verbal pretraining practice. This hypothesis is consistent with the findings reported by Brown and Lenneberg (1954) and Lantz and Steffire (1964) which indicate that the ease of naming visual stimuli is positively related to their recognizability. More generally, this hypothesis implies that as demands upon the memory system are increased, as reflected for example in the use of complex stimuli or in brief presentations of the stimuli during pretraining, the possession of some verbal code or representation becomes increasingly important in determining recognition performance.

As was noted, the hypothesis does not predict absolute gains in recognition performance—which is to say that recognition will be determined by variations in memory load itself, as reflected in such parameters as stimulus complexity, degree of practice, stimulus codability, rehearsal opportunities, or verbal indices of the organizational character of stimuli such as length of a verbalization given to a stimulus. Moreover, the stimuli can be sufficiently impoverished, in the sense that they tend to elicit few if any associations, or sufficiently complex (coupled with low association-producing properties) so that variations in the type of verbal labeling practice would produce only minimal effects on recognition performance. The next section examines the relationship between stimulus recognition and response processes in greater detail.

III. Stimulus Encoding and Response Variables

A. SHAPE RECOGNITION STUDIES

These initial studies suggested the importance of verbal labeling operations under somewhat restricted conditions, namely those in which the verbal label could be regarded as "representative" of the stimuli. The impetus for the next series of studies stemmed principally from the fact that the precise role of the verbal label in predifferentiation studies remained ambiguous. For example, Hake and Eriksen (1955), in examining the role of response specificity, suggested that the perceptual gain resulting from labeling practice was primarily a result of the general labeling process which provides a search task for a subject. Subsequently, Hake and Eriksen (1956) demonstrated that what subjects learn about visual stimuli during pretraining was more reliably tied to labeling performance when the labels were familiar to a subject. Other studies have reported divergent findings. For example, Johnson (1964) found that recognition of random shapes following predifferentiation training varied inversely with the class-similarity and class-label congruence of the shapes. In turn, Arnoult (1956) reported that properties of the verbal label employed during associative training did *not* differentially affect subsequent recognition of the stimuli.

Arnoult's (1956) negative findings were puzzling principally because it appeared reasonable to assume that subject-supplied labels and modal labels would serve as more effective mediators of performance than would nonsense syllables or irrelevant labels, presumably by enabling a subject to select more readily distinctive features of the stimuli. It was conceivable, however, that Arnoult's negative findings were the result of using only a single level of stimulus complexity (intermediate) and a single level of stimulus meaning (undetermined), and that the effects of properties of the verbal label depended upon associative and/or other properties of the stimuli employed. Indeed, it was known that the effect of verbal labeling depends upon the codability and meaningfulness of the forms (Ellis *et al.*, 1966), findings which suggest that properties of the verbal label govern recognition performance for certain critical values of the stimuli. Additional evidence for this kind of interaction was noted by Pfafflin (1960), who found positive transfer from verbal pretraining when the stimuli were low in associative consistency and negative transfer with stimuli of high associative consistency.

An extensive study of the role of verbal pretraining in both stimulus recognition and transfer of training (Ellis, 1968) revealed that the effect of response variables in the recognition task did *not* mirror in any simple fashion the role of these variables in a transfer task. This comparison was of interest because it was known that the theoretical controversy between associative and differentiation theories of perceptual learning was, in part, the result of investigators using different test tasks. Subjects were given paired-associate training in labeling random shapes and then given a recognition or paired-associate transfer test. In the recognition experiments four factors were varied: shape complexity (6- or 24-point random shapes), association value of the shapes (low or high), amount of practice (2, 8, or 16 trials), and type of response associated with the stimulus (meaningful and relevant, meaningful but irrelevant, and CVC trigrams). The last variable allowed separation of the effects of response representativeness from response meaningfulness per se.

The results of the recognition test following the various conditions of pretraining are shown in Fig. 4. The upper two panels show plots

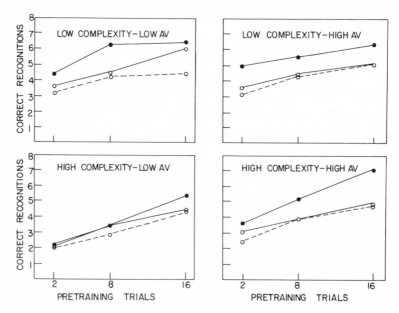

Fig. 4. Effects of three kinds of verbal labeling practice on shape recognition. Labels are either meaningful and relevant words (MR) (●—●), meaningful and irrelevant words (MIR) (○—○), or nonmeaningful and irrelevant trigrams (CVC) (○---○). Data are from Ellis (1968).

for the 6-point shapes, and the lower panels show results for 24-point shapes. The figure shows that the effect of response factors varied with both physical and associative properties of the stimuli, and that response relevance (or representativeness) was generally a more potent variable in influencing recognition than was response meaningfulness.

In the transfer study subjects were given identical pretraining as in the recognition study with only the complex (24-point) shapes of high association value. They received the three types of labeling pretraining described above; there was also an irrelevant-stimulus (C-D) pretraining control and a no-pretraining condition. Only 8 and 16 pretraining trials were given. Following pretraining subjects were given a transfer task which required them to learn an identifying response (pressing a switch) for each of the shapes learned during pretraining. The transfer results indicated that response *relevance* contributed principally to the transfer effects after eight pretraining trials, whereas response *meaningfulness* emerged as the effective variable influencing transfer performance after 16 pretraining trials. Clearly, the role of response variables in the transfer task did *not* reflect in any direct fashion the role of these variables in the recognition task. This indicates that performance in transfer tasks requiring the learning of new responses is mediated by processes that are in part different from those which mediate performance in recognition tasks. In the former case, attaching meaningful-irrelevant labels to the set of shapes provides subjects with sufficient information about the distinctive features of the stimuli to enable them to learn more rapidly the transfer task than subjects given CVC labeling practice. More generally, meaningful-irrelevant labeling practice is regarded as providing for an effective encoding which is critical for performing a new task in which the stimuli are the *same* as those learned during pretraining, but does not when the task requires recognition of a previously learned shape immersed among highly similar distractor items. Although the pretraining conditions are comparable, and thus produce comparable encodings of the shapes, the encodings do not function in a parallel fashion in the two test tasks. These results suggested that verbal labels may serve at least two functions during paired-associate learning. One function is general, in the sense of providing a subject with confirmation of his association, and the other is more specific, and directs a subject's attention to properties of the stimulus depending upon parameters of the shape and label. Moreover, these results are consistent with the view (Vanderplas, 1963) that transfer of training in perceptual learning depends on the relationship between pretraining and transfer-task activities.

B. RECOGNITION OF VERBAL MATERIALS

The cumulative pattern of results presented a clearer picture regarding the effect of associative training on stimulus recognition and transfer. Association of responses representative of the visual patterns led to enhanced recognizability of the stimuli when compared with conditions in which subjects merely observed the stimuli (Ellis & Daniel, 1971; Ellis & Muller, 1964) or when they associated meaningful but nonrepresentative responses or CVC trigrams (Ellis, 1968).

In the context of verbal learning research, however, Martin (1967b) had presented evidence indicating that stimulus recognition was unaffected by the association of responses during paired-associate learning. In his study subjects learned to associate trigram-digit pairs of two types: in one case subjects learned to associate consistent pairs, and in the other the digits were re-paired anew on successive study trials. Martin found that the presence of strong stable associations, as would be expected with the consistently paired items, did not enhance the recognizability of the stimuli. Since the studies of Ellis and Martin differed in a number of ways including type of stimulus items, type of responses, and stimulus meaningfulness, a resolution of the differences was attempted.

In two experiments (Ellis & Shumate, 1973; Ellis & Tatum, 1973) substantial evidence for response-dependent stimulus encoding during associative learning was obtained, indicating that Martin's conclusion was somewhat restricted in generality.

In the Ellis and Shumate study, subjects learned to associate representative or nonrepresentative common words with high- or low-meaningfulness trigram doublets. Doublets consisted of trigram pairs such as RIBHUT and DENGIT, and representative responses were judged as being descriptive, suggestive, or related to the stimulus; a nonrepresentative response was judged as bearing little relationship to its corresponding stimulus mate. These procedures were comparable to those used by Ellis (1968) in shape recognition studies, and in the case of verbal stimuli, the representative response terms were selected so as to be formally and/or acoustically similar to the stimuli. Subjects received eight paired-associate trials, learning pairs consisting of stimuli of either high- or low-M (100% and 12% M-values in Archer, 1960) and representative or nonrepresentative response terms. Following training, subjects received three memory tests including stimulus recognition. Independent groups of subjects were tested immediately after paired-associate training or at 2, 7, 14, and 28 days.

Figure 5 shows the stimulus recognition results. This figure shows a plot of the number of correct recognitions in a five-item forced-choice recognition test as a function of the retention intervals. The figure reveals three findings: (a) there was no loss in recognition performance over the delay intervals employed; (b) stimulus-meaningfulness exerted a pronounced effect on stimulus recognition, with subjects correctly recognizing an average of 86% of the high-M items and only 53% of the low-M items; (c) and, most importantly, the figure reveals an obvious interaction between stimulus-M and response representativeness. The figure clearly shows that associating a representative response to a verbal stimulus aids encoding of that stimulus, as estimated by stimulus recognition, when the stimuli are low- but not high-M.

This interaction is in accord with the conceptual coding hypothesis (Ellis & Muller, 1964) if stimulus-M is regarded as one index of

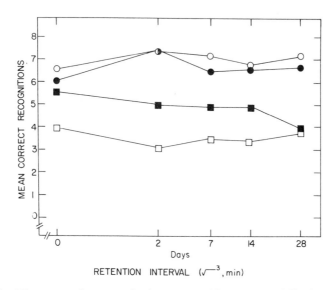

Fig. 5. The temporal course of trigram-recognition memory following associative training with high- and low-meaningfulness trigram-doublet stimuli and representative and nonrepresentative word response terms. High stimulus-M: representative responses (●); high stimulus-M: nonrepresentative responses (○); low stimulus-M: representative responses (■); low stimulus-M: nonrepresentative responses (□). Data from Ellis and Shumate (1973).

codability. This interaction parallels stimulus recognition findings previously reported with respect to stimulus complexity (Ellis & Muller, 1964, Exp. I), degree of training (Ellis & Daniel, 1971, Exps. I & II), and number of items to be stored (Santa & Ranken, 1972, Exp. II), where visual form stimuli were employed. These three studies indicated that the relative effects of associating responses to stimuli on their subsequent recognition (relative to either associating nonrepresentative responses or merely observing the stimuli) increased with high complexity forms, increased with fewer practice trials, and increased with an increasing number of items to be placed in memory, respectively. Finally, in the Ellis and Shumate study, the effect was present with low-M stimuli. All four operations can be regarded as conditions which increase the difficulty of encoding the stimuli, thereby placing increasing demand upon memory load. These relationships are predicted by the conceptual coding hypothesis which proposes that easily encoded stimuli may be encoded virtually free of their context, whereas contextual factors become increasingly important with a decrease in the initial codability of the stimuli.

Although the process of response-dependent encoding of verbal as well as visual pattern stimuli was now established, one remaining issue concerned the earlier described negative results of Martin (1967b); conceivably the differences in results were related to procedural and item differences. Bower (1970) had also examined the issue of response-dependent encoding in the context of imagery research and found that recognition of nouns employed as stimulus terms was essentially independent of various associative training procedures. In view of the Ellis and Shumate results, however, Bower's negative findings seem understandable in terms of the high-M property of nouns which are already easy to encode and hence do not profit from encodings suggested by the training context. The next line of investigation focused, therefore, on an analysis of this problem using Martin's (1967a, 1967b) study-recall procedure.

C. Stimulus Recognition and Association Formation

The final attack on the problem of the relationship between stimulus recognition and association formation was a series of four experiments by Ellis and Tatum (1973). The first question of interest was: Under what conditions does the formation of an association between a stimulus and a response affect the recognizability of the stimulus? The second issue concerned the relationship between stimulus recognition and recall (and/or associative matching) of the responses as a result of paired-associate training. Therefore, the second question of interest was: Is stimulus recognition following associative training a necessary prerequisite for recall of the associated response? Martin (1967a) had argued for this dependency, based upon his finding that the probability of subjects recalling the responses was no better than chance given that they failed to recognize the stimulus. His conclusion was that the activation of an association, and hence the occurrence of the overt response requires, as a necessary antecedent, recognition of the stimulus. This second issue will be discussed in Section IV, A.

1. Role of Response Variables (Experiment 1)

In the first experiment, subjects learned to associate either trigram-digit or trigram-word pairs by a study-test procedure. In the test subjects were first required to recognize the stimuli and then matched the stimuli and responses. The stimuli were CCC's of 45–55% association value. The responses were either digits (1–6), or three- and four-letter words judged as representative of the stimuli. The list consisted of 12 pairs, half of which were consistently paired (Type-C) on successive trials, and half of which were re-paired (Type-R) anew on successive trials. In this fashion, the effects of both consistency of pairings and response representatives on stimulus recognition could be examined. In the recognition test subjects saw both the 12 old stimuli and 12 new stimuli (distractors) of the same class, with a different set of new items on each trial. With the exception of the matching test, the procedure was essentially identical to Martin's (1967b). (In the trigram-word pairs the responses were representative of the stimuli only in the Type-C case because of the confounding of pairing consistency with response representativeness beyond the first test; no problem arises on the first recognition test because there has been no repetition of pairs. This problem is resolved in the second experiment.)

The results of the stimulus recognition test are shown in Fig. 6, which shows a plot of correct stimulus recognitions over eight test trials with pair type as a parameter. The left panel of Fig. 6 shows the proportion of correct stimulus recognitions when digits were used as responses, and the right panel shows the proportion of correct stimulus recognitions when words were used as responses.

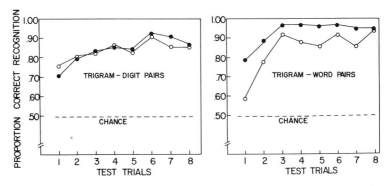

Fig. 6. Correct stimulus recognition as a function of trials for both trigram-digit and trigram-word pairs with pair type (C *versus* R) as parameter. Type C (●); type R (○). Data from Ellis and Tatum (1973).

The figure shows that for the trigram-digit pairs, stimulus recognition for the two pair types was essentially identical, indicating that consistently associating digit response to stimuli did not facilitate stimulus recognition, thus confirming Martin's (1967b) findings. In contrast, the right panel indicates that associating word responses which are representative of the stimuli produced superior recognition compared with training in which re-pairing occurred on each trial. Moreover, this effect was reliable on the first test.

2. Response Representativeness versus Pairing Consistency (Experiment II)

In order to separate the effects of pairing consistency and response representativeness in the Type-C pairings, a second study was conducted. Subjects learned only trigram-word pairs of Type-C, as in the first experiment, and Type-R pairs in which subjects received re-pairings on each trial with new responses that were always representative of the stimuli. (The Type-R pairs were, of course, never representative in the first experiment.) Thus, response representativeness was kept comparable in the two pairing conditions, with only consistency of pairing being varied. The principal results are shown in Fig. 7 which reveal that pairing consistency per se, regardless of the representativeness of the words, did not affect stimulus recognition. Thus, the effect obtained in the first experiment was clearly due to the representative properties of the words enabling a more effective encoding of the stimuli than would otherwise occur.

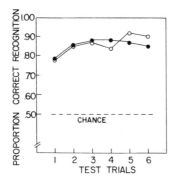

Fig. 7. Correct stimulus recognition as a function of trials when "representativeness" of the response terms is kept comparable. Pair type (C *versus* R) is employed as a parameter. Type C (●); type R (○). Data from Ellis and Tatum (1973).

3. *Procedural Variable* (Experiments III and IV)

The two remaining experiments examined procedural details which conceivably may have affected the results. The procedures and materials were essentially identical to the first experiment with the following changes. In Experiment III, subjects were given a response *recall* test following stimulus recognition rather than an associative matching test, since it was conceivable that they could have made their recognition responses (as well as matching) on the basis of "similarity matching" of the stimuli and responses. The use of a recall procedure precluded this possibility. The fourth study used a forced-choice stimulus recognition to control for a possible response bias operating in the single stimulus test. In both studies subjects learned consistently paired (Type-C) or re-paired (Type-R) lists of trigram-word pairs.

The stimulus recognition results are presented in Fig. 8. As before, this figure shows the relationship between stimulus recognition and association formation with pair type as the parameter. The left panel shows the proportion of correct stimulus recognitions for the single-stimulus test, and the right panel shows a parallel plot for the forced-choice case. In both cases, the effect of the response is still present. Comparison of the two panels suggests results generally similar to those of the trigram-word pairs of the first study with some attenuation of the pair-type effect in the forced-choice case.

In summary, these experiments established clear evidence for response-dependent encoding of verbal stimuli in associative learn-

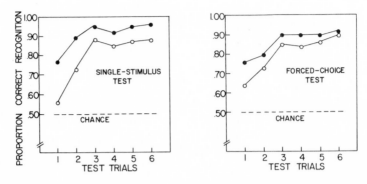

Fig. 8. Correct stimulus recognition as a function of trials for the single-stimulus and forced-choice case with pair type (C *versus* R) as parameter. Type C (●); type R (○). Data from Ellis and Tatum (1973).

ing tasks when the responses bear some relationship to the stimuli. The observed effect is the result of the representative properties of the responses producing a more effective encoding of the stimuli and not to the consistency of pairing per se. Moreover, the encoding effect was present with a forced-choice recognition test, although somewhat attenuated, and thus was not attributable to any potential source of response bias operating in the single stimulus case. Since the distractors were high in formal similarity in the forced-choice case, this more demanding recognition test may have contributed to the attenuation. Finally, when the response terms were digits which bore no evident relationship to the stimuli, the development of strong stable associations did not facilitate recognition.

D.   IMPLICATIONS OF RESPONSE-DEPENDENT ENCODING

The general implications of the finding that properties of an overt response or label can affect the manner in which a nominal stimulus is encoded during associative learning is at least threefold. First, an encoded version of a low- or moderate-M stimulus following A-B associative training with representative responses is not identical with an encoded version of these stimuli following associative training with nonrepresentative responses, despite the nominal identity of A in both lists. Although the entire set of features that may accompany these two encoded versions of A cannot be precisely specified in these experiments, it does follow that A as a result of A-B (representative) training contains significantly more features or attributes than does A otherwise, at least more of those features which are necessary for correct stimulus recognition.

Second, this finding has obvious implications for transfer studies employing the A-B, A-D paradigm. To the extent that the encoding of A is response-dependent, then it follows that the encoding of A during A-D learning may differ from whatever encoding was achieved during A-B learning. Where the encoding of A is likely to be response-dependent, then the onset of A-D learning may serve to disrupt the encoding of A established in A-B training. In contrast, under conditions in which the encoding of A is minimally dependent upon the response, then the onset of A-D learning should minimize the likelihood that a new encoding of A will develop if the already acquired encoding will effectively cue the response. Since the encoding of low-M stimuli are more contextually dependent, it would follow that such stimuli are more likely to be recoded or altered during A-D learning. Although the evidence for this is indirect (e.g., Bryk & Kausler, 1966), direct tests of recoding nominally identical stimuli have not been promising (e.g., Goggin & Martin, 1970; Williams & Underwood, 1970). Perhaps Martin's (1971) admonition is well taken in that rough tests of recoding may provide spurious negative results. Given the clear evidence for response-dependent encoding of stimuli in this study, the concept of stimulus recoding in negative transfer paradigms is of interest.

Finally, it should be noted that the importance of contextual factors in recognition bears upon the issue of retrieval processes in recognition (e.g., Tulving & Thomson, 1971; Winograd, Karchmer, & Russell, 1971). Although the previously described experiments were not directed specifically toward this issue, the finding that recognition is dependent upon contextual changes in the recognition test has been used as the basis for arguing for retrieval processes in recognition. The question of retrieval processes in recognition will be examined from a different stance in the next section, where the relationship between stimulus recognition and recall is analyzed.

IV. Interdependence of Recall and Recognition

A. STIMULUS RECOGNITION A PREREQUISITE FOR RECALL?

In Section III, C the issue of response-dependent encoding of stimuli was examined. A second issue was identified but not developed. This issue concerns the relationship between stimulus recognition and response recall during associative training. Martin (1967a, 1967b) has presented evidence indicating that in a paired-associate task correct responding is contingent upon stimulus recognition. Subjects learned trigram-digit pairs via the study-test method. On study trials eight pairs were presented aurally; on test trials which alternated between study trials subjects were given single-stimulus recognition tests requiring them to first indicate whether or not they recognized the stimulus, and then they had to recall the digit response. The results of both studies were that the probability of a correct recall increased steadily over trials but *only* when a subject correctly recognized the stimulus. In contrast, if a stimulus was not correctly recognized, the probability of a correct recall fell to the level of chance.

In the experiments by Ellis and Tatum (Section III, C) the same measures were obtained, and the relationship between recall and recognition was examined since these data bore directly upon Martin's findings. In the first experiment by Ellis and Tatum, conditional probabilities involving associative matching and recognition were calculated in order to examine the hypothesis that the probability of a correct match will be no greater than chance if a subject fails to recognize the stimulus. Table I shows the proportion of

TABLE I[a]

PROPORTION CORRECT ASSOCIATIVE MATCHINGS (AM) GIVEN
RECOGNITION (R) AND NONRECOGNITION (NR) OF THE STIMULUS

	Pair type			
	C		R	
Contingency	Digit	Word	Digit	Word
P (Chance AM)	.17	.17	.17	.17
P (AM/NR)	.24	.39	.22	.19
P (AM/R)	.35	.90	.29	.31

[a] From Ellis and Tatum (1973).

associative matchings (AM) given recognition (R) and given non-recognition (NR) of the stimulus. The top row of the table shows that the probability that a subject will match the response term correctly by chance was .17, calculated simply on the basis of the six response alternatives. The probabilities of digit and word matching (for the Type-R pairs) given nonrecognition of the stimulus, P(AM/NR), were .22 and .19, respectively. These values do not differ significantly from chance, t (9) $= .56$, $p > .50$, and t (8) $= .58$, $p >$ .50, for digits and words respectively.

In contrast to the Type-R pairs, Table I reveals that for the Type-C pairs, the probabilities of digit and word matching given incorrect stimulus recognition were .24 and .39, respectively. The value of P(AM/NR) for words (but not digits) was significantly larger than chance, $t(5) = 4.08$, $p < .01$, and indicates that associative matching is above chance even when subjects fail to correctly recognize the stimulus. The proportion of correct matchings, given correct recognition, are all above the values for P(AM/NR) and all exceed chance expectancy. [All t-tests were based on responses averaged over subjects, and degrees of freedom vary because those subjects who correctly recognized all of the stimuli were excluded from analysis of P(AM/NR).]

Similar analyses were made on the third and fourth experiments. Conditional probabilities were calculated in order to determine the dependency of response recall upon stimulus recognition and nonrecognition. Table II shows the proportion of correct recalls (CR) given recognition (R) and nonrecognition (NR) of the stimulus. The top row of the table shows the probability of chance response recall, which was again .17 calculated on the basis of the six response alternatives. The probabilities of recall for the single-stimulus and forced-choice conditions (for the Type-R pairs), given nonrecognition, were .22 and .20 respectively, values which do not differ from chance, t (9) $= 1.45$, $p > .10$, and t (12) $= 1.06$, $p > .10$.

Table II shows, however, that for the Type-C pairs, the probabilities of recall for the single-stimulus and forced-choice condition, given nonrecognition of the stimulus, were .53 and .60, respectively. The value of P(CR/NR) exceeds chance for both conditions, t (5) $=$

TABLE II[a]

PROPORTION CORRECT RECALLS (CR) GIVEN RECOGNITION (R)
AND NONRECOGNITION (NR) OF THE STIMULUS

	Pair type			
	C		R	
Contingency	Single stimulus	Forced choice	Single stimulus	Forced choice
P (Chance CR)	.17	.17	.17	.17
P (CR/NR)	.53	.60	.22	.20
P (CR/R)	.84	.92	.26	.23

[a] From Ellis and Tatum (1973).

6.69, $p < .001$, and $t (12) = 7.28$, $p < .001$, respectively, indicating that stimulus recognition is not a necessary prerequisite for response recall when the responses are representative of the stimuli. The proportion of correct recalls for the Type-C pairs, given correct recognition, are all above the values for $P(CR/NR)$ and all exceed chance expectancy.

In summary, the three experiments indicated that the probability of response recall (or matching), given nonrecognition of the stimulus, was significantly higher than chance for the Type-C pairs when a representative word served as the response. This simply indicates that subjects can fail to recognize a stimulus and yet correctly recall its response mate following associative training. (The conditional probabilities for both recall and associative matching, given non-recognition of the stimulus, were higher than chance; therefore, I shall refer collectively to the measures as recall.) In contrast, the probability of recall, given nonrecognition of the stimulus, was no greater than chance when the responses were digits. This latter finding is in agreement with the findings of Martin (1967b), whereas the former result places a restriction on his generalization that recall drops to chance if a subject fails to recognize the stimulus. An interpretation of these results is developed in the next section.

B.   RECALL AND STIMULUS ENCODING

The problem is to account for the fact that when a representative-word response is paired with a stimulus consistently during associative learning, the subsequent recall of that response *does not require,* as an antecedent, correct recognition of the nominal stimulus. First consider the forced-choice situation. If the new stimulus is judged as "old," a subject failed to make a correct recognition, which is synonymous with making a false recognition in the forced-choice case. Since the probability of a correct recall, given nonrecognition of the stimulus, was significantly higher than chance for the trigram-word pairs, the problem of specifying the cue(s) for recall arises in this case, since recognition of the nominal stimulus alone will not suffice.

It is proposed in the case of the trigram-word pairings that recall of the response mate is *not* dependent upon recognition of the *nominal* stimulus per se, but rather that *the probability of recall is dependent upon retrieval of some critical portion of the encoded version of the nominal stimulus.* The importance of this argument is that it emphasizes that a correct recall of a response can be cued even though an erroneous recognition of a stimulus is made, as long as an erroneous recognition is concomitant with the retrieval of an encoded version of the nominal stimulus or some portion otherwise. This process can readily occur in the forced-choice situation. When a subject selected a new stimulus (and thus failed to recognize correctly the old one), he did so because this new stimulus, by virtue of its similarity to the old stimulus, contained a number of features (features suggested by the response term) which enabled him to retrieve the original encoding of the stimulus, or some reasonable approximation of the original encoding, established during associative learning. Therefore, retrieval of this original encoding of the stimulus provided a subject with an encoding on which to cue his recall of the response term. This interpretation is not a simple "stimulus generalization" account of the recall findings, for such an account would predict similar findings with the trigram-digit pairs.

Now consider how this interpretation applies to the single-stimulus case. For the distractor stimuli there were, of course, no "correct" response mates, and so subjects were instructed simply to guess. This case is of little concern since interest is focused only on what a subject does with the old stimuli. What needs to be explained is why, when a subject responds "new" to an old stimulus in the single-stimulus case, he is still able to recall the associated response correctly with greater than chance probability when the responses are representative words.

The interpretation is essentially the same as that for the forced-choice case with one additional assumption. Again, failure to recognize correctly the stimulus does not necessarily imply a failure to retrieve an effective encoding of the stimulus when the response terms are representative words. It is assumed that a subject is still basing his encoding on critical features suggested by the response terms, and he is still able to retrieve his encoding, or some portion of it, during the recognition test. An explanation is possible if it is assumed that when a single-stimulus procedure is used, subjects criterion for a "good match" between his momentary encoding of the test stimulus and retrieved encoding of a stimulus can vary. It is conceivable that he will respond "new" to an old stimulus because his retrieved encoding of the stimulus does not exceed some arbitrary criterion for a "good match" to the momentary encoding of the test stimulus. Since he is required to recall a response, his encoding may nevertheless be sufficient to cue the correct response.

The interpretation as to why subjects fail to recall the digit-response terms at a greater than chance probability, given nonrecognition of the stimulus in Experiment I, is quite straightforward. Failure to recognize the stimulus simply indicates a failure to retrieve an effective encoding, and this means that a subject has no cue for a correct recall; therefore, response recall given nonrecognition does not exceed chance. The discussion has so far emphasized the dependency of recall upon recognition. Another facet of this contingency is examined in the next section.

C. LOCUS OF THE LABELING EFFECT

A final problem involving recognition-recall relations concerned the locus of the verbal labeling effect. It is possible to contend, for example, that the associated verbal response or label aids a subject in making a recognition response, in that if a subject recalls the association appropriate to the encoded input, then the probability of correct recognition will increase. This notion bears some relationship to the verbal-loop hypothesis (Glanzer & Clark, 1962), which contends that the relationship between length of verbalization given to a stimulus and recall of that stimulus is dependent upon a subject's retrieval of the verbalization. Since longer verbalizations may be less accessible in recall (as well as reflecting greater difficulty in encoding), then stimuli which tend to elicit longer verbalizations (in efforts on the part of subjects to describe them) are stimuli that are less likely to be recalled.

The verbal-loop hypothesis has been applied primarily to studies of perceptual recall as distinct from recognition, although it has been suggested by Glanzer and Clark (1964) that the hypothesis applies to recognition as well as recall performance. Price and Slive (1970) have extended this position and proposed that recognition of visual information may be mediated by recall of an association at the time of recognition testing, thus proposing that the effects of verbal coding on recognition memory may actually operate during the recognition test itself. Although it is unrealistic to contend that recognition bypasses the retrieval process entirely (Tulving & Thomson, 1971), it nevertheless appeared unlikely that stimulus recognition was in any simple sense a direct function of a subject's recall of an associated verbal label *at the time* of recognition testing.

An alternative view was that a verbal label exerted its principal effects on stimulus recognition by way of events that occur during the initial encoding of the stimuli. As noted earlier, Ellis (1968) had proposed that a representative verbal label directs a subject's attention to distinctive features of the stimulus pattern, a view emphasizing the process of stimulus selection, and had contended that representative verbal labels aid a subject in more rapidly acquiring a set of functional cues during shape-label associative training by directing a subject's visual search for critical or distinctive features. The point to note is that this hypothesis expresses the view that *the effects of verbal labeling occur during the initial encoding of the input, and that these effects persist in memory because of the more effective encoding established during training.* It would seemingly follow, therefore, that if label recall is forgotten at a rate faster than stimulus recognition, then the evidence would be against a simple mediated recognition account; if the labels are not accessible at recall, then they cannot provide the basis on which a subject makes his recognition response.

The results of two recent experiments argue against a mediated recognition account of the effects of verbal labeling. Ellis and Daniel (1971, Experiment III) have shown that although the temporal course of stimulus recognition shows little forgetting over retention intervals up to 28 days, recall of the associated verbal labels becomes poorer. Moreover, the proportion of correct recalls given correct recognition shows a systematic decline in the recognition-recall contingencies. Table III shows the conditional probabilities which are calculated for both free and aided recall of the verbal labels. For either recall measure the pattern of results is quite clear: the probability of a correct recall, given stimulus recognition, decreases as the

TABLE III[a]

STIMULUS RECOGNITION-RESPONSE RECALL CONTINGENCIES
FOLLOWING PAIRED-ASSOCIATE LEARNING

Retention interval	Proportion of correct recalls given stimulus recognition		Proportion of correct recognitions given correct recall	
	Free recall	Aided recall	Free recall	Aided recall
0	.94	—	.83	—
15 minutes	.94	—	.90	—
2 days	.87	.90	.89	.89
7 days	.72	.72	.75	.72
14 days	.86	.80	.85	.78
28 days	.74	.74	.79	.74

[a] From Ellis and Daniel (1971).

retention interval increases. Thus, although stimulus recognition shows virtually no loss over test intervals, the *associative strength* between labels and shapes weakens during the corresponding period.

In a follow-up study, Ellis and Shumate (1973) showed the same kind of relationship using verbal stimulus (trigram pairs) materials. As noted earlier, subjects were given pair associate training in which the stimulus terms were trigram pairs, and the response terms were familiar nouns. Stimuli of high- and low-M and responses that were either representative or nonrepresentative were employed. Following training, subjects were tested over five retention intervals up to 28 days. The results indicated that recognition did not systematically change over the 28-day period, whereas both free and aided recall of the responses decreased. Since response recall weakened under conditions in which stimulus recognition remained stable, the evidence was against a simple mediated recognition account.

To augment this interpretation, conditional probabilities involving recall and recognition were again examined, as in Ellis and Daniel (1971). Table IV presents the conditional probabilities and

TABLE IV[a]

STIMULUS RECOGNITION-RESPONSE RECALL CONTINGENCIES
FOLLOWING PAIRED-ASSOCIATE LEARNING

Retention interval	Proportion of correct recalls given stimulus recognition		Proportion of correct recognitions given correct recall	
	Free recall	Aided recall	Free recall	Aided recall
0	.90	.87	.71	.72
2 days	.64	.74	.73	.76
7 days	.57	.66	.69	.76
14 days	.37	.58	.66	.68
28 days	.26	.49	.66	.78

[a] From Ellis and Shumate (1973).

reveals two important features. First, there is a systematic and reliable decline in the proportion of correct recall of responses given correct recognition of the corresponding stimuli. This decrease occurs for both the free and aided recall measures, although the decrease is faster for free than for aided recall as reflected in the reliable Task (free vs. aided recall) × Delay interaction. This indicates that the relative importance of the stimulus item as a retrieval cue increases with the length of the retention interval. More importantly, the steady decrease in these conditional probabilities, especially aided response recall given stimulus recognition, argues against the notion that stimulus recognition is in some way mediated by recall of its response mate at the time of recognition testing.

The second interesting finding in Table IV concerns the reverse contingency, the proportion of correct stimulus recognitions given either free or aided correct recalls of the responses. The probability of correctly recognizing a stimulus given recall of the response averaged .71 at the immediate-test condition and .72 after 28 days, and while the contingency is moderately high it reveals simply that neither free nor aided recall of a response guarantees perfect recognition of its stimulus mate. These results lend support to the view that the effect of response-contextual factors on stimulus recognition is during the initial encoding of the stimulus as distinct from processes that may operate at the time of recognition testing.

V. Stimulus Encoding and Stimulus Variables

The analysis of stimulus encoding has thus far focused on the role of response-contextual variables which effect the encoding of stimuli and on the contingencies of recognition and recall. In this section the role of stimulus variables in encoding is examined.

A. STIMULUS MEANING AND RECOGNITION

The first study (Ellis *et al.*, 1966) in this series revealed that stimulus recognition depended upon stimulus-M. Stimulus-M was varied in three ways: the classic Glaze association-value procedure, Noble's production method which defines meaningfulness in terms of the average number of associations given to a stimulus, and associative consistency which describes meaning in terms of intersubject judgmental consistency, a measure similar to one employed by Brown and Lenneberg (1954) in studies of stimulus codability and memory. For the present purposes, the interesting findings of this study were twofold: (*a*) recognition was positively correlated with association value, but not with the production-method scale values, and (*b*) false recognition performance depended upon the way in which M was measured. A significantly higher false alarm rate was given to low-association value shapes compared with those high in association value, whereas the reverse was obtained with measures obtained from the production method. One problem was why presumably similar or correlated measures of M produced opposite performance effects.

Two follow-up studies (Ellis & Feuge, 1966; Feuge & Ellis, 1969) pursued the study of false recognition by examining stimulus variables which influenced gradients of false recognition. A gradient of false recognition refers simply to the proportion of false recognitions given to test stimuli as a function of the similarity of test and training stimuli. In the latter study, subjects were trained in paired-associate fashion to associate responses to stimuli (24-point random shapes) of either low or high association value, and low or high associative frequency (Noble, 1952). Principal interest was focused on the role of stimulus-M (defined either way) on a subject's false alarm rate in the recognition task when the distractor (new) items varied along a dimension of similarity. The results were like those of the Ellis *et al.* (1966) study in that false recognition performance was *greater* for low-association value stimuli (compared with high association value), but *less* for low-associative frequency stimuli when compared with high-associative frequency stimuli. Stimuli from each set were independent and were equated on the other indices of stimulus-M, so the results were not attributable to confounding of scale measurement. These results are portrayed in Fig. 9.

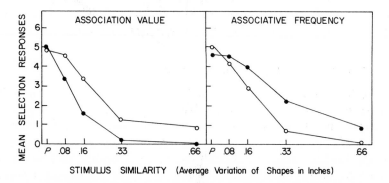

Fig. 9. Gradients of false recognition (selection responses) as a function of degree and type of stimulus meaning. High (●); low (○). Data from Feuge and Ellis (1969).

The problem remains as to how to account for the complex effects of stimulus-M, as well as the dependency of the effects of degree of stimulus-M on the manner in which stimulus-M is scaled. Ideally, it would be desirable to account for the effects of stimulus-M on the slope of false recognition gradients via some general conceptual formulation regarding stimulus-M. This would appear to require, however, that traditional measures of stimulus-M such as the percent of subjects having an association to verbal or perceptual items (Glaze, 1928; Vanderplas & Garvin, 1959) and the number of associations an item elicits (Ellis *et al.,* 1966; Noble, 1952), although commonly regarded as reflecting correlated events, be viewed as contributing to either the storage and/or retrieval of visual information in quite different ways. Indeed, it may well be that association value and production-method scales produce their different effects on recognition memory through differences in the way in which the functional stimulus is acquired and stored during pretraining, or through differences in the manner in which such information is retrieved. In any event, any attempt to account for the effects of both measures of stimulus meaning requires a theory which would predict differing slopes associated with the two measures.

To produce an interpretation consistent with both findings, Feuge and Ellis (1969) suggested that stimulus-M could be defined in terms of the variability of encoding responses made to the stimuli during training, similar to Martin's (1968) hypothesis. They assumed that during associative training, a subject responds to somewhat different portions of the visual stimulus on successive trials in an effort to achieve a functional stimulus. These responses could be viewed as implicit perceptual-encoding responses (e.g., Kendler & Kendler, 1962), although their precise properties remained unspecified. This redefinition of stimulus meaning relates it to a description of an underlying process that is dependent upon a subject's search for a functional stimulus. Stimulus-M is regarded as inversely related to the number of alternative encoding responses made to a nominal stimulus. High-M nominal stimuli were seen as eliciting one, or relatively few, of these responses, where as low-M nominal stimuli were seen as eliciting many of these responses, and thus more alternative functional stimuli. Within this context, high association-value stimuli were viewed as reflecting the influence of a single dominant perceptual-encoding response, low-association value stimuli, in turn, reflecting several. In contrast, high-associative frequency stimuli were seen as reflecting several alternative encoding responses, and low-associative frequency stimuli few. Thus, stimulus-M is directly related to association value (Glaze measure), but was viewed as inversely related to associative frequency (Noble measure). The assumptions allow the prediction that false recognition is inversely related to stimulus-M.

B. Meaningfulness and Perceptual Grouping

Several lines of evidence have suggested that the effects of stimu-
lus-M can be understood in terms of the fractionable *versus* inte-
grated nature of stimuli (e.g., Martin, 1968; Shepard, 1963). It has
been suggested that highly integrated stimuli (e.g., high-M stimuli)
may be encoded quite rapidly because they are processed as a single
unit, where as fractionated stimuli (e.g., low-M stimuli) are encoded
more slowly because the encoding consists of more than one com-
ponent. This account of the underlying dimensions of M bears a
strong resemblance to G. A. Miller's (1956) concept of "chunking,"
wherein units that may be integrated into larger (and, therefore,
fewer discrete) chunks are more easily processed. In a similar vein,
variations in stimulus-M may produce corresponding demands upon
a subject's memory load, with the M-value of stimuli being nega-
tively correlated with memory load. If low-M stimuli are regarded
as more difficult to process because of their fragmentary, uninte-
grated nature, it should be possible to alter the M-value of a unitary
or high-M stimulus, and thus the ease with which it can be encoded
as a unit, by varying the perceptual grouping of a sequence of letters
normally encoded as a unit.

In a series of three experiments, Ellis, Parente, and Shumate
(1972a) examined the effect of stimulus-M on recognition perfor-
mance by varying the fragmented *vs.* perceptually integrated charac-
ter of verbal stimuli. The purpose of this series of experiments was
threefold: (*a*) to demonstrate a positive relationship between stimu-
lus-M and correct recognition; (*b*) to determine if the effect of stim-
ulus-M depends upon the fragmented property of the stimuli, or the
ease with which they may be perceptually grouped as a unit; (*c*) to
determine if fragmented high-M stimuli operate as low-M stimuli in
the sense that their recognition is importantly dependent upon con-
textual cues present during associative training, thus providing a
converging operation with earlier studies.

The first experiment examined the effect of stimulus-M on recog-
nition memory. Although some studies have demonstrated a positive
relationship between M and recognition (e.g., Ellis & Shumate, 1973),
others (e.g., McNulty, 1965) have demonstrated a negative relation-
ship. It was necessary to establish this finding for purposes of the
latter two experiments. Subjects learned a list of 12 trigram doublets
(e.g., RUMWIG, TIJFEQ) with four doublets each of high-, moder-
ate-, and low-M (Archer, 1960). Doublets were presented at 1-second
rate and following presentation of the list, a two-choice recognition

test was given with a highly similar distractor paired with each old doublet. Subjects were given eight trials, with study and recognition testing alternating.

A plot of the recognition learning results of this experiment is shown in the left panel of Fig. 10. The figure shows the differential effects of stimulus-M upon recognition learning, with high-M stimuli producing superior recognition, followed by moderate-M, with low-M showing the poorest performance.

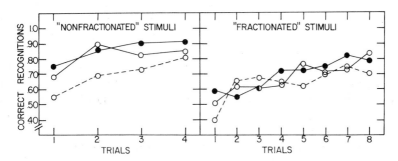

Fig. 10. Recognition learning curves as a function of stimulus meaning with "non-fractionated" and "fractionated" trigram doublets. High meaningfulness (–●–); moderate (–○–); low (– –○– –). Data from Ellis *et al.* (1972a).

The second experiment determined if the positive relationship between stimulus-M and recognition is dependent directly upon the extent to which the stimuli can be encoded. It used a "fractionation" procedure which decreased the probability that stimuli would be encoded as a unit because the fractionated stimuli could be less easily grouped as a perceptual unit. The same doublets were now fractionated so that they appeared as perceptual groupings of one or more letters. For example, the four high-M doublets, BANCOW, CUPNET, RUMWIG, and DENGIT, were presented in the following form, each adhering to a different fractionation rule: [BA NC OW], [C UPN ET], [R UMWI G], and [DE NGI T]. The moderate-M and low-M doublets were also fractionated according to the same rules used with the high-M stimuli. Each stimulus maintained the same form or grouping rule throughout all eight trials. The test trials were administered the same as in Experiment I; however, the distractor items were fractionated according to the same rules as the target items. The right panel of Fig. 10 presents the recognition learning curves for the fractionated stimuli. Clearly the stimulus-M effect is no longer present, even after eight trials, and the mean recognition scores for the three conditions averaged over eight trials did not differ reliably, nor did they differ from the low-M condition of the first experiment.

These experiments provide direct support for the view that the effect of stimuli-M on recognition performance is dependent upon the structural properties of the trigram doublets. High-M stimuli, when fragmented or grouped so that their unitary feature is less readily detected, are recognized at approximately the same level as low-M stimuli, regardless of whether the latter are physically fragmented or presented as a unit. It follows that if the high-M stimuli have indeed become functionally equivalent to low-M stimuli, then they should operate as low-M stimuli under other experimental conditions. Since low-M stimuli are most susceptible to response-dependent encoding (Ellis & Shumate, 1973), it would follow that degraded or fractionated high-M stimuli would show a similar effect. Therefore, it would follow that if *fragmented* high-M stimuli are paired with representative responses during associative training, such training would facilitate stimulus encoding compared with associative training in which the responses were nonrepresentative, because the fragmented high-M stimuli function as low-M stimuli. Subjects learned a paired-associate list consisting of the fragmented high-M stimuli and responses which were either representative or nonrepresentative words as in the study of Ellis and Shumate. Following eight paired-associate trials, subjects were given a forced-choice five-item recognition test, and the four distractors were fractionated in the same fashion as the old item.

The results of the recognition test are shown in Fig. 11, which portrays the mean proportion of correct stimulus recognition following associative training with representative and nonrepresentative responses. The mean recognition scores of the fractionated high-M stimuli for the representative and nonrepresentative response conditions were .78 and .45, respectively, a difference which was reliable. Recognition performances for the fractionated high-M stimuli are roughly comparable to those for low-M stimuli reported by Ellis and Shumate, where corresponding recognition scores were .70 and .50, respectively, for those stimuli associated with representative and nonrepresentative words during training for the immediate test conditions. Also shown in Fig. 11 are stimulus recognition results for the same stimuli obtained under identical conditions, *except* that the trigram doublets were presented as an integrated unit. These data are also taken from Ellis and Shumate and reveal that recognition of integrated high-M stimuli are not differentially affected by associative training with representative *vs.* nonrepresentative responses, as

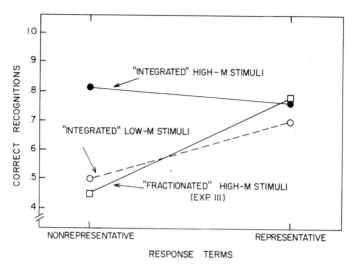

Fig. 11. Recognition memory of trigram doublets following associative training with representative and nonrepresentative responses. "Integrated" high-M and low-M stimuli data from Ellis and Shumate (1973). Other data from Ellis *et al.* (1972a).

the mean proportion of correct stimulus recognitions for these two training conditions were .76 and .82, respectively. Thus, the facilitating effect of associating a representative response to a high-M stimulus on subsequent recognition of that stimulus occurs only when the stimulus is fractionated, effectively making its encoding like that of a low-M stimulus.

C. Nominal Stimulus Variability

Thus far concern has been focused on conditions which modify or vary the hypothesized encodings of stimuli as reflected primarily in recognition tasks. I will now consider that case in which *nominal* stimuli are varied in some systematic fashion and compare the effects of variation on stimulus recognition and recall. By nominal stimulus variation is meant situations in which contextual, background, or other variations are introduced into a set of nominal stimuli which share one or more common features. For example, a set of visual patterns belonging to the same schema family (e.g., Posner, 1969) represent one way of varying nominal stimuli belonging to the same class. Another procedure is to employ photographs of the same person in different clothing and poses (Dukes & Bevan, 1967). Changes in stimulus variation allow comparison with simple stimulus repetition as factors influencing both free and stimulated recall as well as recognition memory.

The most extensive studies of stimulus variation have been conducted by Bevan and his colleagues. In one study Bevan, Dukes, and Avant (1966) showed that recall of stimulus categories was facilitated by variation in the category instances. In a similar study Dukes and Bevan (1967) evaluated the effects of variation *vs.* repetition when the test stimuli were the same as ones seen and when new instances of the class were shown. Their results indicated that when the test stimulus had been presented as a training stimulus, repetition in training yielded greater recall than variation in training. In contrast, when the test stimuli were different from, but related to those in training, stimulus variation produced greater recall than simple repetition of a single stimulus. Common names were associated with each class of faces shown, and a subjects task was to recall the name. They concluded that the superiority of intensive drill on particular stimulus-response (S-R) combinations is evident when the purpose of training is to reinstate a particular response to a specific stimulus, whereas diverse contacts with members of a class of stimuli are important when the purpose of training is to correctly identify new members of the class.

Their results are open, however, to two possible interpretations. The superiority of varied training when the test stimuli are new can be viewed as a case of "generalization." The subjects may simply have acquired a "set to generalize" as a result of varied training, a set less likely to occur with fixed (repetitious) training. Alternatively, the results may be viewed as reflecting unbiased recall estimates. These alternatives can be evaluated, however, by the use of a forced recall procedure which would keep the decision criterion comparable in the two situations.

Several theoretical issues are raised by these findings. Specifically, what is the nature of the encoding established in the varied condition compared with the constant or fixed condition? Presumably, subjects who see varied instances of a stimulus (such as different photographs of the same person) learn to attend to more distinctive or selective features of the stimulus. Since dress, pose, etc., are systematically varied, the likely encoding would be based on more common or redundant features. Thus, varied-stimulus training would produce its effect because subjects focus on certain features common to the entire class of stimuli, whereas repeated presentations of the same nominal stimulus do not necessarily require selection of a specific class of features. Many more cues are relevant and redundant for evoking the appropriate naming responses, and thus precise dimensional control is not necessarily achieved.

The implications of nominal stimulus variation for recognition are different from those of recall. Given that a subject is more likely to select those features common to the stimulus class, which is reasonable since the design (Dukes & Bevan, 1967) makes their study like that of concept identification, then the nature of the encoded representation that a subject acquires will be dependent principally upon these common or redundant features. Indeed, in this kind of situation a subject can be said to be learning a concept, or perhaps, a schema. Other, noncommon, or nonredundant features will be less attended to during training, perhaps attenuated (e.g., Treisman, 1964) in some fashion. A comparison of varied with repetitive training, followed by a recognition test with a probe from the training set, should produce superior recognition under repetition conditions, a finding predictable from simple frequency considerations.

In the studies of Bevan, subjects are shown stimuli of the type ax, bx, fx, jx, where x is the common feature and a, b, f, and j, are the modifying elements. To each stimulus compound subjects learn a common response and then recall that response when shown either one of the training stimuli or new instances of the category such as tx. It is thus not surprising that varied training produces superior recall.

As an alternative, it is possible to vary the physical properties of the nominal stimulus *itself*. In this fashion direct variation of the information to be recalled can be varied rather than the modifying elements. Ellis, Parente, and Walker (1972) have explored the variation-repetition problem with this approach in which the grouping structure of letter sequences composed of trigram pairs was varied. Subjects were given study trials consisting of 12 trigram pairs (doublets) in which the grouping structure was either varied or kept constant on successive trials. Varied training involved presentation of trigram pairs, such as RUMWIG, in groupings which differed on successive trials such as [R UMW IG], [RU MW IG], [RU MWI G], etc. Four different groupings were used, but the intact trigram (RUM, or WIG) was never presented. The letters were always in the same sequence but grouped differently on each trial. Subjects trained under constant (repetition) condition saw the same structure on successive trials. Half the subjects were given a free recall test of the six disyllables and half a forced-choice recognition test interspersed between study trials. (Since there were differences in training procedures, the recognition-recall results are not directly comparable.)

A plot of the free recall and recognition results is given in Fig. 12. The left panel shows the recognition results and the right panel shows recall. Recognition performance was obviously facilitated by repetition conditions, whereas varied training produced significantly greater recall. Recall was scored according to complete recall of all six letters in the proper sequence.

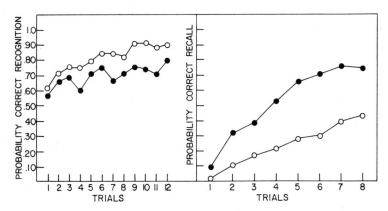

Fig. 12. The effects of nominal stimulus variability *versus* constant presentation (repetition) on probability of correct recognition (left panel) and correct recall (right panel) of trigram doublets. Constant training (○); varied training (●). Data from Ellis *et al.* (1972b).

A subanalysis of the partial recalls is shown in Fig. 13. Partial recalls of correct 5-, 4-, 3-, or 2-letter sequences were calculated in order to examine the effects of varied-constant presentation on size of the recalled chunk. The figure clearly shows that the effect of varied training interacts with the size of the partially recalled sequence. This relationship portrays the expected trade off since the varied condition cannot lead to greater recall of smaller units given that larger units are recalled more frequently. (Figure 13 has differing values on the y-axis and must be interpreted with caution.)

The results are interesting for several reasons. First, they show that the classic assumption that sheer repetition of nominally constant stimuli is important for recall is not the case, at least under these conditions. Second, the results indicated that the effects of nominal stimulus variation depend upon the size of the unit to be

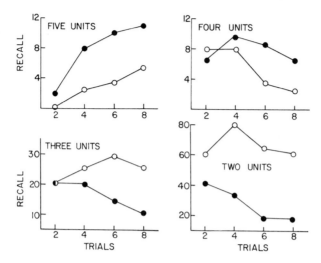

Fig. 13. The effect of nominal stimulus variability *versus* constant presentation on partially correct recall of trigram sequences as a function of size of the chunk recalled. Varied training (●); constant training (○). Data from Ellis *et al.* (1972b).

recalled. And third, the results suggest that recall and recognition may well reflect different processes at either the encoding and/or retrieval stages of memory, and thus would be inconsistent with strength conceptions of recognition memory (Kintsch, 1970). More generally, these findings open a new line of attack regarding the role of differential encodings in tasks of recall, recognition, transfer, and classification.

VI. Encoding and the Transfer of Stimulus Differentiation

A. STIMULUS DIFFERENTIATION

A long-standing view in verbal learning theory (E. J. Gibson, 1940) has been that part of what is learned in a paired-associate task, where two or more pairs are involved, is distinguishing or discriminating among the stimulus terms. Presumably, subjects learn to establish consistent and differentiating representational responses to each stimulus. Obviously, if the stimulus terms are readily discriminable, this process should at best consume only a small portion of the total learning time. In contrast, if the stimuli are difficult to distinguish, then this process becomes increasingly important. Numerous experiments have shown, of course, that as the formal similarity among the items is increased, total learning time is retarded (e.g., Runquist, 1968).

It was further assumed by Gibson that once stimulus differentiation was accomplished that it would transfer to a second task containing the same nominal stimuli. The argument for this proposition was quite straightforward: when subjects began a second paired-associate task that contained the same nominal stimuli as the first, they would profit from already having learned to differentiate the stimuli. Hence Gibson referred to this as the "transfer of differentiation" among stimuli. Gibson recognized that sources of interference existed in this kind of transfer situation, but nevertheless emphasized that the transfer of differentiation, or discrimination, should provide a *source* of positive transfer in a second task containing the same stimulus terms, even though the net effect might be negative transfer.

Most importantly, however, it was emphasized that the source of positive transfer should be greater as the similarity among the stimulus terms increased. If subjects had to expend considerable effort in distinguishing among difficult-to-discriminate stimuli, relative to other subprocesses operating, then this differentiation should provide for a greater source of transfer compared with subject's distinguishing among easy-to-discriminate stimuli, such as colors or familiar words of different classes. It follows from this argument that in transfer studies using the A-B, A-D paradigm, where subjects learn to associate new responses to the same stimuli, that the magnitude of relative positive transfer should be greater under conditions of high intralist stimulus similarity as compared with low similarity. In this instance, performance of the A-B, A-D group is compared with the conventional A-B, C-D condition, a nonspecific transfer control. There can be no transfer of differentiation *specific* to the stimuli in the control condition, since the stimuli are new and are usually unrelated to those of the first task in the sense of containing different elements or features, or having different structural properties.

Despite the long-standing existence of this theory, its critical prediction has received little or no confirmation in earlier studies. Reviews of the predifferentiation literature (Arnoult, 1957; Ellis, 1969) indicated that evidence for such a phenomenon was quite ambiguous, and seemingly a result of highly specialized conditions when present. Moreover, two recent experiments (Del Castillo & Ellis, 1968; Underwood & Ekstrand, 1968) failed to find any substantial evidence for the transfer of differentiation. Using light patterns of varying brightness, Del Castillo and Ellis found no reliably greater transfer when the stimuli were high than low in similarity. Similarly, using trigram stimuli varying in formal similarity, Underwood and Ekstrand found no greater transfer under high than low similarity.

These experiments indicated that although the stimuli were clearly differentiated during first-task learning, such differentiation did not transfer to a second task. One implication would be that hypothetical generalization gradients among the training stimuli, which presumably steepen as a result of such training, are *specific* to the particular responses learned in the first task. Such a position might seemingly imply that a generalizationlike process, following Gibson's thinking at that time, is response specific. An alternative and more contemporary interpretation is that second-task responses act to disrupt the functional encodings of the stimuli established during first-task learning, which seems likely with stimuli whose encodings are response dependent.

The failure to find evidence for the transfer of discrimination raises a general question in the context of contemporary stimulus-encoding conceptions: what does happen to functional encodings of the stimuli when subjects learn a second task containing nominal stimuli identical to first-task stimuli? Are the encodings disrupted? Are they suppressed as new ones are learned? Why do subjects appear not to use learned encodings of stimuli in a new task containing the same nominal stimuli? Accordingly, the long-standing issue of the transfer of stimulus differentiation is related to the issue of stimulus encoding. If stimulus discrimination is viewed as basically a process of establishing stable representational or perceptual encoding responses to nominal stimuli, then a theory of stimulus coding must specify what happens to these representations during transfer learning. These conceptual issues have, therefore, prompted reexamination of the differentiation problem, not with a focus on the classic transfer issue itself, but with a focus on its implications for theoretical conceptions of stimulus encoding.

In a series of experiments, Ellis and Shaffer (1971) have shown that the transfer of differentiation depends critically on the characteristics of the stimulus terms. First, with trigram stimuli of low- and high-intralist similarity they found no evidence for the transfer of discrimination; these results are shown in the upper panel of Fig. 14. Thus, the results corroborate those of Underwood and Ekstrand (1968). In striking contrast they found quite substantial evidence for the transfer of discrimination when 24-point random shapes of high

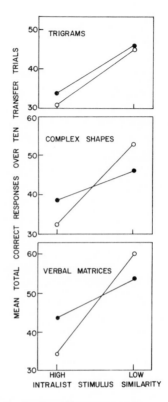

Fig. 14. The transfer of stimulus differentiation in an A-B, A-D paradigm as a function of characteristics of the list stimuli. A-D paradigm (●); C-D paradigm (○). Data from Ellis and Shaffer (1971).

and low similarity were used. The middle panel of Fig. 14 portrays these results in which the usual negative transfer in the A-D paradigm is obtained with stimuli of low similarity. Absolute positive transfer is, however, obtained in the A-D paradigm when the stimuli are high in intralist similarity in accord with the classic hypothesis. The figure portrays a substantial effect and the interaction of stimulus similarity and paradigm is highly reliable. Finally, a similar interaction was obtained with complex matrices of letters called polygrams. The letter arrangements consisted of 3 × 3 matrices comprised of three letters, such as R, T, and M, which allow for high stimulus overlap among the matrices and many relevant redundant cues. The results of the transfer study with letter matrices are shown in the lower panel of Fig. 14.

The results suggest that it is the presence of *multiple redundant cues* in the stimulus compound which is decisive in producing the transfer of differentiation effect. The classical prediction holds provided selection of functional cues is possible from a range of alternative features. This hypothesis was directly tested with stimuli similar to those typically used in concept identification studies. In this experiment the number of relevant redundant cues was varied systematically with the stimulus patterns comprised of either one-element stimuli, or four-elements compounds consisting of shape, color, line tilt, and a trigram. As predicted, the number of alternative encodings determined the transfer of differentiation effect. No such transfer was obtained with the one-element stimuli, but facilitation was clearly present with the four-element compounds.

B. STIMULUS RECODING IN THE FACE OF INTERFERENCE

The finding that the transfer of stimulus differentiation in an A-B, A-D paradigm is dependent upon the presence of multiple redundant cues raises the issue of what manner a subject utilizes the encodings established during first-list learning when he is required to attach new responses to the old stimuli in the second list. One possible mechanism by which subjects may overcome the interference normally encountered in an A-B, A-D paradigm is that of stimulus recoding (Lawrence, 1963; Martin, 1968). Martin's basic proposition is that subjects may recode the nominally identical stimuli in second-list learning and thus avoid interference effects.

If stimulus recoding is to be an effective mechanism, certain conditions appear indispensable. Certainly the stimuli must contain some minimum number of distinguishing characteristics that allow for new functional encodings to develop. Moreover, it is doubtful on theoretical grounds that such a shift of functional encodings in and of itself can be the *sole* mechanism accounting for sources of positive transfer in overall or net negative-transfer situations. Consider, for example, the A-B, A-D transfer paradigm in which a subject learns to associate new responses to the same nominal stimuli in the second task. If a subject simply recodes the A stimulus terms in the second task, developing new functional encodings in order to overcome interference, then the recoded version of the A stimuli associated with new (D) responses become functionally equivalent to a nonspecific transfer paradigm (A-B, C-D). In effect, the A stimuli would now be like C stimuli, and a subject would be essentially starting from "scratch" with respect to the stimuli. Thus recoding could lead to performance equivalent to a nonspecific-transfer control condition, but not superior to it. If this argument is sound, it follows that at least one additional mechanism must be incorporated in order to account for observed effects. (It is possible, however, that the recoding of A stimuli may not be the simple analog of learning the C stimuli, in that a subject may recode A in a manner different from, perhaps faster than, his learning of new C stimuli.)

A weaker proposition would be that shifts in dimensional attention occur in the face of negative transfer in order to overcome conflict, but do not result in absolute positive transfer. Thus, attempts at recoding can be seen as part of a subject's effort to sidestep interference even though this process does not provide for absolute positive transfer. In a study by Bryk and Kausler (1966), indirect evidence for this proposition was obtained, in the sense that less retroactive interference was obtained when the stimuli were low than when they were high in meaningfulness. Such a pattern of findings is consistent with the hypothesis that low-M stimuli were recoded in the second task. Similarly, Schneider and Houston (1968) report that subjects instructed to switch their encodings in the second task showed considerably less interference when tested for recall of first-list associations.

As noted earlier, however, direct tests of recoding nominally identical stimuli have not been promising (e.g., Goggin & Martin, 1970; Williams & Underwood, 1970). In a study of forced-stimulus recoding, Goggin and Martin found that transfer performance in a negative transfer paradigm was poorer for subjects forced to shift their functional encodings. Subsequent attempts to produce shifts in encoding in our laboratory also yielded similar results. In several experiments, subjects were asked at the end of first-list learning to identify what portions of the stimuli they used to "cue" their responses. A similar determination was made at the end of the second-list learning. Subjects could thus be classified as either retaining the same functional cues or shifting their cue selection. It was found that subjects who retained their original codes showed reliably greater transfer than did those who shifted. Thus, resistance to interference appears to depend on the stability rather than on the variability of stimulus encoding. Other experiments examined the role of recoding in interference paradigms using verbal materials as well as shapes. Variations in the tasks including instructions, priming, and stimulus complexity were employed. Again, in all instances, subjects who retained their original codes performed better than those who shifted to new codes. These data cast serious doubt on the Lawrence-Martin hypothesis that stimulus recoding provides a vehicle by which subjects may bypass associative interference in negative transfer paradigms.

C. STIMULUS RECODING AND OVERLEARNING

The finding that stimulus recoding is not a viable mechanism for the bypassing of associative interference had led to consideration of other mechanisms which produce the transfer of differentiation effect when the stimuli consist of multiple redundant cues. It clearly appears that after learning to distinguish difficult-to-discriminate stimuli subjects are quite reluctant to shift their attention to a new set of encodings. How, then, is the transfer of differentiation effect explained? One possibility is the differential overlearning received by the high-similarity stimuli. Although subjects are carried to a common performance criterion, subjects in the high-similarity condition received more training on their discriminations. This training differential, however, exists with the high similarity trigram stimuli (where the effect was not obtained) as well as shapes and verbal matrices. Therefore, overlearning per se could not be the factor that produces these effects. On the other hand, overlearning could produce effects in conjunction with stimulus patterns having relevant redundant cues, and these effects may in turn produce the transfer of differentiation. One possibility is that with extended training subjects begin to "pick up" the additional relevant cues, weaker though they may be (e.g., James & Greeno, 1967). Weaker cues might become part of a stimulus compound, so that subjects could use any one of such components in a transfer task to cue his response. In a sense a subject may shift, but not in the way proposed by Lawrence and Martin. An alternative possibility is that a subject may shift, not from one element to another, but from a compound to one of its elements. Regardless of how the learning of weaker cues might underlie such a process, this proposition may account for the transfer of stimulus differentiation effects obtained with compound stimuli.

VII. Summary and Conclusions

The role of verbal processes in the encoding of visual pattern and verbal stimuli was evaluated in the context of recognition, recall, and transfer experiments. A diverse number of task situations was examined, all of which focused on how human subjects process stimulus information in learning tasks, thus providing a range of situations in which to evaluate several interpretations of stimulus encoding. In the investigation of stimulus encoding processes, the objective or nominal stimuli defined by an investigator must be clearly distinguished from the coded or functional stimuli to which a subject responds. The codes are often verbal, but they may involve other representations such as mental images. Conceivably, subjects may use alternative codes for the same nominal stimuli on different occasions. Most importantly, the choice and variation of codes are significantly influenced by the context and requirements of the learning task.

Studies of verbal pretraining reveal that practice in associating common responses to stimuli of a given class produce a less distinctive encoding of these stimuli, as reflected in their poorer recognition compared with control conditions. This poorer recognition performance is most likely due to the common label encouraging subjects to attend to common features of the stimulus class, producing less distinctive encodings than would otherwise occur. This result is viewed as the outcome of selective attentional processes and is not easily handled by S-R mediational interpretations or observing-response accounts. The effects of labeling stimuli with distinctive verbal labels on their subsequent recognizability depends largely upon the representational properties of the verbal labels as distinct from the meaningfulness of the label, supporting the view that the principal effect of a label is to direct a subject's attention toward those distinctive features of the stimulus which are suggested by the label.

The effect of associating distinctive and representative labels with visual shapes on subsequent shape recognition depends upon shape complexity. With stimuli that are physically complex the effect of labeling is to enhance recognition performance above that of subjects who are instructed merely to observe the shapes during pretraining. In contrast, with physically simple shapes the effects of verbal labeling are either negligible or they produce some lowering of performance. A conceptual coding hypothesis was proposed to account for the dependency of verbal labeling effects upon stimulus complexity, stimulus meaningfulness, amount of associative training, and number of items to be remembered. It was proposed that the relative contribution of verbal labeling practice on stimulus recognition was greatest with stimuli that are initially most difficult to encode.

Studies of verbal pretraining using stimulus recognition tests yield results which do not mirror the findings obtained with transfer tests employing the A-B, A-D paradigm. Under conditions in which verbal labeling of visual patterns produces positive transfer, the same training conditions do not enhance the recognizability of the stimuli. Similarly, response variables unimportant in facilitating stimulus recognition frequently facilitate transfer. Thus, comparable encodings of stimuli, produced by equivalent training conditions, do not produce comparable effects in recognition and transfer tests. These findings are important in theoretical considerations of perceptual learning and stimulus encoding.

In studies of verbal paired-associate learning, stimulus recognition is unaffected by the consistency with which responses are paired with stimuli. Thus, sheer repetition of associations does not enhance the encoding of stimuli. In contrast, the development of strong, stable associations via pairing with representative responses does enhance the recognizability of verbal stimuli. The locus of this encoding effect, in both visual pattern and verbal stimulus recognition, appears to be in the stimulus-selection encoding stages of learning.

Nominal stimulus recognition is not necessarily a prerequisite for recall of responses following associative training. The probability of response recall, given nonrecognition of the stimulus, is significantly above chance when the response terms employed in associative learning are representative of the stimuli. With digit or nonrepresentative responses, this contingency does fall to chance. A retrieval-match model of stimulus recognition was proposed in which it was hypothesized that the probability of recall is dependent upon retrieval of some critical portion of the encoded version of the nominal stimulus.

Stimulus meaningfulness is positively related to correct stimulus recognition, and inversely related to the false alarm rate where meaningfulness is defined as association value. The effect of stimulus meaningfulness depends, in part, upon the type of scale. The integrated-fractionable character of stimuli is an important determinant of the ease with which they are encoded. Moreover, disruption of the spatial grouping of high-meaningfulness stimuli makes them operate like low-meaningfulness stimuli in tests of recognition memory.

Nominal stimulus variability produces different effects on recall and recognition. Nominal variability, defined in terms of perceptual grouping rules, produces free recall superior to that accomplished by sheer repetition of the nominal stimulus. Variation produces inferior recognition, however, when the test item is one from the list studied. If the item is one from the *class* of items, as distinct from truly old, then variation facilitates class recognition. The effect of nominal stimulus variability on recall is dependent upon the size of the unit to be recalled. In general, the greater the size of the unit, the more pronounced are the facilitative effects of variability.

The transfer of differentiation effect is a function of the presence of multiple redundant cues in the stimulus compound. Positive transfer of stimulus differentiation, in accord with the classic hypothesis, is obtained with compound stimuli possessing multiple redundant cues but not with component stimuli. No evidence for a stimulus recoding interpretation of this phenomenon was obtained. In general, subjects who retain their original encodings showed superior performance in transfer. Thus, resistance to interference appears to depend upon the stability rather than the variability of stimulus encoding. A modification of the recoding hypothesis, in which subjects shift from a compound to a component, was proposed as a possible mechanism in accounting for positive transfer of differentiation effects.

The significance of stimulus encoding processes in accounts of human learning, memory, and transfer was outlined. Although investigators in human learning have been historically less interested in stimulus processes, recent developments require a thorough analysis of the conditions which influence the development of stimulus representations, and the manner in which these representations function in tasks of memory and transfer. The fact that comparable encodings of stimuli may function differently in recall, recognition, and transfer complicates this analysis, but nevertheless emphasizes its importance. How stimulus information is perceived, selected, encoded, and elaborated reflects one feature of the paradigm shift in contemporary psychology.

REFERENCES

Archer, E. J. A re-evaluation of the meaningfulness of all possible CVC trigrams. *Psychological Monographs,* 1960, **74** (Whole No. 497).

Arnoult, M. D. Recognition of shapes following paired-associates pretraining. In G. Finch & F. Cameron (Eds.), *Symposium on Air Force human engineering, personnel, and training research.* NAS-NRC Publ. No. 455. Washington, D.C.: Nat. Acad. Sci. —Nat. Res. Counc., 1956. Pp. 1–9.

Arnoult, M. D. Stimulus predifferentiation: Some generalizations and hypotheses. *Psychological Bulletin,* 1957, **54,** 339–350.

Bahrick, H. P., & Boucher, B. Retention of visual and verbal codes of the same stimuli. *Journal of Experimental Psychology,* 1968, **78,** 417–422.

Bernbach, H. Stimulus learning and recognition in paired-associate learning. *Journal of Experimental Psychology,* 1967, **75,** 513–519.

Bevan, W., Dukes, W. F., & Avant, L. The effect of variation in specific stimuli on memory for their superordinates. *American Journal of Psychology,* 1966, **79,** 250–257.

Birge, J. S. The role of verbal responses in transfer. Unpublished doctoral dissertation, Yale University, 1941.

Bower, G. H. Imagery as a relational organizer in associative learning. *Journal of Verbal Learning and Verbal Behavior,* 1970, **9,** 529–533.

Bower, G. H. Mental imagery and associative learning. In L. Gregg (Ed.), *Cognition in learning and memory.* New York: Wiley, 1972.

Brown, R. N., & Lenneberg, E. H. A study in language and cognition. *Journal of Abnormal and Social Psychology,* 1954, **49,** 454–462.

Bryk, J. A., & Kausler, D. H. Stimulus meaningfulness and unlearning in the A-B, A-C transfer paradigm. *Journal of Experimental Psychology,* 1966, **71,** 917–920.

Campbell, V., & Freeman, J. T. Some functions of experimentally-induced language in perceptual learning. *Perceptual and Motor Skills,* 1955, **1,** 71–79.

Carmichael, L., Hogan, H. P., & Walter, A. A. An experimental study of the effect of language on the reproduction of visually perceived form. *Journal of Experimental Psychology,* 1932, **15,** 73–86.

Clark, H. J. Recognition memory for random shapes as a function of complexity, association value, and delay. *Journal of Experimental Psychology,* 1965, **69,** 590–595.

Daniel, T. C., & Ellis, H. C. Stimulus codability and long-term recognition memory for visual form. *Journal of Experimental Psychology,* 1972, **93,** 83–89.

Del Castillo, D. M., & Ellis, H. C. The role of response-produced cues in paired-associate transfer as a function of stimulus similarity. *Psychonomic Science,* 1968, **10,** 197–198.

Dollard, J., & Miller, N. E. *Personality and psychotherapy.* New York: McGraw-Hill, 1950.

Dukes, W. F., & Bevan, W. Stimulus variation and repetition in the acquisition of naming responses. *Journal of Experimental Psychology,* 1967, **74,** 178–181.

Ellis, H. C. Transfer of stimulus predifferentiation to shape recognition and identification learning: Role of properties of verbal labels. *Journal of Experimental Psychology,* 1968, **78,** 401–409.

Ellis, H. C. Transfer and retention. In M. H. Marx (Ed.), *Learning: Processes.* New York: Macmillan, 1969.

Ellis, H. C. Verbal processes in perceptual learning, transfer, and mediated generalization. In J. Linhart (Ed.), *Proceedings of the international conference on the psychology of human learning.* Vol. II. Prague: Inst. Psychol., Czech. Acad. Sci. 1970.

Ellis, H. C., Bessemer, D. W., Devine, J. V., & Trafton, C. L. Recognition of random tactual shapes following predifferentiation training. *Perceptual and Motor Skills,* 1962, **10,** 99–102.

Ellis, H. C., & Daniel, T. C. Verbal processes in long-term stimulus-recognition memory. *Journal of Experimental Psychology,* 1971, **90,** 18–26.

Ellis, H. C., & Feuge, R. L. Transfer of predifferentiation training to gradients of generalization in shape recognition. *Journal of Experimental Psychology,* 1966, **71,** 539–542.

Ellis, H. C., Feuge, R. L., Long, K. K., & Pegram, V. G. Evidence for acquired equivalence of cues in a perceptual task. *Perceptual and Motor Skills,* 1964, **19,** 159–162.

Ellis, H. C., & Homan, L. Implicit verbal responses and the transfer of stimulus predifferentiation. *Journal of Experimental Psychology,* 1968, **76,** 486–489.

Ellis, H. C., & Muller, D. G. Transfer in perceptual learning following stimulus predifferentiation. *Journal of Experimental Psychology,* 1964, **68,** 388–395.

Ellis, H. C., Muller, D. G., & Tosti, D. T. Stimulus meaning and complexity as factors in the transfer of stimulus predifferentiation. *Journal of Experimental Psychology,* 1966, **71,** 629–633.

Ellis, H. C., Parente, F. J., & Shumate, E. C. Meaningfulness, perceptual grouping, and organization in recognition memory. Unpublished manuscript, University of New Mexico, 1972. (a)

Ellis, H. C., Parente, F. J., & Walker, C. W. Nominal stimulus variability in recall and recognition. Unpublished manuscript, University of New Mexico, 1972. (b)

Ellis, H. C., & Shaffer, R. W. Stimulus encoding and the transfer of stimulus differentiation. Unpublished manuscript, University of New Mexico, 1971.

Ellis, H. C., & Shumate, E. C. Encoding effects of response belongingness and stimulus meaningfulness on recognition memory of trigram stimuli. *Journal of Experimental Psychology,* 1973, **98,** 70–78.

Ellis, H. C., & Tatum, B. C. Stimulus encoding and the relationship between stimulus recognition and association formation. *Journal of Verbal Learning and Verbal Behavior,* 1973, in press.

Feuge, R. L., & Ellis, H. C. Generalization gradients in recognition memory of visual form: The role of stimulus meaning. *Journal of Experimental Psychology,* 1969, **79,** 288–294.

Gagné, R. M., & Baker, K. E. Stimulus predifferentiation as a factor in transfer of training. *Journal of Experimental Psychology,* 1950, **40,** 439–451.

Gibson, E. J. A systematic application of the concepts of generalization and differentiation to verbal learning. *Psychological Review,* 1940, **47,** 196–229.

Gibson, E. J. *Principles of perceptual learning and development.* New York: Appleton, 1969.

Gibson, J. J., & Gibson, E. J. Perceptual learning: Differentiation or enrichment? *Psychological Review,* 1955, **62,** 32–41.

Glanzer, M., & Clark, W. H. Accuracy of perceptual recall: An analysis of organization. *Journal of Verbal Learning and Verbal Behavior,* 1962, **1,** 289–299.

Glanzer, M., & Clark, W. H. The verbal loop hypothesis: Conventional figures. *American Journal of Psychology,* 1964, **77,** 621–627.

Glaze, J. A. The association value of nonsense syllables. *Journal of Genetic Psychology,* 1928, **35,** 255–269.

Goggin, J., & Martin, E. Forced stimulus encoding and retroactive interference. *Journal of Experimental Psychology,* 1970, **84,** 131–136.

Goss, A. E. A stimulus-response analysis of the interaction of cue-producing and mediating responses. *Psychological Review,* 1955, **62,** 20–31.

Goss, A. E., & Greenfeld, N. Transfer to a motor task as influenced by conditions and degree of prior discrimination training. *Journal of Experimental Psychology,* 1958, **55,** 258–269.

Hake, H. W., & Eriksen, C. W. Effect of number of permissible response categories on learning of a constant number of visual stimuli. *Journal of Experimental Psychology,* 1955, **50,** 161–167.

Hake, H. W., & Eriksen, C. W. Role of response variables in recognition and identification of complex visual forms. *Journal of Experimental Psychology,* 1956, **52,** 235–243.

James, C. T., & Greeno, J. G. Stimulus selection at different stages of paired-associate learning. *Journal of Experimental Psychology,* 1967, **74,** 75–83.

Johnson, R. Recognition of nonsense shapes as a function of degree of congruence among components of the pretraining task. Unpublished doctoral dissertation, University of Virginia, 1964.

Katz, P. A. Effect of labels on children's perception and discrimination learning. *Journal of Experimental Psychology*, 1963, **66**, 423–428.

Kendler, H. H., & Kendler, T. S. Vertical and horizontal processes in problem solving. *Psychological Review*, 1962, **69**, 1–16.

Kendler, H. H., & Kendler, T. S. Mediation and conceptual behavior. In K. W. Spence & J. T. Spence (Eds.), *The psychology of learning and motivation. Advances in research and theory*. Vol. 2. New York: Academic Press, 1968.

Kintsch, W. Models of free recall and recognition. In D. A. Norman (Ed.), *Models of human memory*. New York: Academic, 1970.

Lantz, D., & Steffire, V. Language and cognition revisited. *Journal of Abnormal and Social Psychology*, 1964, **69**, 472–481.

Lawrence, D. H. The nature of a stimulus: Some relationships between learning and perception. In S. Koch (Ed.), *Psychology: A study of a science*. Vol. 5. New York: McGraw-Hill, 1963.

McGuire, W. J. A multiprocess model for paired-associate learning. *Journal of Experimental Psychology*, 1961, **62**, 335–347.

McNulty, J. A. Short-term retention as a function of method of measurement, recording time, and meaningfulness of the material. *Canadian Journal of Psychology*, 1965, **19**, 188–196.

Malloy, T. E., & Ellis, H. C. Attention and cue-producing responses in response-mediated stimulus generalization. *Journal of Experimental Psychology*, 1970, **83**, 191–200.

Maltzman, I. Theoretical conceptions of semantic conditioning and generalization. In T. R. Dixon & D. L. Horton (Eds.), *Verbal behavior and general behavior theory*. Englewood Cliffs, N.J.: Prentice-Hall, 1968.

Martin, E. Stimulus recognition in aural paired-associate learning. *Journal of Verbal Learning and Verbal Behavior*, 1967, **6**, 272–276. (a)

Martin, E. Relation between stimulus recognition and paired-associate learning. *Journal of Experimental Psychology*, 1967, **74**, 500–505. (b)

Martin, E. Stimulus meaningfulness and paired-associate transfer: An encoding-variability hypothesis. *Psychological Review*, 1968, **75**, 421–441.

Martin E. Verbal learning theory and independent retrieval phenomena. *Psychological Review*, 1971, **78**, 314–332.

Martin, E., & Melton, A. W. Meaningfulness and trigram recognition. *Journal of Verbal Learning and Verbal Behavior*, 1970, **9**, 126–135.

Melton, A. W. Decision processes in retrieval from memory: Comments on the contributions of Lloyd R. Peterson and Charles N. Cofer. In B. Kleinmuntz (Ed.), *Concepts and the structure of memory*. New York: Wiley, 1967.

Miller, G. A. The magical number seven plus or minus two: Some limits on our capacity to process information. *Psychological Review*, 1956, **63**, 81–97.

Miller, N. E., & Dollard, J. *Social learning and imitation*. New Haven: Yale University Press, 1941.

Noble, C. E. An analysis of meaning. *Psychological Review*, 1952, **59**, 421–430.

Paivio, A. Mental imagery in associative learning and memory. *Psychological Review*, 1969, **76**, 241–263.

Peterson, L. R. Search and judgment in memory. In B. Kleinmuntz (Ed.), *Concepts and the structure of memory*. New York: Wiley, 1967.

Pfafflin, S. M. Stimulus meaning in stimulus predifferentiation. *Journal of Experimental Psychology*, 1960, **59**, 269–274.

Posner, M. I. Abstraction and the process of recognition. In G. H. Bower & J. T. Spence (Eds.), *The psychology of learning and motivation. Advances in research and theory*. Vol. 3. New York: Academic, 1969.

Prentice, W. C. H. Visual recognition of verbally labeled figures. *American Journal of Psychology*, 1954, **67**, 315–320.

Price, R. H., & Slive, A. B. Verbal processes in shape recognition. *Journal of Experimental Psychology*, 1970, **83**, 373–379.

Ranken, H. B. Language and thinking: Positive and negative effects of naming. *Science*, 1963, **141**, 48–50.

Richardson, J. Cue effectiveness and abstraction in paired-associate learning. *Psychological Bulletin*, 1971, **75**, 73–91.

Riley, D. A. Memory for form. In L. Postman (Ed.), *Psychology in the making*. New York: Knopf, 1962.

Robinson, J. S. The effect of learning labels for stimuli on their later discrimination. *Journal of Experimental Psychology*, 1955, **49**, 112–115.

Royer, J. M. Associative recall as a function of stimulus recognition. *American Journal of Psychology*, 1969, **82**, 96–103.

Runquist, W. N. Functions relating intralist stimulus similarity to acquisition performance with a variety of materials. *Journal of Verbal Learning and Verbal Behavior*, 1968, **7**, 549–553.

Santa, J. L., & Ranken, H. B. Effects of verbal coding on recognition memory. *Journal of Experimental Psychology*, 1972, **93**, 268–278.

Schneider, N. G., & Houston, J. P. Stimulus selection and retroactive inhibition. *Journal of Experimental Psychology*, 1968, **77**, 166–167.

Shepard, R. N. Comments on Professor Underwood's paper. In C. N. Cofer & B. S. Musgrave (Eds.), *Verbal behavior and learning*. New York: McGraw-Hill, 1963.

Spiker, C. C. Verbal factors in the discrimination learning of children. In J. C. Wright & J. Kagan (Eds.), *Basic cognitive processes in children. Monographs of the Society for Research in Child Development*, 1963, **28**, (2, Whole No. 86).

Trabasso, T., & Bower, G. H. *Attention in learning*. New York: Wiley, 1968.

Treisman, A. Selective attention in man. *British Medical Bulletin*, 1964, **20**, 12–16.

Tulving, E., & Thomson, D. M. Retrieval processes in recognition memory: Effects of associative context. *Journal of Experimental Psychology*, 1971, **87**, 116–124.

Underwood, B. J. False recognition produced by implicit associative responses. *Journal of Experimental Psychology*, 1965, **70**, 122–129.

Underwood, B. J., & Ekstrand, B. R. Differentiation among stimuli as a factor in transfer performance. *Journal of Verbal Learning and Verbal Behavior*, 1968, **7**, 172–175.

Underwood, B. J., & Erlebacher, A. H. Studies of coding in verbal learning. *Psychological Monographs*, 1965, **79** (13, Whole No. 606).

Vanderplas, J. M. Associative processes in task relations in perceptual learning. *Perceptual and Motor Skills*, 1963, **16**, 501–509.

Vanderplas, J. M., & Garvin, E. A. Complexity, association value, and practice as factors in shape recognition following paired-associates training. *Journal of Experimental Psychology*, 1959, **57**, 155–163.

Vanderplas, J. M., Sanderson, W. A., & Vanderplas, J. N. Some task-related determinants of transfer in perceptual learning. *Perceptual and Motor Skills*, 1964, **18**, 71–80.

Williams, R. F., & Underwood, B. J. Encoding variability: Tests of the Martin hypothesis. *Journal of Experimental Psychology*, 1970, **86**, 317–324.

Winograd, E., Karchmer, M. A., & Russel, I. S. Role of encoding unitization in cued recognition memory. *Journal of Verbal Learning and Verbal Behavior*, 1971, **10**, 199–206.

SUBPROBLEM ANALYSIS OF DISCRIMINATION

LEARNING[1]

Thomas Tighe

DEPARTMENT OF PSYCHOLOGY, DARTMOUTH COLLEGE,
HANOVER, NEW HAMPSHIRE

I. Introduction

The research reported in this paper had its origins in the study of discrimination shift learning. The defining feature of the shift experiment is a change in stimulus-reward relations within a multidimensional task, such that a previously learned solution is rendered inappropriate and a new problem posed. A major interest in this research has been comparison of the ease with which organisms solve a reversal (R) shift, which requires reversal of choice response to the cues of the relevant dimension, as opposed to an extra-dimensional (ED) shift, which requires choice of stimulus values on a previously irrelevant dimension (see Fig. 1). During the past decade, an extensive literature has developed on comparative, developmental, and methodological aspects of this comparison, and this research is widely assumed to be of importance for theories of discrimination learning and development.

The present experimental analysis began with an attempt to take

[1] Preparation of this paper was aided by Public Health Service Grants MH-11088 from the National Institutes of Health and K4-HD-43, 859 from the National Institute of Child Health and Human Development. The author is grateful to George Wolford for assistance in the computer simulation of Spence's model and to Jill Nagy for assistance in data collection and analysis. Helpful comments on the manuscript were provided by Louise Tighe and Robert Leaton.

a naive, atheoretical view of the manner in which organisms might learn discrimination tasks of the type depicted in Fig. 1. Experimenters implicitly assume that in learning such tasks the subject treats the individual stimulus pairs (large black *vs.* small white, and small black *vs.* large white) as instances of a single problem. Although this is certainly an intuitively plausible view, it nevertheless appears to rest solely upon intuition rather than on direct tests of a subject's actual mode of processing the task. It is at least logically possible that a subject might view the stimulus pairs as independent problems which happen to occur on alternate trials in the course of training, or that a subject might otherwise discriminate between performance on the problem elements. How might such possibilities be assessed? Examination of Fig. 1 suggests a simple, direct test. Note that while the R shift involves a reversal of stimulus-reward relations on both pairs of the task, the ED shift involves reversal of the reward relations on only *one* of the pairs, the other pair retaining the reward relations which was obtained in the preshift stage. If subjects do learn the stimulus pairs as independent subproblems, then relearning during ED shift should be largely confined to the changed pair.

It would seem to be an easy matter to examine the data from R-ED comparisons to determine whether independent subproblem learning ever characterizes the learning of the problem pairs. But

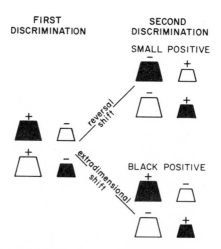

Fig. 1. Illustration of reversal and extradimensional shifts. Each line contains a pair of choice stimuli presented simultaneously. The two pairs of test stimuli and the rewarded stimulus are shown for each phase of the experiment.

despite the very large number of studies involving such comparisons, there was in fact little data available for such an analysis. Experimenters have in fact rarely conducted the R-ED comparison in the straightforward manner indicated in Fig. 1. Rather, for reasons linked to the use of the R-ED comparison in tests of theories of discrimination learning, investigators have almost invariably employed procedures which restructure the problem at the point of shift in stimulus-reward relations. For example, a commonly used procedure is to eliminate within-pair variation of the irrelevant dimension during the shift phase. Such alteration in the manner of stimulus pairing of course precludes application of the subproblem analysis.

We have recently applied the analysis to a comparison of R-ED shifts in 4- and 10-year-old children (Tighe, Glick, & Cole, 1971). The children had been trained in a two-dimension, two-pair R-ED comparison in precisely the manner depicted in Fig. 1. Figure 2

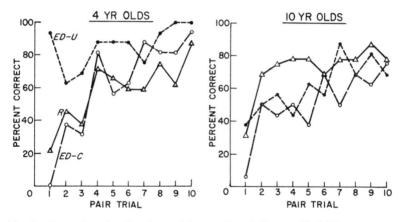

Fig. 2. Group learning functions of 4-year-old and 10-year-old children on reversal (R) shift and on changed (ED-C) and unchanged (ED-U) elements of extradimensional shift. For R, the "pair trial" refers to successive presentations of both stimulus pairs. (From Tighe *et al.*, 1971, by permission of The Psychonomic Society, Inc., Austin, Texas.)

contains the shift performance of each of the age groups in terms of the subproblem analysis. The figure includes the trial-by-trial group learning functions during the shift phase for the changed (reversed) pair of the ED shift (ED-C) and the unchanged pair (ED-U), along with the averaged functions for the two pairs of R shift. Considering the performance of the 4-year-olds, it is apparent that there is a marked difference in the learning on the two ED pairs with subjects exhibiting a high proportion of correct choice on ED-U throughout shift, but a slow acquisition of correct choice to the changed pair (ED-C). It is notable that performance on the pairs of the R shift is similar to that of ED-C. In contrast to the 4-year-olds, the performance of the 10-year-old children suffers on *both* ED-U and ED-C, and this deterioration of performance is marked at the outset of shift learning. Ten of the 16 older children in this sample reversed their choice on their first postshift exposure to ED-U after experiencing nonreward on ED-C. That is, nonreinforcement on ED-C caused these subjects to change response on ED-U even though they had never experienced nonreward on this pair of the task. In contrast, only one of the 16 4-year-olds showed such spontaneous reversal of choice on ED-U. In fact, seven of these subjects never made an error on the unchanged pair throughout shift learning. All of the older children made at least one error on ED-U during learning. (Subjects were trained to a criterion of nine correct out of ten consecutive responses in both original learning and shift phases.)

These data indicate that while the 10-year-old children learned the stimulus pairs in a unitary manner, the 4-year-olds tended to process the pairs as independent subproblems. Coincidentally, Cole, Gay, Glick, and Sharp (1971) observed a strikingly similar degree of independence in the learning of ED shift stimulus pairs by Liberian children. It is by no means clear, of course, just what process underlies such independent subproblem learning. Hindsight, as usual, suggests several possibilities in addition to that which prompted the analysis. For example, subjects may learn the pairs as instances of a single task, yet they may adopt a "compound solution" (Zeaman & House, 1963). Alternatively, the independence between the learning functions on changed and unchanged problem elements might conceivably be derived from Spence's model. Nevertheless, the observations of independent subproblem learning have clear and important implications for the study of learning. First, and most generally, the fact that some subject populations learn such "obviously" related problem elements in unrelated fashion is counterintuitive and underscores that there are serious gaps in our knowledge about the ways in which subjects may treat the material of standard laboratory tasks. Second, independent subproblem learning as in Fig. 2 challenges some widely held formal assumptions regarding the nature of discrimination learning. For example, this pattern strains general expectations from attention theories, which assume that discrimination learning proceeds on the basis of dimensional observing responses common to the task instances. Finally, the subproblem analysis, considered as a technique, promises more direct measure of the transfer processes at work in shift learning and related problems than has been obtained to date. Investigators in this area have focused exclusively on comparisons of overall trial and error scores under various types of shift, and have sought to infer the nature of the learning process from such comparisons. But Fig. 2 delineates patterns of learning which may be basic to understanding shift learning, yet which are in no way indicated by simple compilation of trial and error scores.

In view of these implications, the subproblem analysis of discrimination learning was pursued in relation to a variety of subject populations and test conditions. This paper summarizes and interprets that research program. The paper is divided into two broad sections, the first dealing with studies of animal learning and the second with analysis of children's learning. In presenting the empirical aspects of these sections, the term "independent subproblem learning" *will be used in a purely descriptive sense to refer to unrelated learning functions on the elements of an ED shift problem.* More specifically, the term will be applied to subproblem patterns in which the proportion of correct response on ED-U remains at or near unity throughout learning.

II. Subproblem Analysis of Animal Discrimination Learning

A. Generality of Independent Subproblem Learning

The initial concern in this research was simply to examine the pattern of subproblem learning in several species. These analyses were carried out within comparisons of R and ED shifts in order to test a possible relation between the pattern of subproblem learning and the relative ease of the two types of shift. The general procedure in each of these studies was that shown in Fig. 1. Subjects were trained in simultaneous discrimination tasks involving two visual dimensions plus position. The relevant cues in the pre- and postshift discriminations were always selected from the visual dimensions. All subjects received 20 noncorrection trials per day with food reinforcement and were trained to a rigorous criterion of solution in both the initial discrimination and shift phase (90% correct choice over a 2-day block). Within this general procedure, separate experiments studied the shift learning of rats (Tighe & Frey, 1972), pigeons (Tighe & Graf, 1972), and turtles (Graf & Tighe, 1971). The rats were trained to choose between alleys varying in brightness and in the presence *vs.* absence of chains. The pigeons were trained in a conventional operant (key-peck) conditioning chamber to choose between keys varying in hue and in steady *vs.* flickering light. The turtles were trained in a Y-maze to choose between two endboxes containing light patches varying in hue and in brightness.

Figure 3 presents the outcomes of these experiments in terms of the subproblem analysis. It shows the group learning functions of each species for the changed (ED-C) and unchanged (ED-U) pairs of the ED shift along with the averaged functions for both pairs of the R shift. The data are further broken down by the dimension relevant during the shift phase.

Each species exhibits marked independence in subproblem learning. The performance of turtles with brightness relevant is particularly noteworthy. None of these subjects made an error on the unchanged pair at any time during ED shift but concurrently exhibited an error rate on the other stimulus pair of the same "problem" which closely paralleled the error rate of subjects undergoing full R shift. In general, for each species and test condition, performance on ED-U hovers near or above criterion (90% correct), while there is a gradual, reversal-like acquisition of correct response to ED-C. It is notable that there is some reduction in independence when the relevant dimension is the less salient one (as measured by pre- and postshift learning scores), at least in the case of the rats and turtles. We will return to this point in a later section.

Two additional observations are pertinent to the data in Fig. 3. First, in an experiment just completed we tested subproblem learning in pigeons with the stimuli described above for these subjects but with the four stimulus compounds presented singly under the typical operant "go-no go" procedure. Again, independent subproblem learning was observed during an ED shift. Second, Medin (1972) recently applied the subproblem analysis to rhesus monkeys using the paradigm of Fig. 1 and testing subjects under the usual WGTA[1a] procedures with choice objects differing in color and form. Consistent with the foregoing studies, Medin found that errors during ED shift were confined almost exclusively to the changed subproblem, while performance on the unchanged pair continued at the preshift level. Significantly, total errors on the changed subproblem of ED shift were almost exactly one-half of the total errors on R shift.

Although the question of the significance of reported phylogenetic differences in relative ease of R *vs.* ED shifts is not a primary concern of this paper, it is notable that each of the species tested under

[1a] Wisconsin General Test Apparatus.

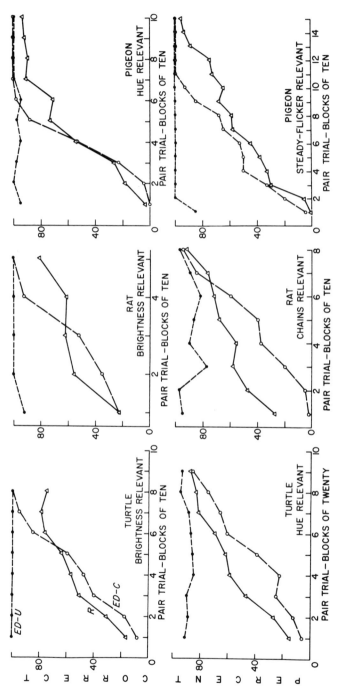

Fig. 3. Subproblem analysis of shift learning in rats, turtles, and pigeons, showing group learning functions on reversal (R, triangles) shift and on changed (ED-C, open dots) and unchanged (ED-U, solid dots) elements of an extradimensional shift. For R, pair trial refers to successive presentations of both stimulus pairs.

the subproblem analysis (including monkeys) was found to accomplish ED shift more readily than R shift. The curves of Fig. 3 indicate that this outcome is not properly interpretable in terms of dimensional or conceptual transfer processes, as generally supposed, but rather in terms of the difficulty of relearning the specific reversal subproblems posed by each condition. In essence, ED was faster than R because ED shift poses one reversal subproblem while R shift poses two reversal subproblems.

To summarize, the answer to our first question is clear—independent subproblem learning is found in infrahuman learning, and moreover this solution mode appears to characterize the shift learning of infrahuman subjects over a wide range of testing conditions (apparatus, stimulus dimensions, conditioning procedures). Having established the generality of the phenomenon under the paradigm of Fig. 1, we next sought to define its limits in animal learning. The general idea was to study subproblem learning in relation to training conditions which, on the basis of general principles, could be held likely to diminish or eliminate independence in subproblem learning. In this research, we focused on subproblem learning in a single species, the rat.

B.   PATTERN OF SUBPROBLEM LEARNING IN RELATION TO TASK CONDITIONS

We earlier noted that independent subproblem learning poses difficulties for attention theories of discrimination learning (e.g., Lovejoy, 1965; Sutherland, 1964; Zeaman & House, 1963). Let us examine this assertion in more detail. Attention theories assume that discrimination learning in all subjects is a chained, two-stage process involving, first, selective response to the task dimensions and, second, instrumental choice of cue values on the dimension(s) sampled. It is further assumed that selective attention to the relevant dimension is prerequisite to learning of the correct choice response, and that strengthening and weakening of the dimensional attention response follow reinforcement and nonreinforcement of the subsequent cue-choice response.

Under this view of learning, choice responses on the pairs of a shift task such as that of Fig. 1 are seen as being linked to an attentional response common to the pairs. At the start of ED shift that attentional response is focused, of course, on the previously relevant dimension. But if this view is correct, then the weakening of attentional response to the formerly relevant dimension as a consequence of nonreinforcement on ED-C should be reflected in disruption of performance on ED-U. Such disruption may or may not occur early in shift learning but would certainly be expected as correct choice on ED-C reaches the chance level. Moreover, at this point a period of chance responding on both ED-U and ED-C would be expected, since following extinction of attentional response to the formerly relevant dimension subjects would have an initial likelihood of sampling both relevant and irrelevant cues (Sutherland, 1964; Zeaman & House, 1963). But the functions in Fig. 3 provide no evidence that transfer learning involved extinction and acquisition of dimensional observing responses (i.e., involved a redirection of attention to dimensions) prior to solution of the ED problem. Rather, these subjects appear to have simply shifted choice responses on the specific stimulus objects affected by the altered reinforcement contingencies. It should be emphasized that it is the sustained correct performance on ED-U that is the critical evidence here. That is, the fact that subjects are more likely to perform correctly on ED-U than on ED-C over the initial phase of shift is consistent with an attentional interpretation; what is damaging to this viewpoint is the fact that eventual recovery of correct performance on ED-C is not accompanied by performance change on ED-U. It is for this reason that it is useful to know not only how many errors are made on ED-U, but at what point in learning they occur, as shown in the subproblem curves.

Independent subproblem learning in animals, then, is clearly inconsistent with the expectations of attention theory. But, more importantly, the argument from the subproblem data could also be directed against any theory of discrimination learning which assumes that subjects solve such tasks by relating a unitary stimulus aspect to reward, however that abstract relation might be mediated. In essence, the point we wish to make here is that observation of independent subproblem learning means that problem solution does not involve abstraction in any conceptual sense. Given this general interpretation of the significance of independent subproblem learning, it is of some importance to determine if our previous observations are representative of infrahuman learning. There are data which could be used to argue that infrahuman subjects do typically abstract at a conceptual level in discrimination learning (e.g., Shepp & Eimas, 1964), and thus one is led to wonder whether the conditions of the foregoing subproblem experiments may not have been such as to bias against an abstract learning mode.

In reviewing our subproblem learning experiments for this possibility, it was noted that all the observations of independence in sub-problem learning were made in shift tasks in which the relevant dimension was one of two or more simultaneously varying visual dimensions. Conceivably, this circumstance gave the cue sets an integral quality (Garner, 1970) which rendered abstraction of the relevant feature difficult for these subjects and constrained them to adopt a more concrete, and perhaps atypical, solution mode. Therefore, our first experiment in this series sought to test subproblem learning on cue sets which could reasonably be held to be readily separable by the organisms involved, and which at the same time would pose relatively simple discrimination-shift problems.

1. Experiment I

a. Apparatus. The subjects were trained in an enclosed cross-maze (see Fig. 4) consisting of 10-inch long start boxes (A1, A2), 9-inch long stems (B areas), and 33-inch long choice arms (C1, C2).

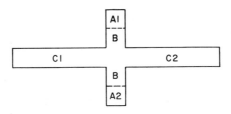

Fig. 4. Schematic diagram of the cross-maze. A1 and A2 are start boxes; C1 and C2 are choice arms.

Each of these units was $3\frac{3}{4}$ inches wide and $5\frac{3}{4}$ inches deep, and all interior walls and floors were painted gray. A standard rat lever protruded through the end wall of each choice arm, and mounted beneath each lever was a metal food dish connected to an automatic 45-mg pellet dispenser. Guillotine doors were located at the juncture of the start boxes and stems and at the entrance to each choice arm, the latter serving as retrace doors. The top of each choice arm was covered by frosted Plexiglas extending over the entire length of the arm. Each arm was independently illuminated by a row of sixteen $7\frac{1}{2}$-W bulbs mounted in a box above the Plexiglas sheet which formed the bottom of the box and the ceiling of the choice arm. A white-noise source with output at 65 dB (re .0002 dynes/cm^2) was located immediately beneath the midpoint of the apparatus.

b. Procedure. The subjects were eight, naive, 90-day-old male rats from the Holtzman, Wisconsin supply. The subjects were reduced to between 80 and 85% of their free-feeding weight 10 days prior to training and were maintained at that level throughout training

The subjects received 4 days of pretraining during which period the maze arms were equally illuminated at a value intermediate to the training values described below. The first 2 days of pretraining were concerned with shaping a reliable bar-press response under CRF in each choice arm. On Day 3, subjects made 10 free-choice runs through the maze from each start box in a random order, each run terminating in food reinforcement via a bar press. The choices on these trials provided a measure of a subject's position preference, and these measures were balanced over the later S+ assignments in discrimination training. Day 4 pretraining was the same as that of Day 3, except that by closing the appropriate choice arm door prior to the start of each run each subject was forced into a pattern of position choices opposite to that exhibited on Day 3.

Discrimination training began on Day 5 and proceeded at the rate of 20, massed, noncorrection trials per day thereafter. Correct choices were rewarded by a single 45-mg pellet contingent upon a bar press. Throughout training, one choice arm was set at a brightness of 4.3 fc and the other at a brightness of 0.28 fc, as measured at the midpoint of the arm by a Macbeth Illuminometer. Half of the subjects' 20 daily trials started from A1 and half from A2. The position of the brightness cues also varied so that on half of the A1 and A2 trials the brighter arm was C1. The order in which these stimulus configurations were presented was random, with the restriction that the same configuration was not repeated more than twice in succession. Subjects were thus confronted with two stimulus pairs at the choice point—bright alley-left vs. dim alley-right, and bright alley-right vs. dim alley-left; and the procedure precluded any possible conjoint operation of extramaze place cues with either the brightness or position cue sets.

Within this training procedure, half of the subjects learned a brightness discrimination followed by a position discrimination, while for the other half this order was reversed. Subjects were trained to a criterion of 90% correct choice on each of 2 successive days in both of their discriminations. This training sequence, of course, comprises an ED shift of the form illustrated in Fig. 1, and thus the second discrimination confronts a subject with a stimulus pairing for which the reward relations of the first task are maintained along with a stimulus pair on which the reward relations are reversed. For example, a subject who is shifted from "bright" as S+ to "left" as S+ continues to be rewarded for choosing the bright alley on the left as opposed to the dim alley on the right but has to learn to reverse response to the pairing of bright alley on the right *vs.* dim alley on the left. Each subject received one of the eight possible S+ sequences (e.g., bright to left).

Abstraction of the relevant cue should be an easier matter in this discrimination task than in those used in the previous studies of subproblem learning. Presumably, in the present experiment there are only two effective cue sets, rather than three, and the relevant dimension is less integral with the irrelevant feature. Thus, the isolation of, say, "go right" in relation to reward requires only that the subject not attend concurrently to bright-dim cues, and both the modality separation and the internal-external separation of these cue sets should render such selective attention relatively easy.

c. Results. Figure 5 shows the group learning functions on the unchanged (interrupted lines) and changed (solid lines) problem elements for each condition of dimension relevance. Table I presents each subject's total number of errors on changed and unchanged pairs and total trials to criterion.

Independence is manifest, and there is little individual variation in performance on the changed and unchanged elements of the problem. Surprisingly, the rats do not appear to have differentiated out the stimulus-reward relation common to the instances of this simple conceptual task; rather, these data point to extremely strong contextual determination of performance on each subproblem—bright right *vs.* dim left and bright left *vs.* dim right.

TABLE I

NUMBER OF ERRORS ON CHANGED (C) AND UNCHANGED (U) ELEMENTS AND NUMBER OF TRIALS TO CRITERION FOR EACH SUBJECT

Dimension relevant in shift	U	C	Trials
	7	109	340
	2	59	160
Position	9	73	220
	4	95	220
	4	66	180
	1	116	300
Brightness	2	57	180
	11	67	180

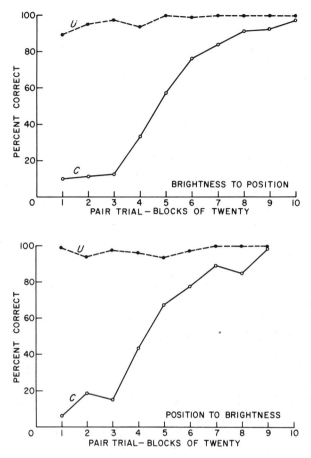

Fig. 5.   Group learning functions of rats on unchanged (U) and changed (C) instances of an extradimensional shift within two-dimensional tasks.

2. Experiment II

In considering the outcome of Experiment I it might be argued that the rat is highly sensitive to each of the cue sets involved and therefore may have attained criterion in the initial discrimination still having a relatively high probability of attending to the irrelevant cues as well as to the relevant cues, regardless of which particular cues were relevant. Under this view, training may have been insufficient to produce isolation of the critical cue-reward relations, and thus subjects may have been likely to utilize an atypical compounding strategy in shift learning. However, with continued training evidence of such abstraction would presumably appear as a consequence of continued strengthening of the appropriate mediating response. Attention theorists have argued that postcriterion training does further develop control of discriminative response by the relevant stimulus class (e.g., Sutherland, 1964), and the well-known overlearning-reversal effect (ORE) is generally cited as an instance of the operation of such further selective learning. Accordingly, it was decided to test this line of argument by repeating Experiment I with overtraining (OT) in the initial discrimination problem.

The ORE literature was consulted to aid determination of the amount of OT to be used in Experiment II. However, facilitation of reversal has by no means been the invariable outcome of OT and the factors underlying the discrepant outcomes are not fully understood. Amount of OT can be expressed both as the absolute number of OT trials and as the ratio of number of OT trials and trials required to solve the discrimination problem. A survey of a score or so studies of rat discrimination-reversal learning found that, with consideration of both OT measures, OT was likely to facilitate learning when between 100 and 150 OT trials were used, while OT was generally without effect when between 200 to 300 trials were used. The strategy followed here was to use two degrees of OT, one from within each of these ranges. The final OT values selected were chosen so that the ratio measures of OT would approximate those of the comparison studies.

a. Procedure. The subjects were 16 naive, 90-day-old male rats from the Holtzman supply. All details of apparatus, deprivation operations, pretraining, and discrimination training were identical to those of Experiment I with the exception of OT. The two degrees of OT, 140 and 320 trials, were imposed within each training sequence (brightness to position and position to brightness) with four subjects assigned to each treatment. OT was administered at the rate of 20 trials per day, and shift training began the day following termination of OT.

b. Results. As in the previous experiments our major concern is with pattern of performance. Figure 6 shows the by-now familiar subproblem analysis for each treatment condition, and Table II provides the total errors on changed and unchanged instances for individual subjects. It is clear that OT did not alter the pattern of subproblem learning, and we therefore reject the hypothesis that the failure to find a dimensional or abstract solution mode in these subproblem experiments is due to insufficient training on the relevant cues.

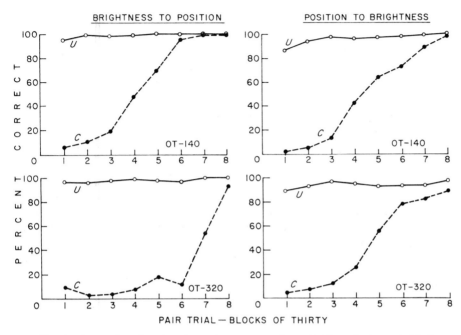

Fig. 6. Group learning functions of rats on unchanged (U) and changed (C) instances of an extradimensional shift within two-dimensional tasks and under two degrees of overtraining (OT).

TABLE II

NUMBER OF ERRORS ON CHANGED (C) AND UNCHANGED (U) ELEMENTS
AND NUMBER OF TRIALS TO CRITERION FOR EACH SUBJECT

Training condition	U	C	Trials	Training condition	U	C	Trials
	3	105	260		10	176	400
Position	0	103	240	Position	3	201	440
140 OT[a]	2	116	320	320 OT	3	158	400
	5	81	280		7	258	580
	7	83	200		11	89	240
Brightness	4	81	200	Brightness	3	112	300
140 OT	7	132	320	320 OT	7	144	360
	13	189	400		32	186	500

[a] OT, overtraining.

Another aspect of the data is worthy of comment. When the curves of Fig. 5 are compared with those of Fig. 6 (bearing in mind that the latter are plotted in 30-trial blocks and the former in 20-trial blocks), it is evident that OT produced a prolongation of the high error rate on the changed instance in the initial stage of shift while at the same time tending to accelerate subsequent reversal of performance on this instance. This pattern is most clearly seen by comparing criterion and 320-OT curves on the brightness to position sequence. The criterion group performance on the changed instance exceeds 50% correct choice by trial 100, while the OT-320 group performance does not attain 50% correct until trial 210. But transition from 20% correct to criterion performance requires about 100 trials for the criterion subjects but only about 60 trials for the overtrained subjects.

This outcome is reminiscent of the prediction from attention theory that while overtraining prior to reversal should increase responses to the former S+, it should also eliminate an otherwise expected period of chance responding following extinction of instrumental response to the former S+ (Sutherland, 1964). The period of chance response is expected in criterion-trained subjects because concomitant with extinction of response to the former S+ there is extinction of the attentional response to the relevant dimension. Consequently, there is likely to be a period of time before a subject resamples the relevant cues, and such resampling is necessary before learning of the correct choice response can proceed. Overtraining, however, is assumed to strengthen selective attention to the relevant dimension to a degree sufficient to insure that a subject is still attending to it upon extinction of response to the former S+; hence the response learning (reversal) can progress rapidly. It is in this way that attention theory accounts for observations of facilitation of reversal learning by overtraining. Patterns of reversal learning consistent with this analysis have been observed in rats (Sutherland, 1964).

What is significant about the data of Experiment II in this regard is that we observe a phenomenon similar to that predicted by attention theorists but in the context of a behavior pattern which indicates that subjects did *not* discriminate on the basis of dimensional mediating responses. Explanation of the ORE, then, does not, as generally supposed, require a mediational model of learning.

3. Experiment III

One interpretation of independence in subproblem learning is that it reflects an incapacity to abstract and use the relevant feature as specified by the particular cues employed. Alternatively, it might be argued that independence occurs not because subjects are incapable of detecting the feature-reward relations, but because separate learning of specific instances is the less difficult of the two solution modes under the given conditions. Under this view, independence in subproblem learning might decrease when irrelevant dimensions are added to the task due to the disproportionate increase in number of subproblems and hence in the relative difficulty of the independent solution mode. This hypothesis was tested in Experiment III by adding a visual dimension to the conditions of Experiment I to increase the number of subproblems from two to four.

a. *Procedure.* The subjects were 18 naive, male albino rats from the Holtzman supply. All details of experimental procedure were the same as in Experiment I. The added visual feature was the presence of alternating black and white 3-inch-wide stripes along the floor of one choice arm as opposed to a solid black flooring in the other. During training placement of the striped flooring was combined equally often with each position and brightness cue to yield four different choice-point stimulus configurations. During the shift phase, then, two of these instances underwent a reversal in stimulus-reward relations, while two maintained the reward relations of the initial discrimination. Six subjects were assigned to each of three ED shift training sequences: stripes (relevant) to brightness, brightness to position, and position to stripes. Within each shift condition, all of the possible S+ sequences were utilized.

b. *Results.* Table III presents the errors on C and U instances for each subject. These data show clearly that the increase in number of subproblems does not affect solution mode for subjects trained on either the stripes to brightness or the brightness to position sequences. It is apparent from the figures in Table III that subproblem curves for these training sequences would closely resemble those seen in Experiments I and II.

However, the position to stripes sequence produced the first clear evidence of nonindependence in subproblem learning. All subjects in this condition showed a high error rate on the unchanged instances as compared to subjects in the other training sequences. There was, however, considerable variation in the proportion of errors on unchanged and changed instances among subjects shifted from position to stripes. For this reason, subproblem curves were determined for individual subjects in this condition (see Fig. 7). Two subjects (Nos. 34 and 41) show marked dependence in subproblem learning, with performance on the unchanged elements declining to

TABLE III

NUMBER OF ERRORS ON CHANGED (C) AND UNCHANGED (U) INSTANCES AND NUMBER OF TRIALS TO CRITERION FOR EACH SUBJECT

	Stripes to brightness			Brightness to position			Position to stripes		
	U	C	Trials	U	C	Trials	U	C	Trials
	4	117	320	1	115	300	35	106	260
	1	82	220	3	48	120	34	109	300
	9	132	320	2	189	400	46	182	520
	6	72	200	6	118	280	108	210	640
	10	79	260	1	96	220	86	185	600
	2	68	200	3	155	340	26	192	540
Mean	5.3	91.7		2.7	120.2		55.8	164.0	

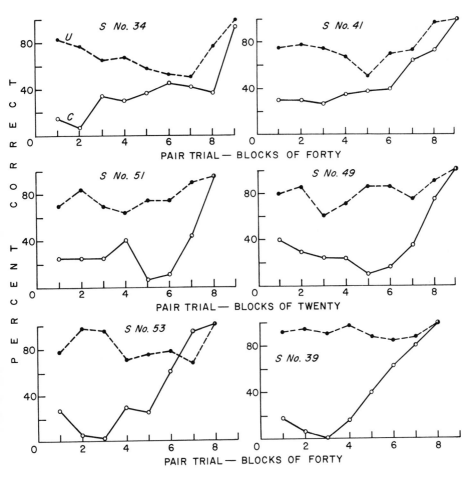

Fig. 7. Individual learning functions of rats on unchanged (U) and changed (C) instances of an extradimensional shift (position relevant to stripes relevant) within a three-dimensional task.

chance. It is notable that for these subjects percentages of correct response for changed and unchanged instances tend toward a complementary relationship. Such a relationship can occur only when subjects choose the same cue an equal proportion of trials under the U and C conditions.

With one exception, the remaining subjects in this group show at least a 30% decrease in correct response in the U condition, indicating considerable negative transfer from nonreinforcement of the former S+ on the C trials. Only Subject No. 39 sustains criterion or near-criterion performance on the unchanged instances throughout shift learning.

Other noteworthy effects of adding the stripes cues are suggested by considering the learning scores in the initial discriminations of Experiments I–III. Considering, first, learning with brightness cues relevant, the median number of trials to criterion in original learning for subjects trained with stripe cues absent (Experiments I and II) and with stripe cues present (Experiment III) were 130 and 200, respectively. A median test on these distributions yielded an exact p of .06. Addition of the stripe cues, then, appears to have slowed learning of the brightness discrimination. Retardation of learning by addition of an irrelevant feature is to be expected and has been repeatedly demonstrated (Bourne & Restle, 1959). But surprisingly, the data do not indicate a similar effect when position cues were relevant. The corresponding median values for this condition were 260 and 190 trials. Addition of the stripe cues did not slow learning but in fact tended to facilitate learning, although the latter trend was not significant by a median test.

In sum, when visual cues were relevant in the initial discrimination, the addition of an irrelevant visual feature slowed learning and resulted in the usual pattern of independent subproblem learning. But when position cues were relevant in the initial discrimination, addition of an irrelevant visual dimension did not retard learning and resulted in nonindependent patterns of subproblem learning. These relations are intriguing but are not convincingly established by the data of Experiment III. Accordingly, it was decided to further test the effect of visual complexity by adding another visual feature to the task on the presumption that the suspected relations should reappear, and likely in augmented form, under a higher degree of visual complexity.

4. Experiment IV

a. Procedure. The subjects were 24 naive, male albino rats from the Holtzman supply. With exception of the following details, the experimental procedure duplicated that of Experiment III. The added visual feature was steady *vs.* flickering light in opposing choice arms. Flicker stimuli were obtained by routing the power which energized the bank of overhead lights through a Grason-Stadler E783F multivibrator slowed by a capacitor circuit to 8 Hz. Subjects received 16 trials per day consisting of two trials of each of the eight possible subproblems generated by the combinations of the three visual features plus position. In the initial and shift tasks subjects were trained to a criterion of no more than three errors over 2 consecutive days. Six subjects were assigned to each of three ED shift training sequences: position to stripes, position to brightness, and stripes to brightness. The first and third of these sequences were used in Experiment III. The position to brightness sequence was added in Experiment IV in order to determine whether the nonindependence observed in the position to stripes sequence of Experiment III was unique to the presence of the stripes cues. An additional group of six subjects was trained with steady-flicker relevant but was not shifted. The latter subjects were added in order to test the discriminability of the flicker cues under the conditions of this experiment. Within each shift condition all of the possible S+ sequences were utilized.

b. *Results.* i. *Learning in the initial discriminations.* Considering, first, learning with position cues relevant, the median number of trials to criterion was 160 ($N = 12$), as compared to a median of 190 trials in Experiment III (two visual features irrelevant, $N = 6$) and a median of 250 trials in Experiments I–II (one visual feature irrelevant, $N = 12$). The difference between the scores of the present experiment and Experiments I–II in this regard is significant by a median test (exact $p < .05$). Experiment IV, then, confirms and extends the trend evident in Experiments I–III: when position cues are relevant, increase in the number of irrelevant visual dimensions does not retard learning, but rather has a facilitating effect. Precisely the opposite relation obtained for the condition of visual cues relevant. The median number of trials to criterion for subjects who had stripe cues relevant in the present experiment was 816, as compared to the median of 460 trials for subjects with stripes relevant in Experiment III (median test, exact $p < .05$). Although these are across-experiment comparisons and therefore might be regarded with some caution, it should be noted that conditions of training, including experimenters, were constant across Experiments I–IV.

It should also be noted that learning proved to be inordinately difficult for subjects trained with visual cues relevant. One index of the task difficulty is the fact that three subjects trained with stripes relevant and five trained with flicker cues relevant required more than 1000 trials to attain criterion in the initial discrimination. In addition, several subjects did not learn visual shift-discriminations within a preset 1000 trial limit (see below). These figures suggest that task difficulty in this experiment approached the limit of the subject's learning capacity (and the experimenter's tolerance).

ii. Subproblem learning.   The patterns of subproblem learning in Experiment IV were largely consistent with the trend seen in Experiment III. It will be recalled that the position to stripes sequence in Experiment III produced nonindependent subproblem learning, and on this basis it might be expected that nonindependence should again obtain under the higher degree of visual irrelevancy in Experiment IV. Figure 8 shows that this expectation was clearly confirmed. (Two subjects in this training sequence did not attain criterion in the shift phase in the 1000 trial limit set and so were discontinued. Since these subjects were still below 50% correct choice on ED-C at the termination of training, their subproblem curves were not included in Fig. 8.)

A similar pattern of subproblem learning might be expected for the subjects trained on the position to brightness sequence on the presumption that nonindependence is likely to obtain for any position to visual sequence. But the data for this condition are not uniform. As seen in Fig. 9, subjects numbered 14, 21, and 54 do show nonindependent subproblem learning, while the curves of subjects numbered 62 and 57 are difficult to interpret in any clear fashion.

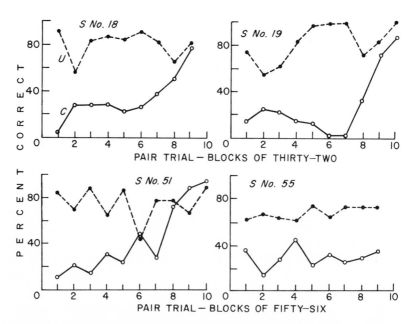

Fig. 8.   Individual learning functions of rats on unchanged (U) and changed (C) instances of an extradimensional shift (position relevant to stripes relevant) within a four-dimensional task.

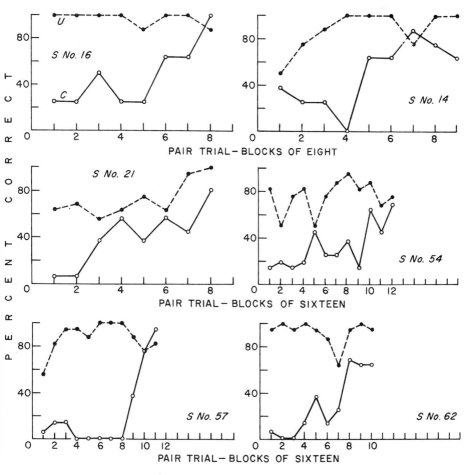

Fig. 9. Individual learning functions of rats on unchanged (U) and changed (C) instances of an extradimensional shift (position relevant to brightness relevant) within a four-dimensional task.

The curves of subject number 16, on the other hand, meet the criterion of independence.

In regard to learning under the stripes to brightness sequence, independent subproblem learning appears to be the dominant solution mode (see Fig. 10), and this outcome is consistent with the data for the "visual to visual" training sequence of Experiment III. (Data from one nonlearner were omitted from Fig. 10.)

The data of Experiment IV point up some limitations to the graphical analysis of pattern of subproblem learning, limitations

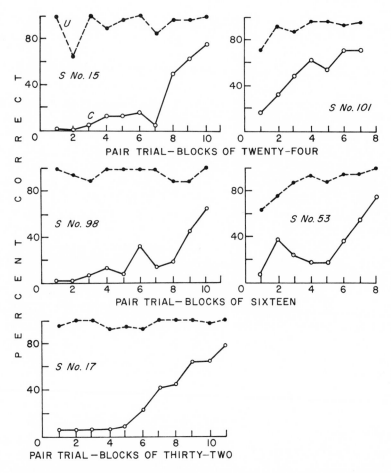

Fig. 10. Individual learning functions of rats on unchanged (U) and changed (C) instances of an extradimensional shift (stripes relevant to brightness relevant) within a four-dimensional task.

which were not apparent with the more uniform data of Experiments I, II, and III. A number of the ED-U curves in Experiment IV present irregular patterns which are difficult to interpret or to classify in terms of independent *vs.* dependent solution modes. For example, several ED-U curves show occasional but sharp deterioration in performance alternating with what is otherwise criterion-level performance. In such cases it would be desirable to have a numerical measure of a subject's overall tendency toward independence throughout shift learning. One such measure is the ratio of errors on ED-C instances to ED-U instances during the shift learning, and Table IV shows this measure for each subject in Experiments I–IV (collapsing over the overtraining conditions of Experiment II).

Table IV helps to clarify the relations between training conditions and pattern of subproblem learning appearing in Experiment IV and the earlier studies, and provides a convenient way to summarize the major findings. First, it is seen that independence (ratios approaching zero) prevails under low degrees of task complexity (Experiments I and II), and despite extensive training prior to the shift phase. Second, increasing task complexity by adding irrelevant visual features (Experiments III and IV) does reduce independence in subproblem learning, but this relation is clearly established only for subjects initially trained with position cues relevant. Third, there are marked individual differences in subproblem learning under high task complexity. This is most apparent for the position to brightness sequence of Experiment IV. This condition includes ratios of .03 and .48, which approach the limits of independence and dependence as seen in these studies; and subjects in this condition are equally divided between independent and nonindependent solution modes. Finally, these observations on subproblem learning should be considered in relation to the finding that increasing the number of irrelevant visual features retarded learning of the initial discrimination when visual cues were relevant but facilitated learning when position cues were relevant.

5. Experiment V

One additional effort to modify the pattern of subproblem learning will be noted. This effort differed from the foregoing studies in that it attempted to reduce independence by altering the standard discrimination training procedure itself. The experiment has been reported elsewhere (Tighe & Frey, 1972) and so will simply be summarized here.

Rats were trained in an R-ED shift comparison of the type illustrated in Fig. 1. The apparatus consisted of two duplicate double-alley discrimination training units connected end to end. The stimulus dimensions consisted of differential alley brightness (black *vs.* white) and presence *vs.* absence of chains in the alleys. Left-right position of these cues also varied and was always irrelevant. Three conditions of training were employed. Condition I involved standard simultaneous discrimination training. The two stimulus pairs (black-chains *vs.* white-no chains, and white-chains *vs.* black-no

TABLE IV

RATIO OF ERRORS BY INDIVIDUAL SUBJECTS ON UNCHANGED TO
CHANGED INSTANCES UNDER EACH TRAINING SEQUENCE
IN EXPERIMENTS I TO IV

	Position to brightness	Brightness to position
Experiment I	.164	.064
	.061	.034
	.009	.123
	.035	.042
Mean	.067	.066

	Position to brightness	Brightness to position
Experiment II	.084	.029
	.049	.000
	.053	.017
	.069	.062
	.124	.057
	.027	.015
	.049	.019
	.172	.027
Mean	.078	.028

	Position to stripes	Brightness to position	Stripes to brightness
Experiment III	.330	.009	.034
	.312	.063	.012
	.253	.011	.068
	.514	.051	.083
	.464	.010	.127
	.135	.019	.029
Mean	.335	.027	.059

	Position to stripes	Position to brightness	Stripes to brightness
Experiment IV	.300	.029	.099
	.239	.479	.042
	.420	.265	.205
	.449	.362	.213
		.161	.054
		.116	
Mean	.352	.235	.123

chains) were presented successively with a constant intertrial interval and with reinforcement for each correct response. In this condition the stimulus pairs were presented only in the first of the two connected discrimination units. Conditions II and III were designed to increase the likelihood that subjects process the stimulus pairs as instances of a single problem. Condition II was identical to I, except that by employing both discrimination training units subjects were made to respond to the two pairs in temporally and spatially defined "runs," with reinforcement following choice to each pair. This procedure was adopted in view of Leary's observation (1962) that monkeys tended to generalize reversal behavior across unrelated stimulus pairs when these were presented within a "list structure." In Condition III the pairs were presented as in II, but a subject was reinforced *only* if there had been correct choice to *both* pairs in the run. This training made reinforcement (and mastery of the problem) contingent upon occurrence of a common response across the constituent pairs.

In Conditions II and III the two discrimination training units always contained the two different stimulus pairs on any run, but the location of a particular pair varied randomly from one run to the next. The order in which the pairs were presented over the entire training sequence and the sequence of left *vs.* right position of pair members were identical for Conditions I, II, and III. Thus, the three conditions provided different degrees of stimulus and response organization of the constituent pairs but within the same overall presentation sequence.

The outcome was clear. Independent subproblem learning was exhibited under all training conditions, and ED was faster than R shift. The subproblem curves closely resembled those shown for rats in Fig. 3.

To recapitulate briefly, the only training condition which has been found to substantially reduce independence in subproblem learning is that in which position cues were relevant within a high degree of visual irrelevance. Under all other training conditions, learning in ED shift was largely confined to the changed elements of the problem.

C. Theoretical Treatment

There are three primary outcomes of the subproblem experiments which any explanatory treatment must resolve: (1) the fact of independent subproblem learning itself, i.e., observations of sustained criterion-level performance on the unchanged instances of an ED problem; (2) the finding that independence in subproblem learning decreases as task complexity increases and chiefly for the case of position to visual training sequences; (3) the finding that increase in visual irrelevance facilitates position discrimination learning but retards visual discriminations.

We have already indicated our belief that current attentional models of learning fail to handle satisfactorily the first of these outcomes in the case of animal learning. The arguments advanced earlier (Section II, B) would hold not only for single-look models (Lovejoy, 1965; Sutherland, 1964; Zeaman & House, 1963) but also for models allowing learning about more than one cue on a trial (Sutherland & Mackintosh, 1971). Although models of the latter type might allow a rat to learn something about, say, position while responding to brightness (as under the conditions of Experiments I and II), such models still imply a decrease in proportion correct on U instances because the consistent nonrewards on C instances must drastically reduce the controlling dimensional responses common to U and C trials. But as we have seen, the proportion correct on U instances remained near unity throughout ED learning in a number of the subproblem experiments.

Conceivably, attention theory might be salvaged in this situation if, as some attention theorists have suggested, cue compounds themselves may on occasion form stimulus dimensions and be processed in the same manner as any single distinguishing feature of stimulation (Zeaman & House, 1963). Thus, in a position-brightness task of the type used in Experiments I and II, the compounds "bright-right, dim-left," and "bright-left, dim-right" could each be considered a dimension. A subject might then learn to reverse choice on the cues within one dimension without interference on the other compound set. While such a view permits application of attention theory in a formal sense, it does so at the price of denying to the learning process the highly selective, abstract character claimed by the theory. Moreover, resort by attention models to such stimulus compounding is without value unless accompanied by specification of the conditions under which stimulus compounds rather than isolated dimensions become the effective stimuli.

Again considering only the first of the three outcomes noted above, i.e., considering only the phenomenon of independent subproblem learning, Spence's theory (1936) would appear to provide a logical alternative to two-stage models. The applicability of Spence's model to the subproblem data was accomplished by computer simulation using a program developed by Wolford and Bower (1969) that simulates, under the assumptions of Spence's theory, the learning of R and ED shifts within a discrimination involving one relevant and one irrelevant dimension. The parameters varied in the simulation are the strengths of the component habits at the outset of the initial discrimination (e.g., the strength of approach to "bright," "dim," "left," etc.).

In the present application, for each set of starting weights a group of 90 "stat rats" was run under the ED shift with the program modified so as to provide an output of the proportion of correct responses on each trial for each of the ED subproblems (i.e., for ED-U and ED-C). The values of the initial habit strengths were varied across the possible combinations of relatively high and low total weight on the relevant and irrelevant dimensions and of relatively large and small difference between the starting weights within the relevant and irrelevant dimensions. Within these combinations, assignment to preferred (higher weight) and nonpreferred cues was also varied. Three degrees of training were used prior to shift—criterion training, criterion training plus 20 overtraining trials, and criterion training plus 100 overtraining trials. In other respects, the simulation was as described in Wolford and Bower (1969).

The most significant outcome was that over a wide range of start vectors the proportion correct on ED-U remained at or near unity throughout shift, while the proportion correct on ED-C climbed in reversal-like fashion. Thus, marked independence in subproblem learning, similar to that seen in the experimental data, was a likely outcome of the model. In addition, independence in subproblem learning was not diminished under overtraining, an outcome consistent with the data of Experiment II. Finally, certain start vectors were likely to depress ED-U performance to the point of overlap with ED-C. In general, errors were induced on ED-U as the combined weight of the relevant cues in the initial discrimination became higher relative to that of irrelevant cues, and as the difference between cue weights on the relevant dimension became larger relative to that in the irrelevant cue set. There is evidence of a similar relation in the subproblem experiments. In Fig. 3, it can be seen that errors were induced on the ED-U functions of the rats and turtles only when the more salient (i.e., the more easily discriminated) of the two dimensions was relevant in the initial discrimination. On the other hand, a significant difference in learning rate on the task dimensions was not always associated with difference in pattern of subproblem learning, e.g., see Experiments I and II.

Although these points of agreement between the simulation and experimental data are impressive, the Spence model is nevertheless inadequate to account for the other major outcomes of the subproblem experiments. Since the model assumes that cue weights (component habit strengths) combine in simple additive fashion, it cannot deduce the observed facilitation of position discrimination by the addition of irrelevant visual cues. Similarly, the model provides no basis to account for the selective nature of this facilitation nor for its apparent link with nonindependent subproblem learning. However, these aspects of the subproblem data could be accounted for within the framework of a basically nonselective learning process if it were assumed that the higher degrees of visual irrelevance rendered differentiation of visual cues sufficiently difficult that subjects were biased to attend only to the less "noisy" kinesthetic channel. If so, addition of the visual features would effectively constrain isolation of the relevant cue by subjects trained on position relevant, since the stimuli associated with "go right" and "go left" are presumably the only consistent kinesthetic cues at the choice point. Such isolation would both favor initial discrimination learning and produce nonindependence in ED subproblem learning, since the effects of extinction on the relevant cue would be independent of its context. In contrast, under the above assumptions the added visual feature should produce contrary effects for subjects learning with visual cues relevant. Because of the "noise" in the visual channel, these subjects are biased toward an ineffective strategy, i.e., toward response to position cues. More importantly, solution of the problem ultimately requires these subjects to differentiate the more complex visual input but without the constraint toward isolation of the relevant cue which operates in the animals assigned to position relevant. The result is retardation of learning in the initial discrimination accompanied by the usual pattern of independent subproblem learning.

The overall data are quite consistent with this analysis. Only for subjects assigned to position under high visual irrelevance was there evidence of both fast initial learning and nonindependent subproblem learning. In contrast, subjects assigned to visual cues under high irrelevance required extensive training to solve the initial discrimination and exhibited independent subproblem learning during shift. Finally, when task complexity was low (Experiments I and II), all subjects showed independent subproblem learning even following overtraining in the initial discrimination.

One point of inconsistency is the performance of subjects trained .

under the position to brightness sequence of Experiment IV. The analysis indicates that these subjects should not learn the task instances independently, but Table IV shows that subjects were split evenly between independent and nonindependent solution patterns. Independent subproblem learning would obtain in this condition, however, for any subject who compounded the position and brightness cues in each task instance of the initial discrimination. It seems likely that some subjects solved the problem by such compound learning since the brightness cues are highly salient relative to the other visual cues (by the learning rate measure). The channel selection process postulated above need not be assumed to have an inflexible, all-or-none character.

The outcomes of the subproblem analysis, then, indicate that animals tend to learn stimulus-reward relations nonselectively and isolate cues only when constrained to do so. The "nonselective learning" may be Spencean in nature with associations established to all task cues in proportion to their discriminability. In consequence, correct choice is developed to a stimulus pattern consisting of the relevant cues and some or all of their associated context. In this way, each task instance with its unique context *potentially* constitutes a different and independent discrimination. To the extent that a subject excludes irrelevant features, then the number of different discriminations (independent subproblems) is reduced. But the present data suggest that even under unfavorable conditions subjects tend toward inclusiveness in the formation of relevant cue-context patterns.

However, the subproblem experiments also indicate that nonselectivity in learning may be sharply limited in ways not predicted by Spence's model, as by a channel selection process. It might be postulated that the filtering out of irrelevant context as a consequence of channel or modality selection is but a special case of a general principle that irrelevant cues of low discriminability are excluded from learned associations. If such a principle does hold, then a subject assigned to learn highly salient visual cues might not process less discriminable visual cues, particularly under high task complexity. Such an effect would be detectable in a training sequence involving shift from salient to nonsalient visual cues. For example, subjects trained on a brightness to flicker sequence under the conditions of Experiment IV might show nonindependent subproblem learning. But the subproblem data also suggest that exclusion of cues is limited to cues *less* discriminable than the relevant cues in that independent subproblem learning obtained for both the brightness to position and the stripes to brightness training sequences in Experiments III and IV.

III.   Subproblem Analysis of Children's Discrimination Learning

A.   PATTERN OF SUBPROBLEM LEARNING IN RELATION TO AGE AND TASK CONDITIONS

As we have seen (Fig. 2), subproblem analysis of children's learning within a two-dimension (height and brightness) simultaneous discrimination found that ED-U and ED-C functions of 10-year-olds overlapped throughout shift learning while those of 4-year-olds showed substantial independence. It seemed reasonable to inquire, as we had for our rat subjects, how children's subproblem learning varies with degree of task complexity. Accordingly, Experiment VI tested 4-year-olds and 10-year-olds in a task of low complexity but under training conditions similar to those which obtained in the experiment which generated the data of Fig. 2 (Tighe & Tighe, 1967).

1. Experiment VI

a. Procedure.   The subjects in this and the subsequent experiments were all from the Hanover, New Hampshire area. The subjects were 22 "4-year-old" children (average age 4 years 10 months, range 4 years 2 months to 5 years 5 months) and 17 "10-year-old" children (average age 10 years 11 months, range 10 years 5 months to 11 years 11 months).

The choice stimuli were two wood cylinders 1.5 inches in diameter and 5 inches in height. Both cylinders were hollow at the base and one was painted black and one painted white. These were presented simultaneously about 8 inches apart in a simple turntable apparatus of the type described in T. S. Kendler and Kendler (1959). Essentially, this consisted of a presentation platform with a perpendicular backing mounted on a swivel base. The experimenter sat opposite the subject at a small table, and in setting up the stimulus pairs for each trial rotated the apparatus so the presentation area was blocked from the subject's view. The left *vs.* right positioning of the black and white cylinders was varied according to a Fellows sequence (1967).

Subjects did not keep the marbles won during training, but at the termination of the experiment were given a bag containing 10 nickels and were allowed to choose a prize from an assortment of inexpensive edibles and manipulatables (e.g., M & M's, jacks set). The following instructions were used:

Listen carefully and I will tell you how the game is played. See, there are two blocks here (the experimenter points to the two blocks which he has swiveled into place in front of the subject). When we start the game you are going to choose one of them and pick it up. If you are right you will find a marble. If you are wrong you won't find anything. You may pick up only one block, then I will turn the box and fix another turn like this (the experimenter turns the box around), but on each turn you may pick up only one block. The game is to see how soon you can get a marble every time you choose. If you get a marble you put it in one of these holes (the experimenter points to a board with holes punched to hold marbles won by the subject). When we finish the game you may have the bag of nickels on the chair and you may choose one of the other prizes. Now remember, the game is to see how soon you can get a marble every time you choose.

During training, the experimenter used two prompts: (1) "Remember you get a marble when you are right and the game is to see how soon you can get a marble every time you choose"; (2) "You may only pick up one block but be sure to look at both blocks before choosing." These prompts were used if S appeared to be choosing impulsively or without attending to the choice stimuli. However, prompt (1) was never used until 25 trials had elapsed and then no more than once in ten trials. Prompt (2) was used no more than twice in ten trials. Prompts were never used once shift learning began.

All subjects were trained in the initial discrimination to a criterion of nine correct responses in 10 successive choices. Then without interruption of procedure or further instruction, stimulus-reward relations were shifted so that a value of the formerly irrelevant dimension became the S+ and training continued to the same criterion as in the initial discrimination. Subjects who did not attain criterion in either training phase within 75 trials were dropped from the experiment and replaced. Five 4-year-olds were dropped on this basis; all 10-year-olds successfully completed both tasks. Eight subjects within each age group were randomly assigned to the position to brightness training sequence and nine subjects to the brightness to position sequence. All possible S+ sequences were used.

The subject populations, apparatus, and general training procedures were the same as those in the experiment which produced the data of Fig. 2. The choice stimuli differed only in the absence, in the present experiment, of height variation.

b. Results. Factorial analyses of variance found no difference between age groups in speed of learning either the initial or the shift discriminations, nor was learning found to vary with the particular dimension relevant within either age group. The overall mean trials to criterion in the initial discrimination for 4- and 10-year-olds were 7.7 and 13.3, respectively; the corresponding means for the shift tasks were 13.9 and 10.0.

Since the proportion of total ED shift errors occurring on ED-U did not vary with the dimension relevant within either age group, the ED-U and ED-C functions were determined for the position and brightness discriminations combined. Figure 11 shows these curves for each age group. An age difference in learning the ED-U subproblem is manifest, with 4-year-olds showing a higher proportion correct on the initial shift trials than the 10-year-olds. Other measures also point to greater independence in the young children's subproblem learning. First, 13 of the 17 10-year-olds showed spontaneous reversal (i.e., reversed response on the first post-shift exposure to ED-U after experiencing nonreward on ED-C), while four of the 17 4-year-olds spontaneously reversed ($\chi^2 = 8.74$, $p < .01$). It will be recalled that a similar age difference in spontaneous reversal behavior was observed in connection with the data of Fig. 2. Second, nine of the younger children solved the shift problem without making an error on ED-U presentations (including those in the criterion run), while all of the older children made one or more errors on ED-U ($p < .001$). Again, a similar outcome was observed in connection with the data of Fig. 2.

In sum, Experiment VI found age differences in pattern of subproblem learning within a two-dimensional (position and brightness)

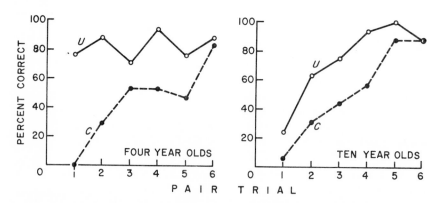

Fig. 11. Group learning functions of 4-year-old and 10-year-old children on unchanged (U) and changed (C) instances of an extradimensional shift within a two-dimensional task.

task which closely resembled those previously observed within a three-dimensional (position, brightness, and height) task.

2. *Experiment VII*

Since reduction in task complexity as implemented in Experiment VI did not eliminate the independent pattern of subproblem learning in young children, it was decided, largely for the reasons considered in the animal experiments, to determine the effect of higher task complexity. The discrimination selected for this purpose involved choice objects similar to those of the foregoing experiment but varying in four dimensions. Since the aim of the experiment was to determine whether *any* training sequence within these stimulus variations would produce in 4-year-olds a pattern of subproblem learning resembling that observed in the more mature subject, it was decided to test the possible training sequences one at a time until either the sequences were exhausted or clear dependency in subproblem learning was obtained. Another consideration contributing to this procedural decision was the anticipation that the task would be extremely difficult for many 4-year-olds. As will be seen, it proved necessary to test only one sequence.

a. Procedure. The subjects were 27 children ranging in age from 3 years 4 months to 5 years 11 months, with an average age of 4 years 5 months.

The choice stimuli consisted of wood blocks varying in brightness (black and white), shape (cylindrical, $1\frac{1}{2}$-inch diameter, and square, $1\frac{5}{8}$-inch sides), height (4 inches and 6 inches), and position (left *vs.* right). The apparatus, stimulus presentation procedures, incentives, instructions, and shift training were as described in Experiment VI. All subjects were trained on the brightness to height sequence. Subjects who did not attain criterion in the initial or shift discriminations within 70 trials were dropped from the experiment. Testing continued until eight children, a predetermined number, had successfully completed both tasks.

b. Results. Sixteen subjects did not learn the initial discrimination, and three subjects did not complete shift. The mean trials to criterion in shift for the eight successful learners was 41.1. The subproblem curves for these subjects are shown in Fig. 12. These functions are strikingly similar to those of the 10-year-old children in Fig. 2. In agreement with the subproblem curves, both the proportion of spontaneous reversers and the number of subjects making errors on ED-U during shift were higher than previously observed

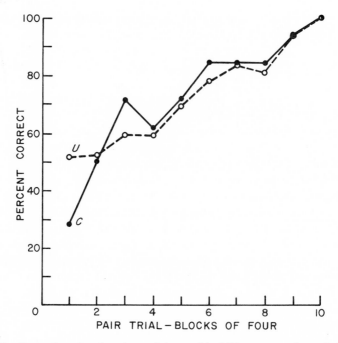

Fig. 12. Group learning functions of 4-year-old children on unchanged (U) and changed (C) instances of an extradimensional shift within a four-dimensional task.

in 4-year-old children. One of the subjects unaccountably shifted response on the *first* shift trial and hence could not be classified as to spontaneous reversal behavior. But of the remaining seven subjects, five showed spontaneous reversal. All of the subjects made one or more errors on ED-U.

These data suggest that the higher task complexity did induce a pattern of learning in 4-year-olds heretofore observed only in older children. However, considering the large number of nonlearners in this experiment, it is possible that the observed changes in subproblem learning were due to subject selection rather than to any alteration of the learning process. A check on this possibility is provided by comparing the proportion of nonlearners in this experiment with the proportion of nonlearners in a fully comparable sample tested on a three-dimensional discrimination (form, color, and position) by the same experimenter. These proportions were .57 for the three-dimensional task and .67 for the present four-dimensional task. The relatively small difference between these proportions indicates that subject selection, if influential, was not the sole determinant of the differential outcome of this experiment. In any event, the data do unequivocally demonstrate that 4-year-olds can be shown to exhibit patterns of subproblem learning like those of 10-year-olds.

3. Experiment VIII

The data of Fig. 2 were taken from an experiment (Tighe & Tighe, 1967) which compared R and ED shift learning in 4- and 10-year-olds with the irrelevant dimension constant vs. variable. The latter condition was the source of the Fig. 2 data, and it represents a degree of task complexity intermediate to the levels in Experiments VI and VII. In the Tighe and Tighe experiment, 4-year-olds were found to accomplish ED faster than R regardless of whether the irrelevant dimension was constant or variable. Caron (1970) attempted to replicate these results but failed to do so for the latter condition: his 4-year-olds accomplished R faster than ED when the irrelevant dimension was variable. Whatever accounts for this discrepant outcome, Caron's data question both the representativeness of the subproblem curves of the 4-year-olds in Fig. 2 and the relation between subproblem learning and relative ease of R and ED shift in young children. For this reason, it was decided to retest the R and ED learning of our subject population under the procedures of Caron's study. Although the latter closely paralleled our earlier study, there were several discrepancies, notably in regard to instructions, prompts, and stimulus presentation procedure on the initial trials. To reduce response to position, Caron presented the same stimulus pair on the first four trials with the pair members reversed in position on trials 1 and 4 vs. on trials 2 and 3. Since Caron's subjects required about half as many trials to learn the initial discrimination as those in Tighe and Tighe's study, it was hoped that this initial position training would speed learning and reduce the number of nonlearners in our subject population.

a. Procedure. The subjects in Experiment VIII were 32 children drawn from the Hanover Nursery School and ranging in age from 3 years 9 months to 5 years 9 months. The average age was 4 years 10 months.

The experimental conditions and procedures were virtually identical to those described in detail by Caron (1969, 1970) and hence need not be stated here. The only notable difference was that in the present study limits were placed on the number and timing of the experimenter's prompts, in the manner described for Experiment VI. Essentially, the children underwent R and ED shifts in a simultaneous discrimination involving choice objects varying in position, height, and brightness, and under training procedures generally similar to those in Experiments VI and VII. Four subjects did not attain criterion in the initial discrimination within a preset limit of 100 trials and were dropped from the experiment. The remaining 28 subjects were randomly assigned to four equal subgroups comprising the combinations of shift condition and dimension relevant (height *vs.* brightness).

  b. Results. Factorial analysis of trials to criterion scores in the initial discrimination showed that shift and dimension assignment had no main or interactive effects ($F \leq 1.40$, $df = 1/24$), thus establishing the initial comparability of the treatment groups. The overall mean trials to criterion in the initial discrimination was 15.9.

Eleven subjects did not attain criterion within a preset 60 trial limit in shift, three on R shift with brightness relevant, three on ED with height relevant, and five on ED with brightness relevant. Following Caron's procedure, these nonlearners were assigned a score of 60 in the analysis of trials to criterion in shift. This analysis found that R was faster than ED shift ($F = 9.47$, $df = 1/24$, $p < .01$) while neither dimension assignment nor the interaction factor were significant ($F = 2.02$ and $F < 1$, respectively). The mean number of trials to criterion in R and ED were 25.4 and 48.5, respectively, and these figures virtually duplicated Caron's scores.

Figure 13 shows the subproblem curves for subjects who learned shift. R refers to the averaged functions on the two pairs of the reversal shift. Like the 4-year-olds' curves of Fig. 2, there is a clear difference in ED-U and ED-C functions in contrast to the corresponding functions of 10-year-olds.

Spontaneous reversal behavior in the 4-year-olds was again infrequent as compared to the levels previously observed in 10-year-olds. Spontaneous reversals were made by five of the 14 subjects assigned to ED shift and by four of the 14 subjects in R shift. Only one subject relearned the ED problem without errors on ED-U.

To recapitulate briefly, Experiments VI–VIII confirm the previously observed age difference in pattern of subproblem learning and suggest that subproblem learning in young children varies with task complexity in a fashion resembling the age trend. For 4-year-olds, increasing task complexity is accompanied by decreasing difference between U and C functions, by increase in frequency of spontaneous shifting, and by decrease in the number of errorless ED-U learners.

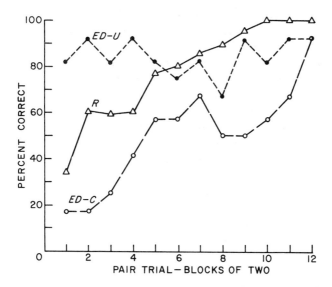

Fig. 13.   Group learning functions of 4-year-old children on reversal (R) shift and on changed (ED-C) and unchanged (ED-U) elements of an extradimensional shift within a three-dimensional task. For R, pair trial refers to successive presentation of both stimulus pairs.

B.   DISCUSSION

There are some obvious similarities between the subproblem data of the younger children and animals. For tasks of low complexity, the subproblem learning of both 4-year-old children and rats was characterized by a relatively low error rate on ED-U, and for both subject populations this error rate increased under high stimulus irrelevance. On this basis, it might be hypothesized that the learning process in young children is similar to that postulated earlier for infrahuman subjects, while the older child discriminates on a conceptual (dimensional) basis (cf. H. H. Kendler & Kendler, 1962). But other aspects of the data question the comparability of learning in younger children and animals. First, the subproblem data of infrahuman subjects is more convincing as to the separability of learning on ED-U and ED-C than that of the young children. In all infrahuman species tested, zero or close to zero error rate on U instances has been observed over long periods of training and in the face of gradual reversal on C instances of the problem (Fig. 3) (Medin, 1972). In contrast, shift learning in young children was generally so rapid in the low complexity condition that separability of U and C learning could be established only for a small number of data points.

Another difference between the younger children's subproblem learning and that of animals concerns its relation to the R-ED comparison. The four infrahuman species tested in the conventional two-dimensional R-ED paradigm have shown both marked independence in subproblem learning and faster ED than R shift. In contrast, Experiment VIII found substantial difference in young children's U and C functions accompanied by faster R than ED. And Cole *et al.* (1971) found independent subproblem learning in young Liberian children accompanied by ED learning equal to R learning. It has been suggested (Tighe & Tighe, 1972) that pattern of subproblem learning may be closely correlated with shift performance, but this interpretation is now shown to be in error for human subjects.

Finally, subproblem analysis of children's learning revealed a response pattern that was never evidenced in analyses of infrahuman learning—spontaneous shifting. Although spontaneous shift was relatively infrequent among younger children, it was nevertheless present in every experimental sample and was particularly evident in these subjects under high task complexity.

The foregoing differences argue against a simple equation of the learning process in animals and young children. But on the other hand, the data of the younger children are not without problems for mediational theory. First, there was evidence of independence in subproblem learning by these subjects in tasks of lower complexity; in Experiments VI and VIII, the U and C functions do not show the complementary relationship expected under the assumptions of mediation theory. However, these are group functions, and it may be argued that they are not convincing regarding the nature of individual performance. Given the rapidity of learning, individual functions on U and C would convey little information, but another measure relevant to the question of individual performance is the proportion of subjects with zero errors on ED-U. For the task of lowest complexity (two dimensions, Experiment VI), nine of the 4-year-olds and none of the 10-year-olds showed errorless relearning on ED-U ($n = 17$ per sample). The 4-year-olds' distribution is within the bounds of attention theory given the following assumptions: (1) that when the instrumental response to the former S+ is abandoned, attention to the formerly relevant dimension is weaker for all subjects (at least momentarily) than to the competing dimension; (2) that a subject has a probability of .50 of then sampling either cue within the latter dimension; (3) that extraneous stimuli are a negligible source of competition. Under these assumptions, 50% of the sample could be expected to show errorless ED-U learning, and this, of course, is the outcome observed.[2] In regard to the proportion of errorless ED-U learners in three-dimensional tasks (Experiment VIII), a similar argument can be advanced to show that a wide range of outcomes consistent with attention theory can be derived from differing assumptions concerning the strengths of attentional responses to the relevant and irrelevant dimensions during shift.

Even if the foregoing reasoning is accepted, there remains the problem of accounting for the observed age difference in proportion of errorless ED-U learners. This difference can be accounted for only if the theory is modified to assume developmental difference in strength of attention response or in the extinction rates of attention *vs.* instrumental response. Thus, if attention theory is to account for the fact that all 10-year-olds made errors on ED-U under the conditions of Experiment VI, it must be assumed that after these subjects abandoned instrumental response to the former S+ they were likely to continue attending to the formerly relevant dimension and to choose the former S—. In contrast, the 4-year-olds must be assumed to no longer attend to the formerly relevant dimension after abandoning response to the former S+.

Another difficulty for attention theory is that high task complexity (four dimensions) appears to have produced in 4-year-olds a pattern of subproblem learning previously seen only in 10-year-olds. It may be that higher levels of complexity enhance control by the relevant task dimension, but there is no basis in present models to predict such an effect.

Finally, the spontaneous reversal data challenge the adequacy of theories of discrimination shift learning which stress the role of dimensional control, whether mediated by attentional or by representational processes. These data clearly indicate that response sets also have an important role in shift behavior. Since the differences between the ED-U and ED-C functions of 4- *vs.* 10-year-olds were most marked over the initial shift trials, age difference in spontaneous reversal may account for a significant portion of the age difference in pattern of subproblem learning. However, two observations indicate that spontaneous reversal is not purely a matter of response learning and transfer, i.e., that it is not independent of stimulus factors. First,

[2] The fit of attention theory is somewhat exaggerated since four subjects spontaneously reversed and thus appear to have violated the first of the above assumptions. Given this consideration, the expected number of errorless ED-U learners is 6.5 rather than 8.5.

Experiment VII suggested that spontaneous shift was more likely under high task complexity. If so, this response set would have the status of a strategy available to young children but appearing as a function of task conditions (Flavell, 1970). Secondly, Tighe & Tighe (1972) found that first-grade children were more likely to spontaneously reverse in a multidimensional shift task if they had received perceptual pretraining designed to highlight the task dimensions.

Spontaneous shift has previously been identified in the learning of stimulus items lacking a common dimensional attribute (Sanders, 1971). Its appearance in the present experiments gives added weight to the argument that response sets (e.g., "lose-shift," "do the opposite") are a primary factor in the development of reversal behavior (Goulet & Williams, 1970; Sanders, 1971).

In sum, while attentional theory can be made to fit much of the data from subproblem analysis of children's learning, the fit is not without strain. The data indicate the need for theoretical modifications in two areas. First, for the young child selective dimensional control appears relatively weak and contextual determinants of response stronger than in the mature subject. In this regard, the data are compatible with a view (Tighe & Tighe, 1972) that subjects concurrently acquire information about both the specific object-reward relations and the dimension-reward relations of the task, with the former more likely to guide choice behavior in the young child. Second, the theory makes no provision for the operation of potent response-shift processes that operate in parallel with dimensional control mechanisms.

IV. Concluding Comment

The subproblem analysis provides a relatively direct measure of the nature of stimulus control in learning problems that have been a major testing ground for theories of learning—theories that differ essentially in conceptions of stimulus control. What has been gained by the subproblem analyses reported here? The data, while not conclusive, do point to significant modification of current conceptions. The subproblem experiments indicate that dimensional control in infrahuman learning is more limited and conditional than generally supposed. While these subjects did not abstract dimensions in the manner indicated by current attentional formulations, neither did they learn in the fully nonselective manner indicated by Spence. Rather, the research suggests that irrelevant cues exert control in proportion to their discriminability, but that with increasing task complexity subjects may reject or filter out cues less discriminable than the relevant cues. In regard to children's learning, the subproblem analysis delineates significant and interrelated age differences in selective stimulus control and problem-solving strategies. Isolation of the relative contributions of these factors poses a major experimental challenge.

REFERENCES

Bourne, L. E., Jr., & Restle, F. A mathematical theory of concept identification. *Psychological Review*, 1959, **66**, 278–296.

Caron, A. J. Discrimination shifts in three-year-olds as a function of dimensional salience. *Developmental Psychology*, 1969, **1**, 333–339.

Caron, A. J. Discrimination shifts in three-year-olds as a function of shift procedure. *Developmental Psychology*, 1970, **3**, 236–241.

Cole, M., Gay, J., Glick, J. A., & Sharp, D. W. *The cultural context of learning and thinking*. New York: Basic Books, 1971.

Fellows, B. J. Chance stimulus sequences for discrimination tasks. *Psychological Bulletin*, 1967, **67**, 87–92.

Flavell, J. H. Developmental studies of mediated memory. In H. W. Reese & L. P. Lipsitt (Eds.), *Advances in child development and behavior*. Vol. 5. New York: Academic Press, 1970. Pp. 181–211.

Garner, W. R. The stimulus in information processing. *American Psychologist*, 1970, **25**, 350–358.

Goulet, L. R., & Williams, K. G. Children's shift performance in the absence of dimensionality and a learned representational response. *Journal of Experimental Child Psychology*, 1970, **10**, 287–294.

Graf, V., & Tighe, T. Subproblem analysis of discrimination shift learning in the turtle (Chrysemys picta picta). *Psychonomic Science*, 1971, **25**, 257–259.

Kendler, H. H., & Kendler, T. S. Vertical and horizontal processes in problem-solving. *Psychological Review*, 1962, **69**, 1–16.

Kendler, T. S., & Kendler, H. H. Reversal and nonreversal shifts in kindergarten children. *Journal of Experimental Psychology*, 1959, **58**, 56–60.

Leary, R. W. "Spontaneous reversal" in the serial-discrimination reversal learning of monkeys. *Canadian Journal of Psychology*, 1962, **16**, 228–233.

Lovejoy, E. An attention theory of discrimination learning. *Journal of Mathematical Psychology*, 1965, **2**, 342–362.

Medin, D. L. Discrimination-shift learning in rhesus monkeys: Subproblem analysis. Paper presented at the Mathematical Psychology meetings, University of California, San Diego and La Jolla, August 1972.

Sanders, B. Factors affecting reversal and nonreversal shifts in rats and children. *Journal of Comparative and Physiological Psychology*, 1971, **74**, 192–202.

Shepp, B. E., & Eimas, P. D. Intradimensional and extradimensional shifts in the rat. *Journal of Comparative and Physiological Psychology*, 1964, **57**, 357–361.

Spence, K. W. The nature of discrimination learning in animals. *Psychological Review*, 1936, **43**, 427–449.

Sutherland, N. S. The learning of discrimination by animals. *Endeavour*, 1964, **23**, 148–152.

Sutherland, N. S., & Mackintosh, N. J. *Mechanisms of animal discrimination learning.* New York: Academic Press, 1971.

Tighe, T. J., & Frey, K. Subproblem analysis of discrimination shift learning in the rat. *Psychonomic Science*, 1972, **28**, 129–133.

Tighe, T. J., Glick, J., & Cole, M. Subproblem analysis of discrimination-shift learning. *Psychonomic Science*, 1971, **24**, 159–160.

Tighe, T. J., & Graf, V. Subproblem analysis of discrimination shift learning in the pigeon. *Psychonomic Science*, 1972, **29**, 139–141.

Tighe, T. J., & Tighe, L. S. Discrimination shift performance of children as a function of age and shift procedure. *Journal of Experimental Psychology*, 1967, **74**, 466–470.

Tighe, T. J., & Tighe, L. S. Stimulus control in children's learning. In A. D. Pick (Ed.), *Minnesota symposia on child psychology.* Vol. 6. Minneapolis: University of Minnesota Press, 1972. Pp. 128–157.

Wolford, G., & Bower, G. H. Continuity theory revisited: Rejected for the wrong reasons? *Psychological Review*, 1969, **76**, 515–518.

Zeaman, D., & House, B. J. The role of attention in retardate discrimination learning. In N. R. Ellis (Ed.), *Handbook of mental deficiency.* New York: McGraw-Hill, 1963. Pp. 159–223.

DELAYED MATCHING AND SHORT-TERM
MEMORY IN MONKEYS[1]

M. R. D'Amato

DEPARTMENT OF PSYCHOLOGY, RUTGERS UNIVERSITY,
NEW BRUNSWICK, NEW JERSEY

I. Introduction: Delayed Matching-to-Sample
and Short-Term Memory

After many years of neglect, even by investigators partial to animal research, memory processes in animals has emerged as a topic of legitimate study and interest. Doubtless the intense research effort devoted to human memory during the last decade or so is a contributing factor, but in any case the study of animal memory has already become sufficiently broad and deep as to warrant a recent volume on the topic (Honig & James, 1971). Moreover, the interest generated by the ancient topic of memory has already breached the insulation which traditionally separates animal and human behavioral research (cf. Winograd, 1971).

And yet our conceptual analysis of memory, animal or human, has

[1] The research reported in this paper was largely supported by National Science Foundation grants GB-7951 and GB-24386X. I wish to thank Robert Worsham for his valuable and sustained assistance in technical and other matters.

not profited greatly from the considerable research effort that has been recently committed to the topic. One might even make the case that the major contribution of a great deal of modern research has been to disinter, or more charitably to rediscover, the time-worn concepts of disuse (in the more respectable garb of "trace decay" or "short-term" memory), and redintegration (now "retrieval"). It seems that psychologists are forever engaged in the battle of establishing the limits of nature's frugality, and memory is no exception. For a time two-process theorists seemed to have the upper hand, but one-process theorists have found in retrieval a concept to rally around (Lewis, 1969; Spear, 1971). But even if the emphasis on short-term memory should ultimately prove a conceptual diversion, there is no denying that it has aroused a good bit of research interest and at times emotion.

My own recruitment into the area came about for reasons that were no more significant than that we had at hand a paradigm—delayed matching-to-sample (DMTS)—that seemed eminently suitable for investigating short-term memory in animals, particularly primates. Thus armed with what looked like a powerful paradigm and the comforting knowledge that little work with DMTS existed, we set out on a series of empirical studies which, somewhat adventitiously, fell into an incomplete but discernible pattern. Actually the matching paradigm has a long history of employment, as pointed out by Weinstein (1941) going back at least to Itard (1932), who more than a century ago used this technique among others in an attempt to train Victor, the "Wild Boy of Aveyron," to the ways of society. But at the time we were ignorant of the venerable history of the matching paradigm, and in any event not much had been done with *delayed* matching, which seemed to place it safely in the area of memory rather than discrimination learning.

II. Nonspecific Sources of Interference in Delayed Matching-to-Sample

Our first discovery of importance (by accident, of course) was that delayed matching could be dramatically facilitated by the simple operation of extinguishing all illumination during the delay (retention) interval. Before presenting these results, let me first describe those aspects of the experimental situation and procedures that are common to all of the studies which I shall report.

A. General Methodology

1. Subjects and Motive-Incentive Conditions

All experimental subjects were capuchin monkeys (*Cebus apella*) who, before their DMTS experience, were in laboratory residence from 1 to 4 years, during which they were exposed to various kinds of experimental training. Motivation was induced by food deprivation, the animals being reduced to a body weight at which they worked with reasonable diligence. Like humans, the propensity for labor among individual monkeys varies considerably, and thus it was necessary in some cases to reduce animals to 80% of their full-ration body weight, while in others adequate performance was achieved though the animal actually gained weight during the experiment. CIBA banana pellets weighing 190 mg served as reinforcers.

2. Apparatus

Two identical experimental chambers were employed in which the subject faced a wall housing five in-line stimulus projectors (Industrial Electronic Engineers, Inc., Series 10,000) located at the four corners and at the midpoint of a 12-cm square (see Fig. 1). Each projector was fitted with a transparent plastic key which served as the response mechanism. A microswitch, with which the subject initiated a trial, was centered below the five projectors. In most experiments presentation of stimuli was arranged by a block tape reader described in an earlier publication (D'Amato, 1965), and programming of trial events and data recording were accomplished by conventional electromechanical equipment. Later experiments were controlled on-line by a PDP 8/e computer.

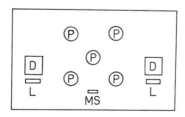

Fig. 1. Diagram of the experimental apparatus. To initiate a trial, the subject completed an FR 15 on the microswitch (MS). The discriminative stimuli appeared on the projectors (P), each of which was faced by a transparent plastic key that served as the response mechanism. On each side of the projectors there was a response lever (L) available, and a display unit (D), which could be illuminated with white light.

3. Sample and Comparison Stimuli

In most of the experiments the stimuli employed were a square, a triangle, a vertical line, and a red disk that illuminated a circular area approximately 2.5 cm in diameter. All forms were composed of 17-mm white lines, approximately 1.5 mm thick, on black backgrounds. Although the sample set frequently consisted of these four stimuli, not more than two stimuli ever appeared together at the time of choice.

4. Procedures

The typical procedure on a DMTS trial was as follows. After completing 15 responses (FR 15) on the microswitch, one of the stimuli (the sample) appeared on the center projector and remained there until the subject pressed the center key for a minimum duration of .3 seconds. The sample then disappeared and the delay (retention) interval began. At the termination of the latter, the sample and a comparison stimulus (another stimulus drawn from the sample set) appeared on two of the four outer projectors. The two "choice" stimuli remained present until the subject responded to one of them. Each correct response was followed by delivery of one CIBA pellet, after which the subject could initiate the next trial by completing the FR 15 on the microswitch. Incorrect responses were followed by a 1-minute time-out, signaled by the dimming of the overhead house-light. At the end of the time-out, the subject was free to initiate the next trial.

It should be pointed out that certain methodological problems arise in delayed-matching studies that can result in the deception of the experimenter with regard to the subject's short-term memory capacity. These have been discussed elsewhere (D'Amato & O'Neill, 1970), and we need only note here that because of precautions taken in our experiments with respect to the sequencing of individual trials and the assignment of stimuli to projectors, we believe that above-chance matching in our animals reflects control by the sample stimuli rather than by other, extraneous, cues.

B. EFFECTS OF DELAY-INTERVAL ILLUMINATION

1. Facilitation of Short-Term Retention by Delay-Interval Darkness

Following up a serendipitous observation in our laboratory, Etkin showed that delayed-matching performance was greatly facilitated when the retention interval was spent in darkness rather than in the normal illumination that prevailed in the experimental chamber. In the latter (houselight-on) condition, the chamber was illuminated by a 15-W overhead houselight which projected a maximum illumination on the floor of the chamber of approximately 6 fc. In the dark (houselight-off) condition, the houselight was extinguished, plunging the experimental chamber in near-total darkness. This simple operation was sufficient to lead to marked differences in DMTS performance over delay intervals as long as 24 seconds (Etkin, 1970, 1972).

O'Neill and I extended this finding for retention intervals as long as 2 minutes (D'Amato & O'Neill, 1971). Three subjects sophisticated with respect to DMTS, were tested in the houselight-on and -off conditions at retention intervals ranging from 16 to 120 seconds. As Fig. 2 shows, retention was greatly superior in two of the three

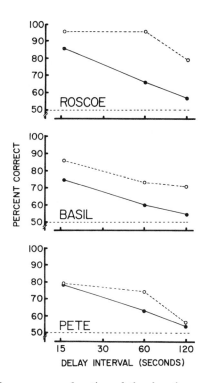

Fig. 2. DMTS performance as a function of the duration and lighting conditions of the delay (retention) interval. Houselight on (●—●); houselight off (○ – – – ○). (From M. R. D'Amato & W. O'Neill, 1971. *Journal of the Experimental Analysis of Behavior* **15**, 327–333. Copyright 1971 by the Society for the Experimental Analysis of Behavior, Inc.; used with permission.)

subjects when the delay interval was spent in darkness rather than in moderate illumination. The effect was rather small for Pete, but it is significant at the 60-second delay interval. A measure of the power of this variable is indicated by the fact that, at a 120-second delay, the performance of all three subjects was at chance levels in the houselight-on condition, whereas all three showed significant retention in the houselight-off condition. Examination of the data with respect to the individual sample stimuli employed in the experiment revealed that all four of the samples profited from the houselight-off condition, which reduced error rate by an average of approximately 36%.

2. Is Facilitation Due to Reduction or Change in Delay-Interval Illumination?

Although we had consistently found that delay-interval darkness enhanced visual short-term retention, we were a little worried that the houselight-off condition might be beneficial, not because it constituted an absence of illumination, but rather because it simply represented an illumination *change* in the sequence of events on a trial. Normally the houselight is on during the period when the sample is presented and during the time that the choice stimuli are available. Consequently, when the houselight remains on during the retention interval, the stimulus conditions of the retention and the "choice" intervals are more similar than when the houselight is extinguished during the former interval. It is possible that responses (e.g., frustration) become conditioned during the retention interval that can later interfere with appropriate matching behavior. If so, it is reasonable to suppose that, because of the greater similarity in the stimulus conditions of the retention and choice intervals, such responses would be more likely to intrude into the choice interval in the houselight-on condition and serve as a source of interference.

This possibility was evaluated in an experiment in which the sample and choice stimuli were presented with the houselight off. With this modification the dark, rather than the illuminated, retention interval more nearly resembled the stimulus situation at the time of choice.

To describe the experiment briefly, two subjects were trained with the houselight off during all phases of a trial sequence except for intertrial periods (the duration between the completion of one trial and the initiation of the next) when the houselight was on, and time-outs when the houselight was dimmed. The retention interval

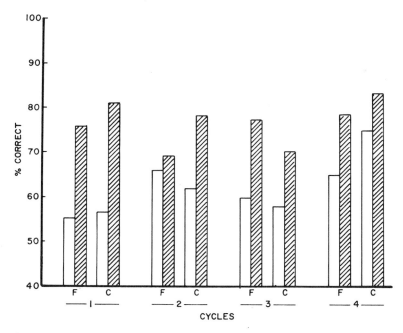

Fig. 3. DMTS performance over the four testing cycles with the houselight either on or off during the retention interval, which was 50 seconds for Fifi (F) and 24 seconds for Coco (C). Houselight on (□); houselight off (■). (From M. R. D'Amato & W. O'Neill, 1971. *Journal of the Experimental Analysis of Behavior* 15, 327–333. Copyright 1971 by the Society for the Experimental Analysis of Behavior, Inc.; used with permission.)

was gradually increased until the subject's DMTS performance reached a level at which the illumination variable could express itself unhindered by a "ceiling effect." The houselight-on and houselight-off conditions were then alternated every other session, each alternation, of which there were four, constituting a "cycle." Figure 3 presents the results of this study (D'Amato & O'Neill, 1971, Experiment 2), which again revealed better retention in the houselight-off condition. The reduction in error rate associated with the latter condition was 33%.

3. Some Other Relevant Data

We were by no means the first investigators to look at the effect of delay-interval illumination on retention. More than 30 years ago Malmo (1942) reported that darkness during the delay interval facilitated delayed-response performance in rhesus monkeys. However, the results obtained in the delayed-response situation since that time have been quite inconsistent (cf. Hornbuckle, 1972; King & Clawson, 1966; King, Flaningam, & Rees, 1968; McDowell & Brown, 1960). We attribute this inconsistency in large measure to the fact that in the delayed-response paradigm the subject is required to remember a spatial location rather than the nature of a visual stimulus. This complicates matters because illumination during the delay interval provides cues by means of which the animal can maintain bodily orientation toward the correct alternative and therefore bridge the retention interval. Indeed, it is possible that the facilitation arising from this source may often be sufficient to outweigh any deleterious effect of illumination on retention. If an animal were to depend entirely upon such orientation, there would be little need to resort to memory processes to account for accurate delayed-response performance. With DMTS, on the other hand, particularly when more than two samples are employed, the likelihood of an animal bridging the delay interval by bodily orientation or by other overt mediating behavior is rather remote. In any event, such mediating behavior cannot be so simple as orienting toward the correct spatial location. Thus, if ambient illumination serves as a nonspecific source of interference for visual memory, it is more likely to be detected in matching tasks than in delayed-response performance.

There are a number of other results which implicate retention-interval illumination as a source of interference in the retention of visual tasks. Mello (1971) recently reported that her rhesus monkeys were capable of successful delayed matching with retention intervals as long as 3 minutes, whereas earlier work with rhesus and stumptail monkeys placed the limit of retention far below this value (e.g., Scheckel, 1965; Weinstein, 1941). It is interesting, therefore, that unlike the earlier investigators, Mello conducted her research in an experimental chamber which, apart from the illumination provided by the experimental stimuli, was almost totally dark. It has also been reported that goldfish retain a form discrimination better when the retention interval is dark rather than illuminated (Düncker & Rensch, 1968).

4. The "Why" of Facilitation

The next question that arises, of course, is the mechanism by which illumination can act as a nonspecific source of interference or, conversely, the mechanism by which delay-interval darkness can facilitate retention. A consolidation theorist would lose no time in pointing out that a period of total darkness provides much more opportunity for consolidation of the trace of the sample stimulus than a period of moderate illumination, during which the visual modality is busy processing a steady stream of visual stimuli. A somewhat related hypothesis is that a dark retention interval may allow the survival of the afterimage of the sample, which an illuminated retention interval would otherwise wipe out. Both of these hypotheses suggest that if illumination is introduced at the beginning of the delay interval, it ought to prove more deleterious than if the same duration of illumination is introduced at the end of an otherwise dark retention interval.

This experiment was done by Etkin (1972), who introduced light probes ranging from 1 to 16 seconds in duration at the beginning or the end of an 18-second retention interval. The light probe consisted of turning on the houselight for the specified interval. Two control conditions were run, one in which the houselight was on throughout the 18-second delay interval, and the other in which the entire delay interval was spent in darkness.

Figure 4 presents his results averaged over the three subjects of the experiment. The first point to be observed is that, as usual, performance was considerably facilitated in the houselight-off condition (D *vs.* L). The difference between placing the light probe at the beginning (B) or the end (E) of the retention interval is small and far

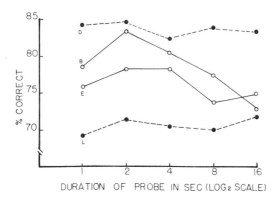

Fig. 4. DMTS performance, averaged over three subjects, as a function of the duration of the light probe (i.e., houselight on) and its location in the 18-second delay interval, either at the beginning (B) or the end (E). L and D indicate that the houselight was on and off, respectively, throughout the delay interval. (From Etkin, 1972, by permission of Academic Press, New York.)

from significant, but in any case it is clear that placing the probe at the beginning of the delay interval does not lead to poorer performance. Except for the data from the 1-second probe, the results suggest that it is the duration of the light probe rather than its location in the retention interval that determines the degree of interference with retention. The relatively poor performance on the 1-second probe most likely can be attributed to the fact that probe duration was confounded with order of testing. Etkin (1970) replicated the 1- and 2-second probe durations under the beginning and end conditions and found no differences among them, the average performance in the four replicated points being close to 85% correct responses.

A somewhat similar result has been obtained by Moise (1970), who required his stumptail monkeys to respond to an illuminated key during the retention interval of a DMTS task. He found little difference in the degree of interference obtained when this activity occurred at the beginning or the end of the retention interval; on the other hand, both of these conditions produced less interference than when the entire retention interval was filled with the interpolated responding (cf. Jarvik, Goldfarb, & Carley, 1969).

There are related data on the human level in short-term memory tasks, but their results are by no means definitive. Corman and Wickens (1968) presented interfering material either at the beginning or the end of a 10-second retention interval. They found only a small and insignificant tendency for greater loss of retention in the former case, and these same authors cite a number of studies in which retroactive inhibition studies with far longer retention intervals also failed to produce a significant relationship between the temporal position of the interpolated learning and the amount of forgetting. On the other hand, Salzberg, Parks, Kroll, and Parkinson (1971) reported that material high in phonemic similarity with respect to the target item produced greater retention deficit than material with low phonemic similarity when the interpolated materials were presented early in a 12-second retention interval; however, the difference disappeared when the same materials were presented late in the retention interval. To paraphrase the position taken by Corman and Wickens (1968), if the temporal position of the interfering material is at all relevant, it is of considerably less importance than such variables as similarity of materials and amount of interpolated material. To offer a more specific suggestion regarding these variables, the temporal location of the interpolated material in the retention interval may be of importance only when the interpolated material is closely similar to the target stimulus.

There is another simple interpretation of the delay-interval illumination effect that can quickly be laid to rest, viz., that darkness during the retention interval leads to less motor activity and hence to better preservation of the memory trace. Etkin (1972) counted the number of times that his subjects interrupted an infrared beam in the experimental chamber during illuminated and dark delay intervals. By this measure of motor activity his animals were somewhat *more* active during the dark retention intervals. Another piece of data that argues against the importance of overt motor activity in delayed-matching performance is the finding by Jarrard and Moise (1970) that stumptail monkeys perform as well on a DMTS task when they are free to move about the experimental chamber as when they are physically restrained in a primate chair.

C.   Effects of Delay-Interval Auditory Input

1. White Noise as a Source of Interference

At this point we stopped, or rather postponed, worrying about what the mechanism underlying the effectiveness of the delay-interval illumination variable might be and turned our attention to the question of whether stimuli in other modalities might also serve as nonspecific sources of interference for visual delayed-matching performance.

The presence of illumination during the retention interval can be considered to be a kind of visual "noise" which interacts with the visual trace of a sample, degrading it in some measure. Unless the visual trace system is well insulated from auditory input, white noise might be expected to produce a similar effect.

Robert Worsham and I therefore conducted a study in which potentially interfering visual and auditory stimuli were introduced during retention intervals of different durations. The experiment followed a factorial design in which the retention intervals were filled with illumination, white noise, both illumination and white noise, or neither. The white noise was introduced into the experimental chamber by means of a 4-inch speaker located at the top of the chamber; it measured approximately 73 dB with a General Radio Sound Survey meter located 16 inches from the speaker. To a human observer the white noise appeared as a loud but not aversive sound.

Jocko, Roscoe, and Basil served in this experiment (Worsham & D'Amato, 1973). Each of the four conditions occurred once in a block of four 24-trial sessions, and a total of five blocks were given at each of the "long" delay intervals (described below). Two procedural changes were introduced into this and the following experiment. Rather than have the sample terminated when the subject pressed the center key, the sample was presented for a fixed duration of time. Onset of the sample occurred when the animal pressed the lever located 12 cm to the left of the projector array (see Fig. 1). Thus, when the subject completed the FR 15 on the microswitch, thereby initiating a trial, the stimulus display unit above the left lever became illuminated. Pressing the lever caused the sample to appear on the center projector for .2 seconds.

The purpose of the second modification was to gain better control over the animals' attending responses. At relatively long retention intervals we found that some subjects would press the left lever without bothering to look at the center projector. This failure to attend to the sample was largely eliminated by programming 2-second delay intervals on 50% of each session's trials, randomly determined. The other 12 trials were "long" delay trials of appropriate duration.

The results of the experiment were gratifyingly clear-cut. Figure 5 shows that the usual result was obtained with respect to the illumination variable, namely, DMTS performance was far better when the retention interval was spent in darkness. On the other hand, white noise had no effect on delayed-matching performance, nor did it interact with the delay-interval illumination variable. Roscoe showed a small separation for the white noise variable, but the difference was far from achieving statistical significance $(F < 1)$.

There are, of course, a number of reasons why one should be reluctant about embracing the conclusion that auditory input during the retention interval is without effect on visual short-term memory in monkeys. For one thing, there is no easy way of deciding whether the difference between the noise and no-noise conditions equalled that of the houselight-on and houselight-off conditions. Even more important is the fact that rather different consequences follow upon introducing illumination and white noise into the retention interval. The presence of illumination during the retention interval allows the subject to perceive visual stimuli in the environment, and very likely it is the processing of visual information that leads to impairment of retention in visual delayed matching rather than illumination per se. If, for example, illumination during the delay interval were introduced by means of translucent contact lenses, precluding perception of visual stimuli, perhaps no effect would be found on delayed matching. The white noise stimulus, on the other hand, probably elicits a bare minimum of auditory processing, if indeed the subjects attend to it at all.

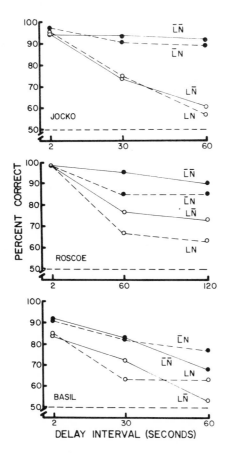

Fig. 5. Individual DMTS performance functions obtained with the houselight on (L), houselight off (L̄) and the white noise on (N), white noise off (N̄) conditions operating during the retention interval. Note the longer retention intervals used with Roscoe. (From Worsham & D'Amato, 1973. Copyright 1973 by the American Psychological Association, Inc.)

2. Vocalization as a Source of Interference

A fairer test of the ability of auditory stimuli to interfere with visual memory can be achieved by employing auditory stimuli that are likely to gain and hold the animals' attention. We attempted to accomplish this objective by recording the normal noises and vocalizations which occur in our monkey colony room (cf. Butler, 1957). From many hours of these recordings we constructed a tape from which long periods of silence and certain atypical sounds were deleted. The resulting tape consisted largely of the monkeys' vocalizations, which ranged widely in content and intensity.

Armed with this "vocalization" tape we repeated the previous experiment, using the sounds on the tape in place of white noise. To minimize adaptation to the vocalization sounds, the segment of the tape played during a given retention interval was chosen in a quasi-random fashion. Only Jocko and Roscoe were run in this experiment (Worsham & D'Amato, 1973) which, apart from the use of vocalization in place of white noise, was very similar to the previous study. Both animals were tested at 2-second delay, a "medium" delay (30 seconds for Jocko and 60 seconds for Roscoe), and a "long" delay (60 and 120 seconds, respectively). A session consisted of eight trials at each of the three delays, and there was a total of 16 sessions, four devoted to each of the four different delay-interval conditions.

Because both subjects' performance on the 2-second delay trials was virtually 100% in all conditions, these trials were not included in the data analysis. Delay-interval illumination once again produced a powerful effect and, unexpectedly, the analysis revealed a significant delay interval by vocalization interaction, the nature of which is shown in Fig. 6. (Ignore for the moment the replication data pre-

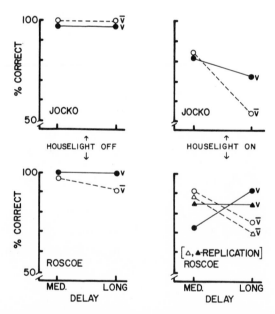

Fig. 6. DMTS performance as affected by the illumination and vocalization-on (V), vocalization-off (V̄) conditions of the delay interval. The medium (med.) delay interval was 30 seconds for Jocko and 60 seconds for Roscoe; the respective long delays were 60 and 120 seconds. The 2-second delay trials are not shown. (From Worsham & D'Amato, 1973. Copyright 1973 by the American Psychological Association, Inc.)

sented in the lower right panel.) Except for Roscoe in the house-light-on condition, there is very little difference between the performance generated by the vocalization-on and vocalization-off conditions at the medium retention interval. On the other hand, a substantial difference exists at the long delay, in favor of the vocal-ization-on condition. Most of the interaction is contributed by the houselight-on condition, although the vocalization by houselight by delay interval interaction did not reach accepted significance levels.

Apart from Roscoe's performance in the houselight-on condition at medium delay, the nature of the vocalization by delay interaction is consistent and is subject to a reasonable interpretation. Conse-quently, Roscoe was returned to the experimental situation for eight sessions in the houselight-on condition, and retested with vocaliza-tion-on alternating every two sessions with vocalization-off. As the data in the lower right panel of Fig. 6 show, this replication pro-duced little difference between vocalization-on and vocalization-off at the medium delay, but a sizable difference in favor of the former appeared at the long (120-second) delay.

It seems reasonable to conclude, therefore, that visual DMTS performance does not necessarily suffer when the retention interval is filled with auditory material to which there is good reason to believe the animals attend, at least for a portion of the delay interval. Indeed, the nature of the vocalization by delay interaction—which constitutes the evidence that the animals attended to the auditory stimuli—suggests that, far from interfering with visual short-term memory, the processing of auditory input may actually preserve visual memories.

One plausible interpretation of the latter finding is that the monkey processes complex sensory materials serially, so that if it is attending to information in the auditory modality, it cannot at the same time process complex visual material. The topic of selective perception is, of course, quite vast, and it is not our purpose here to apply that literature to the issue under discussion. However, given this assumption, to which many attention theorists would subscribe, it follows that the visual short-term memory of our subjects should be less susceptible to interference from the visual stimuli available in the houselight-on condition when vocalization is present during the retention interval than when vocalization is absent.

Because we so frequently code visual material verbally, one must expect in humans a great deal more interaction between the visual and auditory modalities with regard to short-term retention than is the case for animals. Nevertheless, modality-specific interference, not unlike that observed in the present experiments, has been frequently reported in studies of human short-term memory. For example, Salzberg *et al.* (1971) in a study cited earlier, found that when a 12-second retention interval was filled with auditory shadowing, recall was far better when the target stimuli (letters of the alphabet) were presented visually rather than aurally. This same differential susceptibility of visual and auditory target stimuli to interference from the processing of auditory material has led a number of investigators to propose the existence in humans of a "prelinguistic" visual store with a life variously estimated to be from a few seconds up to as much as half a minute (cf. Kroll, Parks, Parkinson, Bieber, & Johnson, 1970; Meudell, 1972; Murdock, 1971; Murdock & Walker, 1969; Scarborough, 1972). Since, however, there is no reason to assume that monkeys recode visual events to auditory counterparts, it would appear from the present experiments that, either human visual short-term memory has been grossly underestimated, or the capacity of primates in this regard greatly exceeds our own.

It naturally occurred to us that the case for modality-specific interference would be much stronger if it could be shown that delay-interval illumination does not interfere with auditory delayed matching. We set about this task some time ago, but after many months of careful training, which involved a variety of shaping techniques, we were unable to get our animals to acquire reliably a discrimination based on tonal frequency differences. Whether our failure is due to the extensive past experience of our animals with visual stimuli or to the nature of the auditory stimuli employed, or perhaps to other factors, we cannot presently say. But in any case our difficulty is another pointed reminder of the nonequivalence of discriminative stimuli (Garcia, McGowan, & Green, 1972; Seligman, 1970).

III. Role of Sample Duration in Delayed Matching-to-Sample

When we began our studies of delayed matching, the empirical and theoretical work on short-term memory in humans had prepared us to expect little evidence of retention in our animals beyond 20 or 30 seconds. After all, Peterson and Peterson's (1959) subjects showed only 10% retention after an 18-second retention interval, and numerous theorists had postulated the limits of human short-term memory in the absence of rehearsal to be in the order of a minute or less (cf. Norman, 1970). And, as we have just noted, the "prelinguistic" visual short-term memory of humans is apparently equally evanescent. We were somewhat surprised, therefore, when several of our monkeys showed clear signs of significant retention with delay intervals as long as 2 minutes, which by no means reaches the limits of visual short-term memory in the more talented of our subjects. Before we were willing to concede to our animals either the ability to rehearse or a visual short-term storage system superior to our own, we thought it best to investigate some of the variables which might account for this unexpected level of DMTS performance.

One likely candidate was the duration of the sample presentation period. It is known that performance on short-term memory tasks is enhanced by increasing the number of practice trials with the material to be retained, a result which holds both for humans (Hellyer, 1962) and for primates (Jarrard & Moise, 1970). In most of our early experiments, the subject terminated the sample by pressing the appropriate response key, and it seemed possible that when tested with long retention intervals the animals might view the sample several times before making the observing response, thereby enjoying the equivalent of several practice trials. Indeed, we noticed in this connection that with long retention intervals, some subjects did allow the sample to remain present for relatively long periods before making the appropriate observing response. We therefore ran an experiment in which we systematically manipulated the duration that the sample was available for viewing, our interest being in whether DMTS performance would turn out to be an increasing function of sample duration.

In this study (D'Amato & Worsham, 1972), which was actually performed before the previous two experiments, after the subject initiated a trial by completing an FR 15 on the microswitch, the display unit above the left lever was illuminated. Pressing the left lever caused the sample to appear on the center projector for a fixed duration of time. At the termination of the sample, the retention interval, during which the houselight was extinguished, commenced. Twenty-four trials were given during each daily session, half of which were 2-second delay trials and the other half were "long" delay trials. The duration of the long delay trials constituted one variable of the experiment and the duration of the sample, the other.

The design of the experiment, which was somewhat complex, can best be described in conjunction with Fig. 7. In Phase I, sample duration was initially set at .15 second, and three sessions were given at the four delay intervals shown in the figure (7.5–60 seconds). The duration of the sample was then reduced to .10 second, and three sessions were again given at the four retention intervals, and finally, this procedure was repeated with the sample duration further reduced to .075 second. It should be pointed out that the sample durations given refer to the nominal time intervals that the bulbs of the appropriate stimulus projectors were powered by a 6-vac source. Oscilloscopic measurement of the voltage applied to the bulbs showed the actual (average) intervals to be .13, .08, and .06 second, for the nominal intervals of .15, .10, and .075 second, respectively. There was a noticeable diminution in the brightness of some of the four sample stimuli at the .075-second interval, and therefore shorter intervals were not employed. It should be further noted that perception of the sample at the very brief sample durations required that the subject focus on the center projector before presentation of the sample began. This presented no problem to our animals, who adopted the procedure of orienting their heads toward the center projector before pressing the left lever.

As Figs. 7 and 8 clearly show, in Phase 1 the DMTS performance of both Jocko and Roscoe was unaffected by the sample duration variable. However, we thought it possible that the relatively high

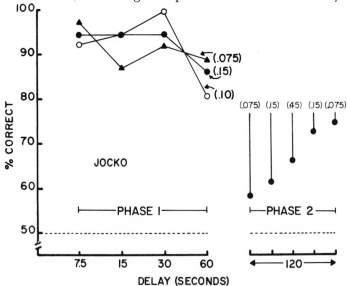

Fig. 7. Jocko's DMTS performance as a function of the duration of the retention interval and the (nominal) sample presentation time. Performance on the 2-second delay trials is not shown. Numbers in parentheses are sample durations in seconds. (From D'Amato & Worsham, 1972, by permission of Academic Press, New York.)

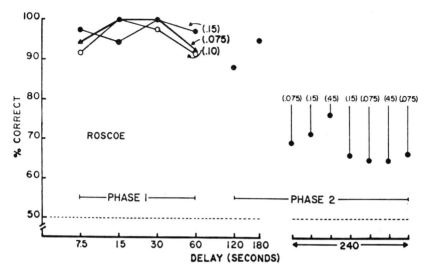

Fig. 8. Roscoe's DMTS performance as a function of the duration of the retention interval and the (nominal) sample presentation time. Performance on the 2-second delay trials is not shown. Numbers in parentheses are sample durations in seconds. (From D'Amato & Worsham, 1972, by permission of Academic Press, New York.)

performance level maintained even at the 60-second retention interval might have prevented the sample duration variable from expressing itself. Consequently in Phase 2 we tested this variable at a delay interval which generated a much lower level of performance and we increased the range of sample durations to include .45 second, a value close to the average latency at which our subjects terminate the sample when an observing response is available.

Unlike Phase 1, each of the data points of Phase 2 is based on 60 long-delay trials (five sessions). In the case of Jocko (Fig. 7), a 120-second retention interval was employed during Phase 2, and though he showed a very striking "practice effect" over the 25 training sessions, sample duration had not the slightest influence on his DMTS behavior. Roscoe's performance (Fig. 8) in Phase 2 at 120- and 180-second delay was quite substantial, and it required a 240-second retention interval to bring his performance down to a level where the sample duration variable could be manipulated. Although Roscoe showed a similar practice effect as sample duration was increased from .075 to .45 second, his performance dropped off when sample duration was reduced to .15 and then to .075 second, giving the impression that in this animal the sample duration variable was perhaps effective. However, observation of Roscoe's behavior at the time of choice suggested to us that a motivational deficit, specific to the long-delay trials, was developing at this exceedingly long retention interval. The deficit manifested itself in rather rapid and "casual" responding to the choice stimuli, which was uncharacteristic of this animal's behavior. As a check of this interpretation, sample duration was again increased to .45 second for five sessions and then reduced to .075 second. As Fig. 8 shows, Roscoe's performance was unaffected by this manipulation. Thus it is safe to conclude that, in this animal as well, matching performance was affected little if at all by the sample duration variable.

These data reveal in our animals a rather remarkable ability to retain for relatively long intervals information presented for very brief periods of time. That their performance was unrelated to sample duration in the interval .075–.45 second was unexpected. We had supposed that the longer sample durations would allow the reception of more features of the sample stimulus than could be attended to at very brief exposures. In the case of the square, for example, a long sample duration might permit the subject to observe the upper horizontal line, the right vertical line, and the angle formed at their apex, whereas with a briefer duration only a portion of the right vertical line might be observed. If the comparison stimulus on that trial was a vertical line, matching performance should generally be superior with the longer sample duration. The fact that this result was not obtained suggests that, perhaps because of the considerable experience both subjects had with the sample set, each stimulus was a highly organized configuration which could be identified even with partial information, just as a human observer can identify a triangle at exposures too brief for him to perceive the entire figure.

In a recent report concerned with visual short-term memory in humans, Scarborough (1972) found that college students retained more of an eight-letter visual display (after retention intervals ranging from 0 to 2 seconds) when the target items were displayed for .75 second rather than for only .25 second. If, as suggested by the author, the increased performance with the longer exposure is attributable to the greater opportunity for "implicit speech coding," then the absence of a sample duration effect in Roscoe and Jocko is not necessarily in conflict with Scarborough's results. Lacking the means to code visual material verbally, increasing the input of a stimulus beyond that necessary for full sensory registration ought not to profit short-term retention in animals.

With relatively complex visual materials, such as pictures of objects, people, and scenes, recognition memory has been found to depend upon stimulus duration time. Potter and Levy (1969) presented their subjects with a series of unrelated pictures for durations ranging from .125 to 2.0 seconds and found that recognition memory increased sharply with stimulus presentation time. Subsequently, Shaffer and Shiffrin (1972) verified this result and in addition showed that it could not easily be attributed to rehearsal of the visual input during the longer presentation times. They varied both stimulus presentation time (from .2 to 4.0 seconds) and the duration intervening between successive stimulus presentations ("blank" time), going so far as to encourage their subjects to use the blank periods, which ranged from 1 to 4 seconds, to "think about" and "remember" the previously presented picture. In spite of the added opportunity for rehearsal of the target material offered by the longer blank periods, Shaffer and Shiffrin found that blank time had virtually no effect on recognition.

The simplest interpretation of the results of these two studies is that the longer stimulus presentation times allowed the subjects to learn more identifying features of the individual stimuli than could be managed with shorter durations. As already pointed out, the stimuli were relatively complex and unfamiliar in the sense that the subjects did not have previous experience with the specific stimuli used in the experiments. Consequently, there likely was ample opportunity for visual learning ("processing"?) to occur at the longer stimulus durations. It is, of course, interesting that the additional learning which took place at the longer presentation times seems not to have undergone rehearsal during the blank periods, which suggests that verbal encoding of the learned features did not occur during the stimulus presentation period or thereafter. In a way this seems strange, for if the subjects did indeed learn more about the stimuli after the longer stimulus durations, they most certainly would have been able to verbalize more features of the stimuli after long presentation intervals if called upon to do so. However, as the data suggest, it does not necessarily follow that in the absence of appropriate instructions such verbal encoding automatically takes place.

A reasonable conclusion that can be drawn from these studies and our own data is that stimulus presentation time will affect visual short-term retention only to the degree that the visual materials are "unfamiliar," thus providing the potential for visual learning. The implication is that if subjects are first given a reasonable amount of experience with the visual stimuli later to be used as target and distractor stimuli, the influence of stimulus presentation time would be greatly attenuated.

Returning to our own study, another point of interest is the marked "practice effect" shown by Jocko during the 25 sessions of Phase 2 (Fig. 7). At the time this animal entered Phase 2 it had had considerable experience in the experimental situation with virtually all of the contingencies about which he could learn. The only significant change in the parameters of Phase 2 over earlier training was the duration of the retention interval, 120 seconds, which initially caused a severe decrement in performance. Jocko's steady and marked improvement indicates that somehow he learned how to reduce the disruption caused by the long retention interval. Improved attending to the sample stimulus cannot be the responsible factor because Jocko averaged 95.5% correct responses on the 2-second delay trials of Phase 2. Another possibility is that Jocko learned to engage in certain behaviors which served to preserve the information which he had received from the sample. For example, he may have learned to remain relatively motionless during the retention interval and perhaps thereby better preserve the memory trace of the sample. We have, however, already described some of the data that argue against the notion that peripheral motor activity interferes with DMTS performance (Etkin, 1972; Jarrard & Moise, 1970). Later on I shall indicate what seems to me a more reasonable explanation of this practice effect. At this point I wish to emphasize that at long retention intervals improved performance with increased practice is a common observation in our laboratory. Previously we had assumed that most of the observed practice effect was due simply to the recovery of attentional responses which had been weakened by the errors attending the introduction of a long retention interval. The present data rule out this interpretation. Rather than learning to attend, the animals appear in some manner to be learning to remember.

IV.   Retrieval Cues and Short-Term Memory
in Monkeys

A.   Reducing the Number of Retrieval Cues from Two to One

Since the impressive short-term memory displayed by our animals could not be attributed to the conditions of input, we next turned our attention to the retrieval cues that are available to them at the time of choice. DMTS is, of course, a recognition memory task. In our version of DMTS, two retrieval cues are available on every trial, the sample and a comparison stimulus. Consequently, an animal can respond correctly on a given trial because he recognizes the sample stimulus or because he recognizes that the comparison stimulus is *not* the sample, or some combination of both processes.

A great many studies of human short-term memory have, on the other hand, employed recall tasks, and while recognition tasks have frequently been used in human research, they often are of the "yes-no" variety. That is to say, the subject is provided with a test stimulus at the end of the retention interval, and he must decide whether or not it corresponds to the target stimulus.

Our first step in evaluating the role of retrieval cues in DMTS performance was to reduce the number of available retrieval cues from two to one. This was accomplished by presenting the animal with a single stimulus at the end of the retention interval, either the sample or a comparison stimulus, and providing the subject with two responses, one to indicate that the presented stimulus was the sample and the other to indicate that it was not. The analogy between this modification of two-choice DMTS, which we shall refer to as yes-no DMTS, and the yes-no signal detection paradigm immediately comes to mind. A mismatch between the sample and the stimulus presented at the end of the retention interval may be considered the "noise" and a match (the sample is presented at the time of choice) the "signal plus noise."

The actual experimental procedure employed for the yes-no paradigm was as follows. When the animal completed the FR 15 on the microswitch, thus initiating a trial, the sample appeared on the center key as usual. Pressing the center key caused the sample to disappear and initiated the delay interval, which was spent in darkness. The test stimulus, either the sample or a comparison stimulus, appeared at the end of the retention interval on one of the two right projectors (the two left projectors being unused in yes-no DMTS), and simultaneously the display unit above the right lever was illuminated (cf. Fig. 1). If the test stimulus was the sample, the correct response was pressing the projector on which it appeared (a "hit" in the terminology of signal detection); pressing the right lever constituted an error ("false rejection"). Conversely, when the test stimulus was not the sample, the correct response was pressing the right lever ("correct rejection"); pressing the projector on which the "nonsample" appeared comprised the second type of error ("false alarm").

The three animals used in the study (D'Amato & Worsham, in press),

Dagwood, Tilly, and Olive, all had some previous experience with DMTS and the standard four-stimulus sample set. It turned out to be a rather simple matter to shape the animals to the yes-no paradigm, which was accomplished by first briefly training the animals to press the illuminated right lever to obtain a reward pellet. The yes-no paradigm was then introduced, using only two sample stimuli, the red disk and the vertical line, and a 0-second delay interval. When the animal reached a criterion of approximately 90% correct responses, which only took a few days, they were shifted to the four-sample set, still at 0-second retention interval.

The experiment proper began after the animals showed mastery on the four-sample set. The two-choice DMTS paradigm alternated with the yes-no paradigm every two sessions, each daily session being comprised of 24 trials. Sixteen such sessions were given at 0-, 1-, 4-, 8-, and 16-second retention intervals in that order. Because of personnel changes, a 2-month break in the experiment followed, after which the animals were quickly reinstated to the experimental procedures. The major change in this portion of the experiment was that 12 of each session's trials, quasi-randomly chosen, were 2-second delay trials. Three blocks of 16 sessions were given with the delay interval on half of a session's trials set at 32, 64, and 128 seconds, for the first, second, and third block, respectively. On half of the trials the sample appeared at the end of the retention interval and on the other half, one of the other three members of the four-stimulus set.

Figure 9 presents the results of the experiment, excluding the data for the 0- and 1-second delay intervals. It is clear that, overall, there is very little difference between the performance of the animals under the two paradigms. An analysis of variance based on the data from the 32- to 128-second retention intervals, which were free of limitations from a ceiling effect, bears this out, in that the only significant main effect was duration of the retention interval; moreover, none of the interactions was significant. Performance on the 2-second delay trials was very high for both paradigms, 97.8 and 96.3% for the two-choice and yes-no tasks, respectively.

1. A Signal Detection Analysis

The analogy between the yes-no DMTS task and the yes-no signal detection paradigm has already been pointed out, and a reasonable correspondence also exists between two-choice DMTS and the two-alternative, forced-choice (2 AFC) signal detection paradigm. This raises the interesting possibility of finding a parallel in signal detec-

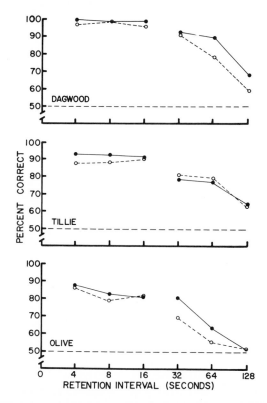

Fig. 9. A comparison of performance on comparable two-choice (●—●) and yes-no (○ - - - ○) DMTS tasks, which alternated every other session. A 2-month break intervened in the experiment between the 16- and 32-second retention intervals. Performance on the 2-second delay trials associated with the last three retention intervals is not shown.

tion theory for the issue raised here regarding the role of retrieval cues in DMTS performance.

According to signal detection theory, assuming comparable experimental parameters, the yes-no and 2 AFC paradigms ought to yield similar measures of sensitivity, d' (cf. Green & Swets, 1966). However, for a fixed value of d', a higher percentage of correct responses will result from the 2 AFC paradigm. For example, for $d' = 1.0$ and no response bias, the yes-no paradigm may be expected to yield approximately 69% correct responses, while the corresponding figure for the 2 AFC task is 76% (assuming that the noise and signal-plus-noise distributions are normally distributed with equal variance). The basic reason why signal detection theory predicts a higher performance level in the 2 AFC task is that in this situation a subject bases his decision on the difference between two independent inputs rather than on only one, which is the case for the yes-no task.

We can apply the signal detection formulation to two-choice DMTS if we assume that the animals base their decisions on the difference in "familiarity" evoked by the sample and the comparison stimulus. This assumption, it should be noted, specifies one way in which the sample and comparison stimulus both serve a retrieval function. In yes-no DMTS, on the other hand, the subjects have available only one value of familiarity, which, in accordance with a signal detection analysis, is referred to the distributions of familiarity in the noise and signal-plus-noise conditions (both presumed to be normal with equal variances) in order to yield a decision. These assumptions are rather similar to those sometimes made in applications of signal detection to human recognition memory (cf. Lockhart & Murdock, 1970; Parks, 1966).

If for some reason the subject makes use of only one of the two stimuli available in two-choice DMTS, presumably his expected percentage of correct responses, for a fixed value of d', would be the same for the two-choice and yes-no tasks. For example, suppose the subject stores one or more unique features of the sample which, at the end of the retention interval, he attempts to match in the stimuli available to him. In this scheme of things the sample serves as the paramount retrieval cue, and the comparison stimulus has little, if any, specific retrieval function.

The present data can be brought to bear on this issue by inquiring whether the difference in percentages of correct responses observed in the two-choice and yes-no DMTS paradigms is what one would expect if the animals were in fact operating in accordance with the signal detection model. As the first step in this analysis, values of d' were obtained for each subject for each of the three longest retention intervals, using the percentages of hits and false alarms produced in the yes-no task. The tables provided by Elliot (1964) were used for this purpose. These values of d' were then located in the 2 AFC table of d' (also supplied by Elliot) in order to obtain the expected percentage of correct responses for the corresponding two-choice DMTS tasks. The average of the latter values turned out to be 75.8%. The average percentage of correct responses actually obtained in the two-choice DMTS task, 74.0, was rather close to the expected value. On the other hand, the average percentage of correct responses obtained in the yes-no task was 69.6.

One may wonder, however, whether the difference in the obtained average percentages of correct responses in the two-choice and yes-no DMTS tasks reflects anything more than the different opportunity for response bias afforded by the two paradigms. Because of the use of four stimulus projectors, the two-choice situation is not conducive to the development of a strong response bias. On the other hand, the two distinctively different response alternatives of the yes-no paradigm are much more likely to generate a response bias, and in fact analysis of the overall percentage of hits and correct rejections made by each subject at the last three retention intervals reveals that all three had a significant response bias, two animals in the direction of preferring the response lever. The following correction was therefore applied to the yes-no data. For each value of d' observed in the yes-no task, the corresponding percentage of correct responses that would have been generated had no response bias existed (i.e., for $\beta = 1.0$) was obtained from the yes-no tables. The resulting percentages were then averaged over the three subjects and the three retention intervals, producing the value of 70.4%, a figure very close to the actual average percentage of correct responses in the yes-no task, 69.6%.

Thus, although the difference in performance on the two-choice and yes-no DMTS tasks was small, even at long retention intervals, the analysis based on signal detection theory suggests that the subjects made some use of both stimuli in two-choice DMTS; that is, both the sample and the comparison stimulus may have served a retrieval function. And yet it is clear that the contribution of the second stimulus is quite small. One stimulus, either the sample or the comparison stimulus, apparently allows the subject to make almost full use of the information that survives the retention interval, and a second relevant stimulus adds only a little to the process.

To return to the issue that prompted the present experiment, it seems unlikely that the impressive visual short-term memory of our animals, as evidenced by their matching performance, is largely a consequence of the fact that DMTS is a recognition task. But to establish that point more convincingly, all differential retrieval cues present at the end of the retention interval should be eliminated. This is what we next set out to accomplish.

B. CONDITIONAL MATCHING—AN ANALOG OF RECALL

Since removing either the sample or the comparison stimulus at the time of choice had so little effect on DMTS performance, we went all the way and eliminated both of these potential retrieval cues, creating a situation which is analogous to recall in human experiments. This was accomplished by employing a "conditional" matching task. In conditional matching, the "match" is based on an arbitrary association between the sample (or "standard stimulus") and a comparison stimulus, rather than being based on physical identity, as in DMTS. As an illustration, in the experiment to be described a red disk and a vertical line served as standard stimuli, and an inverted triangle and a small circle (a "dot") provided the comparison stimuli (D'Amato & Worsham, in press). When the red disk appeared as the sample, the correct comparison stimulus was the inverted triangle, and when the vertical line was the standard stimulus, the dot was correct. With this arrangement the stimuli present at the time of choice provide no information whatever regarding the identity of the standard stimulus. Said differently, the comparison stimuli serve no differential retrieval function.

Simultaneous conditional matching (also called "symbolic" matching) has been investigated in pigeons and rhesus monkeys (Cumming & Berryman, 1965; Ginsberg, 1957; Weinstein, 1945), both of which are capable of high performance levels on this task. However, delayed conditional matching seems to have been studied in animals little, if at all.

A substantial amount of effort was required to train the animals on the conditional matching task. All three subjects, Lucy, Fifi, and Coco, had previous experience with DMTS, while Fifi and Coco also had the benefit of some earlier training on delayed conditional matching (DCM).

To describe the "pretraining" procedures briefly, the three subjects were first introduced to DMTS, the retention interval being gradually increased from 0 to 32 seconds. Training on simultaneous and 0-second DCM followed, in which the vertical line and red disk served as standard stimuli and the dot and inverted triangle comprised the comparison stimuli. During many of these sessions a fading technique was used in which a slow transition was provided from identity to conditional matching. This was accomplished by superimposing the standard stimulus upon the appropriate choice stimulus (e.g., vertical line plus dot), and then gradually fading out the standard stimulus by reducing in small steps the voltage powering the appropriate stimulus bulb. When stable 0-second delay conditional matching was achieved, the delay interval was gradually increased to 32 seconds for Fifi and 60 seconds for Lucy and Coco. The total number of sessions required to complete pretraining ranged between 44 and 138.

In comparing DCM with DMTS one can use identical stimuli in

both paradigms as samples or as choice stimuli, but of course both controls cannot be applied at the same time. In Phase 1 of the present study, the stimuli present at the time of choice (inverted triangle and dot) were the same in both paradigms, while the red disk and vertical line served as standard stimuli in DCM. Phase 1 training began with 0-second delay, the DMTS and DCM tasks alternating every two sessions. Each session consisted of 24 trials, half of which, after a 4-second delay interval was reached, were 2-second delay trials. The retention interval was increased in slightly different ways for the three subjects, and the number of sessions given at a particular delay interval varied between 4 and 16. The total number of training sessions given in Phase 1 ranged between 78 and 128.

Figure 10 presents the results obtained on both tasks on the 2-second and long-delay trials. Coco's performance on the long-delay trials was far better with DMTS than with DCM. However, a significant difference in the same direction also existed on the 2-second

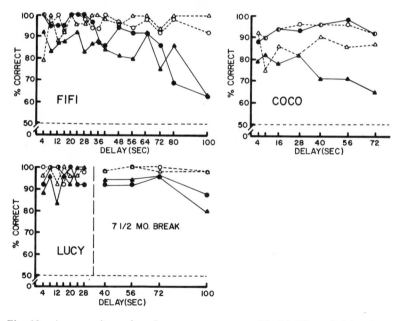

Fig. 10. A comparison of performance on comparable DMTS and delayed conditional matching (DCM) tasks, which alternated every two sessions. In Phase 1, the comparison stimuli were identical in the two paradigms, but the sample stimuli differed. The 2-second delay curve plots performance on these trials as a function of the long delay which occurred with the 2-second delay. ●—● = DMTS, long delays; ▲—▲ = DCM, long delays; ○---○ = DMTS, 2-second delays; △---△ = DCM, 2-second delays.

delay trials, suggesting that the different performance with the two paradigms was due, at least in part, to a failure of association rather than of retention. This interpretation is verified by an analysis of variance (based on the main factors of type of task, 2-second *vs.* long-delay trials, and delay blocks ranging from 8 to 72 seconds) which produced an insignificant F for the interaction between type of task and 2-second *vs.* long delay. Similar analyses were performed on Fifi's data for delay blocks ranging from 28 to 100 seconds, and in her case type of task was significant for long-delay trials as was the interaction between this variable and 2-second *vs.* long-delay trials. However, the difference between the percentage of correct responses obtained in the two paradigms on the long-delay trials is, in absolute terms, quite small, 86.4 *vs.* 82.1%, for DMTS and DCM, respectively.

Because of an unauthorized pregnancy, a $7\frac{1}{2}$-month break intervened during Lucy's experimental training. Focusing on the data obtained after the lengthy break, it is clear that there is very little difference between DMTS and DCM, either for the 2-second or the long-delay trials.

Taken together, the results of Phase 1 suggest that when the conditional relationships between sample and comparison stimuli are well learned—as evidenced by equal DMTS and DCM performance on the 2-second delay trials—retention after relatively long delays is only slightly, if at all, better in the DMTS task. Since DCM eliminates entirely the differential retrieval cues available in DMTS, we may therefore conclude that the formidable visual short-term memory of our subjects does not depend upon, or arise from, the retrieval conditions characteristic of DMTS.

The red disk and vertical line served as standard stimuli for the DCM task, and it is possible to argue that it is easier to differentially store these stimuli than the inverted triangle and dot, which served the same function for DMTS. Although the available evidence does not support this view (D'Amato, 1971; Etkin & D'Amato, 1969), in Phase 2 the standard stimuli were held constant in the two paradigms, and the comparison stimuli varied.

Because of time pressure, only Fifi and Coco were run in Phase 2, which apart from the use of the same stimuli as samples (red disk and vertical line) was very similar in procedural details as those of Phase 1. Eight 24-trial sessions were given at each of the delays indicated on the abscissa of Fig. 11. As the figure shows, Fifi performed somewhat better on the DCM task, both on 2-second and long-delay trials, though analysis of the results for the 28- to 100-second delay blocks did not show this difference to be significant. Coco, on the other

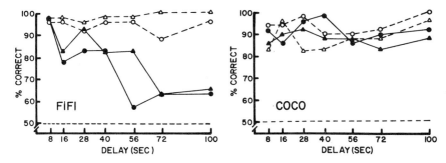

Fig. 11. A comparison of performance on comparable DMTS and delayed conditional matching (DCM) tasks, which alternated every two sessions. In Phase 2 the sample stimuli used in the two paradigms were identical, but the comparison stimuli differed. ●—● = DMTS, long delays; ▲—▲ = DCM, long delays; ○ - - - ○ = DMTS, 2-second delays; △ - - - △ = DCM, 2-second delays.

hand, maintained a higher level of performance on the DMTS task, but as before the superiority of DMTS was approximately equal for the 2-second delay and the long-delay trials. Moreover, the difference between DMTS and DCM was substantially reduced in Phase 2. We may conclude, therefore, that since the present data are in agreement with those of Phase 1, the latter results cannot be attributed to the circumstance that different stimuli served as samples in the DMTS and DCM paradigms.

V. The Development of Short-Term Retention in Monkeys

In Section III we took note of the pervasive "practice effects" that occur in DMTS performance, but their magnitude now needs emphasizing. The most experienced and talented of our subjects is Roscoe, who has been involved with DMTS during most of his adult life. Figure 12 gives a rough indication of the course of the development of visual short-term memory in this animal over the 6 years that he has been exposed to some 30,000 DMTS trials. Initially, he was able to perform only slightly better than chance at a 9-second retention interval. But over the years this limit receded continuously until at his most recent testing, conducted with one long-delay trial per session, Roscoe displayed substantial retention at a 9-minute delay interval in a DMTS task employing six sample stimuli. Nor is there any indication that this represents the limit of his visual "short-term memory."

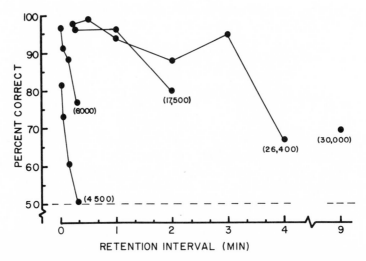

Fig. 12. The development of visual short-term memory in Roscoe over some 30,000 DMTS trials spanning 6 years. The numbers in parentheses are estimates of the total number of DMTS trials received up to that point. The data point on the right is based on 33 trials with a 9-minute retention interval given one trial per day.

An equally striking improvement with practice occurred with the conditional matching task. I have already pointed out the difficulty we encountered in training our animals on DCM, which, unlike DMTS, proved very unstable. An animal performing well at 0-second delay would not infrequently go to pieces when the delay was increased only to 1.0 second. And yet, after sufficient practice these same animals were ultimately able not only to perform well in DCM at lengthy delays but also to equal their DMTS performance.

Something more than Harlow's "learning-sets" seems to be involved here. It is true that with sufficient training monkeys will generalize DMTS to new sample stimuli (e.g., D'Amato, 1971; Mello, 1971; Weinstein, 1945), and this seems to resemble closely the development of learning sets in conventional discrimination tasks. But the fact that primates, with no known rehearsal processes at their disposal, can with practice increase their retention of visual information by a factor of 50 seems to define a different capacity. As yet, we have not the slightest inkling of how they achieve this remarkable feat. In the next section I will comment on some implications of this phenomenon. At this point I would like to raise the question—without attempting an answer—of whether we may have grossly underestimated human retention and other performances by our habit of sampling in our experiments such a thin slice of the subjects' behavior.

VI. Concluding Remarks

A. Is Delayed Matching a Reasonable Short-Term Memory Task?

I have now completed the description of our empirical work, and it remains to suggest what bearing, if any, our results have on the general topic of memory, particularly human memory. A natural starting point is the question of whether any meaningful connection can be made between delayed matching and the short-term memory tasks used with humans. After all, our animals were limited to a very small set of target stimuli with which they had the benefit of extensive experience. Moreover, only a single of these heavily overlearned stimuli was ever presented as the to-be-remembered item.

Perhaps it is only necessary, in rebuttal, to point out that the digits and letters that serve as target stimuli in human studies of short-term memory also constitute relatively small stimulus sets, particularly when one takes into account the different cognitive capacities of monkeys and humans. And no one will argue, I trust, that in regard to familiarity with the stimulus materials employed, the use of digits and letters puts human subjects at a disadvantage. We have already given some consideration to the recognition-recall issue, but let me add here that if the "basic difference between recall and recognition is (probably) whether or not the S can readily generate all possible alternatives [Murdock, 1972, p. 70]," then surely studies in which digits and letters serve as target stimuli are as much recognition tasks as DMTS and DCM. So at least for a significant subset of human short-term memory studies (studies, moreover, which frequently show sizable retention losses for single items over relatively short retention intervals), the delayed matching paradigm would seem to be a reasonable animal analog.

On the other hand, the parallel fades considerably when such short-term memory paradigms as single-trial free-recall and "continuous" recall are considered. In these "multiple-item" tasks the subject is burdened with a series of more or less homogeneous items in rather rapid succession, and the focus of interest shifts from the retention gradient of a single item to the number of items that can survive simultaneously in the short-term store. It is possible that, at bottom, the same processes govern performance in both classes of short-term memory tasks; for example, the retention gradient for a single item may be generated by the increased probability of additional category items entering the short-term store at longer retention intervals. But in any event, on the surface at least delayed matching is not a close relative of the multiple-item short-term memory paradigms.

B. Episodic Memory as Temporal Discrimination

The striking improvement in delayed matching performance which occurs with practice is not unlike the slowly accumulating but ultimately dramatic practice effects which arise in a variety of discriminative tasks. This fact, among others, has led me to wonder whether we might fruitfully view short-term memory as simply another discriminative process, one in which the major discriminative cues are temporal in nature. Taking DMTS as an illustration, at the time of choice the task confronting the subject is to decide which of the two choice stimuli has most recently served in the role of sample. With long retention intervals, this decision becomes more difficult because the "time-to-last-seen" (as sample) of the two stimuli become more similar. Suppose, for example, a square served as the sample on the previous trial, and 1 minute later the current trial, on which the sample is a triangle, begins. If the current and previous retention intervals are both 4 minutes, and the choice stimuli on the current trial are square and triangle, the time-to-last-seen is 9 minutes for the square and 4 minutes for the sample, 2.25 expressed as a ratio. With a 30-second retention interval, on the other hand, this same ratio increases to 18.0. Although the actual situation is bound to be far more complex than is suggested by the present illustration, it seems possible that this general approach could, at least in a qualitative way, account for both retention gradients and the fact that, within limits, performance on animal and human short-term memory tasks increases with longer intertrial intervals (Jarrard & Moise, 1971; Loess & Waugh, 1967).

The ability to discriminate temporal intervals will depend not only on the duration of the intervals themselves but also, of course, on the nature of the events that fill the intervals. For example, when an animal performing at a high accuracy level commits an error, the nonreinforcement encountered could serve to set apart the events of that trial (including the sample stimulus), making them more discriminable after a period of time than they would otherwise be. If a loud tone were sounded simultaneously with the presentation of the sample stimulus, the latter might be more discriminable (from other sample stimuli) on subsequent trials than if the demarcating event, which will be referred to as a "time marker," did not occur. Time markers, of which the clock and the day-night cycle are powerful illustrations, are exceedingly important in our own temporal discriminations, that is, our memory for the temporal ordering of events. We may not easily recall exactly what day we met so and so but, because we happened to look at our watch, we are certain it was at noontime. Without such time markers it would be extremely difficult to sort past events into their proper temporal sequence, which even with all of the aids at our disposal, natural and artificial, still is often accomplished only imperfectly.

My current view, then, is that the kind of memory evidenced in delayed matching—which in the terminology of Tulving (1972) falls in the category of "episodic" memory—is based on discriminative processes no different in kind from those operative in other, more familiar, discriminative tasks. Although I have developed the argument in relation to two-choice DMTS, I think it applies as well to yes-no DMTS and to DCM, only in the latter cases the subject has to consult (to a greater or lesser degree) internal representations of the individual members of the target stimulus set. And there seems little difference in principle between our animals trying to decide in the DCM task whether they last saw the red disk or the vertical line and a human subject trying to reproduce the correct digit at the time of recall.

C. Some Implications of the Temporal Discrimination Hypothesis

Are there any concrete advantages to be gained from viewing short-term memory in terms of discriminative rather than "storage" processes? I think there are. On the conceptual side, by translating short-term memory—or more generally episodic memory—to discriminative processes, we collapse two behavioral categories into one. Rather than thinking of episodic memory as a capacity separate from that of discrimination, we can encompass them in the same class and presumably the variables that are effective in one will be effective in the other. Whatever knowledge we have about discrimination learning (which unfortunately is not overwhelming) should be applicable to memory, and vice versa.

1. Shaping and Practice Effects

Although the implications of this view may not be startling, they can be helpful. For example, the importance of "shaping" in establishing a difficult discrimination is well known in the discrimination learning literature. Two decades ago Lawrence (1952) showed that rats can be more efficiently trained on a difficult brightness discrimination if they are first taught an easy brightness discrimination rather than starting from scratch on the difficult task. "Errorless" discrimination learning and its applications (e.g., Sidman & Stoddard, 1967; Terrace, 1963) represent further developments of this result. Applied to short-term memory, or at least to the delayed-matching version, the implication is that successful performance on a long retention interval can be accomplished much more efficiently by distributing the same amount of practice over gradually increasing delays rather than by introducing the subject at once to the terminal delay value. There can be little doubt that this implication is correct. Conversely, we ought to expect that performance on short-term memory tasks will generally improve as a function of practice. And this is how we are disposed to account for the practice effect produced by Jocko in the experiment described in Section III. His performance suffered when the delay interval was abruptly increased to 2 minutes because the temporal discrimination task was thereby rendered more difficult. Continued practice at the 2-minute retention interval resulted in improved performance for the same reasons that, with practice, performance improves in other discriminative tasks.

Unfortunately, it is not altogether clear why discriminative performance either in or out of the laboratory generally improves with practice, although many current theorists emphasize the importance of learning to attend to the relevant discriminative cues (cf. Sutherland & Mackintosh, 1971). Perhaps by assigning temporal parameters as part of the relevant stimulus dimension, attention theory can be applied to the present problem. The perceptual differentiation view of the Gibsons and their associates (cf. Gibson, 1969) may also be applicable in this connection.

I have already questioned the wisdom of our general experimental procedures which sample only a few minutes of the subject's behavior. It would be interesting in light of the profound practice effects observed in our experiments to expose human subjects to analogous retention tasks for periods of weeks or longer to gauge the extent of practice effects obtainable in these so-called short-term memory tasks. My guess is that they would greatly exceed our present expectations. It is of some interest that Shepard (1967) found that even after a 1-week delay his subjects could discriminate at an extremely high level between "new" and "old" meaningful pictures. If we may view his experiment, in which the target stimuli were presented to the subjects for a 10-second period, as a visual "short-term" memory task, we perhaps receive some support for the previous conjecture. Adult human subjects have a lifetime of experience with complex meaningful stimuli, with establishing and maintaining temporal discriminations among them.

2. Delay-Interval Illumination

Delay-interval illumination was one of the most powerful variables investigated by us, and the question naturally arises as to whether its effects can be accommodated by what we have referred to, somewhat grandly, as the temporal discrimination hypothesis. In Section II,B we dismissed explanations based on visual aftereffects, trace consolidation, and changes in peripheral motor activity. The interpretation I currently favor is that, insofar as visual target stimuli are concerned, delay-interval darkness simply decreases, sometimes dramatically, the effective duration of the retention interval. It seems intuitively reasonable that visual events will appear more recent after an interval spent in darkness than after a like period filled with a myriad of visual perceptions. If this speculation is correct, it would account for both the facilitation of visual DMTS performance by delay-interval darkness, and the fact that a dark probe is equally effective whether it occurs at the beginning or the end of an otherwise illuminated retention interval (Etkin, 1972).

3. The Limits of Short-Term Memory

I have stressed in several places the accomplishments of our subjects with regard to visual short-term memory, and now it is time to acknowledge their limitations. Even when assisted by delay-interval darkness, given a sufficiently long retention interval (approached slowly) their DMTS performance declines to chance or near-chance levels. Why is this? If an animal can "remember" the target stimulus for 2 minutes, why not for 20 minutes, or 20 hours for that matter? If the basis for such short-term memory as is displayed by our subjects resides in a recycling (rehearsal) mechanism, there ought not in principle be any limit to their short-term memory capacity. One could perhaps appeal to the assumption that the recycling process is imperfect in that each recycling carries with it the possibility of some loss of the stored information. But then the problem becomes one of accounting for the virtually flat retention gradients that are sometimes observed over considerable ranges of delay intervals (cf. Figs. 5, 6, 8).

A plausible interpretation of the inevitable limits of delayed matching performance is inherent in the temporal discrimination hypothesis. Just as there are limits to the fineness of discrimination possible in the more familiar modalities of vision and audition, temporal discriminations cannot be performed with infinite resolution. When our subjects' DMTS performance declines to near-chance levels, this is to be taken as indication that their temporal discrimination "difference threshold"—under the contemporary experimental conditions—is being approached. In a similar vein, I would prefer to view the vastly superior DMTS performance of primates over pigeons (cf. Cumming & Berryman, 1965; Roberts, 1972) as arising from a difference in the temporal discriminative skills of the two species rather than from a difference in memory or storage capacities.

4. Short-Term Memory and Delay of Reinforcement

The interpretation of episodic memory as a special case of discriminative behavior has suggested the following interesting parallel. One of the most significant variables which affects animal discrimination learning is delay of reinforcement. In a particularly striking demonstration, Grice (1948) showed that if conditioned reinforcement cues were eliminated, rats that ordinarily required only 20 trials to master a visual discrimination failed to learn the task even after 1400 training trials when reinforcement was delayed for 10 seconds. The deleterious effect of delay of reinforcement on a wide range of behaviors was widely acknowledged theoretically and practically. The issue re-emerged recently when it was found that learning (conditioned aversion) could occur with delays (CS–US intervals) of several hours (cf. Garcia et al., 1972). This striking difference in the effects of delay of reinforcement has led to an entire reorientation in learning theory, one feature of which is the denial of the existence of laws of learning of any general significance.

Without commenting on the merit of this new orientation, it seems strikingly curious to me that ordinary laboratory discrimination learning can be so grossly interfered with by short reinforcement delays when our subjects show themselves capable of a high level of DMTS performance with retention intervals in the order of minutes. If our animals can remember the identity of the sample stimulus for 2 minutes, why could they not remember for the same duration the identity of a stimulus to which they respond, which is the essential requirement of a delay of reinforcement experiment? Or, in discriminative terms, if they can discriminate among temporal events separated by at least 2 minutes in the DMTS situation, why could they not perform at an equal level in a discrimination learning task which places comparable demands on their temporal discriminative ability?

We began looking at this problem, running a few subjects on a simple two-choice discrimination task with a 0-second reinforcement delay, until their performance achieved a high level of accuracy. Our strategy was then to increase reinforcement delay on the same discrimination, giving the subjects the practice they needed in order to span substantial reinforcement delay intervals. After the animals had achieved this goal, our plan was to introduce a fresh discrimination, starting from scratch with the long delay of reinforcement. As it turned out, however, we never got past the first phase. Very much to our surprise, when delay of reinforcement reached 10 or 20 seconds, some animals inexplicably began committing large numbers of errors, although they had had hundreds of training trials on the simple discrimination and had performed virtually errorless at shorter delays. Indeed, in some cases the animals actually began responding more to S— than to S+.

My interpretation of their behavior is that a relatively long delay of reinforcement has aversive properties, and since the delay is contingent on pressing one of the two discriminative cues, the aversiveness becomes associated with S+, because this is the stimulus to which the animal consistently responds. Ultimately the aversiveness reaches a level which exceeds, at least momentarily, the aversiveness of S— (developed earlier by nonreinforced responding to that stimulus). One weakness of this interpretation, and there may be others, is that it is difficult to understand why the subjects persist in responding to S— for so long, inasmuch as by this action the subject is forced to endure not only the delay of reinforcement but also the 1-minute time-out period which followed incorrect responses.

Regardless of the merit of this interpretation, it is clear to me that the emotional consequences of delayed reinforcement very likely outweigh its effect on cognitive processes, and before one can intelligently investigate the role of reinforcement delay in associative processes, the former will have to be dealt with. It is only a short step to the further realization that similar emotional processes may be at work in short-term retention tasks, with similar contaminating effects. In retrospect, the decline in Roscoe's DMTS performance with the 4-minute retention interval (Section III), which we attributed to a lack of motivation, quite likely is a manifestation of the disruptive emotional responses which longer retention intervals tend to generate. But to return to the central point, it is apparent that conventional discrimination learning with delayed reinforcement and DMTS tap a common process, which in my view is the ability to form temporal discriminations. By employing shaping procedures designed to develop the necessary temporal discriminative skills and overcome the emotional consequences of lengthy reinforcement delays, it should be possible to demonstrate rapid discrimination learning with delays of reinforcement of the same order of magnitude as the retention intervals used successfully in our studies. We are currently working on this problem.

In closing, let me observe that, although the temporal discrimination hypothesis is vague and couched only in generalities, it perhaps is significant that a number of writers have recently stressed, with different degrees of explicitness, the importance of temporal variables and discriminations in memory phenomena (e.g., Bower, 1967, pp. 319–320; Gleitman, 1971, p. 30; Hilgard & Bower, 1966, pp. 510–511; Murdock, 1972, pp. 88–90; Winograd, 1971, p. 267). Whether these are minor ripples in the sea of thought surrounding the topic of memory or harbingers of a new tide, remains to be seen.

REFERENCES

Bower, G. H. A multicomponent theory of the memory trace. In K. W. Spence & J. T. Spence (Eds.), *The psychology of learning and motivation: Advances in research and theory.* Vol. 1. New York: Academic Press, 1967.

Butler, R. A. Discrimination learning by rhesus monkeys to auditory incentives. *Journal of Comparative and Physiological Psychology,* 1957, **50,** 239–241.

Corman, C. D., & Wickens, D. D. Retroactive inhibition in short-term memory. *Journal of Verbal Learning and Verbal Behavior,* 1968, **7,** 16–19.

Cumming, W. W., & Berryman, R. The complex discriminated operant: Studies of matching-to-sample and related problems. In D. I. Mostofsky (Ed.), *Stimulus generalization.* Stanford: Stanford University Press, 1965. Pp. 284–330.

D'Amato, M. R. Direct programming of multiple stimuli—the tape block reader. *Journal of the Experimental Analysis of Behavior,* 1965, **8,** 230.

D'Amato, M. R. Sample familiarity and delayed matching in monkeys. *Psychonomic Science,* 1971, **25,** 179–180.

D'Amato, M. R., & O'Neill, W. Matching behavior: Some methodological problems. *Behavior Research Methods and Instrumentation,* 1970, **2,** 162–164.

D'Amato, M. R., & O'Neill, W. Effect of delay-interval illumination on matching behavior in the capuchin monkey. *Journal of the Experimental Analysis of Behavior,* 1971, **15,** 327–333.

D'Amato, M. R., & Worsham, R. W. Delayed matching in the capuchin monkey with brief sample durations. *Learning and Motivation,* 1972, **3,** 304–312.

D'Amato, M. R., & Worsham, R. W. Retrieval cues and short-term memory in capuchin monkeys. *Journal of Comparative and Physiological Psychology,* in press.

Düncker, G., & Rensch, B. Verzögerung des Vergessens erlernter visuellen Aufgaben bei

Fischen durch Dunkelhaltung. *Pflugers Archiv für die Gesamte Physiologie des Menschen und der Tiere,* 1968, **301,** 1–6.

Elliot, P. B. Tables of d'. In J. A. Swets (Ed.), *Signal detection and recognition by human observers.* New York: Wiley, 1964. Pp. 651–684.

Etkin, M. W. Ambient light-produced interference in a delayed matching task with capuchin monkeys. Unpublished doctoral dissertation, Rutgers University, 1970.

Etkin, M. W. Light produced interference in a delayed matching task with capuchin monkeys. *Learning and Motivation,* 1972, **3,** 313–324.

Etkin, M., & D'Amato, M. R. Delayed matching-to-sample and short-term memory in the capuchin monkey. *Journal of Comparative and Physiological Psychology,* 1969, **69,** 544–549.

Garcia, J., McGowan, B. K., & Green, K. F. Biological constraints on conditioning. In A. H. Black & W. F. Prokasy (Eds.), *Classical conditioning II: Current research and theory.* New York: Appleton, 1972. Pp. 3–27.

Gibson, E. J. *Perceptual learning and development.* New York: Appleton, 1969.

Ginsberg, N. Matching in pigeons. *Journal of Comparative and Physiological Psychology,* 1957, **50,** 261–263.

Gleitman, H. Forgetting of long-term memory in animals. In W. K. Honig & P. H. R. James (Eds.), *Animal memory.* New York: Academic Press, 1971. Pp. 1–44.

Green, D. M., & Swets, J. A. *Signal detection theory and psychophysics.* New York: Wiley, 1966.

Grice, G. R. The relation of secondary reinforcement to delayed reward in visual discrimination learning. *Journal of Experimental Psychology,* 1948, **38,** 1–16.

Hellyer, S. Supplementary report: Frequency of stimulus presentation and short-term decrement in recall. *Journal of Experimental Psychology,* 1962, **64,** 650.

Hilgard, E. R., & Bower, G. H. *Theories of learning.* (3rd ed.) New York: Appleton, 1966.

Honig, W. K., & James, P. H. R. (Eds.) *Animal memory.* New York: Academic Press, 1971.

Hornbuckle, P. A. Delayed-response performance as a function of sensory stimulation in the squirrel and owl monkey. *Journal of Comparative and Physiological Psychology,* 1972, **79,** 99–104.

Itard, J. M. G. *The wild boy of Aveyron.* (Transl. by G. & M. Humphrey) New York: Century, 1932.

Jarrard, L. E., & Moise, S. L., Jr. Short-term memory in the stumptail macaque: Effect of physical restraint of behavior on performance. *Learning and Motivation,* 1970, **1,** 267–275.

Jarrard, L. E., & Moise, S. L. Short-term memory in the monkey. In L. E. Jarrard (Ed.), *Cognitive processes of nonhuman primates.* New York: Academic Press, 1971. Pp. 3–24.

Jarvik, M. E., Goldfarb, T. L., & Carley, J. L. Influence of interference on delayed matching in monkeys. *Journal of Experimental Psychology,* 1969, **81,** 1–6.

King, J. E., & Clawson, J. R. Delayed response by squirrel monkeys under various delay lighting conditions. *Psychonomic Science,* 1966, **6,** 429–430.

King, J. E., Flaningam, M. R., & Rees, W. W. Delayed response with different delay conditions by squirrel monkeys and fox squirrels. *Animal Behavior,* 1968, **16,** 271–275.

Kroll, N. E. A., Parks, T., Parkinson, S. R., Bieber, S. L., & Johnson, A. L. Short-term memory while shadowing: Recall of visually and of aurally presented letters. *Journal of Experimental Psychology,* 1970, **85,** 220–224.

Lawrence, D. H. The transfer of a discrimination along a continuum. *Journal of Comparative and Physiological Psychology*, 1952, **45**, 511–516.

Lewis, D. J. Sources of experimental amnesia. *Psychological Review*, 1969, **76**, 461–472.

Lockhart, R. S., & Murdock, B. B., Jr. Memory and the theory of signal detection. *Psychological Bulletin*, 1970, **74**, 100–109.

Loess, H., & Waugh, N. C. Short-term memory and intertrial interval. *Journal of Verbal Learning and Verbal Behavior*, 1967, **6**, 455–460.

McDowell, A. A., & Brown, W. L. Intervening darkness and delayed response performance by rhesus monkeys. *Journal of Genetic Psychology*, 1960, **97**, 59–65.

Malmo, R. B. Interference factors in delayed response in monkeys after removal of frontal lobe. *Journal of Neurophysiology*, 1942, **5**, 295–308.

Mello, N. Alcohol effects on delayed matching to sample performance by rhesus monkeys. *Physiology and Behavior*, 1971, **7**, 77–101.

Meudell, P. R. Short-term visual memory: Comparative effects of two types of distraction on the recall of visually presented verbal and nonverbal material. *Journal of Experimental Psychology*, 1972, **94**, 244–247.

Moise, S. L., Jr. Short-term retention in *Macaca speciosa* following interpolated activity during delayed matching from sample. *Journal of Comparative and Physiological Psychology*, 1970, **73**, 506–514.

Murdock, B. B., Jr. Four-channel effects in short-term memory. *Psychonomic Science*, 1971, **24**, 197–198.

Murdock, B. B., Jr. Short-term memory. In G. H. Bower (Ed.), *The psychology of learning and motivation: Advances in research and theory*. Vol. 5. New York: Academic Press, 1972. Pp. 67–127.

Murdock, B. B., Jr., & Walker, K. D. Modality effects in free recall. *Journal of Verbal Learning and Verbal Behavior*, 1969, **8**, 665–676.

Norman, D. A. (Ed.) *Models of human memory*. New York: Academic Press, 1970.

Parks, T. E. Signal-detectability theory of recognition-memory performance. *Psychological Review*, 1966, **73**, 44–58.

Peterson, L. R., & Peterson, M. J. Short-term retention of individual verbal items. *Journal of Experimental Psychology*, 1959, **58**, 193–198.

Potter, M. C., & Levy, E. I. Recognition memory for a rapid sequence of pictures. *Journal of Experimental Psychology*, 1969, **81**, 10–15.

Roberts, W. A. Short-term memory in the pigeon: Effects of repetition and spacing. *Journal of Experimental Psychology*, 1972, **94**, 74–83.

Salzberg, P. M., Parks, T. E., Kroll, N. E. A., & Parkinson, S. R. Retroactive effects of phonemic similarity on short-term recall of visual and auditory stimuli. *Journal of Experimental Psychology*, 1971, **91**, 43–46.

Scarborough, D. L. Memory for brief visual displays of symbols. *Cognitive Psychology*, 1972, **3**, 408–429.

Scheckel, C. L. Self-adjustment of the interval in delayed matching: Limit of delay for the rhesus monkey. *Journal of Comparative and Physiological Psychology*, 1965, **59**, 415–418.

Seligman, M. E. P. On the generality of the laws of learning. *Psychological Review*, 1970, **77**, 406–418.

Shaffer, W. O., & Shiffrin, R. M. Rehearsal and storage of visual information. *Journal of Experimental Psychology*, 1972, **92**, 292–296.

Shepard, R. N. Recognition memory for words, sentences, and pictures. *Journal of Verbal Learning and Verbal Behavior*, 1967, **6**, 156–163.

Sidman, M., & Stoddard, L. T. The effectiveness of fading in programming a simultaneous form discrimination for retarded children. *Journal of the Experimental Analysis of Behavior*, 1967, **10**, 3–15.

Spear, N. E. Forgetting as retrieval failure. In W. K. Honig & P. H. R. James (Eds.), *Animal memory*. New York: Academic Press, 1971. Pp. 45–109.

Sutherland, N. S., & Mackintosh, N. J. *Mechanisms of animal discrimination learning*. New York: Academic Press, 1971.

Terrace, H. S. Discrimination learning with and without "errors." *Journal of the Experimental Analysis of Behavior*, 1963, **6**, 1–27.

Tulving, E. Episodic and semantic memory. In E. Tulving & W. Donaldson (Eds.), *Organization of memory*. New York: Academic Press, 1972. Pp. 381–403.

Weinstein, B. Matching-from-sample by rhesus monkeys and by children. *Journal of Comparative Psychology*, 1941, **31**, 195–213.

Weinstein, B. The evaluation of intelligent behavior in rhesus monkeys. *Genetic Psychology Monographs*, 1945, **31**, 3–48.

Winograd, E. Some issues relating animal memory to human memory. In W. K. Honig & P. H. R. James (Eds.), *Animal memory*. New York: Academic Press, 1971. Pp. 259–278.

Worsham, R. W., & D'Amato, M. R. Ambient light, white noise, and monkey vocalization as sources of interference in visual short-term memory of monkeys. *Journal of Experimental Psychology*, 1973, **99**, 99–105.

PERCENTILE REINFORCEMENT: PARADIGMS FOR EXPERIMENTAL ANALYSIS OF RESPONSE SHAPING[1]

John R. Platt

DEPARTMENT OF PSYCHOLOGY, MCMASTER UNIVERSITY,
HAMILTON, ONTARIO, CANADA

I. Introduction

It is probably obvious to even the casual observer that conditioning and other simple learning phenomena no longer enjoy as central and pervasive a role in experimental psychology as they once did. There are many reasons for this demise of conditioning as a cornerstone of experimental psychology, but it is not the purpose of this article to analyze or even enumerate all of these reasons. However, it is this author's opinion that one of these reasons is a certain stagnation that has often occurred in the literature of conditioning as a result of an implicit and self-imposed view of the conditioning psychologist's task as one of analyzing a rather small set of accepted conditioning paradigms. It is as if familiarity with the common paradigms of classical and instrumental conditioning has bred the view that phenomena occurring in these paradigms are themselves the basic processes of behavioral change. This mistaken equation of paradigm and process tends to make understanding of the paradigms an end in

[1] Preparation of this paper was supported by Grant A8269 from the National Research Council of Canada. The author wishes to thank H. M. Jenkins for critical readings of earlier versions of this paper, although remaining inadequacies are solely the fault of the author.

itself. The almost unavoidable consequence of such a strategy is a diminishing return of new and generalizable knowledge as the details of behavior in accepted paradigms are progressively brought to light. As such a diminution takes place, it is not surprising that students of behavior find less and less reason to turn to conditioning for progress in the understanding of behavior.

A more modest but less limiting view of the role of conditioning paradigms in the study of behavioral change is possible. On this view, a conditioning paradigm is merely a tool which allows experimental analysis of a particular class of variables suspected to be of importance in determining some type of behavioral change. For example, if it is suspected that changes in behaivor may be effected by changing temporal relationships between certain stimulus events, a classical conditioning paradigm would probably be chosen to investigate the effects of this class of variables because such a paradigm is explicitly designed to control temporal relationships between stimulus events. Even within this context, various paradigms may emerge because of various possibilities as to the types of stimulus relationships which produce behavioral change. This point is illustrated by the choice between "unpaired" and "random" control groups depending on whether one wishes to investigate the effects of stimulus contiguity or of stimulus contingency (Rescorla, 1967).

An even more important aspect of the present view of the role of conditioning paradigms is that paradigms are not exclusive, since there is no implication that a particular class of variables determines the only, or even the most fundamental, processes of behavioral change. On the contrary, the present view makes explicit the fact that in order to control a particular class of variables, other potential variables are of necessity left uncontrolled. This point can easily be appreciated when it is recognized that irrespective of one's conviction as to the fundamental importance of changes in temporal relationships between stimuli, it might also be suspected that changes in the consequences of an organism's behavior may effect behavioral change. This latter class of variables is not studied with classical conditioning paradigms because such paradigms necessarily limit the control which can be exercised over relationships between behavior and subsequent stimulus events as a direct result of the control exercised over temporal relationships between stimulus events. In order to study effects of changes in the consequences of an organism's behavior, an instrumental or operant conditioning paradigm is usually used. It is important to note, however, that in moving to a paradigm which controls the consequences of behavior by making presentation of a stimulus event behaviorally dependent, control of temporal relationships between stimuli is necessarily limited. This limitation results from the fact that the dependence of a stimulus event on a behavioral event and on some second stimulus event can only be controlled simultaneously if the behavioral event and the second stimulus event are perfectly correlated.

When it is recognized that a particular conditioning paradigm is not the embodiment of a fundamental process of behavioral change, the need becomes apparent for continually modifying old paradigms and developing new paradigms so as to examine variables not manipulated, or even confounded by existing paradigms. Many examples of the fruitfulness of such an enterprise could be drawn from the recent conditioning literature. One such example is provided by the work of Herrnstein (1970) and others who have made admirable progress toward providing a quantitative statement of the empirical law of effect. This progress was made possible by shifting attention from relationships between response rate and reinforcement rate in simple operant reinforcement schedules to relationships between relative response rate and relative reinforcement rate in choice situations or concurrent schedules of reinforcement. Anyone familiar with this work is aware that although the observation of relative rates in concurrent situations appears considerably more complex and derivative than observation of absolute rates in simple reinforcement schedules, the former approach yields mathematically simpler and empirically more invariant relationships between behavior and its consequences.

The present article presents a class of conditioning paradigms which in this author's view offers considerable promise for experimentally analyzing a class of variables which has long been accepted as fundamental to behavior change, but which has remained inextricably confounded within traditional paradigms of instrumental and operant conditioning. In addition, some early results utilizing these new paradigms will be reviewed, and some examples of applications of these paradigms to specific problems in behavior theory will be proposed.

II. Response Shaping as an Attempt to Control Relationships between Behavior and Reinforcement Criteria

As has already been suggested, conditioning paradigms allow experimental control of selected classes of variables which potentially effect behavioral change. Instrumental or operant conditioning paradigms allow examination of how the consequences of an organism's behavior change subsequent behavior. The basic logic of this type of paradigm was well established by E. L. Thorndike (1898) before the dawn of the twentieth century. This logic involves arranging a situation in which some consequence ensues whenever an organism executes a criterion behavior. In Thorndike's case, the criterion behaviors were usually traversal of a maze or operation of a manipulandum, such as stepping on a treadle or pulling on a string. The consequence was usually access to food. Thorndike would repeatedly expose an organism to one of the situations just described, and on each exposure he would measure the time elapsed before the criterion behavior occurred. If this time changed systematically with repeated exposures, an effect of behavioral consequences was assumed to have been demonstrated.

Without going on to elaborate Thorndike's views about this type of conditioning, there are two features of his paradigm which are relevant to the current development. Both of these features derive from the way in which Thorndike defined criterion behaviors. First, Thorndike's paradigm could only be used to manipulate the probability of behaviors which already had a nonzero probability of occurrence. That is, the consequence whose influence on behavior was to be studied would only occur if a criterion behavior occurred. Thorndike was quite aware that it was not the experimenter's criteria for application of consequences which acted to change behavior, but rather actual experience with particular consequences following particular behaviors.

A second feature of Thorndike's paradigm is simply an extension of the first. Although Thorndike realized that the effectiveness of his paradigm in producing behavioral change depended on relationships between an organism's behavior and the experimenter's criteria for applying consequences, the paradigm controlled the criteria rather than their relationships to the organism's current behavior. As the organism's behavior was changed by consequences actually experienced, its relationships to the experimenter's criteria changed so as to modify the distribution of future consequences. For example, a cat repeatedly placed in a box and allowed access to fish following depression of a treadle would on successive occasions depress the treadle with less intervening behavior. The resulting decrease in latency of treadle depressions was taken as evidence of the response selection produced by past treadle depressions having been followed by access to fish. However, this elimination of noncriterion behaviors also meant that a larger proportion of the organism's behavioral output was meeting the experimenter's criterion.

Both a situation in which an organism emits no criterion behaviors and one in which it emits only criterion behaviors are often summarized by saying that the experimenter's criteria for applying consequences are not *contacting* the organism's behavior. Any criteria for applying consequences to behavior partitions potential behavioral events into two or more classes, where class membership is defined by the consequence a particular event is to receive. The minimal case of such partitioning would establish a class of criterion events which would be followed by a particular consequence and a class of noncriterion events which would not be followed by this consequence. In this context, contact between the organism's behavior and the experimenter's criteria for application of consequences refers to some measure of balance between the likelihoods of occurrences from these two classes of behavioral events. Any change in criteria which does not produce a change in class membership for some behavior with a currently nonzero probability of occurrence cannot possibly produce behavioral change. The important point here, however, is that in Thorndike's paradigm changes in degree of contact between an organism's behavior and the experimenter's criteria were not all or none, but occurred to varying degrees in an uncontrolled manner throughout the acquisition process. Exactly what measure of balance between the organism's likelihoods of emitting criterion and noncriterion behavioral events would be most useful as a quantification of contact depends on additional assumptions. Nevertheless, it is clear that over the course of acquisition in Thorndike's paradigm, contact between the organism's behavior and the experimenter's criteria would typically undergo an initial increase and a subsequent decrease.

In the years since Thorndike's pioneering work, his paradigm has been repeatedly refined, extended, and analyzed—particularly by B. F. Skinner and other operant investigators. This work has often given recognition to the problems that have just been discussed and has offered some solution to difficulties caused by these problems in specific instances. However, it is this author's opinion that the basic problem of developing paradigms which control relationships between changing behavior and its consequences has not been adequately treated.

The two main developments in operant research which deal to some extent with the shortcomings discussed for Thorndike's paradigm are the notion of response shaping and the development of a variety of intermittent reinforcement schedules. First consider response shaping. As has been indicated, Thorndike's paradigm was only applicable to producing changes in the probability of behaviors which already had a nonzero probability of occurrence in an organism's repertoire. Skinner (1938, Ch. 8) saw the possibility of removing this limitation by what he called the method of successive approximations—now usually referred to as response shaping. This method involves nothing more than presenting consequences for, or reinforcing[2] behaviors which are successively closer approximations to some target behavior. Skinner's rationale for this method rested on the processes of response generalization and response differentiation which he assumed to be fundamental to operant conditioning paradigms. "Response generalization" refers to the observation that when reinforcing a particular behavior increases the probability of occurrence of that behavior, it also produces increases in the probability of similar behaviors. "Response differentiation" refers to the finding that reinforcing some behaviors while not reinforcing others leads to a reduction in the probability of the nonreinforced behaviors. Whenever an ordering of behaviors with respect to response generalization can be specified between some behavior with a nonzero probability of occurrence and a target behavior, one can then attempt through response shaping to bring the target behavior to a nonzero probability of occurrence. This is done by reinforcing the closest approximation to the target behavior that currently has a substantial probability of occurrence. As a result of response generalization, behaviors which are yet closer approximations to the target behavior should increase in probability. As a result of response differentiation, behaviors which are less similar to the desired behavior should decrease in probability. Once this has happened, a criterion behavior more closely approximating the target behavior can be selected for reinforcement with the whole process being repeated as often an necessary. Such shaping would be expected to succeed so long as the reinforcers used are effective, the target behavior is biologically possible, and the changes in reinforcement criteria do not exceed the range of response generalization.

In terms used earlier, response shaping attempts to present a succession of reinforcement criteria such that the organism's behavior is always in contact with the current criterion. However, response shaping also suggests another relationship between an organism's behavior and reinforcement criteria which may be critical to the effectiveness of reinforcement in changing behavior. This second relationship concerns the uniqueness of criterion behaviors among

---

2 Terms such as "reinforcement" are used throughout this paper to refer to response-contingent presentations of a stimulus, independent of the behavioral effects of such an operation.

behaviors currently being emitted by the organism, and may be referred to as the *selectiveness* of the reinforcement criteria with respect to the organism's behavior. Thus, if only a relatively narrow range of behaviors currently being emitted satisfies the reinforcement criterion, higher selectiveness exists than if a wider range meets this criterion. A minimum of selectiveness would occur when behaviors all along the shaping dimension are reinforced randomly, although contact with reinforcement criteria might be the same as in some situation with high selectiveness, since degree of balance between likelihoods of behavioral events from reinforced and nonreinforced classes could be the same in both cases. Thus, response-shaping methods seek not only to maintain contact between the organism's behavior and reinforcement criteria, but also to maintain selectiveness of the reinforcement criteria with respect to the organism's behavior so as to maximize the desired movement of behavior along the shaping dimension toward the target behavior.

Response shaping is obviously a very powerful extension of Thorndike's basic paradigm and in principle allows for experimental control of relations between behavior and reinforcement criteria such as contact and selectiveness. One might expect that such paradigms have been extensively explored in search of general, quantitative laws. However, this is not the case. Response shaping in both laboratory and applied settings has usually been treated as an art for bringing desired behaviors to a nonzero probability of occurrence so that they may be manipulated by more conventional conditioning techniques. There are almost no attempts to systematically analyze response-shaping paradigms with a goal of abstracting general, quantitative laws. A major effort in this direction is the work of Lane and his associates (e.g., Lane, Kopp, Sheppard, Anderson, & Carlson, 1967). Lane investigated shaping of the duration of vocalizations of the vowel, u, in human adults using monetary reinforcers. The variable of main interest to Lane was the size of changes between successive reinforcement criteria. Lane's findings not too surprisingly indicated that the effectiveness of his shaping procedures appeared to depend on a relationship between the subject's behavior and the criteria for reinforcement. Lane computed a "shaping index" to reflect this relationship. The index was the difference between the criterion duration for reinforcement and the mean duration of responses, expressed in units of the standard deviation of response durations. This index was highly correlated with number of responses required to obtain various shaping criteria and was invariably large when shaping failed.

Although results such as Lane's suggest that the effective variables in response shaping are relationships between the subject's behavior and the experimenter's criteria for reinforcement, shaping studies have usually not attempted to directly control or manipulate such relationships. Shaping is usually done by specifying a series of fixed reinforcement criteria with no reference to the organism's current behavior. These criteria are then changed according to some implicit or explicit rules, either independent of the organism's behavior or based on the organism's past success or failure in obtaining reinforcements. Behaviorally dependent rules have often not been sufficiently explicit to make any conclusions on the basis of results obtained. But even when the rules for changing criteria have been clearly stated (e.g. Weiss, 1967), it has still not been clear what generalizations to other situations might be warranted. The difficulty seems to be that although the success of a particular shaping procedure indicates that behavior did contact the successive reinforcement criteria and that some selectiveness of reinforcement criteria was maintained, the degree and nature of this contact and selectiveness has not been explicitly controlled, manipulated, or even defined in a way applicable to other behaviors or situations.

This problem of defining, controlling, and manipulating relationships between an organism's behavior and reinforcement criteria is not limited to response-shaping paradigms but is characteristic of instrumental and operant conditioning paradigms in general. All of the traditional operant conditioning paradigms are special cases of response shaping in which only a single fixed set of reinforcement criteria is used, rather than a succession of such criteria. That is, one is examining the ways in which consequences act to select responses. Just as was described in the case of Thorndike's paradigm, the contact of an organism's behavior with a reinforcement criterion and the selectiveness of that criterion are free to vary in numerous ways as the behavior is modified by its encounters with that criterion. Operant investigators have devised a variety of intermittent reinforcement schedules which control particular aspects of such relationships. An example is provided by interval schedules which present reinforcement following the first criterion behavioral event after a controlled interval of time has elapsed from the last reinforcement. Such schedules have the property of controlling the temporal density of reinforcement, provided criterion behaviors occur at least as often as reinforcements are available. Thus, if degree of contact between behavior and reinforcement criteria is considered to be constant so long as every reinforced behavioral event is accompanied by a fixed average period of nonreinforced behavioral events, interval schedules can be said to control this contact over a range of response rates which are sufficient to produce all reinforcements made available by the schedule. Unfortunately this same approach is not applicable to the case of response shaping in which the problem is what to regard as a criterion behavior, rather than what instances of a criterion behavior to reinforce. That is to say that such intermittent schedules do nothing to control selectiveness. The approach is also not directly applicable to instances in which one wishes to reinforce all or a fixed proportion of criterion behaviors or to differentially reinforce certain features of a criterion behavior.

In view of the limitations of traditional intermittent reinforcement schedules in controlling relationships between behavior and reinforcement criteria, it is not too surprising that operant investigators have often chosen to concentrate on "steady states" (Sidman, 1961) in which reinforcement criteria have been in effect long enough for relations between behavior and the criteria to achieve an equilibrium. This of course provides little information about acquisition processes or other "transition states" (Sidman, 1961) which Thorndike's paradigm was originally intended to elucidate. An exclusive concentration on steady states is also open to the criticism that steady-state behavior may depend on details of preceding transitional states. Such dependencies would be difficult to identify, let alone analyze, if only steady states were to be investigated. It thus seems reasonable to assert that operant conditioning in general, and response shaping in particular, could profit from new paradigms designed to experimentally manipulate those relationships between behavior and reinforcement criteria, which have been referred to here as contact with and selectiveness of reinforcement criteria.

III. Nontemporal Concepts of Relationships between Behavior and Reinforcement Criteria

There are innumerable ways one might approach the problem of defining and experimentally controlling relationships between behavior and reinforcement criteria during response shaping. Any *a priori* judgment as to which approach would ultimately prove most useful is highly questionable, but there are some rational considerations. One approach would be to correlate various shaping indexes, such as that used by Lane *et al.* (1967), with effectiveness of shaping under a variety of conditions. Indexes which provided the highest correlations could then be proposed as quantitative definitions of such relationships as contact and selectiveness. Further research could identify sizes and rates of changes in reinforcement criteria which correlate highly with the value of these shaping indexes, and hence, ones which could be used to control and manipulate the value of the indexes. A more direct approach would be to define reinforcement criteria in terms of an organism's current behavior in such ways as to directly control particular aspects of the behavior's relationship to reinforcement criteria. For example, Lane's shaping index could be directly controlled by reinforcing any behavior whose value on the shaping dimension exceeded by a fixed number of standard deviation units the mean of values currently being emitted.

Having decided to investigate behavior-dependent reinforcement criteria which directly control some aspects of their relationship to behavior, the question still remains of how these aspects are to be selected. Of course, the above-mentioned consideration of selecting aspects of the relationship which correlate highly with shaping success is important. However, an even more important consideration is that the aspects chosen for investigation be definable for a variety of behaviors and situations. For instance, a concept of behavior's contact with reinforcement criteria implied by a particular class of behavior-dependent reinforcement criteria can only have systematic significance and general usefulness to the extent that it can be manipulated for various behaviors in different situations and shown to obey similar laws. A shaping index such as Lane's does not fare well on this latter point. The use of concepts of mean and standard deviation and of mathematical operations of subtraction and division limit applicability of the index to shaping along dimensions measured on a ratio scale. Use of parametric descriptive statistics also assumes that the shape of the distribution of current behavior along the relevant dimension is either constant or unimportant.

Definitions of behavior's relationships to reinforcement criteria which will be offered in this paper attempt to minimize assumptions about the dimension along which behavior is to be shaped. It will be assumed that there is a set of behaviors which can be at least *ordered* with respect to response generalization. This assumption of an ordinal dimension is the minimum allowed by the concept of response generalization. Thus "response shaping" has no meaning if at least an ordinal dimension of response generalization is not specified. All behavior-dependent reinforcement criteria introduced in the remainder of this paper will require only ordinal properties of behavior.

Having dealt with the preliminary considerations just discussed, a first attempt at defining contact with, and selectiveness of reinforcement criteria, and development of a paradigm to control these relationships can be undertaken. By assumption, a situation is available for which a set of behaviors can be specified such that any member of the set can be rank ordered with respect to all other members on the dimension along which behavior is to be shaped. For brevity, members of such a set will simply be referred to as "measurable behaviors." One sense in which the contact of this set of measurable behaviors with reinforcement criteria could be held constant would be to reinforce a constant proportion of their occurrences. This very simple concept of contact with reinforcement criteria is the one implied in the earlier discussion of Thorndike's paradigm. In that discussion it was indicated that contact with reinforcement criteria changed with repeated trials in the sense that a larger proportion of behavioral events were drawn from the reinforced class.

Since the measure of contact just proposed is based on the relative frequencies of occurrence of reinforced and nonreinforced behavioral events, with no regard for their distribution in time, a companion concept of selectiveness should have similar nontemporal properties. Such a measure of the selectiveness of reinforcement criteria with respect to a set of measurable behaviors can be defined in terms of the proportion of measurable behaviors being emitted which fall within the range of reinforced values on the shaping dimension. Thus any criteria which reinforce all behavioral events within a range of values on the shaping dimension containing a particular proportion of measurable behaviors currently being emitted would represent the same degree of selectiveness. Criteria which reinforce all behavioral events within a range of values containing a larger proportion of current measurable behaviors would represent both less selectiveness and a different degree of contact, although contact could be equated without changing selectiveness if only an appropriate random proportion of behavioral events within the less selective range were reinforced.

In order to control contact with, and selectiveness of reinforcement criteria in response shaping under the definitions just proposed, a paradigm would have to have three major features. First, it would have to control the proportion of measurable behavioral events reinforced. Second, it would have to control the proportion of measurable behavioral events falling within the range of reinforced values on the shaping dimension. Third, it would have to allow some separation of these two variables. A paradigm having these properties is suggested by a fundamental theorem of nonparametric statistics (Smith, 1953). This theorem states that the expected proportion of a population falling between two ordered observations in a random sample from that population is

$$\phi = 1/(m + 1) \tag{1}$$

where m is the sample size. In other words, percentile points of a random sample are estimates of percentile points of the population from which the sample was drawn. In order to see the relevance of this theorem to the present problem, assume that each occurrence of a member of a set of measurable behaviors is randomly selected from a theoretical distribution described the then current probabilities of occurrence of various measurable behaviors. Under these circumstances, Eq. (1) implies that the probability of a particular behavioral event falling between any two ordered observations in a random sample of size m from the same theoretical distribution would be $1/(m + 1)$. This expression also specifies the probabilities of a particular behavioral event falling above the largest or below the smallest observation in the sample. Thus, by reinforcing each occurrence of a measurable behavior if and only if its value on the measurement dimension exceeds a fixed number of ordered values in a random sample from the same theoretical distribution, one would control the proportion of measurable behaviors in the reinforced class and the proportion of behavioral events falling within the range of reinforced values on the shaping dimension at any particular time. These expected proportions would be independent of changes in the distribution of measured behaviors and would have a value of

$$P(S^R) = 1 - [k/(m + 1)] \tag{2}$$

where k is the number of ordered values in the sample to be exceeded for reinforcement and m is the sample size.

The main problem in actually implementing the paradigm just described is that of obtaining a random sample from the theoretical distribution of probabilities of occurrence of the various measurable behaviors. An adequate approximation to such a sample may be had by considering an organism's m most recently emitted measurable behaviors. This sample might not be random because of low-order sequential dependencies between values of successively emitted behaviors. In addition, observations in this sample would probably not all be from exactly the same theoretical distribution, because shaping may have been effective in modifying this distribution over the course of the last m responses. Any tendency for these two factors to change the proportions defining contact and selectiveness could be minimized by making m larger than the period of any major sequential dependencies, but small relative to rates of change expected in the distribution of measurable behaviors actually emitted. Both actual data from the author's laboratory (Alleman & Platt, 1973) and results of computer simulations suggest that in most situations a wide range of m values will produce good control of proportion of occurrences of measurable behaviors actually reinforced.

The type of shaping paradigm just described will be referred to as a "percentile reinforcement schedule," because reinforcement of any occurrence of a measurable behavior is determined by its rank order or percentile score in respect to immediately preceding occurrences. The m most recent measurable behaviors in such a paradigm will be called the "control memory." The paradigm can perhaps be made more concrete by some actual examples. To this author's knowledge there are only two published reports in which a paradigm similar to the percentile reinforcement schedule just described has actually been used. One of these reports (Fields, 1970) was concerned with shaping PR, PP, and RR intervals of the rat EKG. The procedure of particular interest here involved punishment, rather than reinforcement. In some cases rats were presented with tail shock or aversive brain stimulation following either PR, PP, or RR intervals which were *shorter* than a fixed number of the last 512 such intervals. In other cases the aversive event occurred when the current interval was *longer* than a fixed number of the last 512 intervals. It was reported that percent change in baseline cardiac intervals was about the same for the three types of intervals and for the two directions of shaping. The variable of major interest was the proportion of the last 512 intervals at which the criterion for shock was set. As the proportion to be shocked increased from .01 to .1, maximum percent change from baseline interval increased almost linearly from 0 to about 22%. When the proportion of intervals to be shocked was further increased from .1 to .5, maximum percent change from baseline interval decreased in a negatively accelerated manner to a value of about 7.5%. It was also reported that changes in cardiac intervals produced by this procedure sometimes occurred gradually as one might expect for a response-shaping process. However, about 40% of the rats showed very rapid, almost all-or-none transitions from baseline to maximum change.

The Field's study certainly demonstrates the feasibility of percentile reinforcement schedules and the potential relevance of the concepts of contact and selectiveness which these schedules represent. However, this study did not attempt to separate these two concepts. Also, a highly regulated response system such as cardiac activity is probably not an ideal testing ground for response-shaping paradigms, and the function relating maximum percent change in cardiac activity to proportion of intervals followed by shock may have been complicated by unconditioned effects of shock on cardiac output.

Another series of experiments using percentile reinforcement schedules similar to those proposed here has been carried out in the author's laboratory (Alleman & Platt, 1973). The primary purpose of these studies was to experimentally separate effects of differential reinforcement of the interresponse times (IRT's) of pigeons' key pecks (selectiveness) from effects attributable to the proportion of key pecks reinforced (contact). The basic procedure of these experiments involved presenting food to food-deprived pigeons following key pecks which terminated IRT's more extreme than a fixed proportion of the bird's m most recent IRT's. In some cases the longest extreme was reinforced, while in others it was the shortest extreme. The only major deviation from the percentile reinforcement schedules proposed here was the addition of small changes in extremity of reinforcement criteria depending on whether the cumulative proportion of key pecks actually reinforced was above or below a nominal value. Although such an addition was made to further insure control of the proportion of key pecks reinforced, subsequent data collected in this author's laboratory shows that such a procedure does little to improve the control of this variable already provided by the percentile schedule.

The first experiment reported by Alleman and Platt investigated alternate shaping of longer and shorter IRT's as a function of percentile-reinforcement criterion. Different birds were reinforced for IRT's more extreme than 50, 75, 90, or 95% of their m most recent IRT's. The resulting conditions were designated as IRT $>$ 50, IRT $>$ 75, etc., when longest IRT's were reinforced. When shortest IRT's were reinforced, the designations were IRT $<$ 50, IRT $<$ 75, etc. In all cases, the value of m was proportional to the extremity of the reinforcement requirement, so that contents of all control memories would be recycled about the same average number of times per reinforcement. For example, m was 4 for IRT $>$ 50, while it was 40 for IRT $>$ 95. Birds were shaped in one direction for 20 sessions and then shaped in the opposite direction for 20 sessions for a total of 80 sessions or three reversals in direction of shaping.

Figure 1 shows the response rates or reciprocal of mean IRT's

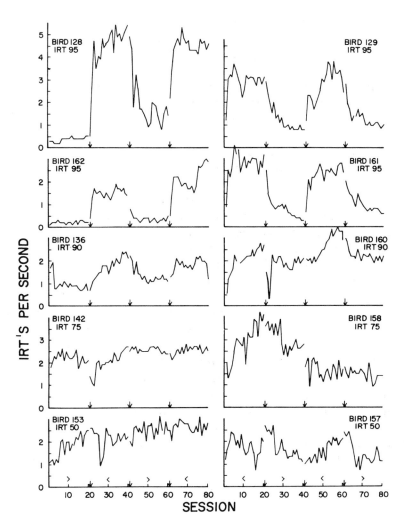

Fig. 1. Key-pecking rates by sessions for individual pigeons in Alleman and Platt's (1972) first experiment.

across sessions for each bird in Alleman and Platt's first experiment. The left side of the figure shows birds initially reinforced for longer IRT's, while the right side shows birds initially reinforced for shorter IRT's. IRT > 95 produced IRT's averaging from 4 to 12 times as long as those produced in the same birds by IRT < 95. Substantially smaller differences were produced by IRT > 90 *vs.* IRT < 90, while no consistent evidence of effective shaping was forthcoming when IRT's more extreme than 50 or 75% of recent IRT's were reinforced. Two additional results may not be obvious from Fig. 1. First, shaping of longer IRT's was most effective when shorter IRT's had not previously been shaped. Second, response rates were systematically related to the extremity of the reinforcement requirement when longer IRT's were reinforced, but not when shorter ones were. This last result suggests that differences between behaviors resulting from reinforcing longer *vs.* shorter IRT's were mainly the result of effectiveness in shaping longer IRT's.

This experiment again makes clear the feasibility of using percentile reinforcement schedules to control the proportion of occurrences of measurable behaviors reinforced during response shaping. The results also indicate that as the reinforcement requirement became more extreme, shaping was more effective. Of course, there is probably some extremity of such requirements which would not produce sufficient reinforcements to maintain key pecking. This point raises a question about treating Alleman and Platt's results in terms of response shaping. Perhaps long IRT's produced by IRT > 95 were not the result of differentially reinforcing longer IRT's, but simply due to a small proportion of key pecks being reinforced. This could not be true in any simple sense, since IRT < 95 reinforced the same proportion of key pecks, but produced much shorter IRT's. Nevertheless, this point does make clear that the percentile schedules described thus far confound contact and selectiveness. As selectiveness is increased by reserving reinforcement for smaller and smaller proportions of occurrences of measurable behaviors, contact is also changing. The role of these two variables could be distinguished by independently manipulating reinforcement probability and relative extremeness of reinforced behaviors.

Two additional experiments reported by Alleman and Platt attempted to separate the role of contact from that of selectiveness. The conditions were essentially the same as in the first experiment with one exception. Only some of the IRT's which were more extreme than a criterion proportion of the last m IRT's were actually reinforced. The random proportion of IRT's meeting a percentile criterion which were actually reinforced was chosen in such a way that different percentile criteria would produce reinforcement for the same proportion of key pecks. For example, for IRT > 95, all IRT's exceeded 95% of the last m IRT's were reinforced, while for IRT > 50 only a random 10% of the IRT's which exceeded 50% of the last m IRT's were reinforced. Thus, about 5% of all IRT's were reinforced in all cases so that contact was held constant while selectiveness was manipulated.

The results of these experiments are not reprinted here because they were essentially identical to those for the first experiment, in spite of the fact that the same proportion of key pecks was reinforced in all conditions. For shaping of key peck IRT's, selectiveness of reinforcement criteria appears to be a potent variable, while no effect of contact with reinforcement criteria was obtained over the range of values employed. This rather surprising result should of course be checked for generality to shaping on other response dimensions— particularly spatial and topographical, as opposed to temporal dimensions.

IV. Implementation Details and Refinements

The percentile reinforcement schedules described in the last section of this paper are logically quite simple, but some details about their implementation and some possible refinements may be instructive to the reader wishing to make use of such procedures. Implementation of the schedules requires a facility for storing and retrieving both the ordinal value and the order of occurrence of an organism's last m measurable behaviors. When a measurable behavior occurs, an "immediate" decision must be made as to whether its value is more extreme than a specified proportion of those values in the control memory, and this new value must then replace the oldest value in the memory. In a discrete-trial situation with widely spaced trials, these requirements can be met by paper and pencil techniques. Before starting a trial the experimenter would look up the value of the behavior having the desired rank in a list of the last m occurrences of measurable behavior. Just as in a standard fixed-criterion paradigm, this value would be entered into whatever device is appropriate to gating reinforcement on the basis of the sign of inequality between a fixed value and the value of the next occurrence of a measurable behavior. When the trial was completed, the value of the measurable behavior occurring on that trial would be added to the list comprising the control memory, and the oldest value on the list would be deleted.

When implementing percentile reinforcement schedules in situations involving closely or unpredictably spaced occurrences of measurable behaviors, as in a free responding situation, the paper and pencil technique just described is usually too slow. In such cases a small laboratory computer or its equivalent is necessary. A variety of approaches to programming percentile schedules in such situations have been considered, and one approach seems consistently more efficient than others. Values of the last m occurrences of measurable behaviors are stored in m consecutive locations in core memory. A circular arrangement is used such that each new value is written over the oldest value via an address pointer whose contents are incremented for each occurrence of a measurable behavior. When the value of the pointer becomes larger than the last address in the control memory, the pointer is reset to the value of the first address. This type of circular memory and an address pointer to the location containing the oldest value removes the necessity of storing an explicit value indicating the order of occurrence of each measurable behavior or of moving contents of locations in the control memory when a new value replaces the oldest value.

Another aspect of programming percentile schedules which requires comment is the algorithm for deciding whether to present reinforcement following a particular occurrence of measurable behavior. The logic of the schedule might suggest rank ordering values in the control memory, but this is highly inefficient and unnecessary. One would thus not want to use the technique described for paper and pencil whereby a fixed criterion value for the next response is determined by looking up the kth ordered value in the control memory. The most efficient technique seems to be to wait until a measurable behavior is actually recorded by the computer. This value is then compared to each value in the control memory to determine sign of inequality, and an appropriate counter is incremented whenever the desired sign is detected. The value of this counter can then be compared to a value of k determined by manipulating Eq. (2) such that

$$k = (m + 1)(1 - P(S^R)) \qquad (3)$$

If the counter is equal to or greater than k, reinforcement is given. The actual time required to find the sign of the $m + 1$ inequalities required produces no behaviorally significant delay of reinforcement for any reasonable values of m with current computer speeds. It should not be forgotten when using this programming technique that reinforcement for a response should be determined before the value of that response is placed in the control memory.

Turning to some refinements and extensions of percentile reinforcement schedules, some readers may have noticed that Eq. (3) seems to place some restrictions on the size of the control memory. The number of values in a control memory to be exceeded for reinforcement is only directly interpretable as a positive integer. Equation 3 indicates that k will be a positive integer only for certain combinations of m and $P(S^R)$. This limitation arises because only certain sample sizes will contain an observation with a particular percentile score. Of course one could carefully choose values of m and $P(S^R)$ so that k was always an integer. However, a slightly more complicated decision rule will avoid this limitation and is also useful in other ways. Regardless of the values of m and $P(S^R)$, there will always be two ordered values k_1 and k_2 such that a desired percentile point lies between these two values. In Eq. (3), k_1 and k_2 will simply be the largest integer less than or equal to k and the smallest integer greater than or equal to k. Of course, k_1 and k_2 have the same value if k is an integer. The important point to note is that measurable behaviors with values more extreme than k_2 of the values in the control memory should clearly be reinforced, while those less extreme than k_1 of the values should definitely not be reinforced. The best that can be done with values that exceed k_1 but not k_2 values in the control memory is to reinforce them randomly with a probability which will not change the expectation for $P(S^R)$. This can be accomplished by the following decision rule. Compute k as in Eq. (3) and call the integer part of k, k_1. If the number of values in the control memory which are less extreme than the current behavior is strictly greater than k_1, reinforce. If this number is exactly equal to k_1, subtract the fractional part of k from 1.0 and reinforce with this probability. If the number of memory values less extreme than the current value is strictly less than k_1, nonreinforce. It is recommended that this more complex decision rule always be used, not because it is difficult to select values of m and $P(S^R)$ which yield integer values of k, but because it solves two other problems. First, this decision rule can be adapted to situations in which a large number of measurable behaviors have the same values. Second, this rule is applicable to any value of m so as to avoid any need for arbitrary decision rules prior to the control memory being filled.

One final refinement of percentile reinforcement schedules concerns the fact that they appear to preclude shaping to a target behavior. This occurs because in gaining control over a relationship between behavior and its consequences, control of the absolute values of behaviors actually reinforced has been sacrificed. Thus, shaping continues indefinitely in a specified direction until processes or factors not controlled by the experimenter create a steady state. While lack of a target behavior may often be quite compatible with an experimental analysis of shaping processes, it sometimes may not be. Lack of a specified target behavior would certainly prevent application of the current procedures as instruments for bringing about a specified behavior. This limitation could of course be removed by making reinforcement available on both a percentile schedule and a fixed reinforcement criterion. The percentile schedule would then shape behavior to a desired value where it would be maintained by the fixed criterion. Obviously such a procedure would cease to control contact with or selectiveness of reinforcement criteria as the target behavior was approached. These limitations could be avoided with a slightly more elaborate type of percentile schedule. Until now percentile reinforcement has been discussed as reinforcing one or another extreme of the measurable behaviors currently being emitted by an organism. There is no reason for this other than that it presumably would maximize response shaping. One could for instance reinforce a fixed proportion of an organism's measurable behaviors about the current median value. Such a procedure would still control contact with, and selectiveness of reinforcement criteria by the present definitions and would presumably produce a reduction in the dispersion of measurable behaviors. This notion can be extended further to include shaping to a target value. One would simply reinforce values falling between a specified proportion of recent values centered on some target value. When all of the organism's last m occurrences of measurable behaviors fell above or below the target value, the procedures would be the same as described earlier. When the target value fell within the distribution of values for the last m occurrences, a value would be reinforced only if it fell within the range of a fixed proportion of values whose median value was closest to the target value. Ignoring additional factors, such a procedure should *shape* and *maintain* a tight distribution of values of measurable behavior while continuously controlling the proportion and rank of measurable behaviors actually reinforced.[3]

V.   Temporal Concepts of Relationships between Behavior and Reinforcement Criteria

The percentile reinforcement schedules discussed in the last two sections sought to control relationships between an organism's be-

[3] The mathematics of a fixed target value interacting with ordinal statistics on a distribution of responses are considerably more complex than for other percentile schedules presented in this article. Depending on the exact nature of the decision rules employed, random variations in the order statistics can interact with a fixed target value to bias the expected probability of reinforcement. Until general solutions are available for any particular procedure, extensive simulation with known response distributions is advisable before applying the procedure to actual subjects.

havior and reinforcement criteria during response shaping on the basis of nontemporal definitions of those relationships. The amount of data available on effects of such relationships (Alleman & Platt, 1973) already suggests that the important variable in shaping is not degree of contact with reinforcement criteria, but the usually confounded variable of selectiveness of reinforcement criteria with respect to the organism's behavior. There are of course many other concepts of contact with reinforcement criteria which could be profitably proposed and investigated. The concept developed in the last two sections still seems to this author to be the most promising for discrete-trial situations such as Thorndike's original paradigm. There is good reason to doubt, however, that this concept is optimal in free behavior situations such as those often used by operant investigators. The fact is that a wide variety of operant research and theory point to temporal density of reinforcements being a more fundamental variable in free responding situations than is the proportion of responses falling in the reinforced class. It would thus be desirable to develop a response-shaping paradigm which controlled contact with reinforcement criteria in the sense of controlling the temporal density of behaviors in the reinforced and nonreinforced classes.

A response-shaping paradigm which controls temporal density of behaviors in the reinforced class can be constructed in a manner quite parallel to that used in developing percentile reinforcement schedules. A set of measurable behaviors with the same properties required for percentile reinforcement is assumed to be available. A control memory is kept which contains the values of occurrences of measurable behaviors during the most recent t units of time. Again assuming that the values in the control memory were randomly sampled from the current theoretical distribution of values, one can specify the proportion of occurrences of measurable behavior which would have to be reinforced to produce an average interval of T time units between reinforcements. This proportion would be

$$P(S^R) = t/Tm \tag{4}$$

where m is again the number of occurrences of measurable behaviors in the control memory. Equation 3 in Section III specified the number of values in a control memory which would have to be less extreme than a reinforced value in order to reinforce the most extreme specified proportion of measurable behaviors. One can thus substitute the value for $P(S^R)$ from Eq. (4) into Eq. (3) to obtain the number of values in the control memory which the current value must exceed for reinforcement if an average interval T is to be maintained between reinforced behavioral events. This value is

$$K = (m + 1) [1 - (t/Tm)] \tag{5}$$

A paradigm based on Eq. (5) might be called an interval-percentile reinforcement schedule, since it uses the rank order of a response among recent responses to determine reinforcement, but in such a manner as to control the average interval between behaviors in the reinforced class rather than the proportion of behaviors in the reinforced class. This control, of course, depends on the occurrence of at least one measurable behavior per desired reinforcement interval, just as with the more usual interval schedules of reinforcement used in operant research.

This author knows of no published reports of response shaping with interval-percentile schedules. Work is under way in the author's laboratory using such paradigms, but reporting of results would be premature at this time.

VI. Other Applications of Percentile-Type Schedules

The paradigms presented in this paper have been developed to deal with problems of controlling contact with, and selectiveness of reinforcement criteria during response shaping, but similar behavior-dependent schedules seem particularly well suited to a number of problem areas in which effects of behaviorally confounded relationships between events must be separated. Several such potential applications will be briefly indicated as examples.

The first application to be discussed is very closely related to response-shaping issues presented earlier. It is sometimes desirable to differentially reinforce responses along some dimension which could reflect the overall probability of occurrence of that response class. In such cases questions arise as to whether observed changes in response values represent a strengthening effect of reinforcement on reinforced response values, or a change in the probability of occurrence of the entire response class as a result of reinforcement parameters arising from relationships between the organism's behavior and the reinforcement criteria. A clear example of this problem arises with respect to differentially reinforcing IRT's. When reinforcement is made dependent on responses with IRT's longer than some value t, organism's often come to emit responses whose IRT's are distributed closely around the value of t. This result could be taken to indicate that reinforcement of particular IRT values directly increases the probability of occurrence of those values. This interpretation has formed the basis for extensive theories about how reinforcement schedules determine response rates (Morse, 1966). One alternative interpretation is that selective reinforcement of particular IRT values has no effect other than to establish a negative feedback system which modulates the probability of the entire response class by varying the proportion of occurrences of that class which are reinforced. For instance, Wilson and Keller (1953) described the following possibility. Each occurrence of an IRT shorter than t is nonreinforced, so that the resulting decrease in probability of a response produces longer IRT's. When IRT's eventually become as long as t, responses are reinforced so that the entire class increases in probability and IRT's become shorter. Such a process should go into an oscillatory steady state with probability of response alternately waxing and waning about a mean value determined by the reinforcement criterion in such a manner as to produce IRT values distributed about the value of t.

There are many ways to attack the Wilson and Keller interpretation just presented, but one of the most direct is that used in the Alleman and Platt (1973) studies discussed earlier in which key-peck IRT's were shaped with percentile reinforcement schedules. These studies clearly indicated that the effects of differentially reinforcing IRT's was independent of proportion of key pecks reinforced for the range of parameter values investigated. This example should suffice to indicate the potential usefulness of percentile-type reinforcement schedules in separating effects of reinforcing a subclass of behaviors from the effects of confounded variations in reinforcement parameters for the entire class.

A closely related application of percentile-type schedules occurs when the dependency of a stimulus on behavior must be manipulated independently of the frequency of occurrence of that stimulus. An example of this type of problem is suggested by a recent study of temporal discrimination (Platt, Kuch, & Bitgood, 1973). In this study it was found that differential reinforcement of lever holding in rats produced holds with durations more closely approximating the value required for reinforcement when a brief intertrial interval followed each lever release. A number of possible explanations for this effect of intertrial intervals were proposed. Some of these explanations, such as intertrial intervals having increased the delay of reinforcement following short holds, clearly depend on intertrial intervals following nonreinforced responses. Other explanations, such as the lower density of reinforcements produced by intertrial intervals having increased the proportional change in reinforcement density resulting from a given change in hold duration, depend simply on the overall frequency of intertrial intervals.

It might seem that the two classes of explanations just described could be distinguished by orthogonally manipulating the presence vs. absence of intertrial intervals following reinforced and nonreinforced responses. The resulting 2×2 factorial design would seem to isolate the relative effectiveness of the two loci of intertrial interval presentations and any interactions between them. If both loci were equally effective in increasing lever holding, one might conclude that only the overall frequency of intertrial intervals was important. However, the logic of this approach is fallacious. The problem is that the frequency of intertrial intervals occurring at a given locus depends on the rat's behavior. For example, when first exposed to a lever-holding requirement, the rat's probability of reinforcement may be very low. Thus, only rats with intertrial intervals programmed to follow nonreinforced responses would actually receive many such intervals. If these rats increased their lever holds more than did others, the effect could be due either to intertrial intervals having followed nonreinforced responses, or to the high frequency of intertrial intervals. One way to avoid these problems would be to examine the intertrial interval conditions just described in a percentile reinforcement schedule for shaping lever holding. Since the proportion of responses reinforced in such a paradigm is continuously controlled by the experimenter, no problem arises in respect to separating effects of locus and relative frequency of intertrial intervals on effectiveness of shaping.

Yet another area of application for percentile-type reinforcement schedules is in situations requiring the separation of variations in reinforcement parameters from behavioral changes produced by those variations. A good example of this type of problem occurs in the area of behavioral contrast. It has long been known that decreasing the temporal density of reinforcement for one alternative in a successive discrimination problem often increases response rates to the other unchanged alternative. However, considerable disagreement has occurred as to whether this phenomenon is due to the decrease in reinforcement density for one alternative (Reynolds, 1961), or the resulting decrease in response rate on that alternative (Terrace, 1968). Various procedures have been used in attempts to break the usual correlation between reinforcement density and response rates, and both Reynolds' and Terrace's views have received some support. Most of these procedures have attempted to drive reinforcement density and response rates in opposite directions by differentially reinforcing either particular response rates or periods of time without responses. Bypassing consideration of the implications of this strategy, the interval-percentile schedules described in Section IV of this review would appear to be particularly well suited for this purpose. An interval-percentile schedule for IRT's on one alternative of a successive discrimination problem should allow response rates to be driven high or low with continuous, independent control of reinforcement density. Such procedures should provide clear indication of any role for either reinforcement density reduction or response rate reduction in determining behavior contrast.

These few examples should suffice to indicate the potential variety of uses for paradigms which define reinforcement criteria in terms of an organism's current behavior so as to control particular relationships between behavior and reinforcement criteria. Such paradigms will undoubtedly seem strange to the instrumental or operant experimenter accustomed to thinking in terms of controlling what physical values of behavior are reinforced. If the transition between these two modes of thought is difficult, perhaps it would help to think of paradigms such as those proposed in this paper as also controlling values of behavior which are reinforced. However, these latter values are measured on a behavioral scale provided by the organism's recent behavior. In these terms it is hoped that the reader has been convinced that such behavioral values of reinforced responses may be more useful than their physical values in understanding such processes as response shaping. Of course the ordinal behavioral scale implied by percentile-type reinforcement schedules is only one of a variety of possibilities which should be considered. But this scale does have the advantages of being definable for almost any dimension of behavior and of being manipulable within a mathematical system which is well understood as a result of work in nonparametric statistics.

References

Alleman, H. D., & Platt, J. R. Differential reinforcement of interresponse times with controlled probability of reinforcement per response. *Learning and Motivation,* 1973, **4**, 40–73.

Fields, C. Instrumental conditioning of the rat cardiac control systems, *Proceedings of the National Academy of Sciences, U.S.,* 1970, **65**, 293–299.

Herrnstein, R. J. On the law of effect. *Journal of the Experimental Analysis of Behavior,* 1970, **13**, 243–266.

Lane, H., Kopp, J., Sheppard, W., Anderson, T., & Carlson, D. Acquisition, maintenance, and retention in the differential reinforcement of vocal duration. *Journal of Experimental Psychology,* 1967, **74** (2, Whole No. 635).

Morse, W. H. Intermittent reinforcement. In W. K. Honig (Ed.), *Operant behavior: Areas of research and application.* New York: Appleton, 1966. Pp. 52–108.

Platt, J. R., Kuch, D. O., & Bitgood, S. C. Rats' lever press durations as psychophysical judgments of time. *Journal of the Experimental Analysis of Behavior,* 1973, **19**, 239–250.

Rescorla, R. A. Pavlovian conditioning and its proper control procedures. *Psychological Review,* 1967, **74**, 71–80.

Reynolds, G. S. Behavioral contrast. *Journal of the Experimental Analysis of Behavior,* 1961, **4**, 57–71.

Sidman, M. *Tactics of scientific research.* New York: Basic Books, 1961.

Skinner, B. F. *The behavior of organisms.* New York: Appleton, 1938.

Smith, K. Distribution-free statistical methods and the concept of power efficiency. In L. Festinger & D. Katz (Ed.), *Research methods in the behavioral sciences.* New York: Dryden, 1953.

Terrace, H. S. Discrimination learning, the peak shift, and behavioral contrast. *Journal of the Experimental Analysis of Behavior,* 1968, **11**, 727–741.

Thorndike, E. L. Animal intelligence: An experimental study of the associative processes in animals. *Psychological Monographs,* 1898, **2**, No. 8.

Weiss, B. Digital computers in the behavioral laboratory. *Biomedical Symposium Proceedings,* 1967, June.

Wilson, M. P., & Keller, F. S. On the selective reinforcement of spaced responses. *Journal of Comparative and Physiological Psychology,* 1953, **46**, 190–193.

PROLONGED REWARDING BRAIN STIMULATION

J. A. Deutsch

DEPARTMENT OF PSYCHOLOGY, UNIVERSITY OF CALIFORNIA,
SAN DIEGO, LA JOLLA, CALIFORNIA

I. Historical Introduction

In some of the pioneering work on rewarding brain stimulation, Bower and Miller (1958) and Roberts (1958) discovered that a brain stimulus which the animal would attempt to obtain when it was brief was apparently aversive when it was prolonged. A rewarding brain stimulus is turned off if it persists. As a result of their work on this phenomenon, Bower and Miller (1958) suggested that an initially rewarding stimulus becomes aversive and further that while the animal could learn to escape such a stimulus it could not learn to avoid it. However, Stein (1962) proposed that the brain stimulus adapts and that therefore the rat must interrupt it in order to feel the next onset and further reward. Valenstein and Valenstein (1964) incline against the explanation in terms of aversiveness because they found rats to respond without hesitation when reward durations beyond those spontaneously tolerated were self-administered. Their position is supported by the results of Keesey (1964) and Hodos (1965). Keesey (1964) found that rats would perform at a higher rate on a variable-interval reinforcement schedule when brain stimulation was of durations which would be spontaneously turned off by the rats. Hodos (1965) reports that rats would perform at higher ratios on a progressive ratio test when given brain reward of longer duration than they would spontaneously tolerate. However, such results are somewhat inconclusive because, as Bower and Miller (1958) suggested, rats are able to escape such stimulation but are unable to avoid it. What Bower and Miller would find more difficult to explain would be that a stimulus which would be classified as aversive is actually more efficient as a positive reinforcer than a stimulus that seems to be less aversive or actually positive. However, this forms no insuperable objection. There seems to be a growing consensus (Gallistel, 1973) that brain reward has at least two components, as originally suggested by the writer (Deutsch, 1960). The first is a rewarding or reinforcing function and the second a motivational or drive effect. Deutsch and Howarth (1963) and Gallistel (1973) have shown that the second component cumulates as stimulation continues, and it is this component that makes for efficient performance on interval or ratio schedules. We could then argue that the motivational or drive component cumulates as the brain stimulus is prolonged in spite of the emergence of an aversive component which the rat would escape but cannot learn to avoid. Whatever the status of such arguments, the notion that prolonged brain stimulation is aversive has been accepted by many workers in the field of brain reward. For instance, Mendelson (1969) states unequivocally: "Short durations of stimulation are rewarding while longer durations become punishing."

II.   Aversiveness or Adaptation

A more cautious view would be that, given the evidence up to now, it is not possible to decide between the two rival hypotheses. What makes the "aversion" hypothesis more attractive is the fact that many animals with electrode implants which do not show positive effects show aversive effects instead. Therefore, by extrapolation, one might expect aversive components even in rats where positively reinforcing properties predominate.

On the other hand, the hypothesis that brain stimulation adapts out seems not to have analogies grounded in our experience of brain stimulation. The notion of adaptation has to be imported from studies of sensory receptors. This lessens its *prima facie* plausibility. We do not think of receptor stimulation as being similar to the direct stimulation of central neurons, and we therefore tend to dismiss analogies between these two cases. What altered the balance of plausibility in this case for the writer was a wholly unexpected observation. Kestenbaum, Coons, and I became interested in the possibility of the behavioral measurement of the refractory period of pathways which mediate aversion in the central nervous system. Stimulating with very brief (.1 msec) negative pulses, I had found (Deutsch, 1964) that a second pulse had no behavioral effect in brain reward unless a small critical delay had elapsed. Further, the length of this critical delay differed depending on whether we measured the rewarding (reinforcing) properties of the stimulation or the drive (motivational) properties. Because the critical delays were within the range of the refractory period of axons as classically measured by the neurophysiologists, I assumed that the refractory periods of two classes of axons accounted for my results. If aversion explained the behavior of rats under prolonged brain stimulation, then it would be interesting to see whether we could not measure yet another critical delay associated with the evocation of aversion. The simplest way to go about this appeared to be the measurement of such a critical delay in the case of electrodes which produced only aversion. Then we could look for the appearance of this delay in the more complex case where reward and drive critical delays were also present. Electrodes were implanted aimed at the spinothalamic fibers in the dorsolateral tegmentum or the medial lemniscus. Stimulation through such electrodes was clearly aversive to the rat. The rat was then placed in a Skinner box where he could turn off such stimulation for a period of 3 seconds by pressing a lever. Surprisingly, when the rats were placed in this situation they were apparently quite unable to learn to press the lever to stop the stimulation. The paradox was that often the rat would press a few times at the outset but then stop completely. We hypothesized that perhaps the electrical stimulation of the neural tissue surrounding the electrode had some kind of effect on memory. However, this venture into mnemonic fantasy was cut short when Coons noticed that the rats were actively avoiding the region of the lever and would resist attempts to make them approach it. This showed that the rats had learned, but they had learned the diametrical opposite of what we, the experimenters, had thought they should learn. Further observation showed why we had obtained the curious inversion. When the brain stimulus was first applied the rat appeared in some pain or discomfort. However the signs of such discomfort quickly subsided, and after a little squealing and running, the rat would begin to groom and sniff around as if the electrical stimulus had disappeared. When we turned off the stimulus by pressing the lever, there was no reaction on the part of the animal. However, such a reaction came unmistakably at the end of the 3 seconds when the electrical stimulus came on automatically. Again there were signs of pain and discomfort which again soon subsided. The interpretation of these rats' behavior then forced itself on us. The pain stimulus quickly adapted and remained adapted, while the brain stimulation continued. Once the brain stimulation ceased, deadaptation took place and the subsequent onset of the stimulation was again punishing. The rat therefore learned that staying away from the lever was the least aversive course of action. However,

Kestenbaum was able to rescue the experiment by the following interesting stratagem. He used a wider spacing of the stimulating pulses. Now why should this work? We had begun by using the same parameters of stimulation as had been used in the work on positive reinforcing stimulation (Deutsch, 1964). Here the pulse pairs occurred once every 10 msec. If we assume that adaptation occurs, we have to assume that each pulse produces some aftereffect which reduces the effectiveness of the next pulse. We also have to assume that this aftereffect of a pulse is not permanent. Rather, this aftereffect decays as some function of time. Otherwise the nervous system would cease to convey signals as a function of the amount of preceding stimulation without recovery. However, we had seen that such recovery was fairly rapid. Therefore, if we spaced out the individual pulses, we should at some interval reach a point at which the aftereffect of one pulse on the next was zero or close to zero. This whole line of reasoning was confirmed when the rats promptly learned to press the lever to turn the stimulation off when the incoming pulses were spaced in time. Their discomfort was no longer transient but appeared to persist. However, at this time we regarded this curious adaptation to stimulation more as an experimental nuisance, to be surmounted rather than to be investigated in its own right. Once we had surmounted it we went on with our original plan and indeed obtained some interesting results (Kestenbaum, Deutsch, & Coons, 1970). However, this somewhat striking example of what seemed like adaptation to intracranial stimulation altered for me the baseline probability of an "adaptation" explanation of behavior under prolonged rewarding brain stimulation.

Another piece of evidence which pointed to possible adaptation during rewarding brain stimulation was presented by Gallistel (1969). Using a runway situation he found that increasing the length of the rewarding brain stimulus did increase reward value past a fairly short train of stimulation. While increases of the train length produced pronounced changes in running speed for the brain stimulation, there was a fairly abrupt cutoff past which any further stimulation produced no further increment. (The data could not be explained on the basis of a ceiling effect of running speed.) No further increment of reward was found after 64 pulses were given at 200 pps. Thus, extending the duration of brain reward beyond .32 second had no further additional effect on the magnitude of that reward. However, Gallistel did not interpret his data in terms of an adaptation effect, choosing instead to regard it as an inability of the reward system to integrate over a longer period. However, whatever his hypothesis, it is clear that his data could be regarded as a case of rapid adaptation in the reward produced by direct brain stimulation. Nevertheless, even if we interpret Gallistel's data as an instance of adaptation, this does not in itself show that prolonged brain stimulation is turned off because of such an adaptation effect and not because of aversion. To do this we must design an experiment which addresses itself more directly to the question.

To make the problem clearer, let us avail ourselves of an analogy. Suppose we observe a man with his hand immersed in a steaming bucket. We observe that he takes his hand out from time to time only to immerse it again. We are now given the problem of finding out why he does so. Does the heat of the water become painful after a while so that he takes his hand out to escape the aversive sensation? Or does he take his hand out because the water does not feel warm after a while and because by taking it out he can again enjoy the sensation of warmth when he reimmerses his hand? One way to find out is to give him an extra option. Give him a choice of pouring some hotter water into the bucket in addition to taking his hand out. If the hot water in the bucket begins to hurt after a while, it would seem most unlikely that he would opt for an increase of temperature in the bucket. We may be sure that he would take his hand out instead. If, however, his hand no longer feels warm, having adapted to the temperature of the water in the bucket, then the most rapid way to recapture the sensation of warmth again is to pour some hotter water into the bucket. We can use this paradigm on the rat undergoing prolonged brain reward. We can give him a choice between turning the brain stimulus off or increasing its intensity. This should tell us whether the stimulus has faded or become aversive.

III. Further Experiments to Test Adaptation Theory

A. Choice of Increment Rather Than Decrement of Prolonged Stimulation

In our first experiment we ran rats in a T-maze, giving, in our most important condition, a choice between an offset of stimulation and an increase in stimulation after prolonged stimulation (Deutsch & Hawkins, 1972). Four rats were run in six conditions each. In the first three conditions, there was no prolonged brain stimulus at the outset. The rats were rewarded with a train of pulses in the goal box. The purpose of the first three conditions was simply to ascertain whether the intracranial stimulus was rewarding and whether the more intense stimulus was actually more rewarding. In the first condition, the rats were given a choice of 200 pps in one goal (lasting for 1 second) *vs.* no stimulation in the other goal box. Out of 64 trials (32 on each side), the rats chose the 200 pps on a mean of 62.75 trials. This showed that 200 pps was rewarding. Similarly, in the second condition, it was shown that 100 pps for 1 second was more rewarding than no stimulation in the other goal box. The mean (out of 64 trials) was 62 trials. In the third condition, a reward of 200 pps for 1 second was compared directly with a reward of 100 pps for 1 second in the other goal box. 200 pps was evidently much more rewarding because it was preferred on 59.25 trials out of 64 on the average. We used an increase of pulse frequency, keeping voltage constant, to produce a more intense reward rather than an increase in individual pulse amplitude, keeping frequency constant. If amplitude of pulse is increased, additional fibers further away from the electrode become stimulated. An increase in amplitude thus stimulates a partially different group of fibers. On the other hand, if amplitude is kept constant but frequency increased (up to a point determined by the refractory period), then the same population of neurons is stimulated but at a higher rate. This results in a more intense reward, as our experiment confirms.

In the second three conditions, the rats were detained in the start box while they were stimulated with 100 pps continuously, at the voltage used previously, for varying periods of time. (It turned out that the time the rats were detained did not affect their choice.) We planned the fourth condition to show that the rats would choose to turn off the stimulation under the conditions of our experiment. If the rat ran to the end of one goal box, the 100 pps stimulus continued until he turned around and ran to the end of the other goal box. There, interruption of a light beam turned off the brain stimulus which then remained "off" until the start of the next trial 8.5 seconds later. The rats chose the side with the offset of stimulation on an average of 45 trials out of 64. In Condition 5, we made a slight change. There was no offset of 100 pps stimulation at the end of one alley and offset of the stimulation in the other alley. However, we inserted a 1-second train of 200 pps for a second before all stimulation terminated for 8.5 seconds. This led to a large increase of the choice of the alley where the stimulus terminated. The addition of a 200 pps stimulus for 1 second before offset boosted the choice of the "offset" alley to a mean of 62.5 out of 64 from a mean of 45 in Condition 4. An increase in the level of stimulation before offset seems to be very rewarding. In Condition 6, we compared the effectiveness of simple offset in one alley with an increase to 200 pps for 1 second before offset in the other alley. The side on which the stimulus increased to 200 pps was chosen over the side in which the stimulus simply terminated on a mean of 53.5 trials out of 64. This result again shows that an increase of stimulation is rewarding and more rewarding than a simple offset of stimulation.

As a test of the generality of our results, we performed another experiment using a Skinner box with two retractable levers. The two levers were mechanically pushed into the box through two slots 15 seconds after the rat had made a choice. Four rats were run under two conditions. In the first condition, one lever provided an increase of stimulation from a steady 100 pps to 200 pps for 1 second. The other lever produced an offset of 1 second of the steady 100 pps intracranial stimulus. As we did not have to move the rat back to the starting point as in the maze experiment, we did not have to turn off the steady 100 pps after the increase to 200 pps for 1 second. The rats preferred the stimulus increase over stimulus offset for 71% of the time. In the second condition, one lever produced an offset for one second of the steady 100 pps, and the other lever produced no change. The rats preferred to press the stimulus lever which produced a 1-second offset over the one which produced no change 66% of the time. The second experiment therefore confirms the effect of the first.

The two experiments together do not support the notion that a rat turns off prolonged stimulation because it becomes aversive. Instead, they are directly predictable from the hypothesis that a rat turns off the intracranial stimulus because reward disappears through a process of adaptation. The reward can be brought back under two conditions. First, the rat can turn the intracranial stimulation off so that the neural substrate can recover from adaptation and so obtain a reward at the next onset of stimulation. Reward here is delayed because the response of turning the stimulation off is not rewarded immediately but only when the stimulation comes on again. In the second condition, the reward which has adapted out can be obtained again immediately if the intensity of the stimulus is raised.

Now, while the experimental results do not support the "aversive" theory, is there any way in which the experimental results can be reconciled with the theory by the use of subsidiary assumptions? We could argue that the increment in reward which occurs when there is an increase from 100 pps to 200 pps outweighs the aversiveness of the stimulation which builds up more gradually. Let us suppose there are two processes, one which is rewarding and which is set off rapidly when stimulation is applied and the other punishing, and which develops gradually after stimulation is applied. A rapid increment in stimulation, if sufficiently large, will immediately produce an increment in reward without producing a similar increment in punishment because this takes a longer time to develop. This rapid increment in reward may be sufficiently large to outbalance the punishing effects of the stimulus that have already developed.

While this line of defense is involved, it does serve to crystallize the issues and forces the "aversive" hypothesis to be more explicit if it is to remain tenable. These assumptions of the aversive hypothesis can also be tested in the following way. We can measure the threshold of preference in intracranial stimulation during prolonged stimulation or during discrete stimulation. Let us suppose that the rat prefers to turn on 120 pps over 100 pps. In this case, no aversion has built up, so that the rat is simply comparing two reward magnitudes. If the difference is less than 20 pps at 100 pps, then suppose that the rat does not display preference as we define it. Now let us place the rat in a situation where prolonged stimulation has been applied beyond the point in time at which it would spontaneously turn off the stimulus. The rat is then given a choice between turning off the stimulus or increasing the stimulus by some fraction. On the aversion hypothesis, the increment in reward would have to outbalance the steady growth of the aversive factor past the neutral point at which the rewarding and aversive factors were balanced. Such an increment in reward would have therefore to be larger than the threshold of reward increase as measured in the first experiment where two rewards were compared without previous prolonged stimulation. The experiment can be devised in the following way. In the first part, preference can be measured in the following way. At an interval of, say, 14 seconds, the rat is given a free stimulus of 100 pps which lasts for 2 seconds. If the rat presses a lever within the first second, the stimulus during the second second increases, say, to 120 pps. This increase in pps is varied from one set of trials to the next. This way, we can measure the threshold number of pps which represent a just noticeable increase in reward before aversive factors have built up. In the second part of the experiment, the 100 pps would be left on continuously for, say, 10 seconds. After this, the rat would be presented with a lever. If the rat did not press it within 1 second, the stimulus would be turned off within 1 second. If the rat did press within 1 second, the stimulus would increase by some number of pps during a second second. In this case, the increment in pps would have to offset the postulated aversive component. The increment would have to be large enough to make it worthwhile to the rat to endure the aversive component for the extra second. Four seconds after the lever had become available, the continuous 100 pps stimulus would resume. In a third part of the experiment, the rat is again subjected to continuous 100 pps stimulation for 10 seconds. At the end of this time he would be presented with a single lever. If he presses within the first second, an increment of frequency occurs for the second second. If not, the 100 pps, instead of turning off in the second second, is left on during the second second. In this third condition, the increment in frequency does not have to counterbalance the disappearance of the postulated aversiveness during the second second in the second condition. As the rat will have to endure the maintenance of the intracranial stimulus whatever he does, he should choose an increase in reward which does not have to compensate for a disappearance of the aversive component. In this condition, we should again measure the incremental threshold for reward in a relatively pure form as distinct from the second condition (at least on the aversion hypothesis). On the other hand, on the adaptation hypothesis the thresholds should be much the same, as no compensation for aversiveness in the second condition is postulated.

B. The Speed of Adaptation of Rewarding Brain Stimulation

If adaptation of the intracranial stimulus is the cause of the turning off of prolonged brain reward, then we should be able to demonstrate such adaptation in other situations. We should also be able to measure how quickly such adaptation takes place. Further, if we are really dealing with adaptation, a fading of the effect of the stimulation should be a function of its frequency. In adaptation we must assume that each pulse produces an aftereffect which decays with time, which sums with the aftereffect of the successive pulse, and which prevents the successive pulse from having an effect depending on the cumulation of the preceding aftereffects. To test these hypotheses in a preliminary manner, we set up the following situation. A rat was given a choice of two levers. Each lever produced a train of pulses at the identical frequency. While the length of the train of pulses remained fixed on one lever, it was possible for the experimenter to shorten the train of pulses obtained by pressing the other lever. The rat was thus able to compare rewards which were identical except in duration. If rewarding stimulation adapts to zero at a certain duration, then stimulus trains beyond that certain duration should not be preferred to stimuli of that duration. A test like this, then, can tell us whether rewarding stimulation adapts and how quickly such stimulation adapts.

Six male albino rats (Sprague Dawley strain) were used, implanted with monopolar electrodes. They were placed in a box with three levers, two set symmetrically on one wall and the third in the middle of the opposite wall. Only the first press on any of the three levers produced a reward. The single lever on the opposite wall had to be pressed to reset the two reward levers. This "reset" lever also provided a priming stimulus to maintain the behavior. What we used was essentially an automated T-maze. The rat was given a choice between 500 msec of 125 pps on one lever against the same or shorter duration (500 msec, 300 msecs, or 100 msecs) on the other lever. In another set of conditions interspersed randomly, the same set of comparisons was done at the basic frequency of 750 pps.

It turns out that at 750 pps, a brain stimulus .3 second long is chosen about as frequently as one .5 second long. Further, at 750 pps a stimulus .1 second long is almost as good as one .5 second long, being chosen 34.4% of the time. In contrast, a stimulus .1 second long at 125 pps is chosen much more rarely over a stimulus .5 second long (only 16.1% of the time). The results are presented in Fig. 1. The results confirm those of Gallistel's (1969) experiment and show, in addition, that the results are also a function of the frequency em-

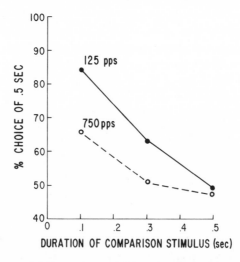

Fig. 1. Percentage of choice of lever yielding .5 second of intracranial stimulus at either 750 or 125 pps as compared with choice of the same pulse frequency at .1, .3, or .5 second. Average of six rats.

ployed. We have also tested some animals with a larger number of frequencies. The rate at which adaptation occurs is quite clearly a monotone function of frequency. The higher the frequency the faster the adaptation until we approach the limit in frequency imposed by the refractory period.

C. REFRACTORY PERIODS OF STIMULATION THE RAT TRIES TO TURN OFF

It seems, then, that we have good evidence that some type of adaptation of the intracranial reward does occur, and such adaptation would be sufficient to account for the phenomena of switching off of prolonged rewarding brain stimulation. We have made the "adaptation" explanation of this phenomenon more probable, but have by no means proved it. We must therefore explore other ways of investigating the phenomenon. One way of doing this is to measure some of the characteristics of the system, activity in which the rat is attempting to turn off the stimulation, and to compare these characteristics with those of other systems which we can measure in the phenomena of rewarding brain stimulation. It should be said by way of introduction here that by no means all rats learn to switch off a prolonged rewarding brain stimulus. But some of those that do will learn not only to turn it off temporarily but also to reduce the intensity temporarily. Given such rats, we can then ask what the animal regards as a reduction in the stimulus that it is attempting to turn off. (Notice that this approach does not presuppose any hypothesis about the reason for the attempted diminution of the prolonged stimulus.) The rat is given a choice of two levers in a Skinner box when it is undergoing prolonged rewarding stimulation. Either both levers reduce the prolonged 200 pps to 100 pps or only one of the levers does. After the rat has been trained under these conditions and shows a stable difference in behavior between them, we introduce 100 pps when the rat presses one lever and 100 pps with each pulse followed by another by some fraction of a millisecond. The rat can thus obtain a reduction of the prolonged 200 pps by pressing one lever to obtain 100 pps. The other lever provides 200 pps but spaced somewhat differently. Instead of obtaining pulses at 5-msec intervals, the rat is given 200 pps in pairs. The pairs occur at 10-msec intervals. In one condition, the first pulse of each pair (the C or conditioning pulse, to use the convention of the neurophysiologists) precedes the second pulse of the pair (the T or test pulse) by .3 msec. In this condition, the T-pulse seems to have no effect. The rat, given a choice

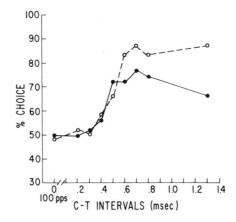

Fig. 2. Percentage of choice of levers when C-T interval is varied on one of the levers (average of three rats). Solid line with solid circles indicates condition where there is constant 200 pps stimulation, and response on one level produces a temporary reduction to 100 pps. A response on the other level produces 200 pps, but spaced so that pulses come in pairs with the spacing between alternate pulses of 10 msec. The second pulse of each pair follows the first at various intervals (.2–1.4 msec). The solid curve indicates the percentage of choice of 100 pps over 200 pps as a function of the spacing of the second pulse. The graph composed of a broken line with open circles indicates the performance of the rats when there is no constant stimulus, and the rats are choosing between exactly the same stimuli as in the first condition (100 pps as against 200 pps variously spaced). In this case the curve indicates the percentage of choice of 200 pps over 100 pps, as the second pulse in the 200 pps condition occurs later after the first pulse of each pair.

between 100 pps and 200 pps spaced in this manner, chooses between the two equally. In another condition, the C-T interval is 1 msec. In this condition, the rat chooses the lever which delivers the 100 pps train, as if the insertion of a T-pulse 1 msec after the C-pulse produced a pulse train equivalent to 200 pps. The purpose of the first part of the experiment is to find out just how far the T-pulse must be placed from the C-pulse before it is registered by the nervous system. The results (Fig. 2) show that the period during which the T-pulse has no apparent effect lasts for about .4 msec.

IV.   Discussion

What further predictions would the two hypotheses make here? If the turning off of the steady 200 pps is due to the adaptation of the rewarding stimulation, the rat should choose that lever which decreases the stimulus and ignore the lever which maintains the stimulus. A momentary decrease in the level of stimulation should enable the stimulated pathway to deadapt at least partly. The rat should therefore prefer that stimulus in which the second pulse of a C-T pair produces no stimulation. If the stimulation is of the reward system which adapts, then the rat should ignore the C-T lever which gives stimulation equivalent to 200 pps and which therefore produces a more intense stimulation of the reward system than the 100 pps lever. The adaptation hypothesis would therefore predict that the C-T interval which would not be sought in the case where stimulation has been prolonged is the C-T interval which would be more rewarding in a situation which there has been no preceding stimulation. The "adaptation" hypothesis would predict that the C-T intervals which would be preferred after prolonged stimulation with 200 pps would be the very ones which would be less preferred in a normal choice situation without preceding prolonged stimulation.

What would the aversive hypothesis predict? As prolonged stimulation is turned off, according to the hypothesis because it has become aversive, the animal should act to reduce such aversiveness. The C-T interval below which stimulation should be chosen should be characteristic of the system which produces the aversive component. On the other hand, when the rat chooses between two C-T intervals without previous prolonged stimulation, then the C-T interval above which the reward system can respond to both the C- and T-pulse will determine which C-T interval is preferred. (Reward is operationally defined in terms of preference. We say that A is more rewarding than B if A is consistently preferred over B.) Now in order to explain the first experiment reported here, where a rat chooses an increase of a prolonged rewarding stimulus over its cessation, the aversive theory would have to postulate two components, a reward component and some other slowly changing component which becomes aversive. Mendelson (1969) assumes that such a component is drive. Therefore the "aversion" theory, instead of predicting an identity of the characteristic C-T interval in both turn-off and turn-on experiments, would have to say that the C-T intervals in the two conditions should be unrelated. If the two C-T intervals turned out to be identical, then such an identity should be due to chance.

Now, as can be seen by the results shown in Fig. 2, the critical C-T interval in both the turning-off and turning-on experiments seem identical. The rat begins to prefer the 100 pps lever when the C-T interval on the other lever exceeds .4 msec when undergoing prolonged stimulation of 200 ppc. On the other hand, the rat begins to prefer the lever which produces a C-T interval greater than .4 msec over the lever which gives 100 pps when there is no previous stimulation. This is what is predicted by the adaptation theory. The "aversion" theory must regard the result as a coincidence.

How likely is such a coincidence? So far, the C-T interval necessary to surmount a refractory period of the stimulated tissue has been measured for a number of functions which can be evoked by hypothalamic stimulation. The refractory period determined for the priming, drive, or motivational effect of rewarding brain stimulation ranges from .8 to 1.1 msec (Deutsch, 1964; Gallistel, 1973; Rolls, 1970). The refractory period of the reward effect hitherto obtained is about .5–.6 msec. The refractory period of evoked eating or drinking is somewhere between that of the priming, or drive, effect (Hawkins & Chang, unpublished; Hu, unpublished; Rolls, unpublished). The present determination of the refractory period of the reward effect is slightly shorter than those so far obtained. This may be because of the high voltage used in the experiment relative to threshold. The determination of the refractory period by behavioral means explores an effect which is bound to be statistical. A higher voltage may stimulate axons earlier in the relative refractory period. Further, a higher voltage will stimulate a larger number of fibers. As such fibers will not all be identical but show some kind of distribution of refractory periods, a higher voltage will stimulate a larger number of fibers with shorter refractory periods, and this will reflect itself in the behavioral effect. However, the point here is not that the measurements of the refractory period are identical with those of other experiments, but that the two measurements in the experiment reported here are nearly identical, and that different functions have so far been found to have different refractory periods.

So far, the experiments reported here lend support to the hypothesis that prolonged rewarding stimulation is turned off because the rewarding aspect of the intracranial stimulus adapts. The evidence so far does not conclusively rule out the possibility that an aversive component is present, at least in the case of some animals. It is possible that such an aversive component of a steady nature is present, and when the rewarding aspect of the intracranial stimulus adapts, the aversive component provides some of the motivation for the rat to turn off the stimulus. It would be surprising if the adaptation of the reward component was not found to be the main ingredient of the turning-off phenomenon. A steady or more slowly adapting aversive component may also be present in differing degrees, depending on the electrode locus. Whether this aversive factor is actually present remains for further work to determine.

REFERENCES

Bower, G. H., & Miller, N. E. Rewarding and punishing effects from stimulating the same place in the rat's brain. *Journal of Comparative and Physiological Psychology,* 1958, **51,** 669–674.

Deutsch, J. A. *The structural basis of behavior.* Chicago: University of Chicago Press, 1960.

Deutsch, J. A. Behavioral measurement of the neural refractory period and its application to intracranial self-stimulation. *Journal of Comparative and Physiological Psychology,* 1964, **58,** 1–9.

Deutsch, J. A., & Hawkins, R. D. Adaptation as a cause of apparent aversiveness of prolonged rewarding brain stimulation. *Behavioral Biology,* 1972, **7,** 285–290.

Deutsch, J. A., & Howarth, C. I. Some tests of a theory of intracranial self-stimulation. *Psychological Review,* 1963, **70,** 444–470.

Gallistel, C. R. Self-stimulation: The neurophysiology of reward and motivation. In J. A. Deutsch (Ed.), *Physiological basis of memory.* New York: Academic Press, 1973.

Gallistel, C. R. Rewarding brain stimulation. In J. A. Deutsch (Ed.), *Physiological basis of memory.* New York: Academic Press, 1972.

Hodos, W. Motivational properties of long durations of rewarding brain stimulation. *Journal of Comparative and Physiological Psychology,* 1965, **59,** 219–244.

Keesey, R. Duration of stimulation and the reward properties of hypothalamic stimulation. *Journal of Comparative and Physiological Psychology,* 1964, **58,** 201–207.

Kestenbaum, R. S., Deutsch, J. A., & Coons, E. E. Behavioral measurement of neural poststimulation excitability cycle: Pain cells in the brain of the rat. *Science,* 1970, **167,** 393–396.

Mendelson, J. Lateral hypothalamic stimulation: inhibition of aversive effects by feeding, drinking and gnawing. *Science,* 1969, **166,** 1431–1433.

Roberts, W. W. Both rewarding and punishing effects from stimulation of posterior hypothalamus of cat with same intensity. *Journal of Comparative and Physiological Psychology,* 1958, **51,** 400–407.

Rolls, E. R. Absolute refractory period of neurons involved in MFB self-stimulation. *Physiology and Behavior,* 1970, **7,** 311–315.

Stein, L. An analysis of stimulus-duration preference in selfstimulation of the brain. *Journal of Comparative and Physiological Psychology,* 1962, **55,** 405–414.

Valenstein, E., & Valenstein, T. Interaction of positive and negative renforcing neural systems. *Science,* 1964, **145,** 1456–1458.

PATTERNED REINFORCEMENT[1]

Stewart H. Hulse

DEPARTMENT OF PSYCHOLOGY, THE JOHNS HOPKINS UNIVERSITY,
BALTIMORE, MARYLAND

I. Introduction

It is a commonplace in the psychology of learning that repetitions of given bits of behavior are rarely, if ever, associated with the same set of reinforcing events. The things that animals and people do are sometimes associated with rewards (both big and small), sometimes with punishers (both strong and weak), and sometimes with neutral events, "neutral" either because they or their properties are ignored, or because we do not have the necessary knowledge to fit them into some proper scheme of things. The key concept here, most would agree, is that of *change;* the things we associate with behavior which we place in the class *reinforcer* easily assume a rich variety of affect and intensity. While all this may be true, psychologists have been curiously satisfied to severely restrict the general properties of the reinforcing event they have undertaken to bring into the laboratory. Reinforcing arrangements, whether of the instrumental or Pavlovian type, which have been so extensively studied over the past 30 years or

[1] The preparation of this article and the research reported in it were supported by National Science Foundation Research Grant GB-26187.

so, have a common limitation: if any variation in the reinforcing stimulus is introduced at all, *successive instances of a response are associated with one of just two possible reinforcing events.* We have watched many pigeons peck keys, many rats press levers and run runways, and many monkeys (and people) poke and prod their environments in great profusion; but the reinforcing event, be it reward, punishment, or whatever, associated with any peck, press, poke, or prod is invariably just one of (at most) two things: *something* or *nothing,* and the "something" is most often an event which remains constant and unchanging for a given subject in a given experiment. Granted that psychologists have shown incredible ingenuity arranging contingencies of reinforcement based on various permutations and combinations of reinforcing stimuli and the attributes such as amount, delay, intensity, probability, distribution in time, and so forth which can be assigned to them. But the fact remains that if any variation is introduced into the reinforcing event at all, variation usually takes the simple form of the successive presence or absence of something.

In this article, I wish to explore the ramifications of a scheme which entertains the notion that the events which are used to reinforce or maintain behavior need not be so simplified, that at the very least the outcomes of successive instances of a response need not be immutably all or nothing. The scheme is just that, a scheme. It is not a formal model from which logical deductions or predictions can be drawn. It is, instead, a plan for reorganizing part of the context in which many of us work in the realm of reinforcement. The plan is necessarily simple at this stage of things, and it owes much to a number of things which have preceded it, yet it has led to some work which might not have been done without it, and it may lend itself to more formal treatment at some future time.

In Section II of the article, I shall develop the basic scheme itself. Then, I shall discuss some research others have done which seems relevant, together with some work we have undertaken based upon some ideas which follow directly from it. Finally, I shall show how it may help to further our understanding of some older phenomena within the domain of reward and punishment in the psychology of learning.

II. Patterns of Reinforcement

The scheme to be developed is based on the concept of a *pattern* of reinforcement. Two general classes of patterns of reinforcement are to be identified—*subordinate* patterns and *superordinate* patterns —and, within each class, two subcategories—*pooled* or *averaged* patterns, and *sequential* patterns.

A *subordinate pattern* of reinforcement exists whenever a response is followed by a reinforcing stimulus which changes in some respect from one occasion of the response to the next, or whenever some feature of the contingency between a response and a reinforcing stimulus changes from one occasion of the response to the next. If a subordinate pattern exists, the specific reinforcing stimulus which follows the response on any given occasion, or the specific response-reinforcer contingency which is in effect on any given occasion of the response, is called an *element* of the pattern. Elements have, in turn, general *attributes* which place them into one or another category of the reinforcing event. Thus, elements may come from the class of positive reinforcers or rewards, or they may come from the class of negative reinforcers or punishers. (We assume some suitable definition of reward and punishment.) Elements may also have additional attributes, such as quality or intensity, which are definable within broader classifications such as reward or punishment.

If a subordinate pattern of reinforcement is based upon elements consisting of contingencies between a response and a reinforcer, probability of reinforcement or delay of reinforcement provide potential attributes beyond those associated with simple reward or punishment. And, in this regard, the concept of a subordinate pattern of reinforcement constructed from elements based on changing contingencies between response and reinforcer can be generalized to the domain of Pavlovian conditioning provided that here, of course, the elements would consist of variations in the contingency between a conditional stimulus (CS) and an unconditional stimulus (UCS).

A subordinate pattern of reinforcement is constructed according to certain rules which determine the manner in which the component elements of the pattern are put together. There are limitless ways in which a limitless variety of elements could be arranged with respect to each other, but the most common one is called a schedule of reinforcement, a pattern based on the principle of simple intermittency. The reinforcing element associated with each of a series of responses assumes just two values: a finite amount of a positive or negative reinforcer, or nothing, the two elements arranged according to timing or counting contingencies. Voluminous amounts of data and theory have been produced, of course, with partial reinforcement and with the various ratio and interval contingencies, among others, which can be generated on the intermittency principle (e.g., Amsel, 1967; Capaldi, 1967; Ferster & Skinner, 1957; Schoenfeld, 1970), and this is hardly the place to expand upon subordinate patterns of this basic type. Suffice it to say that all of this work has been based upon a highly specialized class of subordinate pattern.

While most of the work with simple subordinate patterns has been based on a two-element pattern and the principle of intermittency, there is no logical reason to restrict things to this simple, special case. A pattern may be built from elements which consist of different magnitudes of reinforcement, different UCS intensities, different delays of reinforcement, and so on, and there is no reason to restrict the pattern to a combination of just two elements. It could be composed of many. It could be generated from elements picked from the same reinforcement dimension, such as m magnitudes of reinforcement where m is greater than 2, or it could be developed by combining elements from two or more dimensions of reinforcement, such as m magnitudes of reinforcement intermixed in some fashion with d delays of reinforcement, and, if intermittency were to be added, with p probabilities of reinforcement.

Within the realm of subordinate patterns, two further subcategories have proved useful to identify. These are *averaged* or *pooled* subordinate patterns and *sequential* subordinate patterns. In an *averaged* pattern elements are arranged to follow responses according to an order which is independent and random from one response to the next. Averaged patterns may be derived from an array of elements which vary in an attribute like magnitude of reward or intensity of punishment. Similarly, they may be derived from elements which specify the relationship in time between a response and a reinforcing stimulus. A pattern based on changing delays of reinforcement provides a good example of the latter instance. The elements of the pattern may be picked according to some general rule, that is, parameters of the pattern as a whole may be set, like a *mean* or *range* of reward magnitudes, but the specific order in which the individual elements of the pattern are presented to a subject is not a defining property of the pattern, and is often haphazard or random.

There is a second important characteristic of an averaged pattern. Subjects exposed to an averaged pattern learn about the pattern or about its general properties from repeated exposures to all its elements. Presumably, whatever abstraction develops about the pattern must depend upon the subject's ability to *pool* or *average* features of the elements which enter into the pattern, hence the pattern's label.

A variable ratio schedule of reinforcement provides a very simple example to use to develop the foregoing points. In such a schedule, there is an *a priori* rule which sets the overall ratio of the frequencies of the two elements of the pattern (reinforcement and nonreinforcement), but beyond that restriction, the distribution of the two elements across successive responses is haphazard or random. As such a pattern is used in an experiment, whatever the subject learns about it must come from whatever can be garnered from repeated exposures to its elements. Typically, exposure continues until some feature of behavior stabilizes, such as response rate.

In a *sequential subordinate pattern,* the elements of the pattern change systematically, sequentially, or progressively over time or over successive responses. In contrast to an averaged pattern in which the order or arrangement of the elements is often random or haphazard, order and the attributes of order provide the essential defining property of a sequential pattern. Thus, to pick simple examples, sequential patterns can be built from progressive changes in the probability with which a response is reinforced, from sequential changes in magnitude and delay of reinforcement, and so on. Subjects could, of course, be exposed to a given sequential change over and over again after the fashion of averaged patterns, but as we shall see, it is also useful to consider the behavioral properties of sequential patterns when a subject is exposed to the sequential change of elements just once.

Having defined subordinate patterns in general and two subcategories of them in particular, it is easy to define a second major pattern we wish to identify. A *superordinate pattern of reinforcement* is, quite simply, a pattern of reinforcement constructed from elements which are themselves subordinate patterns of reinforcement. Once again, it is possible to identify two subcategories of superordinate patterns: *averaged* or *pooled* and *sequential* superordinate patterns. In an averaged superordinate pattern, the component elements are arranged from instance to instance without any special regard to their order, while in sequential superordinate patterns, there is a consistent order or sequence to the arrangement of the elements. As a hint of things to come, superordinate patterns have proved interesting because they generate effects which could not be predicted from a knowledge of the behavioral consequences of their component parts. We shall see that they can have *emergent* properties in the full Gestalt sense of the term.

III. Subordinate Patterns of Reinforcement

We turn now, however, to a detailed consideration of some properties of subordinate patterns of reinforcement. As we go, there is a trap to be avoided. And that is the fact that much of what is to be said can be facilely retranslated into the lingo of the operant laboratory. If that is done, it will be done at the risk of missing a major point of this article which is that schedules of reinforcement are quite important but quite restricted instances of a much broader class of events in the reinforcement domain. In developing the concept of a pattern of reinforcement and its several varieties, we hope to show that there are useful things to be learned about behavior if a broader brush spreads things beyond the two elements of reinforcement and nonreinforcement.

A. Averaged Subordinate Patterns

It is convenient to develop the concept of averaged subordinate patterns by looking at two areas toward which some experimental attention has been aimed. The first of these is the study of reinforcement mechanisms which modulate the persistence of behavior (Amsel, 1967), while the second concerns the concept of reinforcement contrast and, in particular, some new data that have recently been obtained concerning this phenomenon.

1. Persistence of Behavior

It is well known that the simplest form of averaged pattern is one based on just two elements, fixed reward and nonreward, and this is hardly the place to further harrow the important but already well-plowed field of response units, partial reinforcement effects, frustration, sequential hypotheses, and so on. It is important, instead, to develop the notion that the arena is, in fact, based on a highly special case which ought to be recognized as such—even though theory may become much more complicated in the process. In this section, then, we shall emphasize research which has examined the general problem of the persistence of behavior when patterns based on other than simple intermittency have been used, and, in particular, when patterns have been adopted which incorporated more than just two elements.

Logan, Beier, and Kincaid (1956) and Yamaguchi (1961) did some very early work in which patterns were studied incorporating *variable magnitudes* of reward, though the patterns were restricted to two elements. Logan *et al.* showed that a two-magnitude pattern of food reward served to increase resistance to extinction much like a two-element pattern in which one of the elements was zero magnitude (nonreinforcement), while Yamaguchi showed that persistence in extinction tended to increase as the range in magnitude increased between the two elements of the pattern. Logan (1960) was probably the first to note that intermittent reinforcement was, in fact, a simple, special case of varied magnitudes of reward, the special case in which at least one of the reinforcing elements to which a subject is exposed is nothing at all. Logan's theoretical comment has been echoed from time to time, most recently perhaps by Leonard (1969) and Rettig and Clement (1971). Leonard, working within Capaldi's (1967) theoretical framework, showed that a two-magnitude pattern of food reward would increase resistance to extinction relative to regular reinforcement with one magnitude, while resistance to extinction was even greater if a third element of zero magnitude were added to the pattern. His results were associated in part with the order in which the elements were presented to his animals, however, so his work does not fall strictly within the domain of averaged patterns.

The use of averaged patterns is by no means restricted to the realm of positive reinforcement. There are a few experiments in which averaged patterns of punishing stimuli have been used, and the persistence of some feature of behavior has been studied. An experiment by Boe (1971) provides a good example. Boe conditioned rats to press a lever for food pellets on a ratio schedule, then introduced variable punishment according to one of five general patterns: (1) for three groups of rats, three fixed intensities of shock were delivered after each 11 lever presses; (2) for three other groups of animals, shock intensity was fixed at 80 V, but the ratio of shocked to unshocked responses varied from 1 to 21; (3) for one group of rats, shock intensity was fixed, but punishment was delivered on a variable ratio ranging from 1 to 21 responses; (4) for one group, punishment was delivered after every 11 responses, but five shock intensities were used which varied haphazardly from 50 to 110 V (arithmetic mean of 80 V); (5) for a final group, both shock intensity and ratio of punished to unpunished responses varied simultaneously. The results showed, first of all, the not unexpected effect that as fixed intensities of punishment increased and as fixed ratios of punishment decreased, lever pressing for food succumbed to punishment to an ever increasing degree. The results showed, next, that the group subjected to a fixed intensity of shock presented on a variable ratio schedule was suppressed just about as much as the group presented with the comparable fixed ratio of shock. Most interestingly, however, the group exposed to the five-element pattern of varying shock intensities was markedly more suppressed than the group punished with a fixed 80-V shock, the middlemost element of the variable pattern, and the group exposed to *both* variable intensity and variable ratios of shock was suppressed to the same degree. In both cases, the suppression was almost as great as that produced by a fixed intensity shock at the most extreme level, 110 V.

The use of averaged patterns need not be restricted to patterns which are developed by changing attributes of the reinforcing stimulus itself. As we have indicated, a pattern can be derived by introducing change in the relationship between a response and its reinforcer, such as introducing one or more delays of reinforcement. In this particular instance again, a two-element pattern seems to be most commonly studied (e.g., Amsel, 1972; Capaldi, 1967; Donin, Surridge, & Amsel, 1967; Shanab, 1971), and, among other things it seems usually the case that the introduction of a delay serves to increase the persistence of the response when positive reinforcement is removed altogether during extinction. Logan (1960) has, once again, pointed out that intermittent reinforcement can be derived as a special case of varied delays of reinforcement, that case where delay of reinforcement is occasionally set at infinity; so perhaps in a general way at least it should not be surprising that two-element patterns based on intermittency and on varied delays should generate some phenomena in common.

In a related vein, one experiment has been done in which variable intervals between a CS and UCS were used to generate an averaged pattern of reinforcement. This experiment, which was done by one of the writer's students (Zill, 1967), had the virtue of deriving a pattern from more than two elements, and it serves to introduce the concept of patterned reinforcement into the realm of Pavlovian conditioning. Zill studied the development of a conditioned emotional response (CER) as a function of a fixed CS-UCS interval of 12 seconds, a fixed CS-UCS interval of 60 seconds, and as a function of CS-UCS intervals which varied haphazardly for the same subject across 12, 42, 78, and 108 seconds with the restriction that all four intervals were presented equally often. Hungry rats were first trained to lick sweetened milk from a drinking tube, then the licking response was placed on a random ratio schedule (Schoenfeld & Cumming, 1960) in which individual licks were reinforced with drops of milk (Hulse, 1960) if they occurred during two regularly spaced, .13-second "t-d" periods each second. If they fell outside these periods, they were not reinforced. With this two-element schedule, Zill was able to generate stable baseline licking behavior in which his rats licked almost continuously for periods of 45 minutes to 1 hour. Following initial training, the animals were exposed to four pairings of CS and UCS during each of 10 daily half-hour experimental sessions. The CS was white light from a 7 W bulb, and the UCS was a .5 mA scrambled shock of .75 second duration delivered at the end of the CS-UCS interval independent of licking behavior. The four presentations of the CS and UCS were spaced at variable intervals throughout a daily session, and the CS went off with the onset of the UCS so that CS duration and the CS-UCS interval were identical in length. Conventional suppression ratios were computed for data analysis, and the course of suppression was also evaluated within successive 6-second segments of the CS.

Analysis of suppression ratios averaged across the four trials of Day 1 showed that the development of suppression was most rapid in the group conditioned with a fixed, 12-second CS-UCS interval. On this day, it was reliably more suppressed than both the fixed, 60-second group and the variable CS-UCS group, the latter two groups not differing between themselves. By the second day, however, the fixed, 12-second group did not differ from the variable CS-UCS group, and over the last 5 days of training, the fixed, 12-second group and the variable CS-UCS group were equally and reliably more suppressed than the fixed, 60-second group. Figure 1 shows the results of breaking CS-UCS intervals into successive 6-second segments and averaging over the last 4 days of the experiment. Note

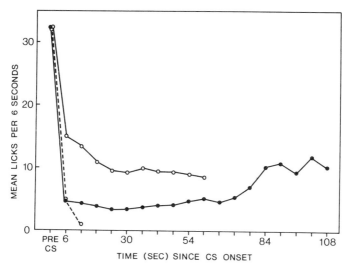

Fig. 1. The course of response suppression following establishment of a conditioned emotional response with variable (●—●) or fixed CS-UCS intervals (60-second, ○—○; 12-second, ○---○).

that as the longer durations are reached for the variable CS-UCS group, fewer data are included since, for example, only four trials were run at the extreme, 108-second interval. Thus, for this group, a CS-UCS interval of 12 seconds contributed to just the first two 6-second segments, while an interval of 108 seconds contributed to each point on the curve.

The most remarkable point to be noted from the data of Fig. 1 is that variable CS-UCS intervals produced suppression that was fully comparable with that produced by a fixed, 12-second CS-UCS interval, both producing reliably more suppression than a fixed, 60-second interval. This was true even though the probability of a shock was just .25 through the first two intervals plotted for the variable group, while it was 1.0 for the fixed 12-second group. The variable group shows some recovery from suppression as the longer intervals in the pattern are approached (the means for the last two CS segments are reliably, $p < .05$, greater than those for the segments covering 49–60 seconds), and the variable group is not reliably different from the fixed, 60-second group over the range from 49 to 60 seconds, indicating increasing probability that licking would resume. But the salient feature of the data is that suppression produced by a four-element pattern of CS-UCS intervals is very great and most characteristic of the shortest interval included in the pattern if that interval is used just by itself.

2. Reinforcement Contrast

In this section, we want to apply the concept of averaged patterns of reinforcement to the phenomenon of reinforcement contrast. By reinforcement contrast we refer to the well-known phenomenon that a shift in reinforcement magnitude to some lower or higher value during the course of acquisition or performance of a response results in an overshoot of performance below or above that of a control group maintained on the low or high value throughout the experiment. Much of the background development that we wish to emphasize at first is owed to Bevan and his associates (Bevan, 1966, 1968; Bevan & Adamson, 1960), and we can do little better than to turn to their work to introduce the topic.

Bevan's work rests primarily on the concept of adaptation level (Helson, 1964) and the general notion that reinforcing stimuli exist in a context which determines their effectiveness at any given point in time. Bevan assumes, basically, that subjects will *pool* their collective experience with the elements of a reinforcement pattern, that which we have called an averaged pattern in particular, to form an adaptation level, and that the utility of any given element at any particular point in time depends upon how it compares relative to the current adaptation level for the pattern as a whole. Normally, adaptation levels are derived from some averaging process, an averaging process described formally by some index of central tendency of the pattern such as a geometric or arithmetic mean of the strengths or intensities of the component elements.

Bevan and Adamson (1960) set out to test some of this thinking as it applies to the reinforcement process. They showed first of all that if different groups of human subjects were exposed initially to a series of either strong, medium, or weak intensities of shock as part of a preadaptation series, then required to learn a bolthead maze with errors punished with the medium intensity shock for all groups, performance was poorest in the group preadapted with the strong shock and best in the group preadapted with the weak shock. For the former, the medium shock was *relatively* weak and so functioned as a less effective punisher as compared with the control condition of medium intensity shocks throughout both preadaptation and learning. For subjects preadapted to the weak shock, the converse was true, of course, and so the medium intensity shock was relatively strong and a relatively effective punishing stimulus. In another experiment in the same series, Bevan and Adamson punished subjects for errors on a bolthead maze with elements from a five-element averaged pattern of shock intensities. The elements were arranged for three groups, in a positively skewed (weakest to strongest) fashion, or symmetrically about a mean intensity. For a fourth group, a single shock intensity was used set at the mean value of the group exposed to the symmetrical pattern. As subjects traced the maze, they were punished for errors with the elements of the several patterns chosen at random, subject, of course, to the frequency constraints imposed by the skewed or symmetrical characteristics of the patterns. The results showed, once again, that the effectiveness of the reinforcing stimuli depended in part upon the context in which they appeared. Subjects exposed to a positively skewed distribution (and, therefore, to a low average intensity of shock) were punished with a relatively weak "average" reinforcer, and so performed much better. Neither group performed as well, however, as the constant-intensity group or the group exposed to a symmetrical distribution, *both of which were exposed to mean intensities less than that associated with the negatively skewed distribution.* Consequently, an adaptation level interpretation is not confirmed completely by all the data. Neither did the experiment include groups punished at a constant level equal, for example, to the means of the two skewed conditions.

It would be interesting to know how much effectiveness of punishment was associated with some measure of central tendency of the patterns, and how much it was associated with parameters of the *shape* of the distribution, that is, with the distribution's skewedness, range, and so forth. Adaptation level speaks primarily to the importance of pooling mechanisms and measures of central tendency, but the pattern imposed on the distribution may be important in its own right. In any event, Bevan has made a signal contribution to reinforcement theory by showing that, as stimuli, reinforcers are profitably viewed as "stimuli in context," and that will be a theme running through much of the remainder of this article.

To further develop the concept of reinforcement contrast in averaged patterns of reinforcement, we turn now to some research that was initiated by an experiment of Collier and Marx in 1959. Collier and Marx (1959) exposed rats during magazine training in a lever box to one of three concentrations of sucrose. Different groups of rats received twenty .4-ml drops of either a 4%, 11.3% or 32% sucrose solution. Then all animals were trained to lever press for a common 11.3% reinforcer, and the course of acquisition of free-operant lever pressing was followed through ten 20-minute sessions. The results showed that the rats magazine trained with 4% sucrose learned to lever press fastest, those magazine trained with 32% sucrose learned slowest, while those magazine trained with the intermediate 11.3% solution learned middling well.

There are three important things about this experiment. First, it seemed to show clear positive and negative reinforcement contrast: rats magazine trained on the 4% solution, for example, were "elated" to find a relatively better reinforcer and so learned to lever press faster that the 11.3% control. Second, it introduced an important technique for the study of reinforcement contrast and, most probably, other reinforcement phenomena as well (Bevan & Adamson noted this fact, and incorporated the procedure in one of their experiments). Basically, an experimental variable is introduced during an early phase of an experiment, and the effects of that variable are assessed during a later phase by a transfer-of-training paradigm in which all subjects are shifted to a common set of experimental conditions and tested there. With the Collier and Marx procedure, transfer is to the *de novo* learning of a response following experience with the stimuli which are to appear later under the guise of reinforcers. Finally, the Collier and Marx experiment contained a serious artifact which renders its results useless so far as the phenomena of reinforcement contrast is concerned.

As Dunham and Kilps (1969) were first to point out, although all animals worked for a common 11.3% concentration of sucrose, the learning curves separated early in learning and *stayed* apart. One might expect contrast to appear in the *initial* portion of the learning period, but since it is normally a transitory affair, the animals ought eventually to have settled down to some common level of performance. The key, said Dunham and Kilps, lay in the method Collier and Marx had used to establish hunger in their animals. Hunger was defined in terms of a 1-hour feeding period to which the animals were exposed following their daily session in the apparatus. This food was combined, however, with the calories obtained from the sucrose used in the experiment proper, higher concentrations of sucrose providing more calories, of course. Consequently, in terms of their total caloric intake, the higher concentrations of sucrose led to a richer daily diet and therefore to *less hunger*. Using this reasoning, the results of the experiment showed different levels of motivation instead of different degrees of the effectiveness of reinforcing stimuli, and it would follow from the procedures used that differential hunger would maintain itself throughout the experiment, assuring the continued separation of the "learning" curves. When Dunham and Kilps repeated the experiment defining hunger in terms of a fixed percentage of body weight which adjusted for calories associated with the several concentrations of sucrose, they obtained learning curves which, for all intents and purposes, were superimposed upon each other.

The story does not end here, however. We reasoned (Hulse, 1973) that nothing in either the Collier and Marx or the Dunham and Kilps experiment had been done to teach the animals prior to the introduction of the lever-pressing contingency that reinforcement magnitude was a relevant dimension in the experiment at all. This, as a matter of fact, is a characteristic of a great many, if not most, experiments dealing with reinforcement contrast effects which do not incorporate discrimination procedures. Earlier work (Hulse, 1962a, b) shows, however, that if a reinforcing stimulus is singled out for a rat by the simple expedient of including it in a two-element pattern of intermittent reinforcement, then changes in the magnitude of the reinforcer are reliably followed by the behavior of the animal, e.g., an upward shift in reinforcement magnitude produces an immediate upward shift in response rate. If, however, no discriminative training of this very simple kind is forced upon the animal—that is, if all responses are followed by a reinforcing stimulus so that discrimination is not compelled by the bare contrast between reinforcement and nonreinforcement—then a shift of any kind in the magnitude of reinforcement produces at least a momentary collapse of behavior even if the shift is to a larger magnitude of reinforcement. This background obviously owes much to Lashley and Wade (1946); with it in mind, we repeated the basic Collier and Marx experiment using a two-element averaged pattern of reinforcement magnitude during magazine training so that through simple stimulus contrast afforded by successive instances of the two magnitudes, the dimension of reinforcement magnitude was defined for the animal prior to the shift to the *de novo* learning of the lever-pressing response.

In the first experiment, three groups of rats maintained at 80% normal body weight were magazine trained under one of the following conditions. For Group C-10, a 5-second 3000-Hz tone was followed immediately by the automatic delivery into a food cup of 10 Noyes .045 mg food pellets. Fifteen pairings of tone and food were given each day for a total of 14 days. The procedure was identical for Group C-1, except that just one pellet of food followed the tone. For groups V-10 and V-1, the experimental treatment was identical during magazine training: a 3000-Hz tone was paired a random half of the time with a 10-pellet quantity and half the time with a one pellet quantity, so that these animals had experience with a two-element averaged pattern of reinforcement magnitude. Tone-pellet presentations were spaced 90 seconds apart.

Following magazine training, a discrete-trial lever-pressing contingency was introduced. Now, food pellets could be obtained only if a lever was pressed. Entrance of the lever into the box was signaled by a 5-second, 3000-Hz tone, the lever disappearing from the box as soon as a response occurred. For groups C-10 and C-1, reinforcement consisted of the same 10-pellet and one-pellet quantities used during magazine training. For group V-10, reinforcement was always a constant 10-pellet magnitude, while for Group V-1, it was always a constant one-pellet magnitude. The animals had an 80-second opportunity to press the lever, and trials were spaced by 10-seconds. There were 16 trials on each of 9 successive days of learning.

In a second experiment, the C-1 and V-1 procedures were repeated except that trials during magazine training were spaced by 20-seconds, and during the lever-pressing phase of the experiment, the animals had a 60-second opportunity to press the lever followed by a 60-second intertrial interval. Fifteen trials were run on each of 5 successive days. The results of the two experiments for the animals who learned to lever-press for a one-pellet reward are shown in Figs. 2, 3, and 4.

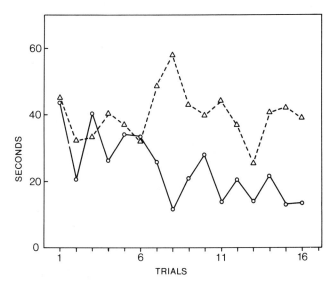

Fig. 2. Response latencies on the first day of acquisition of a discrete-trial lever pressing response. Rats were exposed during magazine training to a constant one-pellet condition [C-1(O)] or to a variable one- and 10-pellet condition [V-1(△)]. All rats worked for one pellet during the acquisition of the lever-pressing response. Data from Experiment 1.

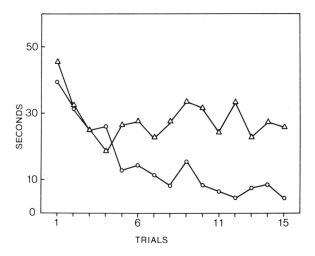

Fig. 3. Same conditions and symbols as those shown in Fig. 2 with data from Experiment 2. All rats worked for one pellet during the acquisition of the lever-pressing response.

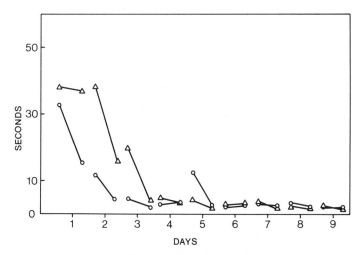

Fig. 4. The course of acquisition of the lever-pressing response after the first day of acquisition in Experiment 1. Rats working for one pellet following training with a variable one- and 10-pellet [V-1(△)] condition were still slower to respond through 3 days of lever pressing than those magazine trained with a constant one-pellet [C-1(○)] condition.

Figures 2 and 3 show mean latencies to respond for one-pellet on each of the trials of the first day of lever-press training. It is readily apparent that the V-1 condition produced learning which followed the course of that produced by the C-1 condition for five or six trials, then slowed to remain at a constant level for the remainder of the day. The C-1 condition generated learning which progressed steadily toward a short latency by the end of the day, and by that time, the two conditions produced differences in latency which were highly reliable. Figure 4, based on the data of the first experiment, shows that the effect was hardly transitory; it lasted for at least 3 days (4 days in the second experiment). Both experiments show, in short, a durable negative reinforcement contrast effect of substantial magnitude; Figs. 2 and 3 show mean differences on the order of 20 seconds or so by the end of the first day of learning.

The data do not reveal positive reinforcement contrast, however. The latencies for all rats that learned to press the lever for a 10-pellet reinforcer are essentially identical throughout learning for the experiment in which this element was used to reinforce new learning. Thus, the data add to the frequent observation that positive reinforcement contrast under procedures comparable to those used here is an ephemeral phenomenon at best (Dunham, 1968). As we shall see, other procedures are required to produce positive contrast with patterns of reinforcement.

Obviously, the results of these experiments seem to lend themselves to an interpretation in terms of adaptation level. There are at least two things which suggest that adaptation level may not do a totally adequate job, however. First, of course, the data show no suggestion of positive reinforcement contrast, and there is nothing in the procedures used in the experiments, such as ceiling effects on response latencies prior to the introduction of a shift in reinforcement magnitude, to mitigate against the appearance of positive contrast. Another glance at Figs. 2 and 3 suggests, too, that it took several learning trials before contrast began to enter the picture. The data seem to show, contrary to a simple adaptation level interpretation, that at first the one-pellet reinforcer was an equally effective reward for all animals, that it was not modified by its value relative to some pooled average carried over from magazine training for the rats exposed to both one- and 10-pellet elements at that earlier time. An alternate explanation is that rats with the two-magnitude background did not begin to show a slowing of learning until it became highly probable that, as compared with their earlier experience, the 10-pellet magnitude was not forthcoming. The data suggest that it took five or six trials for the animals to reach this conclusion, a conclusion for which the rats seemed therefore to have required a p of about .03. We are, of course, being a trifle facetious here, but experiments we will discuss later suggest that at some primitive level, at least, rats are capable of sorting out elements of a pattern and responding to more detailed relationships among them than some simple psychological impression of their central tendency.

We shall return to the problem of reinforcement contrast. Now, however, we turn to our second variety of subordinate pattern of reinforcement for its development.

B. Sequential Subordinate Patterns

In a sequential subordinate pattern, the elements of the pattern, or some feature of the correlation between a response and the reinforcing stimulus, change systematically, sequentially, or progressively over successive responses. Order and the attributes of order provide the essential defining property of sequential patterns and serve to distinguish them from average patterns. To pick simple examples, sequential patterns can be built from progressive changes in the probability with which a response is reinforced, from sequential changes in magnitude and delay of reinforcement, and so on.

Curiously enough, however, the two-element world of schedules of intermittent reinforcement has relatively little to say about sequential patterns. Only three varieties seem to have been identified at all, progressive-ratio, progressive-interval, and cyclic-interval schedules of reinforcement, and they have received almost no experimental attention. Since it is convenient to begin with the simplest case, however, we shall use them to introduce the available evidence concerning sequential patterns based on intermittency of reinforcement. Then we shall move on to some other places in which sequential patterns have been used.

1. Progressive-Ratio, Progressive-Interval, and Cyclic-Interval Schedules

Progressive ratio schedules were first described by Findley (1958) and Hodos (1961). In brief, a progressive-ratio schedule is a two-element schedule based on reinforcement and nonreinforcement in which successive reinforcing stimuli are contingent upon progressively greater numbers of nonreinforced responses. The available data are based on simple arithmetic progressions in which the number of nonreinforced responses required to produce successive reinforcers is some convenient multiple of the number required to produce the first one. Hodos showed that this schedule could be used to assess the motivational properties of a set of drive and reinforcement variables. In effect, he pointed out, successive increases in the responses required for successive reinforcers are analogous to progressively severe obstructions in the sense that Warden (1931) used the term. If one animal were willing to progress to a higher ratio in the schedule than another, for example, this would indicate that the animal was more motivated—either through drive-producing operations per se or because of some greater incentive value of the reinforcing stimulus. Using a 15-minute pause as an index of a "breaking point" on a given run, Hodos was able to show sensible and regular changes in the number of responses in the largest completed ratio run as a function of the concentration of a water-condensed milk mixture and of level of hunger drive. Rats worked their way up to higher and higher ratios the more palatable the reinforcer and the greater their loss from normal body weight.

Hurwitz and Harzem (1968) added another feature of interest to the basic progressive-ratio procedure. They provided rats with an alternative response which could be used at the animals' discretion to reset the progressive-ratio schedule to its initial value. They reasoned that on the principle of least effort, rats ought to choose to reset the ratio the larger the arithmetic multiplier in a progressive-ratio schedule and, for any given progressive ratio, the greater the number of reinforcements already obtained on the schedule, that is, the farther along the animal was on a given run through the schedule. Their data showed, first of all, that animals most often chose to reset the ratio just after they had obtained a reinforcer; they rarely interrupted a run until the next available reinforcer had been obtained. The results also showed that except for a schedule with a small multiplier in which the ratio increased by just five responses after each reinforcement, rats generally came to reset the ratio schedule after they had obtained the first reinforcer. Those on the smaller multiplier were not quite so efficient, but they too rarely worked for more than three reinforcers before resetting the ratio.

These experiments show, in general, that sequential patterns can be put together which provide sensitive indices of the motivational state of an animal. Said differently, animals are sensitive to the motivational properties of stimuli or of experimental conditions like drive when they appear in the context of a progressive-ratio schedule. Rats are apparently also able to discriminate the fine features of such schedules remarkably well, since Hurwitz and Harzem have shown them to be extremely efficient at optimizing the reinforcement available within them.

Progressive-interval schedules are directly analogous to progressive-ratio schedules. They are two-element patterns in which the interval of time between one reinforced response and the availability of the next reinforcer increases according to some rule. Harzem (1969) provides the available data about them. He shows that if a simple arithmetic progression of interval is used for a rat, the animal is capable of following the schedule in the sense that it postpones its first response following a reinforcement for a longer and longer period of time. It also tends to wait for longer and longer intervals between responses as the end of a given interreinforcement period approaches. The rat is not, however, capable of timing things more accurately than this under these conditions. If a progressive-interval schedule is used in which the intervals change *geometrically,* however, rats become remarkably accurate in timing their behavior appropriately.

The first response following a reinforcement tends to be delayed according to a geometric progression in time, and, as compared with an arithmetic progression, the animal makes proportionately more and more of its responses with longer interresponse intervals as the end of a given interreinforcement period approaches. Harzem notes on the basis of these results that animals seem better able to follow changes in the *relative* as opposed to the absolute magnitude of progressive intervals, a fact which is reminiscent of the Weber-Fechner law in psychophysics. He points out the important fact that since animals are able to so successfully follow time intervals which *change* according to some sequential rule, it is unlikely that they discriminate time in interval schedules by bringing collateral or chained mediating behavior into play. Instead, he argues, they must be able to make direct discriminations of time intervals.

Cyclic-interval schedules (Innis & Staddon, 1971; Staddon, 1964) are analogous to progressive-interval schedules. They differ only in that time intervals between the availability of successive reinforcers first become longer, say, according to some mathematical rule, then move in the opposite direction and become shorter according to some mathematical rule. The question of interest, once again, is whether the organism can "track" the intervals in such a schedule by adjusting postreinforcement pauses to conform to the changing time intervals between successive reinforcers. Under a variety of procedures and for a variety of rules governing the course of the cyclic change in successive time intervals, Innis and Staddon (1971) found that pigeons were remarkably skillful in tracking. The duration of postreinforcement pauses increased or decreased with increases or decreases in successive intervals, more accurately so if differential external stimuli signaled the increasing *vs.* decreasing portions of the cycle. They also observed that a power function held between interval duration in their schedules and the duration of the postreinforcement pause. This experiment, together with Harzem's work, clearly calls for some further analysis with psychophysical models.

As we indicated at the outset of this section, the foregoing schedules provide essentially all the available treatment of sequential patterns within the class of two-element schedules of reinforcement. They show clearly that animals respond to sequential changes in time or in probability of reinforcement much as if sequential change has stimulus properties which can be responded to directly. There are some other sources of information which suggest the same things, and we turn to them now.

2. *Sequential Magnitudes of Reward*

Jensen and Rey (1968, 1969) reported two experiments, one a replication of the other, which offer information about patterns based on sequential changes in magnitude of a positive reward. Their work deserves more attention than it seems to have received because it injects some proper cognition into the world of the 4-foot straight runway. Perhaps that is why it has been neglected. The essential design is provided by the second experiment. Three groups of rats were trained to run a runway for food pellets and then, on the same day, extinguished. Food pellets were administered to the three groups according to the following conditions. For one group run under "horn of plenty" conditions, the food cup in the goal box always contained one pellet of food. This treatment received the "horn of plenty" label because, so far as the rats were concerned, the food cup sprouted an endless supply of pellets as the experiment progressed. They received only one pellet per trial, however. For a second group run under "diminishing food supply" conditions, the food cup also contained one food pellet on each trial, but a supply of food pellets located in a Plexiglas tube mounted just above the food cup diminished by one food pellet on each trial. By trial 24, the last training trial, the tube was empty. The rats in the experiment were carefully observed to sniff and bite the tube, giving every indication that they were aware it contained food pellets and was a relevant source of stimulation in the experiment. A third group, a "full tube horn of plenty" group, was analogous to the second; it differed only in that the supply of food pellets in the tube did not diminish over the course of acquisition. The second group, then, provides a pattern of reinforcement in which the total available food supply diminishes in an obvious way over time. It is not, strictly speaking, a pattern in which magnitude of reinforcement per se changes, since all animals were always reinforced with a single food pellet, but information was available to the rats concerning a salient sequential change in the magnitude of reinforcement to be introduced into the experiment. The results of the experiment are shown in Fig. 5, which also includes running speeds obtained on 10 extinction trials which were run immediately after acquisition ended.

It is readily apparent that all three conditions produced common performance at the outset of training, but remarkably different (and reliably so) performance by the time extinction began. The "horn of plenty" animals ran with increasing speed throughout acquisition,

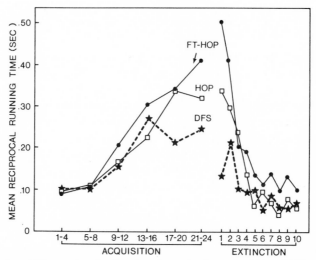

Fig. 5. Acquisition and extinction data from the Jensen and Rey (1969) experiment. During acquisition, rats ran under "full tube horn of plenty" conditions (FT-HOP), under "horn of plenty" conditions (HOP) or under "diminishing food supply" conditions (DFS). (From Jensen and Rey, 1969, by permission of the American Psychological Association, Washington, D.C.)

topped only by the "full tube horn of plenty" animals who presumably had the extra incentive associated with the visual and olfactory cues of a full tube of pellets. The behavior of the rats in the "diminishing food supply" condition was in striking contrast, however. These animals slowed their speeds relative to the other groups as the end of acquisition approached and were reliably slower than either of the other groups on the very first extinction trial. Their speeds on that trial, as a matter of fact, are scarcely different from an operant level defined by the speeds on the first *acquisition* trial. In effect, they showed no resistance to extinction at all.

The experiments of Jensen and Rey suggest that animals respond to a food pellet depending upon their ability to locate it with respect to some context. Clearly their rats responded to something associated with the sequential change per se in the pattern of decreasing numbers of food pellets in the diminishing food supply condition. Final pellets in the sequence had much different efficiencies as reinforcing stimuli than did those at the beginning of the sequence or those which appeared in the other contexts incorporated in the experiment. Similar things have been observed from time to time in the literature on punishment to which we now turn briefly.

3. Sequential Magnitudes of Aversive Stimuli

An early experiment by Miller (1960) provides a convenient start-ing place. Miller was interested in whether rats could learn to get used to fear in a conflict situation. He trained them to run an alley-way for food, then shocked them in the goal box under one of several conditions in order to establish an approach-avoidance conflict. For some rats, shock was introduced suddenly at full strength. For others, it was introduced gradually, beginning at a low level and then in-creasing until it was at the level used from the outset for the first group. The results of the experiment show that suddenly introduced shock had an immediate and fairly permanent effect: it introduced a marked conflict which greatly reduced the speed of approach to the goal. Gradual introduction of punishment, however, substantially reduced its suppressive effects. Animals continued to run quickly even when they were finally running into the same strong shock as the animals which were introduced to the shock all at once. This effect was confined, however, to the introduction of shock in the ex-perimental apparatus; if shock was gradually introduced outside the test alley, its effects were not attenuated.

Another experiment lends some possible further insight into the phenomenon Miller observed. Church, LoLordo, Overmier, Solo-mon, and Turner (1966) used an electric shock as an unconditioned stimulus in dogs paralyzed with tubocurarine and studied the effect of shock intensity on the magnitude of the unconditioned cardiac reflex. Heart rate changes to the shock stimulus were presumed to be potential indices of the functional severity of the shock. Some dogs were exposed to a maximal intensity from the outset of the experi-ment, and some were exposed to the same intensity introduced at a later point (as a control for possible sensitization or for wearing off of the curare). Under a third condition, dogs were exposed to shocks that gradually increased in intensity such that there was a final, com-mon, maximal intensity for all three groups over the last blocks of trials. The results showed that dogs exposed all at once to the maxi-mal intensity of shock produced maximal unconditioned cardiac re-sponses. Those exposed to gradually increasing intensities, however, showed reliably attenuated unconditioned reflexes. The important point about this experiment, as Church *et al.* point out, is that under conditions where competing responses or counterconditioning could not occur to produce the effect, because of the paralysis produced by tubocurarine, the gradual introduction of shock effectively reduced the magnitude of the unconditioned response to a very strong unconditioned stimulus. They therefore postulated the very important point that the gradual introduction of shock reduces the *"subjective severity* of subsequent, intense shocks."

An experiment by Davis and Wagner (1969) provides an important control that was missing in the Church *et al.* experiment. Davis and Wagner reasoned that the earlier phenomenon could have been due to the simple fact that the group subjected to the gradual introduction of shock simply received fewer strong shocks in the experiment than the groups exposed to the strong shock all at once. Davis and Wagner duplicated the essential design that Church *et al.* had used, exposing rats to 4000-Hz tones of gradually increasing intensity, but added a group which controlled for the total amount of stimulation obtained by exposing animals to the same intensities selected at random from trial to trial. The response in question was the startle response measured by stabilimeter. The results showed that the gradual introduction of stimulus intensity produced markedly greater attenuation of the startle response than that produced by the random application of the same intensities (or, for that matter, constant intensities at the mean of the random group or at the most extreme intensity). Apparently, there was something about the *sequence* per se of a gradually increasing series of stimulus intensities which modified the effectiveness of a strong stimulus on the response systems studied by Miller, Church *et al.*, and Davis and Wagner. Furthermore, the effect seems a fairly general one in that, more broadly, it holds for response systems as diverse as approach-avoidance conflict, cardiac reflexes, and startle responses, and over stimulus dimensions as diverse, at least, as electric shock and sound intensity. Certainly, the effect is not confined to some low-level physiological mechanism. The Church *et al.* experiment suggests, as a matter of fact, that the effect may be a cognitive one associated with some ongoing, centrally mediated mechanism.

C. An Overview

What is to be made of the foregoing? First of all, if there is a single generality to be drawn from the research under discussion, it is that the utility of a reinforcing stimulus for the acquisition or maintenance of a response depends upon the *context* from which it comes or in which it is embedded. A reward or a punishment is not some absolute thing; it does not exist in a vacuum. It is certainly not some static, physical event, some constant to be plugged into a

Newtonian system as Hull, for example, would once have had us do. Nor, perhaps, is it independent of context in even so simple a locale as a two-element schedule of reinforcement. Is the reinforcing stimulus itself the same functionally when it appears in the context of a fixed-ratio as compared with a fixed-interval schedule? The answer, curiously enough, remains to be obtained.

The notion of context has, at least, been fairly well developed by Bevan for the case of averaged patterns of reinforcement. We have seen how adaptation-level theory purports to account for phenomena such as the pooling or averaging of the effectiveness of reinforcing events. Unfortunately, however, the available data, scant though they are, do not appear to support a pooling model for multielement averaged patterns of reinforcement completely convincingly. Instead, a general overview suggests the alternative possibility that as an organism is exposed to an averaged pattern, its performance becomes characteristic of that associated with the element of the pattern producing the most extreme performance level when that element is used by itself as a reinforcing event. Thus, as we have seen, while the work of Bevan and Adamson (1960) indicated that the effectiveness of a pattern of reinforcement may sometimes be associated with some measure of the central tendency of the components of the pattern, this was by no means consistently the case. Two groups with a common relatively low mean intensity of punishment nevertheless made fewer errors on a maze problem than another group with a substantially higher mean intensity of punishment. And Black, Adamson, and Bevan (1961) found a similar inconsistency for rats learning to escape from shock in a runway. On the other hand, Boe (1971) found that a pattern of punishment based on a distribution of shock intensities produced response suppression characteristic of that produced by the strongest intensity in the pattern when that was used by itself, while Zill (1967) found that the strength of a CER based on a pattern of varying CS-UCS intervals was characteristic of that produced by the *shortest* CS-UCS interval when that was used by itself. This is hardly the place to take adaptation-level theory to task in general, nor its application to the problem of reinforcement in particular, but the available facts seem to indicate an inconsistent picture at best with respect to some of the details that Bevan proposed. This seems to be the case, at least, with respect to the pooling principle as it applies to an organism that is actively learning a response with a multivalued array of reinforcing stimuli.

Two other generalizations about averaged patterns seem safe to make however. First, all the data indicate—whether from two-

element patterns or from patterns with greater than two elements—
that the persistence of behavior is positively correlated with vari-
ability among the elements of a pattern. Thirty years or more of
research have amply demonstrated this fact for resistance to extinc-
tion following patterns incorporating zero reinforcement as one of
their elements, and all the work on variable magnitudes and delays
of positive reinforcement initiated by Logan seems best cast in the
same mold. The generalization holds over a broader field, however,
since Boe (1971) was able to show that recovery from the effects of
punishment was retarded by the use of a multielement pattern of
punishment, and Zill (1967) showed the same thing for recovery
from a CER following a multielement pattern of CS-UCS intervals.
Apparently, the reinforcement of a response with a variegated set of
events arranged in a random or haphazard fashion assures that the
response will continue to occur when transfer is made to some other
situation such as extinction or the recovery from the emotional or
suppressive effects of punishment. Today, all of these facts are rea-
sonably well documented (although, once again, the two-element
pattern is represented out of all proper proportion), and all have
received their share of theoretical scrutiny. Their generality con-
tinues to grow, however.

Second, and most important, the available work with averaged
patterns of reinforcement shows that they are important tools to use
in the study of reinforcement contrast. The data which come from
organisms exposed to patterns as they acquire a response may be
equivocal, but that which appears when organisms are asked to com-
pare some current set of reinforcement conditions against some prior
context of patterned reinforcement shows consistent negative rein-
forcement contrast. Bevan's work is at its clearest and best in this
regard (although he never looked at contrast following a truly pat-
terned set of reinforcement conditions), and the work falling in the
progression of Collier and Marx, to Dunham and Kilps, and to the
more recent work of the author underlines this fact.

The fact that earlier experimentation has, in fact, appeared in the
context of "learning to adjust to fear" or in the context of response
habituation has apparently fostered two interesting gaps in our
knowledge. First, all the work has been based on sequential patterns
of stimuli which *increased* in intensity. There is nothing in the
literature, apparently, in which the effects upon a response system
of sequential *decreases* in stimulus intensity have been scrutinized, a
fact which is perhaps not surprising given the context in which the
earlier research originated. There does not seem to be anything

particularly intriguing, either theoretically or empirically, about decreasing the intensity of an electric shock in a punishment experiment or in an experiment in which accommodation to aversive stimulation is the point at issue. It is possible, however, that some interesting things might emerge from such a procedure; the appropriate experimental question has simply never been asked.

The identification of the first gap in our knowledge leads to the identification of the second. There is literally no information available at all about *contrast effects* which could be generated using sequential patterns of reinforcement. What would have happened in the Church *et al.* experiment if, for example, the dogs had been suddenly returned to the initial weak shock after having undergone the sequentially increasing series of shock intensities? Would this past history make a suddenly weak shock weaker still? More sensibly, perhaps, would the sudden reintroduction of a strong fear-producing stimulus following a sequential *decrease* in the intensity of a stimulus produce an *exaggerated* fear reaction or an *exaggerated* perceived intensity of shock?

D. Contrast in Sequential Patterns

Figure 6 shows three sequential patterns of reinforcement in which the attribute of successive elements of the pattern is a systematic change in magnitude, intensity, or probability of reinforcement. Pattern 1 is a sequential pattern in which successive elements are decreases in magnitude, say of a positive reinforcer according to a curvilinear rule, while patterns 2 and 3 are patterns in which magnitude increases according to a linear rule on the one hand, and a positively accelerated curvilinear rule on the other. At the "transfer point" we assume a shift to some other experimental condition in which we make a test for the effects of experience with the several patterns. The figure shows shifts to the conditions of reinforcement with which each of the three patterns began and suggests a test for positive and negative reinforcement contrast. The shift could occur within some unitary response system, such as lever pressing itself, or it could occur after the plan of Collier and Marx and take place as part of a transfer across two response systems, that is, from magazine training to the *de novo* acquisition of a lever-pressing response. Thus, for example, we might look at changes in lever-pressing rates when some rats have had the probability of reinforcement decrease from 1.0 to 0 across successive responses according to the rule implied by pattern 1, and then have had the probability suddenly re-

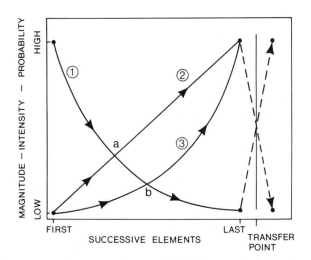

Fig. 6. Three hypothetical functions for sequential changes in the magnitude, intensity, or probability of the successive elements in a sequential pattern of reinforcement. At the "transfer point," a shift to the initial element of the pattern is indicated. At points a and b, patterns 1 and 2 and patterns 1 and 3, respectively, contain common elements.

turned at the "transfer point" to 1.0. We could compare rate changes at transfer with those of a control group maintained at a constant probability of reinforcement of 1.0. Or, we could introduce the pattern during magazine training, exposing some rats to a cue which is followed on successive occasions by reinforcement which arrives with a sequentially decreasing probability, exposing other rats to a cue which is always followed by reinforcement, then comparing the rate at which both sets of animals learn to lever press for a common, $p = 1.0$ probability of reinforcement. Here we would look for positive contrast. Obviously, we could also introduce changes according to patterns 2 or 3 and look at performance following a shift at the transfer point to some minimally effective condition of reinforcement such as a very tiny magnitude of reward. Here, we would be looking for negative contrast. If, to continue, animals were sensitive to differences in the rate of change of the attributes of elements within the pattern, we might also expect patterns 2 and 3 to generate different degrees of negative reinforcement contrast. Clearly, in this particular regard, the number of rules which could be used to build sequential patterns is limitless.

Some other things could happen at the transfer point besides a simple return to an initial condition of reinforcement. As we have indicated, the transfer could include a shift from one response system to another, but it could just as well consist of a shift to some entirely new set of contingencies, such as the sudden introduction of the requirement that a response be *omitted* to assure the continued occurrence of some element of the pattern. A shift could also be made to zero reinforcement and into extinction, a transfer procedure which could be used to check on the persistence of behavior. Intuition suggests that persistence might well be quite different following exposure to patterns 1, 2, and 3, on the assumption that subjects can abstract something about the sequential nature of the patterns per se, and that this would modify their persistence in the total absence of reinforcement.

Finally, in this regard, points a and b mark points of intersection of patterns 1 and 2 on the one hand, and patterns 1 and 3 on the other. At these points, both patterns contain a common element. Here one might wonder most simply if the element would be of equal effectiveness if used to reinforce the acquisition of some response, say, or if its effectiveness would depend in part upon the sequential context in which it had been appearing. More complicated speculations are not hard to develop.

As a beginning step in the experimental study of the multitude of things suggested by the foregoing analysis, we did an experiment which incorporated sequentially changing probabilities of reinforcement and used them to demonstrate a positive reinforcement contrast effect. The patterns were introduced during the magazine-training phase of a discrete-trial lever-pressing task, and their effects were assessed as rats learned to press the lever. Each day of a 2-week period of magazine training, rats were exposed to 40 pairings of a 5-second, 3000-Hz tone with the automatic delivery of a food pellet according to one of the following arrangements ($N = 8$ in each group): (1) $p = 1.0$ that a food pellet would arrive; (2) $p = 0$ that a food pellet would arrive (the rats just listened to tones and never experienced any food directly at all throughout magazine training, although they were certainly exposed to the odor of food in the apparatus); (3) $p = .5$ that a food pellet would arrive; (4) $p = 1.0$ that a food pellet would arrive initially, but in 2-day segments of magazine training, the probability of a food pellet decreased linearly until $p = 0$ that a food pellet would arrive on the last 2-day segment of magazine training; (5) this condition was exactly like (4), except that $p = 0$ of a food pellet initially, and $p = 1.0$ at the end of magazine training. On a day in which both elements, 1 and 0 food pellets, of the pattern occurred in conditions (3), (4), and (5), their distribution was random within the frequencies imposed by the probabilities in effect on that day. Note that in the last three conditions, all rats had identical experience with zero- and one-pellet elements of their respective patterns by the time that magazine training was complete. All that differed among the groups was the pattern with which the elements were arranged.

Following this preliminary experience, all rats learned a discrete-trial lever-pressing response with a single pellet of food as a reinforcing stimulus. There were thirty 30-second trials per day for 6 days with 30 seconds between each trial. A 5-second, 3000-Hz tone signaled the insertion of the lever into the box, the tone going off as the lever began its excursion into the animal's environment.

The results are somewhat complicated, but they are fascinating. Over the 30 trials of the first day, the rats in group $p = 1.0$ showed very little, if any, sign of learning the lever-pressing response. The animals in the group all pressed the lever at least once, but none formed the association between lever pressing and the arrival of a food pellet. The rats in group $p = 0$ learned to lever press in the strange sense that there were reliably more lever presses over the entire course of the day than there were in group $p = 1.0$, but there was no indication of any systematic decrease in response latency over the day. It was much as if the animals were active, therefore stumbled into the lever, stumbled onto the food pellet at some later time, too, but never formed an association between the two events. The rats in group $p = .5$ and group $p = 0 \rightarrow 1$ all learned in the sense that both the frequency of lever pressing and the latency of lever pressing changed in appropriate directions during the course of the day. The rats in group $p = 1 \rightarrow 0$, however, were truly galvanized. They not only learned by any criterion, but the rate of learning was much faster than in any other condition, and the animals were, in general, responding almost twice as fast as those in any other group by the end of the day. Figure 7 shows the course of learning over the first day for groups $p = .5$, $p = 1 \rightarrow 0$, and $p = 0 \rightarrow 1$, while Fig. 8 shows the same thing for groups $p = 0$, $p = 1.0$, and, once again, $p = 1 \rightarrow 0$.

Latencies tended to converge among the groups over the remaining 5 days of the experiment, but in group $p = 1.0$, three animals (out of eight) never learned the lever-pressing response at all, and this group was reliably slower than any other.

There are several points to be made about this experiment. First of all, the behavior generated by the $p = 1.0$ condition is puzzling. This is particularly true in the light of the fact that rats in the ex-

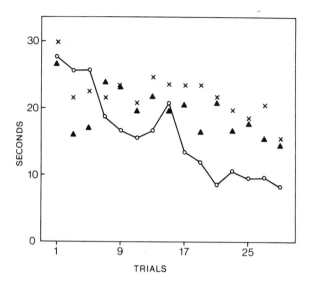

Fig. 7. Day 1 response latencies for every-other trial for the $p = 0 \to 1$(x), $p = 1 \to 0$(○), and $p = .5$(▲) conditions. All rats worked for one pellet of food.

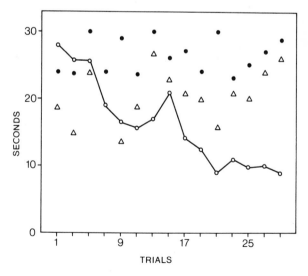

Fig. 8. Day 1 response latencies for every-other trial for the $p = 1 \to 0$(○), $p = 0$(△), and $p = 1.0$(●) conditions. The data for the $p = 1 \to 0$ condition are repeated from Fig. 7 for comparison purposes. All rats worked for one pellet of food.

periment with averaged patterns described earlier were clearly able
to learn following magazine training with a constant one-pellet mag-
nitude. It may be that some peculiarity of intertrial interval or the
number of trials used each day may have produced the difference,
since both differed rather substantially across the two sets of research.
Subsequent experience in our laboratory with these general tech-
niques shows, however, that if magazine training with a constant
one-pellet of food does not always lead to poor learning, it does seem
pretty consistently to make the acquisition of a discrete-trial lever-
pressing response relatively difficult.

In any event, the $p = .5$, $p = 1 \rightarrow 0$, and $p = 0 \rightarrow 1$ groups all
learned. And the most dramatic result of the experiment appears in
the behavior of the $p = 1 \rightarrow 0$ group. If food pellets first exist in an
animal's environment, but disappear gradually over a period of time,
they are extraordinarily effective as reinforcers for the learning of
some new response when they suddenly reappear. The procedure of
"fading out" the probability of a reinforcer seems, in other words, a
highly effective procedure for generating *positive* reinforcement con-
trast in the subsequent acquisition of a response.

One possible contributing factor to these results may have arisen
from the fact that the $p = .5$, $p = 0 \rightarrow 1$, and $p = 1 \rightarrow 0$ groups all
had the common experience of a two-element pattern of food and no
food during magazine training. Some earlier work (Hulse, 1962a,
1962b) shows clearly that a reinforcing stimulus becomes a highly
discriminated event in its own right if it is "brought to the attention"
of a subject through the simple process of discrimination by contrast,
and that such discriminative control can contribute to the formation
of contrast effects. The present results would add to this the fact that
rats can also learn to respond to sequential changes in the probability
of an intermittent reinforcing stimulus, and that the nature of the
response may be in part an "emotional" one which enhances the
utility of food pellets when they are reintroduced as reinforcing
stimuli.

Another possible interpretation of part of these data follows from
a suggestion of Thomas (1972). He argued that "free" food reinforce-
ment during the magazine-training phase of an operant experiment
may engender a state of affairs analogous to the "helplessness" which
response-independent shock can produce in a learning situation based
on aversive stimulation (Maier, Seligman, & Solomon, 1969; Seligman
& Maier, 1967). Thomas trained some pigeons in a "welfare state"
where they had access to a food magazine on a variable-interval sched-
ule, and trained some others to perform a treadle-pressing response
to get food on the same schedule. Then both groups of pigeons (as

well as some others which had no prior training at all) learned to key-peck according to autoshaping procedures. The "welfare state" birds were very, very slow to learn relative to the others. Thomas suggests a cognitive state may have developed where the bird, in effect, acquired a self-satisfied, lazy, do-nothing view of the world which impeded acquisition of the key-peck response when that contingency was introduced. Although Thomas did not use the term, we would call this cognitive state "learned indolence."

Applying the above reasoning to the experiment at hand, the $p = 1.0$ group could certainly have acquired an indolent view of the world with respect to the environment's production of food pellets, and the rate at which the animals in that group learned when asked to do so was certainly slow relative to all the others. Some did not learn at all. Apparently, however, learned indolence must be reserved only for those patterns where free food pellets are always there on cue because stably intermittent, increasing, and especially, decreasing probabilities of food pellets generated moderate to exceptionally rapid learning even though all were totally "free" insofar as they were response independent during magazine training. Learned indolence must give way in part to learned "apprehension" over an irregular or steadily disappearing free food supply, apprehension which reinstates the utility of food pellets when they are subsequently used to foster new learning. And, to remain in the same cognitive vein, the reintroduction of food pellets—though they had to be earned—seems to have been a relatively "joyous" event for those animals which had watched them disappear. Cognitive constructs seem well applied here, since animals seem to be able to respond to patterned events, but the constructs are not simple ones, and perhaps that is as it should be.

IV. Superordinate Patterns of Reinforcement

A. Averaged and Sequential Superordinate Patterns

In this section, we explore some features of the concept of a superordinate pattern of reinforcement. A superordinate pattern of reinforcement consists of at least two elements, the elements being subordinate patterns of reinforcement. Both *averaged* and *sequential* superordinate patterns can be identified, with the order of the elements being unimportant in the former and a basic defining property of the pattern in the latter.

There are many familiar examples of averaged superordinate patterns. These include most of the compound schedules of reinforcement based on intermittency such as multiple and tandem schedules, among others. And there are many familiar, useful, and important things to which these patterns have been directed and applied. These include the experimental analysis of conditioned reinforcement through comparisons among multiple, tandem, and chained schedules (Kelleher, 1966a, 1966b; Kelleher & Gollub, 1962), and the discovery of behavioral contrast in multiple schedules (Reynolds, 1961) with the enormous amount of work on that phenomenon which has since ensued.

There is one apparent general feature of superordinate patterns which, with one exception, all hold in common so far as they have been subjected to scrutiny in the laboratory. Experimental attention has been restricted very narrowly for the most part to an analysis of behavior going on *within* elements of the compound schedules, or perhaps, to the influence of what is going on within one component upon what is going on within a neighboring component. The phenomenon of behavioral contrast provides an excellent example of this point where argument rages as to whether it is response or reinforcement rate in one component of a multiple schedule—or some correlate thereof such as frustration (Amsel, 1971)—which produces exaggerated increases or decreases in rate of response in its neighbor. The single clear exception to this general rule of thumb is the so-called *second-order* schedule of reinforcement (Kelleher, 1966b), in which simple schedules of reinforcement are treated as "units" much like responses and placed themselves on schedules of reinforcement. These have been receiving an increasing amount of attention recently. Thus, we can have a compound schedule in which successive fixed-interval schedules are arranged such that a response in the nth is reinforced with food. Here, too, we have a very good example of a sequential superordinate pattern of reinforcement in which the *order* of the component subordinate patterns can provide the critical defining property of the superordinate pattern. As a matter of fact, the "superordinate feature" of second-order schedules based on a stringing together of a number of fixed-interval schedules and reinforcing the string on a variable-interval basis is the familiar scallop within the successive fixed intervals, but a fairly steady rate of responding when behavior is scanned across successive fixed-interval components of the second-order schedule (Stubbs, 1971).

B. EMERGENT PROPERTIES OF SUPERORDINATE PATTERNS

The foregoing property of second-order schedules of reinforcement in the domain of intermittent reinforcement has not received the explicit attention it deserves and provides the point which we choose to emphasize, not only for the case of intermittent schedules of reinforcement, but also for patterns of reinforcement based on other reinforcement variables. The point, more specifically, is this: far too little attention has been directed to behavioral properties of superordinate patterns which may emerge from the pattern viewed as a whole, as a *Gestalt* if you will. While a great deal of effort has been expended examining local changes in rate in neighboring components of multiple schedules—as the study of behavioral contrast shows, for example—there has been virtually no attempt to study how organisms react to the grand experience of *being placed on a multiple schedule per se.* Is there some emergent property of a multiple schedule which, at the simplest level, distinguishes it from a tandem schedule, for example? Better yet, to borrow the literal line from Gestalt psychology, is there some emergent property of a multiple schedule which could never be predicted from an examination of the experimental features or the behavioral properties of any of its component schedules? The limited data which are available from the study of second-order schedules suggests, at least, that animals can abstract some emergent features associated with the patterning of component schedules; but in this case, the animals simply treat the subordinate schedules as "response units" and respond to them in a fashion which mirrors the behavior produced when they are used as subordinate schedules alone (Blackman, Thomas, & Bond, 1970; Stubbs, 1971). But maybe the proper experimental question has simply never been asked. What would happen, for example, if one cue were paired with one entire second-order schedule and another cue were paired with a second second-order schedule, and then the cues were used as stimuli to modify yet some other response system? What would happen if the cues were internal ones derived from experience with the patterns themselves instead of external cues under the direct control of the experimenter? These are the superordinate questions we wish to emphasize, and we turn now to some experimentation in order to establish the validity of the points they raise.

C. "Super" Extinction

In an experiment done with Herbert Petri and David Fruin, we set out to establish some superordinate patterns based on the simple subordinate patterns of continuous reinforcement (C), 50% random reinforcement (R), and single alternation of reinforcement in which every other response was reinforced (S). The experiment was done using discrete-trial lever pressing. It was prompted in part by some early work done by Theios (1962) and Jenkins (1962) which showed that if a period of continuous reinforcement were interposed between a period of random reinforcement and extinction, resistance to extinction was little different from that obtained following the use of random reinforcement alone. We thought it might be interesting to add a single-alternation pattern to this mix because, while single alternation is a form of intermittent reinforcement, it is a form which can lead to no greater resistance to extinction than continuous reinforcement (Tyler, Wortz, & Bitterman, 1953). Specifically, we trained rats on a discrete-trial lever-pressing response under one of four conditions. The animals in group RSC were exposed in phase 1 of acquisition to 50% random reinforcement, in phase 2 to a single-alternation pattern of reinforcement, and in phase 3 to continuous reinforcement. The rats in group CSR were exposed to the same subordinate patterns but in reverse order. In a third RRR group, rats received 50% random reinforcement throughout training, while in a fourth CCC group, the animals received, similarly, continuous reinforcement throughout training. Phases 1, 2, and 3 lasted 7, 9, and 7 days, respectively, and 50 responses occurred each day. Then all animals were extinguished for 5 days; on each day of extinction, the rats worked until they produced 50 responses, or until 30 minutes elapsed.

First, some results preliminary to the fundamental and major conclusions to be drawn from the experiment. Baseline behavior for the RRR and CCC control groups was remarkably similar throughout acquisition. By the end of phase 1, both groups gave a mean latency on the last day of 1.6 seconds, and on the last day of phase 3 they gave latencies of 1.1 seconds and 1.2 seconds, respectively. Further, there was clear evidence that the rats in both the RSC and CSR groups discriminated the sequence of reinforcement and nonreinforcement while they were on the single-alternation pattern. By the end of phase 2 for both groups, latencies on trials which were to be reinforced were reliably ($p < .001$) shorter than latencies on trials which were not to be reinforced. By the end of phase 3 for these groups, however, latencies had returned to a common level, and, in fact, all four groups entered extinction with response latencies which did not differ reliably.

Figure 9 shows the data on the first day of extinction. The number of lever presses that the animals produced is broken into successive fifths of the time the animals were in the box; the data are essentially identical if response latencies are plotted.

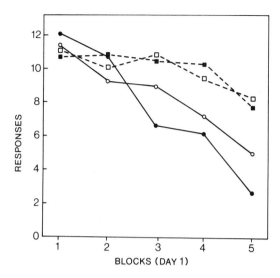

Fig. 9. Numbers of responses during successive fifths of the first day of extinction. Superordinate patterns of reinforcement during acquisition were built sequentially from continuous (C), single-alternation (S), or random (R) subordinate patterns of reinforcement. CSR(□---□); RRR(■---■); CCC(○—○); RSC(●—●).

If conditioning ended with a pattern of random reinforcement, no matter what pattern may have prevailed earlier, resistance to extinction was reliably greater than if conditioning ended with a pattern of continuous reinforcement. In general, the R and CSR groups never differ reliably from each other, but each differs reliably from the C and RSC groups on blocks 4 and 5 of day 1. This is a standard observation for partial *vs.* continuous reinforcement: the former generates greater resistance to extinction than the latter.

It is transparently clear, however, that the RSC order of conditioning led to extraordinarily rapid extinction, "super" extinction if you will. The performance of the rats in this group quickly dropped below all others—even those conditioned with pure continuous reinforcement—by the third block of extinction trials of day 1. Furthermore, the reliable difference persisted in the data throughout the remaining 4 days of extinction. In other work, we were able to duplicate the essential Theios-Jenkins phenomenon using an RC as compared with a CC pattern, so the phenomenon at hand must have something to do with the ordering of the *three* patterns of reinforcement that were used.

There are any number of explanations which could be used to account for "super" extinction, although it is difficult to see offhand how Amsel's frustration theory or Capaldi's sequential hypothesis could do the job in an uncomplicated fashion. We have favored an approach which emphasizes two facts: intermittency of reinforcement draws the organism's attention to the reinforcing stimulus per se (Hulse, 1962a, 1962b), and the highly discriminated reinforcing stimulus become increasingly predictable as exposure continues through the successive subordinate elements of the sequential RSC superordinate pattern. Given the fact that the animal is in a sense taught to be "set" for changes in the reinforcing stimulus, it is relatively easy for the animal to discriminate a shift to zero reinforcement at the outset of extinction, and behavior drops off accordingly. It is also possible that extinction in this case contains a negative reinforcement contrast effect generated by the shift from a sequentially increasing certainty of reinforcement to zero reinforcement. The latter would emphasize some motivational–emotional component of the shift to extinction.

Regardless of the theoretical explanation that one chooses, however, the important fact remains that extinction performance observed in this experiment *emerges* from the use of the tripartite superordinate pattern. It is characteristic of the pattern as a whole, and it is not characteristic of the extinction performance to be expected following the use of any of the subordinate patterns by themselves. It is apparently not characteristic either for the use of pairs of the subordinate patterns—at least the RC and CC pairs—but further work must be done before this can be asserted for sure.[2]

D. "SUPER" CONTRAST

The final experiment to be described is a combination of some further experimentation with subordinate patterns and some new work with superordinate patterns. It incorporated the by now familiar combination of magazine training and transfer to descrete-trial lever pressing. The experimental plan is outlined in Table I.

Table I shows, first of all, that the experiment studied the properties of two reinforcement dimensions—probability and magnitude of reinforcement. During magazine training for the first two groups, which incorporate the fixed-reinforcement conditions run in the

[2] We note in passing that "emergent" factors are a potential variable in any experiment in which subjects have a past history of exposure to patterns of reinforcement, two-element patterns, or otherwise. This fact has implications for any experiment in which other than naive subjects are used.

TABLE I

Experimental Plan for Study of a Sequential Superordinate
Pattern of Reinforcement

Probability, p, that M food pellets follow tone		Number of food pellets following each lever press
$p = 1.0$	$M = 11$	9
$p = 1.0$	$M = 1$	1
$p = 1 \to 0$	$M = 11$	9
$p = 1 \to 0$	$M = 11$	1
$p = 1.0$	$M = 11 \to 0$	9
$p = 1.0$	$M = 11 \to 0$	1
$p = 1 \to 0$	$M = 11 \to 0$	9
$p = 1 \to 0$	$M = 11 \to 0$	1
$p = 0 \to 1$	$M = 0 \to 11$	9
$p = 0 \to 1$	$M = 0 \to 11$	1

changing-probability experiment described earlier, probability of the delivery of food pellets following a tone was set at 1.0, while magnitude was fixed at 11 pellets and one pellet respectively. For the next four conditions shown in Table I, either probability, p, or magnitude, M, was fixed, but the other dimension varied sequentially from 1 to 0 or from 11 to 0. Thus, for example, some rats received pellets with probability fixed at 1.0, but the number they received decreased in a linear fashion from 11 pellets at the outset of magazine training to a magnitude of 0 pellets at the end of magazine training. For the last four conditions *both* probability and magnitude changed simultaneously; they either both decreased on the one hand or, on the other, they both increased. The last four conditions thus satisfy the requirements for superordinate patterns composed of probability and magnitude of reinforcement.

Following magazine training, the rats learned to lever press for a one-pellet reward or for a nine-pellet reward. This called for splitting the groups in the last four magazine-training conditions, so the experiment incorporated 10 groups $(N = 8)$ during its lever-pressing phase. Equipment limitations prevented the use of an 11-pellet reinforcing stimulus. It was assumed that the stimulus change from 11 pellets to nine pellets would be minimal, particularly when combined with the introduction of the lever-pressing contingency.

The details of procedure were quite similar to those described for earlier work. A 5-second, 3,000 Hz tone signaled the arrival of food pellets during the magazine-training phase of the experiment, and trials were spaced by 80 seconds. Because of the large quantities of food to be ingested under some of the conditions, just 15 trials were run each day. Magazine training lasted for 14 days, with probabilities and magnitudes changing linearly in seven 2-day steps. Within each 2-day segment, the probability that food pellets would follow the tone was random, subject to the restrictions imposed by the probability level in effect for that day. During the lever-pressing phase of the experiment, a 5-second, 3,000 Hz tone signaled the subsequent introduction of the lever into the box at the beginning of each trial, and the lever retracted if it was pressed or if a 60-second interval elapsed, whichever occurred first. An intertrial interval of 60 seconds spaced successive trials. Fifteen trials were run each day for 6 days. All rats were run at 80% of normal body weight.

The data of primary interest were the response latencies on the first day of lever-press training. The data show no reliable differences among the groups trained with simple *subordinate* patterns of reinforcement and a one-pellet reinforcing stimulus. That is, for example, the group magazine trained with a constant 11-pellet stimulus which occurred with decreasing probability and lever press trained with a one-pellet reinforcer, was not reliably different from the group magazine trained with a constant one-pellet stimulus. The failure to obtain differences here which were so markedly evident in earlier work we have described may be due to the fact that far fewer trials were run during magazine training than in the earlier work, or, and more likely perhaps, a one-pellet reinforcing stimulus represented a sharp reduction in magnitude compared to the magnitudes that had been presented during much if not all of the magazine training. In any event, the picture is clarified for the same subordinate conditions in which a nine-pellet reinforcing stimulus was incorporated. The relevant data are shown in Fig. 10.

Figure 10 shows quite clearly that animals exposed to one or another of a sequentially decreasing subordinate pattern learned the lever-pressing response faster than a group exposed to an 11-pellet stimulus which appeared with a probability of 1.0. There is a suggestion, furthermore, that a sequential reduction in magnitude was somewhat more effective in enhancing initial learning than a sequential reduction in probability of reinforcement. Again, however, the data do not show reliable differences for the first day of lever pressing, although $p < .10$ for the difference between the $p = 1.0/M = 11$ group and the two patterned groups taken as a whole. Apparently, once again, 15 trials per day during the 14-day magazine-training phase of the experiment simply did not provide enough exposure to the several experimental conditions for differences to emerge which

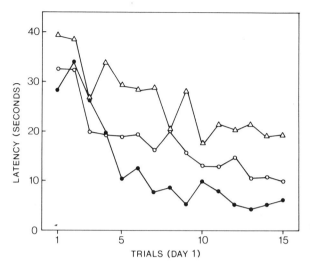

Fig. 10. Trial-by-trial response latencies for Day 1 of acquisition of discrete-trial lever pressing. Rats learned following magazine training in which both probability, p, and magnitude, M, of food pellets were constant [$M = 11$, $p = 1.0(\triangle)$] or in which one was constant while the other changed [$M = 11$, $p = 1 \rightarrow 0$, ($\bigcirc$)]; [$M = 11 \rightarrow 0$, $p = 1.0(\bullet)$]. All rats worked for nine pellets of food during lever-press training.

had emerged clearly in the earlier experiment with sequentially changing probabilities of food pellets.

A look at the data for the four groups exposed to the *superordinate* patterns of reinforcement shows a remarkably different picture. Figure 11 tells the story. The curves marked *increasing* and *decreasing* refer to data for groups in which both probability and magnitude of food pellets following the tone increased and decreased, respectively, during magazine training. The data for the groups which learned to lever press for one food pellet are shown in the left panel of the figure, while the data for the groups which learned to lever press for nine pellets are shown in the right panel of the figure. Clearly, simultaneous sequential changes in *both* probability and magnitude of food pellets produced enormous differences in the effectiveness of food pellets as reinforcers for the learning of the lever-pressing response. If probability and magnitude increased during magazine training, learning was substantially retarded, particularly for the group which learned to lever press for a one pellet reinforcer. The reliability of the effect is shown by a significant ($p < .001$) interaction between trials and increasing or decreasing superordinate patterns.

At a general level, then, the experiment shows most clearly that

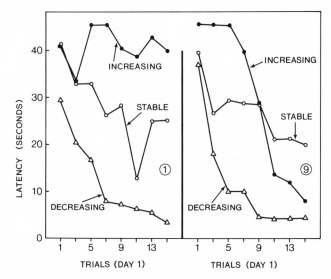

Fig. 11. Trial-by-trial response latencies for Day 1 of acquisition of discrete-trial lever pressing. Data are shown for animals which learned following magazine training in which *both* probability and magnitude of food pellets were constant, increased, or decreased. Data in the left panel are for rats which worked for one pellet, data in the right panel are for rats which worked for nine pellets during lever-press training.

remarkably large positive and negative contrast effects can be obtained relative to either a constant-probability, constant-magnitude control, or to subordinate patterns in which just one reinforcement dimension changes. This is an *emergent* effect in the sense that it does not appear with any particular salience in this experiment if just one of the dimensions of reinforcement changes. Both must change together.

The experiment also serves to underline some earlier comments concerning the possible applicability of "learned indolence" to the data. Clearly, rats in the stable, unchanging conditions of reinforcement were "indolent" as compared with those rats exposed to decreasing probabilities and magnitudes of food pellets during magazine training. They were, relatively speaking, very slow to learn the lever-pressing response. But what is to be made of the animals exposed to the *increasing* probabilities and magnitudes of reinforcement? Do we have "super" indolence, indolence combined with some emotional "super" contrast effect (as we have suggested), or just what? These are all questions awaiting further empirical and theoretical development.

V. Some Speculations about Certain Stimulus Functions in Patterned Reinforcement

In much of the work examined thus far, there are two classes of stimuli to which we now want to draw special attention. The first class is represented by the 3000-Hz tone that was used in some of the experiments to signal the impending arrival of food pellets during magazine training and, later, to signal the impending entry of the lever into the lever box. The second class is a bit more difficult to specify exactly because it consists of whatever internal cognitive state an organism is able to develop as a representation of a pattern of external reinforcing stimuli. For convenience, however, we can call such internal states *abstractions* of patterns of reinforcing stimuli.

First, let us look at some properties of the 3000-Hz tone. According to the analysis of Rescorla and Solomon (1967) and of Trapold and Overmier (1972), among others, that tone had the operational qualifications for a Pavlovian CS, a CS paired in time with food pellets as appetitive unconditional stimuli. According to the same analysis, the tone probably functioned to modulate the acquisition of lever pressing according to a straightforward transfer-of-training or transfer-of-control paradigm, the general experimental procedure that was, of course, used in many of the experiments described in this article. Since, however, the experiments were not designed with Pavlovian questions in mind (the tone was first conceived of simply as a convenient warning signal to mark the arrival of the lever into the animal's environment), conditions may not have been truly optimal for modulation of the acquisition of lever pressing by the CS. For example, the tone preceded entry of the lever by 5 seconds and went off before the animal had the opportunity to press it. Consequently, the CS could function to modify learning only on the basis of its trace, and the trace had to endure for variable periods of time determined from trial to trial by the animal's ultimate response latency. There is no reason to doubt, however, that the tone could have functioned as a CS within the constraints imposed by the procedures used.

If the foregoing is granted, then an interesting fact emerges. Patterns of reinforcement, whether subordinate or superordinate, as they have been incorporated in much of the research discussed in this article, have, in operational terms at least, been patterns in which attributes of an *unconditional stimulus* vary from one occasion to the next. A check of the literature shows that virtually nothing is known about the behavioral properties associated with patterns of unconditional stimulus intensity, for example; yet according to the present analysis that is precisely the model for what was going on as the number of food pellets varied from trial to trial during magazine training. While there must be hundreds of experiments in which UCS intensity has been manipulated, some work by Passey (e.g., Passey & Wood, 1963) apparently provides the only instance in which UCS intensity was varied for the same subject in such a way that a pattern of reinforcement was generated. Most experiments, in contrast, make certain that a given subject is exposed to just one UCS intensity, and the "effects" generated by different UCS intensities become apparent not from the behavior of a given subject exposed to them all, but from the behavior of a statistical test which compares the performance of a number of subjects each exposed to a single, isolated stimulus intensity. Within the context of some Pavlovian experiments, transfer-of-control experiments among them (e.g., Trapold & Overmier, 1972), things are a trifle better, because two-element "patterns" are sometimes used in the sense that a CS+ will be developed based on delivery of a UCS, while a CS— will also be developed based on the programmed absence of the UCS; but even here, these procedures do not define a pattern of reinforcement in the sense in which we have developed the concept in this article. Present practice would call for the association of a changing multielement UCS with an unchanging CS, and that is not characteristic of these procedures. At any rate, there appears to be much to be learned from experiments in which patterns of reinforcement are generated from changing attributes of a UCS. This is probably true within a traditional Pavlovian setting incorporating dog, and meat powder, or eyeball and airpuff, and it is certainly true within the transfer-of-training procedures which have come under such close scrutiny recently.

This brings me to a consideration of the second source of stimulation mentioned above—the internal abstractions which occur given experience with patterns of reinforcement. The rat seems to be able to encode the fact that a reinforcing stimulus such as food can change sequentially in attributes such as magnitude or probability, and the rat seems also to respond in a different way to the two dimensions used alone and used together. Furthermore, the work with sequential combinations of random, single-alternation, and continuous reinforcement shows that if the pattern is based on sequential changes in the certainty with which a reinforcing stimulus can be predicted, the rat also seems to be able to abstract stimulus certainty as a general feature of the pattern. And, apparently, the rat can apply the internal abstraction of the pattern so as to incorporate its influence into the behavior which appears in a new situation. The consequences of the application of the pattern range from "learned indolence" to "super" contrast (both positive and negative) to "super" extinction.

Put a bit more formally, the foregoing suggests that exposure to the elements of a pattern of reinforcement can lead to the formation of an internal abstraction of the pattern which is encoded as a stimulus evokable as a whole. Call that internal stimulus S^I. The internal abstraction can, in turn, come to be elicited by an external stimulus, call it S^E, which is paired with successive elements of the pattern as the internal abstraction of the pattern develops. An external stimulus acquires, in other words, the ability to elicit a complex internal cognitive state. It follows from this and from the experiments we have described, that when S^I is elicited by S^E, it functions as a mediator to modify whatever class of behavior is underway at the time S^E appears. Presumably, and the data indicate this to be so, S^I functions in a way which is ultimately predictable from the features of the pattern of reinforcement from which it is derived.

There are several things which follow from the above analysis. If it is correct, first, it suggests that the pairing of a CS+ with a simple positive reinforcer, say, and a CS— with the absence of that reinforcer, then using the two stimuli in a transfer-of-control experiment, is a very special case of a potentially much more complex state of affairs. The work reported in this article suggests that rats can respond to and develop internal representations of very complex patterns of reinforcing stimuli, that these are elicitable as a whole, and that they function as such when triggered by an S^E in a new situation. It suggests, second, that patterns of reinforcement ought to be usable in differential conditioning, i.e., CS^1 ought to be attachable to an S^I derived from one *pattern* of reinforcement, CS^2 to an S^I derived from a second *pattern* of reinforcement, and the two CS stimuli used to modify behavior differentially. A parallel analogy in instrumental conditioning would be to use stimuli associated with multiple schedules of reinforcement (or from patterns derived according to some of the rules we have suggested in this article) to modify responses other than the one for which they were used initially. It suggests, third, that there may be *both* "associational" and "emotional" components of the state of affairs elicited by a CS in a transfer-of-control experiment. That is, S^I may have two distinguishable properties. Trapold and Overmier (1972) speculate that the "emotional" or "motivational" properties associated with a transfer-of-control procedure may be superfluous as explicators of what transpires there, and they may, of course, be correct. Some of the experiments we have looked at in this article, however, certainly suggest that parallels to contrast effects of the type called "elation" and "depression" can be generated in transfer-of-control experiments, and if one assumes that these represent emotional or motivational states of affairs, then such things ought to be included in our theorizing. In any event, whether the motivational properties of S^I turn out to be important or not, the present work certainly lends weight to the notion that associational features of S^I are very important in such experiments.

VI. Conclusions

We end where we began with the comment that this article portrays the general shape of a scheme designed to broaden the conceptual framework which we use to think about changing conditions of reward and punishment. The scheme need not supplant the familiar concept of the schedule of reinforcement, but it will have served one of its purposes if it identifies some of the potential limitations of that concept. It will have served another if it has successfully produced some research which might not otherwise have been conceived and explored. It will have served its most useful function if it has suggested some paths along which investigation may procede in the future.

VII. Addendum

Since the bulk of this article was prepared, the work I have attributed to Thomas (1972) has appeared in print (Engberg, Hansen, Welker, & Thomas, 1972). They showed, as we indicated earlier, that pigeons acquired an "auto-shaped" key-peck response more slowly if they had previously received noncontingent food from a hopper in the apparatus than if they had not received such training. Their report adds that a third group specifically trained to perform another, treadle-pressing response for contingent food then learned the key-peck response fastest of all when contingencies were switched to that response. The treadle-press group adds an important control for possible interference with acquisition of key-pecking in the noncontingent group: the noncontingent animals were apparently not retarded in acquisition of key-pecking because they had adventitiously acquired some "superstitious" response which kept them in the vicinity of the food hopper and away from the key when the key-pecking contingency began.

In discussing their work, Engberg et al. coin the phrase "learned laziness" for the behavior of the noncontingent group, and they speak of "learned laziness" as an analog to "learned helplessness," the factor presumably accounting for slow acquisition of avoidance responses after exposure to noncontingent shock (Maier *et al.*, 1969; Seligman & Maier, 1967). I think the present work indicates that "learned indolence" may be the more appropriate connotative term, but in any event, both "learned laziness" and "learned indolence" insofar as their defining operations are restricted to a stable, unchanging set of reward conditions during noncontingent training are obviously but special cases of a much more general and complicated state of affairs. Clearly, if reward conditions are changed according to some of the sequential rules discussed in this article, "learned indolence" can be changed into something which is apparently its polar opposite.

We close with the thought that analogous things may hold for the phenomenon of "learned helplessness." What would happen if unavoidable *punishers* were patterned according to some of the procedures we have described and developed, then used to reinforce new learning? One possible prediction, for example, would be that a sequentially decreasing series of shock intensities during noncontingent exposure to shock, followed by the sudden reintroduction of strong shock at the outset of avoidance training, ought to generate extremely *rapid* learning of the avoidance response. Under conditions of patterned reinforcement, in other words, something might emerge in learning which would be in marked contrast to that observed when things are based on simple, fixed, single-element conditions of reinforcement.

REFERENCES

Amsel, A. Partial reinforcement effects on vigor and persistence. In K. W. Spence & J. T. Spence (Eds.), *The psychology of learning and motivation: Advances in research and theory.* Vol. 1. New York: Academic Press, 1967. Pp. 1–65.

Amsel, A. Positive induction, behavioral contrast, and generalization of inhibition in discrimination learning. In H. H. Kendler & J. T. Spence (Eds.), *Essays in neobehaviorism: A memorial volume to Kenneth W. Spence,* New York: Appleton 1971. Pp. 217–236.

Amsel, A. Behavioral habituation, counterconditioning, and persistence. In A. H. Black & W. K. Prokasy (Eds.), *Classical conditioning. II: Current theory and research.* New York: Appleton 1972. Pp. 409–426.

Bevan, W. An adaptation-level interpretation of reinforcement. *Perceptual and Motor Skills,* 1966, **23**, 511–531.

Bevan, W. The contextual basis of behavior. *American Psychologist,* 1968, **23**, 701–714.

Bevan, W., & Adamson, R. Reinforcers and reinforcement: their relation to maze performance. *Journal of Experimental Psychology,* 1960, **59**, 226–232.

Black, R., Adamson, R., & Bevan, W. Runway behavior as a function of apparent intensity of shock. *Journal of Comparative and Physiological Psychology,* 1961, **54**, 270–274.

Blackman, D. E., Thomas, G. V., & Bond, N. W. Second-order fixed-ratio schedules. *Psychonomic Science,* 1970, **21**, 53–55.

Boe, E. B. Variable punishment. *Journal of Comparative and Physiological Psychology,* 1971, **75**, 73–76.

Capaldi, E. J. A sequential hypothesis of instrumental learning. In K. W. Spence & J. T. Spence (Eds.), *The psychology of learning and motivation: Advances in research and theory.* Vol. 1. New York: Academic Press, 1967. Pp. 67–156.

Church, R. M., LoLordo, V., Overmier, J. B., Solomon, R. L., & Turner, L. H. Cardiac responses to shock in curarized dogs: effects of shock intensity and duration, warning signal and prior experience with shock. *Journal of Comparative and Physiological Psychology*, 1966, **62**, 1–7.

Collier, G., & Marx, M. H. Changes in performance as a function of shifts in the magnitude of reinforcement. *Journal of Experimental Psychology*, 1959, **57**, 305–309.

Davis, M., & Wagner, A. R. Habituation of startle response under incremental sequence of stimulus intensities. *Journal of Comparative and Physiological Psychology*, 1969, **67**, 486–492.

Donin, J. A., Surridge, C. T., & Amsel, A. Extinction following partial delay of reward with immediate continuous reward interpolated at 24-hour intervals. *Journal of Experimental Psychology*, 1967, **74**, 50–53.

Dunham, P. J. Contrasted conditions of reinforcement: A selective critique. *Psychological Bulletin*, 1968, **69**, 295–315.

Dunham, P. J., & Kilps, B. Shifts in magnitude of reinforcement: confounded factors or contrast effects? *Journal of Experimental Psychology*, 1969, **79**, 373–374.

Engberg, L. A., Hansen, G., Welker, R. L., & Thomas, D. R. Acquisition of key-pecking via autoshaping as a function of prior experience: "learned laziness"? *Science*, 1972, **178**, 1002–1004.

Ferster, C. B., & Skinner, B. F. *Schedules of reinforcement*. New York: Appleton, 1957.

Findley, J. Preference and switching under concurrent scheduling. *Journal of the Experimental Analysis of Behavior*, 1958, **1**, 123–144.

Harzem, P. Temporal discrimination. In R. M. Gilbert & N. S. Sutherland (Eds.), *Animal discrimination learning*. New York: Academic Press, 1969. Pp. 299–334.

Helson, H. *Adaptation-level theory: An experimental and systematic approach to behavior*. New York: Harper, 1964.

Hodos, W. Progressive ratio as a measure of reward strength. *Science*, 1961, **134**, 943–944.

Hulse, S. H. A precision liquid feeding system controlled by licking behavior. *Journal of the Experimental Analysis of Behavior*, 1960, **3**, 1–3.

Hulse, S. H. Discrimination of the reward in learning with partial and continuous reinforcement. *Journal of Experimental Psychology*, 1962, **64**, 227–233. (a)

Hulse, S. H. Partial reinforcement, continuous reinforcement, and reinforcement shift effects. *Journal of Experimental Psychology*, 1962, **64**, 451–459. (b)

Hulse, S. H. Reinforcement contrast effects in rats following experimental definition of a dimension of reinforcement magnitude. *Journal of Comparative and Physiological Psychology*, 1973, in press.

Hurwitz, H. M., & Harzem, P. Progressive ratio performance with reset option. *Psychological Record*, 1968, **18**, 553–558.

Innis, N. K., & Staddon, J. E. R. Temporal tracking on cyclic-interval reinforcement schedules. *Journal of the Experimental Analysis of Behavior*, 1971, **16**, 411–423.

Jenkins, H. M. Resistance to extinction when partial reinforcement is followed by regular reinforcement. *Journal of Experimental Psychology*, 1962, **74**, 441–450.

Jensen, G. D., & Rey, R. P. Runway performance under "horn of plenty" conditions versus gradual diminution of reward supply. *Journal of Experimental Psychology*, 1968, **76**, 7–11.

Jensen, G. D., & Rey, R. P. "Horn of plenty" conditions versus gradual diminution of reward supply with extended training. *Journal of Experimental Psychology*, 1969, **80**, 190–191.

Kelleher, R. T. Chaining and conditioned reinforcement. In W. K. Honig (Ed.),

Operant behavior: Areas of research and application. New York: Appleton, 1966. Pp. 160–212. (a)

Kelleher, R. T. Conditioned reinforcement in second-order schedules. *Journal of the Experimental Analysis of Behavior,* 1966, **9,** 475–485. (b)

Kelleher, R. T., & Gollub, L. R. A review of positive conditioned reinforcement. *Journal of the Experimental Analysis of Behavior,* 1962, **5,** 543–597.

Lashley, K. S., & Wade, M. The Pavlovian theory of generalization. *Psychological Review,* 1946, **53,** 72–87.

Leonard, D. W. Amount and sequence of reward in partial and continuous reinforcement. *Journal of Comparative and Physiological Psychology,* 1969, **67,** 204–211.

Logan, F. A. *Incentive.* New Haven: Yale University Press, 1960.

Logan, F. A., Beier, E. M., & Kincaid, W. D. Extinction following partial and varied reinforcement. *Journal of Experimental Psychology,* 1956, **52,** 65–70.

Maier, S. F., Seligman, M. E. P., & Solomon, R. L. Pavlovian fear conditioning and learned helplessness: effects on escape and avoidance behavior of (a) the CS-US contingency and (b) the independence of the US and voluntary responding. In B. A. Campbell & R. M. Church (Eds.), *Punishment and aversive behavior.* New York: Appleton, 1969. Pp. 299–342.

Miller, N. E. Learning resistance to pain and fear: effects of overlearning, exposure, and rewarded exposure in context. *Journal of Experimental Psychology,* 1960, **60,** 137–145.

Passey, G. E., & Wood, D. L. Effects of patterns of reinforcement on the conditioned eyelid response. *Journal of Experimental Psychology,* 1963, **66,** 241–244.

Rescorla, R. A., & Solomon, R. L. Two process learning theory: relationships between Pavlovian conditioning and instrumental learning. *Psychological Review,* 1967, **74,** 151–182.

Rettig, E. B., & Clement, P. W. Effects of variable amounts of reinforcement on a lever-pulling response in children. *Proceedings, 79th Annual Convention, American Psychological Association,* 1971, **6,** Part 2, 687–688.

Reynolds, G. S. Behavioral contrast. *Journal of the Experimental Analysis of Behavior,* 1961, **4,** 57–71.

Schoenfeld, W. N. (Ed.) *The theory of reinforcement schedules.* New York: Appleton, 1970.

Schoenfeld, W. N., & Cumming, W. W. Studies in a temporal classification of reinforcement schedules: summary and projection. *Proceedings of the National Academy of Sciences, U.S.,* 1960, **46,** 753–758.

Seligman, M. E. P., & Maier, S. F. Failure to escape traumatic shock. *Journal of Experimental Psychology,* 1967, **74,** 1–9.

Shanab, M. E. Positive transfer between nonreward and delay. *Journal of Experimental Psychology,* 1971, **91,** 98–102.

Staddon, J. E. R. Reinforcement as input: cyclic variable-interval schedule. *Science,* 1964, **145,** 410–412.

Stubbs, D. A. Second-order schedules and the problem of conditioned reinforcement. *Journal of the Experimental Analysis of Behavior,* 1971, **16,** 289–313.

Theios, J. The partial reinforcement effect sustained through blocks of continuous reinforcement. *Journal of Experimental Psychology,* 1962, **64,** 1–6.

Thomas, D. R. The pigeon in a welfare state. Paper presented at the meeting of the Psychonomic Society, St. Louis, November 1972.

Trapold, M. A., & Overmier, J. B. The second learning process in instrumental learning. In A. H. Black & W. F. Prokasy (Eds.), *Classical conditioning II: Current theory and research.* New York: Appleton, 1972. Pp. 427–452.

Tyler, D. W., Wortz, E. C., & Bitterman, M. E. The effect of random and alternating partial reinforcement on resistance to extinction in the rat. *American Journal of Psychology*, 1953, **66,** 57–65.

Warden, J. *Animal motivation: Experimental studies on the albino rat.* New York: Columbia University Press, 1931.

Yamaguchi, H. The effect of continuous, partial, and varied magnitude reinforcement on acquisition and extinction. *Journal of Experimental Psychology*, 1961, **61,** 319–321.

Zill, N. The effects of temporal uncertainty on conditioned suppression and preference for warned shock in rats. Unpublished doctoral dissertation, Johns Hopkins University, 1967.

AUTHOR INDEX

Numbers in italics refer to the pages on which the complete references are listed.

SUBJECT INDEX

A

Adaptation, of brain stimulation, *see* Brain stimulation

Age, subproblem learning and, 214-221

Associations, computer simulation for learning, 21-22
  continuous paired, 96-99
  encoding and formation of, 146-150

Attention, stimulus pretraining and, 132-137

Auditory input, effect on delayed matching, 237-242

Aversiveness, of brain stimulation, 298-301

B

Brain stimulation, adaptation theory of, 308-311
  aversiveness and, 298-301
  increment of prolonged stimulation and, 301-305
  refractory periods of stimulation and, 307-308
  speed of adaptation and, 305-307
  historical aspects, 297-298

C

Children, discrimination learning in, *see* Discrimination learning

Classification learning, computer simulation for, 22-23

Clustering, 99-101

Coding, *see* Encoding, Recoding

Cognition, intelligence and, 87-90, 94-96, 114-120
  acquisition and retrieval from long-term memory and, 104-106
  clustering and, 99-101
  continuous paired associates and, 96-99
  correlational studies, 109-114
  distributed memory model of, 90-94
  encoding and, 101-102
  manipulation of information in short-term memory and, 103-106
  semantic coding and proactive interference and, 102-104
  susceptibility to inferences and, 106-108

Cognitive processing, reaction time in measurement of, 46-49

Contrast, patterned reinforcement and, 322-329, 339-345, 350-354

D

Delayed matching, *see under* Memory

Discrimination, labeling and, 131-132
  temporal, 260-266

Discrimination learning, 183-187
  subproblem analysis in children, 221-224
    in relation to age and task conditions, 214-221
  subproblem analysis in animals, independent learning, 187-190
    in relation to task conditions, 190-209
  theory, 209-214

E

Encoding, 124-128
  cognition and, 101-102
    proactive interference and, 102-104
  conceptual, stimulus pretraining and, 139-140
  mediation and, 126
  recall and, 154-156
  response-dependent, 150-151
  response variables and, in shape recognition, 141-144
    in stimulus recognition and association formation, 146-150
    in verbal recognition, 144-146
  selection and, 125
  self-terminating memory model and, 49-50
  stimulus variables and, meaningfulness, 159-165
    nominal stimulus variability, 165-169
  transfer of stimulus differentiation and, 169-173
  recoding and, 173-175

Extinction, patterned reinforcement and, 347-350

F

Facilitation, of short-term memory, 230-237

6
B 7
C 8
D 9
E 0
F 1
G 2
H 3
I 4
J 5